THE 'A

Common-law judgments tend to be more than merely judgments, for judges often make pronouncements that they need not have made had they kept strictly to the task in hand. Why do they do this? *The Intricacies of* Dicta *and Dissent* examines two such types of pronouncement, *obiter dicta* and dissenting opinions, primarily as aspects of English case law. Neil Duxbury shows that both of these phenomena have complex histories, have been put to a variety of uses, and are not amenable to being straightforwardly categorized as secondary sources of law. This innovative and unusual study casts new light on – and will prompt lawyers to pose fresh questions about – the common law tradition and the nature of judicial decision-making.

NEIL DUXBURY is Professor of English Law at the London School of Economics. He is author of *Patterns of American Jurisprudence* (1995), *Random Justice* (1999), *Jurists and Judges* (2001), *Frederick Pollock and the English Juristic Tradition* (2004), *The Nature and Authority of Precedent* (2008), *Elements of Legislation* (2013), and *Lord Kilmuir* (2015).

THE INTRICACIES OF *DICTA* AND DISSENT

NEIL DUXBURY

London School of Economics and Political Science

CAMBRIDGE
UNIVERSITY PRESS

CAMBRIDGE
UNIVERSITY PRESS

University Printing House, Cambridge CB2 8BS, United Kingdom

One Liberty Plaza, 20th Floor, New York, NY 10006, USA

477 Williamstown Road, Port Melbourne, VIC 3207, Australia

314–321, 3rd Floor, Plot 3, Splendor Forum, Jasola District Centre, New Delhi – 110025, India

103 Penang Road, #05–06/07, Visioncrest Commercial, Singapore 238467

Cambridge University Press is part of the University of Cambridge.

It furthers the University's mission by disseminating knowledge in the pursuit of education, learning, and research at the highest international levels of excellence.

www.cambridge.org
Information on this title: www.cambridge.org/9781108841498
DOI: 10.1017/9781108882590

First published 2021

A catalogue record for this publication is available from the British Library.

Library of Congress Cataloging-in-Publication Data
Names: Duxbury, Neil, author.
Title: The intricacies of dicta and dissent / Neil Duxbury, London School of Economics and Political Science.
Description: Cambridge, United Kingdom; New York, NY: Cambridge University Press, 2021. | Includes bibliographical references and index.
Identifiers: LCCN 2020058039 (print) | LCCN 2020058040 (ebook) | ISBN 9781108841498 (hardback) | ISBN 9781108794886 (paperback) | ISBN 9781108882590 (ebook)
Subjects: LCSH: Common law – Methodology. | Dissenting opinions. | Judicial process – England.
Classification: LCC K588 .D89 2021 (print) | LCC K588 (ebook) | DDC 340.5/7–dc23
LC record available at https://lccn.loc.gov/2020058039
LC ebook record available at https://lccn.loc.gov/2020058040

ISBN 978-1-108-84149-8 Hardback
ISBN 978-1-108-79488-6 Paperback

For Ted White

He became involved in the intricacies of the law, reading as avidly as though the pages were full of easy gossip. He was interested in the workings of his colleagues' minds, their strategies, the words they chose. A few times he was disappointed by the arguments which were not followed through, by the vague assertions and the weak grasp of case law. There were several judgments which he read after lunch, written by his younger colleagues on the High Court, judgments he could not have written himself, since they were so detailed and all-embracing in their knowledge of technical matters such as patents, copyright and the intricacies of tort and property rights. He was more interested, however, in broader questions, in the cases which could raise much larger issues than the mere right and wrong of the arguments presented to the court.

Colm Tóibín, *The Heather Blazing*

As many truths as men. Occasionally, I glimpse a truer Truth, hiding in imperfect simulacrums of itself, but as I approach, it bestirs itself & moves deeper into the thorny swamp of dissent.

David Mitchell, *Cloud Atlas*

CONTENTS

II Dissent

PREFACE

The trouble with Roscoe Pound, Karl Llewellyn once observed, is that he seemed torn between seeking 'to travel on the level of considered and buttressed scholarly discussion' and feeling compelled to write 'bed-time stories for the tired bar'.[1] Perhaps Llewellyn would have thought this my affliction too. *Dicta* and dissent are topics which yield plenty of anecdotes and *aperçus*, and, when writing some parts of this book, I found myself trying to guard against mimicking a fireside narrator. I suspect I did not succeed – and certainly know why I might not have succeeded – in resisting this impulse entirely. Flick through the book and it should be obvious that it belongs to the tradition of Pound the scholar. Yet my main imaginary readership while writing it has not been academics. Rather, it has been barristers and, especially, judges: I am trying to account for certain types of judicial pronouncement – why judges make them, what other judges and counsel do with them. My wished-for audience – the courtroom participants who produce and utilize *obiter dicta* and dissenting opinions – will surely never turn up, or certainly not in large numbers. Nevertheless, this book is a performance with that audience very much in mind, by someone who cannot help but wonder what its judgment would be were it ever to materialize.

For helpful written advice on Essay I, I am immensely grateful to Ross Cranston, Matthew Harding, Philip Sales, and Stephen Sedley. As regards Essay II, the same goes to Tatiana Cutts, Brenda Hale, Nick Sage, and (for comments on Section 2) Jan Zglinski. George Leggatt went above and beyond by providing detailed comments on both essays. Cambridge University Press's four anonymous readers provided incisive feedback on the original proposal and the overall project. I made uninterrupted progress on the book early in 2020 because the LSE Law Department kindly granted me leave for the Lent term. Although, at the end of that

[1] Karl N. Llewellyn, 'A Realistic Jurisprudence – The Next Step' (1930) 30 *Columbia L. Rev.* 431, 435 n. 3.

term, a scheduled visit to the University of Virginia inevitably went the way of travel plans worldwide, Kent Olson in Virginia's Law School library still generously fulfilled by email the various esoteric requests that I had planned to land physically on his desk.

To make some sentences less cumbersome, I occasionally write about 'English' judgments or dissents when I really mean judgments or dissents by judges in the appeal courts of England and Wales, and even though I know that some of the judges doing the judging or dissenting are not English. When presenting abstract scenarios involving the use of singular pronouns I am deliberately inconsistent, in some instances opting for the female and in others for the male. Stylistic quirks confined to particular passages in the book are accounted for in local footnotes. When referring to cases reported since 2001, I use the neutral citation only, unless there is a reason to do otherwise. While the time at which I put the book to bed (late September 2020) has little or no bearing on most of the project, it might be worth keeping it in mind when reading the penultimate section of Essay I. The cover art, finally, will seem a curious choice. Any suitably intrigued reader might want to look at it alongside the Hopper which graces my first book, published in 1995.

TABLE OF CASES

The table is confined to cases which feature (or which contain observations featuring) in the main text, and cases considered in footnotes.

PROLOGUE

Not until the nineteenth century did the doctrine of precedent become an established feature of the common law. Before then, English lawyers understood the common law to be not case law but general customs which, though not written down as laws, were legally enforceable in the courts of the realm – those customs, according to William Blackstone, 'by which proceedings and determinations in the king's ordinary courts of justice are guided and directed'.[1] The common law was, by definition, within the common knowledge of judges, and so there was no reason for lawyers to mention it in writs or pleadings.[2] Cases tended to be treated not as common law but rather as evidence of what the common law was.[3] While nobody today would dismiss the proposition that decisions of courts can be common law, case law and the common law are certainly not one and the same. When the Austrian law professor, Josef Redlich, reported in 1914 on the use of the case method of instruction in American law schools, he had a simple explanation for its success: American law is common law, and the common law is case law.[4] Even

[1] Blackstone, 1 *Commentaries*, 68. (*Commentaries* = William Blackstone, *Commentaries on the Laws of England*, 4 vols. (University of Chicago Press, 1979 [1765–9]).)

[2] So it was that Henry Finch considered it 'not good' legal technique to 'plead that there is a custom among merchants throughout the realm' regarding the recognition of bills of exchange, for 'that which is current throughout the realm, is common law, not custom'. Henry Finch, *Law or a Discourse Thereof* (New York: Kelley, 1969 [1627]), 77.

[3] See, e.g., Edward Coke, *The First Part of the Institutes of the Lawes of England. Or a Commentarie upon Littleton* (London: Societe of Stationers, 1628) at 254a ('our book cases are the best proofs what the law is'); Matthew Hale (d. 1676), *The History of the Common Law of England*, ed. C. M. Gray (University of Chicago Press, 1971), 45 ('Judicial decisions . . . are less than a law, yet they are a greater evidence thereof than the opinion of any private persons'); also *Jones* v. *Randall* (1774) Lofft. 383, 385 *per* Lord Mansfield ('precedent, though it be evidence of law, is not law in itself').

[4] Josef Redlich, *The Common Law and the Case Method in American University Law Schools: A Report to the Carnegie Foundation for the Advancement of Teaching* (Boston: Merrymount Press, 1914), 35 ('[I]n all the states of the Union, the law of America has still remained, above all things, common law . . . *[C]ommon law is case law and nothing else than case law*'). (Emphasis in original.)

case-method practitioners, the constituency whose initiatives Redlich was lauding, baulked at so reductive a description of the common law. That the common law equates with case law is 'hardly even a half truth', one US law professor responded, for the 'common law on any point existed . . . before any case in which it may be applied'.[5]

Just as common law is more than mere case law, case reports are not only composed of common law. Many, as often as not most, of the judicial pronouncements contained in a judgment are not judge-made law, or even determinations as to applicable statutory or customary law. This book is composed of two long, labyrinthine essays on two such types of pronouncement: *obiter dicta* and judicial dissent. The point of the book is not to offer a specific theoretical perspective on these phenomena, or to advance normative claims about them, but rather to try to understand *dicta* and dissent as contributions to common law, primarily English common law, judicial reasoning.

Between *dicta* and dissent there are likenesses and differences. Both are contained in cases and produced by judges. While neither is binding authority, judges in English courts are not entirely averse to following them when no primary legal source supplies an answer to a disputed question. In a rudimentary sense, they are one and the same in that dissents do not belong to the *ratio* of a judgment and so must be *obiter dicta*. They are certainly distinguishable in so far as *dicta* are tangential to a *ratio* whereas a dissent is antithetical to it – though this distinction is somewhat muddied by the fact that a judge's opinion might amalgamate assent and dissent (as when a judge dissents from only part of the decision, or when she concurs on the outcome but rejects the majority's reasoning in support of it). Other characteristics, though they do not distinguish *dicta* and dissents, are more regularly ascribable to one rather than the other. Dissents are usually entire judicial opinions, for example, whereas *dicta* are more likely to be opinions within opinions.

Although dissents are *dicta*, it is uncontroversial to think of *dicta* and dissents as different legal species. One might reasonably ask why it is worth thinking about *dicta* at all. Certainly very little has been written about them. Jurisprudential debate has focused primarily on how to identify the *ratio decidendi* of a case – the content of the case, that is, which is not *obiter dictum*. To purport to discern the *ratio* of a case is, by

[5] Simeon E. Baldwin, 'Education for the Bar in the United States' (1915) 9 *Am. Pol. Sci. Rev.* 437, 447. Baldwin was, at this point, a law professor at Yale. For his own perspective on case law teaching, see Simeon E. Baldwin, 'The Teaching of Law by Cases' (1900) 14 *Harv. L. Rev.* 258.

default, to maintain that one knows its *obiter* content too. Yet determining which judicial pronouncements fall into which category is an exercise fraught with difficulty. It cannot be for a judge deciding a case to make these determinations, for if this were feasible his capacity to make law would be unconstrained: he would be able to expound on any legal matter whatsoever and then assert that his proclamations were not to be treated as *obiter dicta.*

In modern common law theory, the standard response to this predicament is that while judges are free to expound on the law however they wish in the course of deciding a case, only the reasoning necessary to their decisions can bind as precedent. Legal reasoning cannot be necessary to a decision simply because a judge who advances it deems it to be so. There is, however, no rigorous test enabling us objectively to identify the reasons necessary to judgments.[6] It is understandable that modern jurists should have been exercised by the indeterminacy of *ratio decidendi* as a concept, given that the *ratio* is the binding part of a judgment. What is perhaps more surprising is how little attention has been accorded to the similarly indeterminate nature of the concept of *obiter dicta.* For the fact of its indeterminacy is significant: whether a case is distinguished or is followed as precedent will sometimes be attributable to the fact that today's court has been convinced, or has convinced itself, that an element of the reasoning contained in the case should, or should not, be classified as *obiter dictum.* Exceptionally, and controversially, a court might even conclude that although the reasoning in the earlier case indeed is *obiter dictum*, it should be followed as if it were not.

Common-law judges have generally seemed unfazed by the absence of a boundary between *ratio* and *dicta.* They are content, by and large, to let others discern for themselves what the *rationes* of their judgments are, and they are equally at ease extrapolating *rationes* from other judges' judgments. The process of extrapolation would be easier, of course, if judges were to try to confine themselves to making legal pronouncements bearing upon the case to be decided by the court. But judges often make legal observations which have no connection to the court's decision: they will very deliberately pronounce *obiter.*

Judges have all sorts of reasons for making *obiter* observations. They might be seeking to bring some nuance to a judgment, or signalling to the lower courts and the legal profession how they would rule on a matter not

[6] See Neil Duxbury, *The Nature and Authority of Precedent* (Cambridge University Press, 2008), 67–90.

yet litigated were it to come to them for decision, or hoping to influence how the common law develops or how the language of a statute is construed. They could even be settling scores with other judges. A judge will also, with certain types of *obiter* pronouncement, be making a calculation. The *dictum* might obfuscate the judgment. It might come back to haunt the judge who delivers it, or be passed over by later courts in favour of other, competing *dicta*. Much that is *obiter dictum* in a judgment invites no comment. But the *dictum* which makes a legal point has a fate: it is ignored, or received indifferently, or accorded significance, perhaps considerable significance, by those who can change the law to which the *dictum* speaks, or who argue over what that law is or how it might be improved.

As compared with *dicta*, judicial dissent is a more readily graspable topic – one about which lawyers, and others, have had a good deal to say. At the heart of the topic there is a simple dichotomy. When a judgment is not unanimous, there will be a majority and a minority. Not everyone in the minority need be a dissenter. A judge in the minority is only a dissenter if she was unable to reconcile herself to the court's decision. As secondary legal sources, the dissentient content and the *dicta* in a case are distinguishable: in the context of the case, dissenting judicial opinion is rejected legal reasoning, whereas judicial opinion expressed *obiter* is neither rejected not accepted. This is not to maintain that, measured against *dicta*, dissenting opinions are inferior persuasive authorities. Dissent is a challenge to a *ratio*. It can render a precedent fragile or the trajectory of the common law unsettled – perhaps especially when, in a dispute which raises strong legal arguments pulling in different directions, the consequence of dissent is a decision by bare majority.

Analysts of judicial dissent – few of whom focus on the activity specifically or even primarily as a feature of English judgments – have tended to concern themselves with a cluster of issues: whether courts do better or worse to allow dissent, how different legal systems conceptualize and register dissent differently, comparative dissent rates among judges, courts, and court systems, what judges' motivations for dissenting might be, and – the most enthusiastically addressed issue of all – what it means to speak of 'great' dissents and dissenters. All of these issues are intriguing. But dissent as an English case-law phenomenon raises other issues besides. Judges in English appeal courts are never obliged to deliver composite unanimous judgments apart from in some criminal law cases. While, since the late-twentieth century, it has become more common for these courts to produce single (unanimous or majority) judgments, appellate judges have traditionally delivered – and very often still do deliver – separate opinions from which the judgment is to be ascertained. A tradition of separate opinion writing means that judges can dissent. But it can also make it difficult, or create a disincentive, to dissent. If I am the sole dissenter on a five-member court, and the other four judges deliver individual opinions, the majority's *ratio* is likely to be more dispersed, more difficult to identify, and therefore less easy to dissent against, than would be the case had I only to contend with a single majority judgment. That I can produce a separate opinion also means that I can be creative: I might dissent on some legal points but not on others, or I might not dissent at all but nevertheless deliver an opinion containing dissent-like *dicta*. One of the more interesting lines of enquiry regarding dissents in English courts – though it is not unique to these courts – concerns why and how judges might avoid dissenting, and the manoeuvres they might undertake if they want to exhibit dissentient inclinations without delivering a dissenting opinion.

The rest of this study is supposed to make these preliminary remarks seem less obtuse. There are junctures in both Essays, particularly in the second one, when the focus shifts to settings outside England – even, occasionally, to matters outside law. But do not be deceived. Both Essays are rooted in, are fundamentally about, English case law. One can only wonder how that pre-eminent critic of judge-made law, Jeremy Bentham, might have reacted to them. To think of cases as law, he maintained, is to entertain a ludicrous fiction.[7] A study which accords significance to the detritus strewn across the wilderness of single instances,[8] to the case-content which even the content's producers do not treat as law, would surely have left him – his walk-on part in the middle of the first Essay all but confirms this – with his head in his hands. Yet even Bentham had his charitable moments. '[N]othing could be much further from the truth', he wrote to James Madison, 'than if, in speaking of the *matter* of which the English common law is composed, a man were to represent it as being of no use . . . [I]t affords,

[7] See Jeremy Bentham, *A Comment on the Commentaries and a Fragment on Government*, ed. J. H. Burns and H. L. A. Hart (London: Athlone Press, 1977 [*c.*1774–*c.*1776]), at 119–20, 330; also Gerald J. Postema, *Bentham and the Common Law Tradition* (Oxford: Clarendon Press, 1986), at 271–5, 286–9.

[8] See Alfred Tennyson, *Aylmer's Field* (New York: Macmillan & Co, 1891 [1793]), 14 ('the lawless science of our law/That codeless myriad of precedent/That wilderness of single instances').

for the manufactory of real law, a stock of materials which is beyond all price'.[9] *Dicta* and dissent certainly do not belong to Bentham's theory of law and adjudication. But he did not, or did not always, dismiss them as juridical irrelevances. While, he insisted, nothing good can come of treating judicial utterances as 'real law', he appears eventually to have accepted that it would be foolish to maintain that legislators – the makers of real law – should discount them as sources of legal knowledge and reasoning.

[9] Jeremy Bentham, 'To the President of the United States of America' (1811), in *The Works of Jeremy Bentham*, 11 vols ed. J. Bowring (New York: Russell & Russell, 1962 [1838–43]), IV, 453–67 at 460–1 (emphasis in original).

ESSAY I

Dicta

Introduction

We digress when, in intending to make a point, we either temporarily or permanently deviate from it. Digressions can be deliberate or unconscious. They can be to good or bad – or a mixture of good and bad – or to no effect. Distinguishing the digressive from the non-digressive is not always straightforward: comments offered as asides can strike at the very heart of a matter, just as narrative which a reader thinks peripheral might be the author's *fil conducteur*. Common-law judges often digress in the course of making legal decisions. The standard characterization of these digressions is that they are observations which are not integral to a decision that has been reached – that they could be taken out of a judgment without that judgment being undermined. The full legal Latin term for these observations is *obiter dicta*.

Legal theorists have not had a great deal to say about the concept of *obiter dicta*. Much of what can be said yields not just no interesting conclusions but no conclusions at all: observations about *obiter dicta* frequently meet with no less plausible observations running in the opposite direction, and the virtues and drawbacks of *dicta* often end up being sides of the same coin. There is no immediately obvious reason to focus on *dicta* when analysing law, moreover, for the history of common-law jurisprudence repeatedly reinforces the message that *dicta* are not law. In 1980, an eminent English judge admitted doubting that *obiter dicta* had any legal value whatsoever.[1] This did not mean that he had compunctions about uttering them: in that one year alone – and in many before and after – judges and counsel can be seen commending, doubting, or disapproving of remarks which he clearly made *obiter*.[2] But nor did it mean that he was hypocritical. It is hardly surprising that a judge

[1] *R* v. *Sang* [1980] AC 402, 444 *per* Lord Salmon.

[2] For 1980 alone, see *Re Ever's Trust* [1980] 1 WLR 1327 (*dictum* of Salmon LJ applied); *Re Holliday* [1981] Ch 405 (case decided May 1980) (*dictum* of Salmon LJ doubted); *Teesside*

who regards *dictum* dismissively should also be a source of it, for judges are no different from anybody else in being innately digressive. One would have to be a freakishly austere mouthpiece of the law, perhaps the most robotic common-law judge ever, to serve a career of any significant length without so much as once offering an *obiter* opinion in the process of contributing to a decision. Our minds wander, and we often speak our minds. Our thoughts about something often lead us to think about something else, and we end up articulating those tangential thoughts as well as – possibly even instead of – our primary ones. To digress is to be human, and judges are only human. Do these truisms not intimate everything we need to know about *obiter dicta* – that it is just a type of noise which judges cannot help but produce from time to time? What else is there to say?

It is easy to see why studying judicial exhibition of a standard human trait might look like a classic case of academic overthinking. This is especially so when one contemplates *dicta* as something produced. *Dicta* will hardly ever be completely pointless: judgments reserved and written before delivery will often contain carefully formulated *obiter* observations, as, indeed, might some judgments delivered orally (oral delivery of judgments being the norm in English courts until the second half of the twentieth century).[3] Nevertheless, many *obiter dicta* – even ones which are scripted rather than delivered extempore – will be casually cast out and borne of minimal reflection. There is the risk of hearing chimes emanating from silent bells once one starts delving into the motives that judges might have had for making observations which, in many instances, were delivered in the moment and off the cuff.

Yet, as we will see in this Essay, judges often do have distinct reasons for making – and, indeed, for declining to make – *obiter* pronouncements: it would be a mistake to assume that *obiter dicta* are only ever evidence of a judicial predilection for digression. The reasons for according *dictum* significance become obvious when one thinks of it as

Times Ltd v. *Drury* [1980] ICR 338, 354 *per* Goff LJ ('I would agree with the *dictum* of Lord Salmon [in *De Rosa* v. *Barrie* (1974)] . . . that there must be continuity of employment down to the time of the transfer . . .'). For the relevant *dicta*, see *De Rosa* v. *Barrie* [1974] ICR 480, 500 ('[I]f the transferors had given due notice to determine [the respondent's] employment . . . paragraph 10(2) of Schedule 1 to the [Contracts of Employment] Act of 1963 would have had no application to his case. I do not wish, however, to express any concluded view on this point because it has not been argued'); also (the *dicta* being referred to in *Re Ever's* and *Re Holliday*) *Rawlings* v. *Rawlings* [1964] P 398, 419 *per* Salmon LJ.

[3] See Roderick Munday, 'Permutations of the Court and Properties of Judgment' (2002) 61 *CLJ* 612, 614–15.

something not produced but received. One of the main purposes of this Essay is to examine how *obiter dicta* have been interpreted in English law. For what reasons are particular judicial observations classified as *obiter dicta*? To what uses might *dicta* be put? Precisely what legal status do *dicta* have? Has their legal status altered over time? Are there gradations of *dicta*? Answers to these questions offer some intriguing insights into the nature of the common law. The legal status of *dicta* is that they have secondary (or epistemic) authority: they are a source of legal information, opinion, and argument, but they are not an actual source of law. However, the judicial decisions in which they appear are a source of law. Other forms of secondary legal authority – juristic writings, foreign legal sources, legislative history, third-party or *amicus* interventions in judicial proceedings, dissenting judicial opinions, and concurring opinions produced separate from majority judgments – all differ from *obiter dicta* by virtue of being discrete; distinguishing these secondary sources from primary ones poses no significant difficulty. What sets *obiter dicta* apart is that they are not set apart. They are mixed into the substance of the common law.

Although there exists a broadly shared and largely reliable approach to distinguishing *dicta* from whatever content of a judicial decision contributes to the common law, it is not an approach which resolves every uncertainty as to what is the case-law component of a case (Section 7). Lawyers and judges do not always agree on – indeed are not always sure – what is and what is not *obiter* in a judgment. Yet it matters that a distinction between the binding and the non-binding content of a judgment can be drawn – not only because it is impossible, without the distinction, to recognize what it is within a judgment that will count as law in a court,[4] but also because, if it were impossible to identify some of the material within a judgment as *obiter dicta*, the lawmaking power of judges would not be confined to the facts of particular cases. Decided cases, as rule formulations applied to specific facts, are a source of law. But the possibility of these cases occasioning *obiter dicta* means that they may contain judicial observations on the law which are not part of, but which are unlikely to be presented separate from, the rule formulation that any particular case yields. If it were impossible to treat – because it was impossible to identify – these observations as distinct from the binding content of a judicial decision, courts would in effect have an unfettered lawmaking function.

[4] H. L. A. Hart, *The Concept of Law*, 3rd ed. (Oxford University Press, 2012; 1st ed. publ. 1961), 105.

1 The Civilian Dimension

One of the clearest explanations of this last point – of why it is important to be able to distinguish *obiter dicta* from whatever case-content forms part of the common law – is to be found in a rather unlikely source. In his landmark *Méthode d'interprétation et sources en droit privé positif*, first published in 1899, François Gény declared it beyond doubt that the French judges of his day enjoyed considerable interpretive freedom when applying the positive law.[5] But did those judges have any degree of freedom to make law? They 'have the power to create it for a specific situation', Gény believed, but they could never 'produce a general rule',[6] because a judicial power not confined to the 'individualization of private rights' would violate the 'superior principle of separation of powers'.[7] Yet if case law can 'supply the gaps in formal sources, and direct the whole movement of legal life' when those sources are silent, Gény wondered, might we not accurately speak of French judicial decision-making as 'constituting . . . a kind of common law'?[8]

Gény resisted this conclusion. The latitude that judges enjoy when individualizing private rights (their capacity, to use Gény's favoured term, to engage in *la libre recherche scientifique*)[9] entails 'necessary limitations'[10] – what legal theorists sometimes, for somewhat obscure reasons, refer to as *le 'compromis Gény'*.[11] The judicial decision, like

[5] François Gény, *Méthode d'interprétation et sources en droit privé positif: Essai critique*, 2nd ed., 2 vols. (Paris: LGDJ, 1954 [1919]), I, 207–8.

[6] Ibid. II at 35.

[7] Ibid. I at 213, 208.

[8] Ibid. II at 89.

[9] See, e.g., ibid. I at 222, 224; II at 34, 69, 78.

[10] Ibid. II at 34.

[11] See, e.g., Duncan Kennedy and Marie-Claire Belleau, 'François Gény aux États-Unis', in *François Gény, Mythe et Réalités, 1899–1999*, ed. C. Thomasset et al. (Montréal: Yvon Blais, 2000), 295–320 at 297.

> According to Philippe Jestaz, the 'Gény compromise' is as follows: judges and doctrinal writers could pursue free scientific research [*la libre recherche scientifique*], thereby exercising an enormous social power. But there is a price to be paid for the exercise of this considerable power. The price is that neither case law [*jurisprudence*] nor juristic analysis [*la doctrine*] can . . . occupy anything other than a secondary or even tertiary place in the hierarchy of legal sources.

In identifying the source of the term *le 'compromis Gény'*, Kennedy and Belleau refer to a chapter by Philippe Jestaz in the same the volume ('François Gény: Une image française de la loi et du juge', in ibid. at 37–53). But nowhere in Jestaz's chapter, nor in a larger study in which that chapter was subsequently republished (Philippe Jestaz and

doctrinal writing, is a 'moral'[12] or 'second-order authority'[13] which 'often contributes to the formation'[14] of the 'formal source[s] of positive law'.[15] '[T]aken on its own', however, precedent cannot be 'authority ranking among the formal sources of our positive private law'[16] because 'case law ... remains subject to variations and contradictions'[17] – because judges, when engaged in 'the practical ... implementation of positive law',[18] produce opinions which, like juristic speculation, are essentially a form of 'free inquiry'[19] which can become 'disconnected from ... concrete questions'.[20]

The price paid for the judge's freedom to produce *obiter dicta* – the compromise – is that there cannot be a French common law. To treat a recorded judicial decision as 'positive common law'[21] risks 'an encroachment on the domain of legislative power',[22] for the record might contain, along with the ruling on the issue in dispute, incidental judicial commentary on legal difficulties which, though not presently before the court, might at a later date need to be resolved or revisited. If the whole of a recorded judicial decision, including the orthogonal commentary, is considered to be 'a formal source of private positive

Christophe Jamin, *La doctrine* (Paris: Dalloz, 2004)), can Jestaz be found referring to *le 'compromis Gény'*. Perhaps Jestaz used the phrase when speaking at the Gény centenary colloquium in Montreal in late October 1999 – the content of the *Mythe et Réalités* collection, including Jestaz's chapter, is drawn from that event – and perhaps Kennedy and Belleau, participating in the colloquium, heard it and assumed that it would appear in the published version of his remarks. Whatever the case, others have subsequently co-opted *le 'compromis Gény'*, sometimes attributing the phrase to Kennedy and Belleau, sometimes to Jestaz, and sometimes to all three: see Jacco Bomhoff, *Balancing Constitutional Rights: The Origins and Meanings of Postwar Legal Discourse* (Cambridge University Press, 2013), 59 (Kennedy and Belleau); Aboudramane Ouattara, 'Prolégomènes pour une épistémologie du droit en Afrique' (2013) 11 *Revue droit Sénégalais* 249, 284 n. 110 (Jestaz); and Ward Alexander Penfold, 'An Ineluctable Minimum of Natural Law: François Gény, Oliver Wendell Holmes, and the Limits of Legal Skepticism' (2011) 37 *Hist. Eur. Ideas* 475, 476 (all three).

12 Gény, *Méthode d'interprétation*, I, 234 ('une autorité purement morale'), also II, 67 ('une simple autorité morale').

13 Ibid. II at 69.

14 Ibid.

15 Ibid. II at 53, also II at 72–3; on *travaux de doctrine*, see ibid. II at 54–5.

16 Ibid. II at 35.

17 Ibid. II at 48.

18 Ibid. II at 79.

19 Ibid. II at 88.

20 Ibid. II at 79.

21 Ibid. II at 90.

22 Ibid. II at 40 ('un empiétement sur le domaine du pouvoir législatif').

law, independent and *sui generis*',[23] the judicial rule-making power is not confined to determining the actual litigation before the court. Judges, like legislators, would have a general lawmaking function.[24]

In the English common law, as is well known, the distinction between the binding *ratio decidendi* of a case and the non-binding *obiter dicta* pronounced in the course of deciding the case serves as a brake against judges formulating common-law rules *ultra vires*. The *ratio decidendi* is the court's reasoning underpinning its decision on how the law applies to the facts, whereas *obiter dicta* are observations made by the deciding judge, or judges, which bear on matters other than the law as it applies to those facts. Since *obiter dicta* do not pertain to the legal determination of the facts which frame the dispute before the court, they cannot bind as precedent. We will consider in the next section how the distinction between *ratio decidendi* and *obiter dicta* emerged quite late in the history of the English common law, though the reason for its late arrival on the scene is easy enough to deduce: identification of some of the content of a case as *obiter* only becomes a pertinent task once cases come to be understood as sources of law. Perhaps more surprising, and worth reflecting on at least briefly before we turn to the English legal experience, is the fact that the concept of *obiter dicta* featured in the civil law tradition before it became established in the common lawyer's lexicon.

If we were to 'commend unto' the law student 'some special writers of the law', William Fulbeck observed in 1600, at the top of the list ought to be Oxford's then Regius professor of law, Alberico Gentili, 'who . . . hath in his learned labours expressed the judgment of a great statesman'.[25] After alluding to Theodosius II's endorsement of the so-called Law of Citations (426 CE) – that the opinion held by the greater number of jurists shall prevail when conflicting juristic opinions are cited in court[26] – Fulbeck notes that Gentili, though a critic of humanist jurisprudence, wisely joined with one of its most renowned proponents, Andrea Alciato, in considering the Law of Citations unsound. For Gentili and Alciato alike, according to Fulbeck, if a juristic opinion is to stand as legal authority then its status as such ought to depend not on the number of jurists sharing the opinion but rather on the weight the opinion holds

[23] Ibid. II at 72.

[24] Article 5 of the French Civil Code prohibits judges from assuming this function. On *obiter dicta* in the French ordinary courts, see Essay II (Section 3).

[25] William Fulbeck, *Direction or Preparative to the Study of Law* (London: Clarke, 1829), 68–9. The book was written in 1599 and first published in 1600.

[26] C. Theod. (438 CE) 1. 4. 3.

when 'examined' in 'accord with reason'.[27] This rejection of Theodosius' proclamation seems, on the face of it, to amount to nothing. The Law of Citations – or certainly Theodosius' version of it – is more nuanced than Alciato (and, following him, Gentili and Fulbeck) appeared to concede. Although the *Codex Theodosianus* treats the majority juristic opinion as the one which a court has to follow, it does not dismiss the weight of juristic opinion entirely: where opinions before a court are evenly split, the opinion reflecting that of Papinian (the jurist 'of superior genius') is presumed the weightier and is therefore supposed to prevail.[28] By the late sixteenth century, furthermore, it was unlikely to have been immediately obvious that Theodosius' reiteration of the Law of Citations was worth reckoning with, for the Law was a force long spent. 'The Law of Citations in this revised [i.e., Theodosian] form . . . was . . . [r]endered obsolete by the publication of the *Digest*' of Justinian, and, though 'it was included in the *Codex [Justinianus]* of 529 . . . it was excluded from the *Codex* of 534'.[29]

For Gentili, however, this was a Law easily underestimated. The early medieval period seems to have marked the beginning of its reappraisal – even its occasional revival (in the late eighth century, for example, the Law of Citations was incorporated into the *Lex Romana Curiensis*, a set of laws compiled for the Germanic population of Rhaetia in eastern Switzerland).[30] During the middle-ages and early Renaissance, civilian jurists were by no means entirely sold on the Law of Citations, but nor were they wholly dismissive of it; followers of the fourteenth-century Italian jurist, Bartolus, for example, were inclined to argue that Bartolist opinions ought to be upheld by the courts because they were *communis opinio doctorum* – opinions held by a juristic majority.[31] Fulbeck was commending Gentili for his willingness to align himself with Alciato – himself a prominent Bartolist,[32] and a jurist from whom Gentili

[27] Fulbeck, *Direction or Preparative*, 84.

[28] C. Theod. 1. 4. 3. If neither opinion was endorsed by Papinian, the court would determine how the case was to be decided.

[29] Fritz Schulz, *History of Roman Legal Science* (Oxford: Clarendon Press, 1946), 282.

[30] See Peter Stein, *Roman Law in European History* (Cambridge University Press, 1999), 39. According to Vinogradoff, the incorporation was garbled: Paul Vinogradoff, *Roman Law in Medieval Europe*, 2nd ed. (Oxford: Clarendon Press, 1929), 21–3.

[31] See, e.g., Matthaeus Gribaldus Mopha, *De Methodo ac Ratione Studenti* (Lugduni: Coloniensi, 1544), book I, ch. 13 at 75–7.

[32] Alciato is frequently accredited with having composed a verse beginning with the proposition that in law, first place goes to Bartolus ('In iure primas comparatus caeteris hartes habebit Bartolus'). See, e.g., Christop Hegendorf, *Epitome tyrocinii iuris civilis*

distanced himself on other matters[33] – in expressing distaste for a rule which favoured the most widely shared legal opinion over the one most satisfactorily reasoned. For Fulbeck, the significance of Gentili's stance would have been more than merely historical, for even in the late sixteenth century, the period in which both Gentili and Fulbeck wrote, the rule still had its defenders. In 1591, for example, the Venetian jurist, Angelo Matteacci, asserted that although some medieval lawyers had been willing to attach weight to opinions of particular jurists, it was still the case that the majority juristic opinion had a stronger foundation (*fit fundata*) than the opinion of jurists set against it, even if the opinion of the jurists in the minority was inherently fairer and could be said to strive for stronger rights (*quae validioribus nititur iuribus*).[34]

Instinctively, one might presume that, for those civilians who placed store in *communis opinio*, the minority or unfavoured opinion was tantamount to a dissenting opinion. But medieval civil lawyers seem to have conceived of the majority opinion as a form of *ratio* and the unfavoured one as akin to *obiter dictum*. Gentili himself considered it a fact – albeit a lamentable fact – that opinions which, after discussion, become established as the reasoned judgments of a community (*deuentum*) of lawyers will carry more authority than 'anything entering into the calculation which is *obiter*, the incidental *dictum* of some Doctor'.[35] That the majority juristic opinion carried more authority than the *dicta* of outlier jurists did not mean that the authority of *communis opinio* was unassailable. In Justinian's *Corpus Iuris*, the opinions of Papinian, and of other Roman jurists who complemented his labours, are, like judicial rulings, taken to be true statements of the law, or *necessary* authority ('as good as law, ... as if their studies were derived from imperial constitutions').[36] By contrast, the *communis opinio* to be discerned from the writings of medieval glossators and doctors was *probable*

(Basel: Westhemerus, 1540), 32; Mopha, *De Methodo ac Ratione Studenti*, 75; Richard Hall, *De quinquepartita conscientia, libri III* (Duaci: Bogard, 1598), 158.

[33] See Donald R. Kelley, *The Human Measure: Social Thought in the Western Legal Tradition* (Cambridge, Mass.: Harvard University Press, 1990), 187–8.

[34] Angelus Matthaeacius, *De via et ratione artificiosa iuris universi libri duo* (Venice: Meles, 1591), 123. See also ibid. at 124–5 ('*[C]ommunis* ... *opinio* ... has been bold enough ... to give guidance and legal answers to the world's councils and to prescribe courses of action to those seeking legal advice. You may easily infer from this in what great regard the jurists are to be held').

[35] Alberico Gentili, *Lectionum et epistolarum quae ad ius civile pertinent. Liber I* (London: Wolf, 1583), 218.

[36] C 1. 17. 1. 6. On judicial rulings as true statements of the law, see D 1. 5. 25; also D 50. 17. 207.

authority.[37] According to the fourteenth-century logician, John Buridan, probable authority 'is the judgment of the wise or of the expert in some art concerning things that pertain to that art ... [O]f the person or persons who have this condition, we say that they have authority' because 'it is probable that what is said is true'.[38] Buridan was analyzing this conception of authority as set forth in Boethius' *De differentiis topicis*, though he appreciated that the distinction between necessary (apodictic) and probable (plausible) authority could be traced to Book 1 of the *Topics*,[39] where Aristotle demarcates demonstrations from premises which are self-evidently true and dialectical arguments based on premises considered authoritative because they reflect generally accepted reputable opinion. Since the refutation of *communis opinio* by contrary reasoning was never entirely impossible – this was a position regularly taken by civilian jurists during the Renaissance – it could only ever have probable authority.

Arguments not belonging to *communis opinio* on a legal matter had neither necessary nor probable authority. Fulbeck had been expressing his 'wish' that, 'as Gentilis and Alciat do require, ... the authorities and cases of the learned writers of the law should rather be weighed than numbered'.[40] His point was not that the force of an argument depended, but that ideally it ought to depend, on the quality of the reasons supporting the argument

[37] See, e.g., Nicolaus Everardus (Everaerts), *Topicorum seu Locorum Legalium Opus de Inventione* (Basel: Pernam, 1544 [1516]), 243–54; also Otto Maria Vervaart, *Studies over Nicolaas Everaerts (1462–1532) en zijn Topica* (Gouda: Sanders Instituut, 1994), 111.

> 'The authority of a cited person is compelling when it concerns an authority with the competence to give judgments with the force of law [i.e., *lex*], a person with *potestas legis condende* [i.e., original legal power] ... [A]uthority without this lawmaking power, for example when one cites a doctor, no matter how famous or learned ... is only *probabile*, to be proved, and not compelling, *necessarium*. The same goes for the gloss ... One should only trust an expert in their area ... An unlikely authority does not mean anything: a theologian has no business speaking out on juridical matters, and the same goes for a medical doctor in relation to theology, so says Everaerts'.

I am grateful to my colleague, Jacco Bomhoff, for translating this passage from Vervaart's study into English.

[38] John Buridan (*c.*1295–1361), *Summulae de dialectica*, trans. G. Klima (New Haven: Yale University Press, 2001), 480–1.

[39] See ibid. at 481. For similar medieval arguments about probable authority (arguments which sometimes betray other influences besides Aristotelian reasoning), see Daniel Garber and Sandy Zabell, 'On the Emergence of Probability' (1979) 21 *Archive for History of Exact Sciences* 33, 44–7.

[40] Fulbeck, *Direction or Preparative*, 84.

rather than on how many jurists subscribed to it.[41] Those medieval and Renaissance legal writers who rejected this position seemed never to go so far as to claim that any modern jurist – even Bartolus – could be quite on a par with Papinian.[42] It was accepted, nevertheless, that *communis opinio*, even though only probable authority, could determine the outcomes of legal disputes. Even where the judgment yielded by *communis opinio* is evidently mistaken, Nicolaus Everardus observed, it is still – in the absence of a judgment delivered by an actual court[43] – the opinion carrying the most authority (*maxime auctoritates*); and so if a judge were to eschew *communis opinio* in favour of a fresh analysis which revealed errors in it, he might be at risk of incurring personal liability for ruling contrary to a body of interpreters who spoke as one on the legal issue at stake.[44] While *communis opinio* could be de facto binding, juristic *obiter dicta* were never accorded elevated legal status – or, indeed, any legal status. Nicolaus Vigelius, echoing his contemporary, Montaigne, maintained that whatever the quality of disparate legal arguments standing some distance from an original source of law, the fact that they are but incidental accumulations (*per accidentium congeriem*) on the *ratio legis* militates against reading them as probable authority; the locus of this authority, he insisted, could only ever be consensus of opinion among medieval doctors.[45] Juristic opinions which, for whatever

41 Jurists of the period were certainly often willing to accept that on some non-legal matters, such as the interpretation or translation of religious texts, not all informed opinion carried the same weight: see, e.g., Constantius Rogerius, *Tractatus de iuris interpretatione* (Lyon: de Roxio, 1549 [1463]), 42–5.

42 Although in Portugal during the 1440s, legislation was enacted according Baldus' works special weight in the case of tie breaks much as the Law of Citations had done with positions taken by Papinian: see Mário Júlio de Almeida Costa, 'Romanisme et Bartolisme dans le droit portugais', in *Bartolo de Sassoferato: Studi e documenti per il VI Centenario*, 2 vols., ed. D. Segoloni (Milan: Giuffrè, 1962), I, 314–45. Veneration of Papinian himself endured: see, e.g., Antoine Favre, *Iurisprudentiae Papinianae scientia* (Lyon: Borde, Arnaud & Rigaud, 1658 [1607]); Jacques Cujas, *Opera*, 4 vols. (Hanover: Marnium & Aubri, 1602), II. iv. 41; also Giambattista Vico (1668–1744), *Opere scientifiche latine* (Milan: Bravetta, 1837), lxii ('Papinian, whose faculties were above those of all other jurists . . .').

43 Everardus joined with civilian juristic contemporaries in considering judicial (or certainly supreme court) rulings to be as good as law: see Philippe Godding, 'L'origine et l'autorité des recueils de jurisprudence dans les Pays-Bas méridionaux (XIIIe-XVIIIe siècles)', in *Rapports belges au VIIIe Congrès international de droit comparé* (Brussels: CIDC, 1970), 1–37 at 29–30.

44 See Nicolaus Everardus, *Centum modi argumentandi topicorum* (Lyon: de Millis, 1545), 358–60. On speaking as one, see ibid. at 360 ('doctores pro una parte, sicut pro alia').

45 See Nicolaus Vigelius, *Dialectices juris civilis libri III* (Basel: Gemusaeum, 1597), 440–3. See also Michel de Montaigne, *The Complete Essays*, rev. ed. trans. M. A. Screech (London: Penguin, 2003 [1580–1595]), iii. 13 (1210–12).

reason, did not form part of this consensus were *obiter*, and *obiter* opinions could never be dispositive.

It is difficult, if not impossible, to know to what extent the common-law concept of *obiter dicta* is traceable to civilian juristic analysis. Certainly the evidence of civilian influence in Fulbeck's work ought to be treated cautiously, for his familiarity with civil law writing was by no means typical of his English contemporaries. Once English judges and lawyers began to conceive of legal reasoning and judgment as having a digressive dimension, moreover, their reflections on *obiter dicta* quickly became distinguishable from the comparatively meagre observations that had been offered by civilian authors. Juristic *obiter dicta*, in so far as they registered in the civilian legal consciousness, were only ever presented negatively: they counted for nothing. But in England, a different picture emerges: there is clearly discernible, in eighteenth-century case reports, the notion that judicial *obiter dicta* sometimes counted for something – though it would be another century again before judges started to show any significant inclination to articulate what this 'something' might be. Civilian and common lawyers were alike in insisting that *dicta* could not constitute necessary, or binding, legal authority. Common lawyers, however, were, or certainly became, attracted to a variant on the proposition that Fulbeck had admired in the writings of Gentili, and which Gentili had found in the writings of Alciato: that respect given to an opinion should accord with the quality of the reasoning, rather than with the number of lawyers, supporting it.

Before the nineteenth century, common lawyers, unlike their civilian counterparts, showed little, if any, inclination to refer to legal opinion as in any sense authoritative in a court; to this day, indeed, it is not uncommon to find judges declaring that some opinions which form part of the content of a decided case are not even worthy of respect – that they are 'mere *dicta*'. Yet, between the eighteenth century and the present, common-law thinking about *obiter* observations has subtly but significantly altered. For the common lawyer, *obiter dicta* have never acquired the status of probable authority in quite the way that medieval and Renaissance civilians understood that term. Certainly by the twentieth century, however, many English (and other common-law) judges and lawyers are regularly to be found claiming that *dicta* deserving of respect – weighty *dicta* – might sensibly be said to be authoritative. This claim, we will see, almost always trades on a markedly confined notion of authority: *dicta* as authoritative legal information rather than *dicta* as having the authority of law. *Dictum* deemed authoritative in this epistemic sense is typically (though not always) the product of judges reacting to other judges: the standard scenario would be where Judge *A*, usually in an earlier case, has made an observation which is assessed by Judge *B* – possibly because it features in a legal argument presented to *B* in court – and the observation proves helpful to *B* either for the purpose of deciding a case before a court today, or for the purpose of formulating some *dictum* of his own. *B* might well laud *A*'s *dictum* as soundly reasoned. But not necessarily: commendations of *dicta* often refer not to their quality as exercises in legal reasoning but rather identify some proxy feature – such as the utterer's general legal eminence (or expertise in a particular area of the law) or the *dicta* having been regularly endorsed – which is presumed to put any doubts about such quality to rest. What it means to speak of *dicta* as authoritative is examined in detail later (Sections 9–11). We turn first to the emergence, representations, uses, and characteristics of *obiter dicta* in English common law, as well as to the difficulties that the concept has yielded.

2 Case Law As Common Law

The emergence of *obiter dicta* as a common-law concept is sometimes traced to the advent of *stare decisis*. This association of *obiter dicta* with *stare decisis* appears to be underscored by two distinct arguments. The first and most obvious argument – the one set out in the Introduction to this Essay – is that under *stare decisis*, lawyers rely on the concept of *obiter dicta* to identify the non-binding content of precedents: the binding part of the decision is the *ratio decidendi*, the reasons which make for the decision, and any observations offered by the decision-makers in the course of making that decision which are tangential to the decision itself are merely *obiter*.[46] Against the grain of this argument runs the second one: if judicial decisions bind as precedents, judges might be inclined to include in their judgments observations on how the law should apply to a matter similar but not identical to the one for resolution in the immediate case in the hope that, when that cognate matter comes to

[46] See A. W. B. Simpson, 'The *Ratio Decidendi* of a Case and the Doctrine of Binding Precedent', in *Oxford Essays in Jurisprudence (First Series)*, ed. A. G. Guest (Oxford: Clarendon Press, 1961), 148–75 at 160–1 ('[T]here must be some principle which has the effect of reducing the importance of enunciations of the law which have in fact been delivered by judges – either accidentally or deliberately – upon hypothetical issues. Thus the conception of *obiter dicta* grows up; *obiter dicta* are in some sense *ultra vires* enunciations of law').

a later court for resolution, the court might treat the earlier judges' *obiter dicta* as yielding the correct ruling on the matter much as, had the matters to be ruled on been identical in both cases, it would have treated the earlier judgment as binding precedent. One American judge, following this second line of argument, has written of how '*dictum* ... took on a heightened importance with the adoption of "*stare decisis*"[47] – of how "the advent of *stare decisis* ... helped transform *dicta* from trivia into force"'.[48]

Obiter dicta very likely did, as a concept, acquire heightened significance with the advent of *stare decisis*. But it would be a mistake to think of *obiter dicta* and *stare decisis* as legal concepts which emerged in tandem. Even as early as the late fifteenth century, there is evidence that adjudged cases – judgments made by judges on facts – were considered to be a stronger form of legal authority than interlocutory rulings, judicial advice on pleading motions, and the opinions of judges and serjeants as to the correct way to rule on a hypothetical legal problem. Creditable curial advice and respected legal opinion appear to have had a status similar to that of the medieval glossators' and doctors' *communis opinio*. Like *communis opinio*, they were trumped by judicial determinations.[49] In a year book case of 1454, various serjeants and judges attempted to establish the existence of a reversionary term by apparently discounting earlier cases in which the matter was considered settled by thirteenth-century statute law, and instead offered opinions on hypothetical disputes similar to, but not quite the same as, the one being adjudged. The then Chief Justice of the Common Pleas, Sir John Prisot, seemed to become exasperated:

> now you dispute the words of the statute, ... which seems strange to me, considering how many judgments there have been in this case contrary to your opinions before now. For I know well that the cause has been traversed twelve times in our [year] books.[50]

You would have us 'give regard to the opinion of one judge, or two, contrary to so many judgments of many honourable judges on the opposing side', Prisot continued, notwithstanding 'that those judges who

[47] Pierre N. Leval, 'Judging under the Constitution: *Dicta* about *Dicta*' (2006) 81 *NYU L. Rev.* 1249, 1258.

[48] Ibid. at 1256.

[49] See John Baker, 'Legal Discussion in Court', in his *The Oxford History of the Laws of England. Volume VI: 1483–1588* (Oxford University Press, 2003), 385–407 at 389.

[50] *Windham* v. *Felbridge*, YB Mich 33 Hen VI 38 (1454) at 41 (pl. 17).

adjudged these matters in ancient times were much closer to the creation of the statute than we are', and that 'young apprentices' would likely 'never wish to give credence to their books, if such judgment that has been so many times adjudged in their books will now be adjudged the contrary'.[51]

Prisot's observations could be read as indicating that by the end of the fifteenth century, English judges were already amenable to *stare decisis*. But such a reading should be resisted. '[T]he *communis opinio*' of lawyers and judges was tantamount to probable authority: it 'passed for law in the absence of better authority'[52] – and judicial determinations were better authority.[53] But this means only that, as compared with judicial and lawyerly opinion, judicial determinations were a better form of probable authority, not they must have had necessary authority. Note that Prisot never goes so far as to say that the prior judicial decisions had to be followed. By 1500 there may have been a greater expectation than ever before that courts provide authoritative judgments, but at this point legal energies were still focused primarily on the pleadings rather than the decision. A judgment might have been better authority than opinion, but in Prisot's day a judge was far more likely to try to steer disputing parties towards a settlement rather than rule on a point of law.[54]

During the first half of the sixteenth century, a change seemed to be underway in so far as the jury's role as final arbiter of fact and law began to transfer to the courts. Judges gradually stopped exploring points of law before putting a case to the jury and started to determine them after the facts of the case had been found. As a consequence, it became increasingly common for judges to make decisions accompanied by legal reasons.[55] In the prologue to his *Commentaries*, first published 1571,

[51] Ibid.

[52] Baker, 'Legal Discussion in Court', 389.

[53] The picture is complicated by the fact that lawyers and judges sometimes distinguished general common opinion about the law from what every learned lawyer knew about the law. Common erudition or learning, unlike common opinion, commanded legal unanimity, and so would have been indisputable authority. See J. H. Baker, *The Law's Two Bodies* (Oxford University Press, 2001), 67–8; Ian Williams, 'Common Opinion in the Fourteenth Century: Before the Common Learning, Before the Inns of Court', in *English Legal History and Its Sources: Essays in Honour of Sir John Baker*, ed. D. Ibbetson et al. (Cambridge University Press, 2019), 300–17 at 300–1, also 307 ('To dissent from the common learning would have been in a real sense unthinkable').

[54] See David J. Ibbetson, 'Case Law and Judicial Precedents in Mediaeval and Early Modern England', in *Auctoritates: Xenia R. C. van Caenegem oblata* (Brussels: Peeters, 1997), 55–68 at 65–6.

[55] See John Baker, 'Case-Law', in *The Oxford History of the Laws of England. Volume VI*, 473–89 at 486–9; Baker, *The Law's Two Bodies*, 81–4.

Edmund Plowden held out to his readers that his case reports could be relied upon for the 'most firmness and surety of law', because the cases reported were 'upon points of law which [judges] studied, and ... argued and after great deliberation ha[d] given judgment [on]'.[56] A reported case, from this perspective, was a precedent in the sense that it was a judgment of record (which judges could still take issue with) rather than a binding authority.[57] Although, by the end of the sixteenth century, judges are sometimes to be found explaining their decisions by reference to previous cases,[58] no prevalent conception of precedent had yet emerged. Judges and lawyers treated recorded cases in various ways: as binding,[59] as worth considering even if not binding,[60] as a source of law,[61] as not a source of law,[62] as proof of what the law was,[63] as casting doubt on an interpretation of the law,[64] as superior (or as not necessarily

[56] Edmund Plowden, *Les Commentaries* (London: Tottel, 1578 [1571]), iv.

[57] See Baker, 'Case-Law', 486–7.

[58] Ibbetson, 'Case Law and Judicial Precedents', 61.

[59] The instances are rare, and usually take the form of judges confessing either that they intend to decide a case in a particular way unless precedent militating against that decision and adverted to in argument is presented to the court, or that they would have decided a case differently were it not that doing so would put the court at variance with a decision taken on analogous facts in a prior judgment confirmed by the record (confirmation being something which judges appear always to have insisted on): see, e.g., *Stucley* v. *Thynne* (1567), repr. in J. H. Baker, *Reports from the Lost Notebooks of James Dyer*, 2 vols. (London: Selden Society, 1994 [SS vols. 109–10]), I, 127 at 128 *per* Browne J ('[W]e ought not to award the distress, but ... since Jenour prothonotary said ... that there are many precedents ... if I can see such precedents I will subdue my reason to the precedents'); *Hall* v. *Mathor* (1601) BL MS Add 25203, f. 247 *per* Gawdy J; *Sparke* v. *Sparke* (1602) BL MS Add 25203, f. 634^{v} *per* Yelverton J; also Ian Williams, 'Early Modern Judges and the Practice of Precedent', in *Judges and Judging in the History of the Common Law and Civil Law: From Antiquity to Modern Times* (Cambridge University Press, 2012), 51–66 at 53–5.

[60] See, e.g., *Chamberlain* v. *Nichols* (1595) BL MS Hargrave 14, f 89^{v} (King's Bench deferred dispensing with the case pending discovery of the outcome of a case with similar facts decided the previous day in the Court of Exchequer Chamber).

[61] See, e.g., *Browne* v. *Meredith* (1600) BL MS Add 25203, ff 283–4^{v} *per* Gawdy J.

[62] See, e.g., *Browne* v. *Meredith* at f. 283^{v} *per* Popham CJ; also *Slade* v. *Morley* (1602), as compiled in J. H. Baker, 'New Light on *Slade's Case*' (1971) 29 *CLJ* 51, 60–7 at 65 *per* Popham CJ.

[63] See, e.g., *Case of Mines* (1568) 1 Plowden 310 at f. 320^{v} ('For Onslow [apprentice] and Gerard [Attorney General] said that the records of every court are the most effectual proofs of law in things treated in this court').

[64] See, e.g., *Woodland* v. *Mantel and Redsole* (1553) 1 Plowden 94 at ff 95^{v}–96^{v}, where proceedings are reported as having been delayed after counsel for the defendants brought into court a year book case which appears to have made at least two of the judges reconsider their understanding of the relevant law and which the court eventually presented to the jury 'as a good proof' of what the law was.

superior) to the hypothetical case,[65] and very likely in other ways besides.[66] The decidedly unsettled status of reported cases seems to have been on James I's mind in his speech to parliament in 1609. '[A]s a King, I have least cause of any man to dislike the common law',[67] he apparently asserted,

> [y]et could I wish that more certainty were set down ... since the very reports themselves are not always so binding, but that diverse times judges do disclaim them, and recede from the judgement of their predecessors; it were good, that upon mature deliberation, ... such reports were thought fit to serve for law in all times hereafter, and so the people should not depend upon the bare opinions of judges, and uncertain reports.[68]

By this point in time, judges and lawyers were unlikely to reject decided cases out of hand, and, when reasoning, would regularly rely on precedents expecting that others would recognize such reliance to be an acceptable argumentative strategy, even when the precedents were not followed. Increasingly, past decisions guided judges when they ruled on facts materially identical to the ones found in those decisions.[69] There was no fully formed doctrine of precedent by the early seventeenth century, but the seeds of the doctrine are in evidence. So too is the concept of – though not the term – *obiter dicta*. This concept emerges not with the acceptance that decisions by courts could bind as precedents. It emerges, rather, once making decisions becomes a recognizable function of the judiciary.

[65] For preference for genuine cases, see, e.g., *Holwood* v. *Hopkins* (1600), in *Select Cases on Defamation to 1600*, ed. R. H. Helmholz (London: Selden Society, 1985 [SS vol. 101]), 89–92 at 91 *per* Walmsley J ('Our books are good precedents to guide us'); also *Sheffeild* v. *Ratcliffe* (1615) Hob 334, 345, where Hobart maintains that a case which Coke had considered 'a resolution' was 'but a matter of discourse, and ... erroneous', containing 'no point of judgment, or [anything] pertinent to the judgment of that case'. For sixteenth- and early seventeenth-century examples in which hypothetical cases appeared to have been considered on a par with genuine ones, see John P. Dawson, *The Oracles of the Law* (Ann Arbor: University of Michigan Law School, 1968), 71–2.

[66] For a detailed analysis of the various understandings of relevant cases, see Ian S. Williams, *English Legal Reasoning and Legal Culture, c.1528–c.1642* (PhD thesis, Faculty of Law, Cambridge University, 2008), 66–105. I am grateful to Dr Williams for supplying me with this portion of his thesis, which I found immensely valuable when searching for unpublished cases relevant to this section.

[67] *The Kings Majesties Speech to the Lords and Commons* (London: Barker, 1609), 15.

[68] Ibid. at 21.

[69] See Williams, *English Legal Reasoning and Legal Culture* at 80, 94.

3 '*Obiter*' As Legal Entity

In the 1600s, no less so than today, an adjudged case could involve more than the business of judging. If a precedent was to be relied on as a judgment of record, it had to be possible to say what the judgment was – to distinguish the judgment from judicial statements on points of law made alongside the judgment but peripheral to it. '[W]hen … arguing … cases', Fulbeck maintained in his manual for law students, 'the principal case' and 'the points of law' are to be 'orderly distinguished' from 'bye-matters'.[70] Plowden's reports already bore evidence of this way of thinking – perhaps unsurprisingly, given how Plowden eschewed inconclusive cases in favour of reasoned decisions. In a King's Bench case from 1550, a statement by Moile J is reported by Plowden as being considered correct as to the law but 'mise per le voy'.[71] In a case heard by the same court in 1553, Plowden records Bromley J observing of a legal opinion that although it had been 'moved by the way [*move per le voye*] in the years of Henry VII, … there is no principal case adjudged upon this'.[72] Eighty years later, the reporter of *Miller and Jones* v. *Manwaring* distinguished a legal point made in '[Plowden's] Com[mentaries] … *arguendo*' from what was decided in the case containing the point, and recorded that 'St John de Lincolnes Inn' refused to countenance the point stated in argument because he 'den[ied] it to be law' (*ieo denie ceo esse ley*).[73]

Plowden's reports, unlike the report of *Miller and Jones*, appear to contain no direct assertions that an opinion associated with but peripheral to a judgment cannot be law. That an opinion *per le voy* was not considered a source of law in Plowden's time none the less seems clear

[70] Fulbeck, *Direction or Preparative*, 237–8.

[71] *Dive* v. *Maningham* (1550) 1 Plowden 60 at f. 67. In translations of the case the term is rendered as 'put *obiter*'.

[72] *Woodland* v. *Mantel and Redsole* at f. 96. (On the basis of Bromley's observation, one legal historian ventures that by the time of Plowden, '[t]he distinction between *ratio decidendi* and *dicta* seems to have been well defined'. T. Ellis Lewis, 'The History of Judicial Precedent' (pt. IV) (1932) 48 *LQR* 230, 233.)

[73] *Miller and Jones* v. *Manwaring* (1634) 2 *Reports K Bench MS*, Cambridge University Library Manuscripts, Gg. 2. 20. 611, ff. 621–621^{v}. ('St John de Lincolnes Inn' = Oliver St John, called to the bar in 1626 and appointed Chief Justice of the Common Pleas in 1648.) See also *Mary Portington's case* (1613) 10 Co Rep 35^{b} at 40^{a}–40^{b} (where Coke reports that a barrister whom Dyer CJ had apparently 'reproved' as 'not worthy to be of the profession of the law' sought to cite as authority points which 'do not warrant the … conclusion which is made upon them *arguendo* … but to say the truth the contrary … In which case are two great misprisions; one in the citing, the other in the application').

enough. Doubts, if there were any, about the legal status of such opinions are certainly not evident in seventeenth-century decisions. In 1600, Walmsley J appeared to accept adjudged cases as law while refusing to attach significance to an incidental remark which one serjeant testified to hearing uttered in court by – and another claimed to have seen in the handwriting (*escrie ove le main*) of – the then Lord Chief Justice, John Popham.[74] There are 'many authorities' supporting the proposition that infants can be forced to forfeit land until they have reached the age of majority, Gregory J claimed in 1604, and the argument against the proposition 'is only an opinion *obiter*'.[75] Sir John Dodderidge, arguing before the Common Pleas in *Foster* v. *Jackson* (1609), sought to discount 'a judgment which was given in the King's Bench' because 'it was not upon solemn argument of the judges' and so 'not to be compared to other authorities . . . cited'.[76] Dodderidge was serving as a Justice of the King's Bench with Houghton J nine years later when Houghton remarked that 'there is no authority' establishing common-law liability for killing doves, and that judicial opinion on the issue of liability to be found in a Common Pleas decision of 1596 was not part of 'the principal case' but rather expressed 'only on the bye'.[77]

By the early seventeenth century, there is a fair amount of evidence in the law reports – one sees this, for example, in Coke's reports – of judges' and serjeants' 'opinions *obiter*' being declared to be against authority or to pertain to legal matters not for resolution in the case before the court.[78] Some of the reports suggest that opinions expressed *obiter* were not necessarily always thought of as something different from prior decisions

[74] *Holwood* v. *Hopkins*, in *Select Cases on Defamation to 1600*, 90.

[75] *King* v. *Dilliston* (1604) 3 Modern 221, 224.

[76] *Foster* v. *Jackson* (1609) 2 Br & Gould 311, 313–14.

[77] *Earl of Northumberland's case* (1618) Popham 141, 141. The Common Pleas decision – *Boulston's case* (1596) 5 Co Rep 104^{b} – concerned the liability of rabbit breeders for damage caused by their rabbits to neighbouring land. Because breeders could not reasonably be expected to stop their (invariably large numbers of) rabbits straying off their land, there could be no liability. Nor would there have been liability had the case concerned doves, Coke notes (ibid. at 104^{b} n. 6). The content of Coke's note is *obiter dictum*, and in any event goes to the question of liability for damage caused by doves rather than liability for killing them.

[78] See *Clifton's case* (1592) 5 Co Rep 75^{b}, 75^{b}; *Altham's case* (1610) 8 Co Rep 150^{b}, 154^{b}; *Lampet's case* (1612) 10 Co Rep 46^{b}, 50^{a}; *Seymor's case* (1612) 10 Co Rep 95^{b}, 97^{b}; *Newman* v. *Moore* (1625) Hobart 80, 80 ('And it was without argument ruled, . . . by the meaning of the statute against the opinion *obiter* in *Butler's case* and *Baker's*'); also *Pexhall's case* (1609) 8 Co Rep 83^{b}, 85^{a} (where an *obiter* opinion is deemed worth reading so that one might 'better understand the law').

which could be distinguished. In *Foster* v. *Jackson*, for example, Dodderidge appears to have been dismissing an actual judgment rather than an opinion expressed tangential to a judgment. In *Dalton* v. *Bishop of Ely* (1619), an interpretation which Thomas Littleton had put on a land obligations rule originating in the Statute of Merton was discounted as being not an 'authority al cest purpose' but rather only 'un opinion *obiter*' met by 'divers authorities al contrary'.[79] What is not clear is whether the court would have been willing to treat the *obiter* opinion as an authority fit for purpose had there been no authorities running contrary to it. In a Star Chamber report of 1626, a barrister, William Hudson, is recorded as saying that 'Coke has reported the law to be so, but this is only in an *obiter* case.'[80] The reference to a 'case' as *obiter* suggests that early-seventeenth-century lawyers and judges did not always acknowledge a difference between an opinion considered to have no bearing on the present case because it was expressed 'by the way' and a precedent considered to have no bearing on the present case because it was not on all fours with it. It seemed that by around 1650, the term '*obiter*', in so far as it had entered the English legal vocabulary, could carry two distinct meanings: either that an opinion expressed in an earlier decision concerned a matter incidental to that decision (i.e., 'the principal case'), or that the earlier decision might be discounted as not directly relevant to the case currently before the court.

That this ambiguity should be in evidence in the seventeenth-century reports is hardly surprising, given that the cases being described as *obiter* – usually year book cases – were typically records of legal argument rather than records of judgments. In a King's Bench decision of 1660, a case from the 1430s is described as 'an opinion *obiter*', which appears to mean that it is a case containing opinion that, unlike 'an express authority', is not fully on point ('full in this point') with regard to the facts then before the court.[81] By the 1660s, it is nearly always an opinion – usually offered in judicial proceedings or in the course of a judgment – that is

[79] *Dalton* v. *L'Evesq de Ely* (1619) W Jones 45, 50.

[80] 'Hudson, voyer est que Seigneur Coke ad issint report la ley ad estre, mes ceo est forsque in un cas *obiter*'. *Margatts* v. *Bateman* (1626) BL MS Add 48057 at f. 42^{v}. Although the law French version of *Margatts* v. *Bateman* contains the term *obiter*, the English version does not: *Margatts* v. *Bateman* (1626) BL MS Lansdowne 620, f. 26 ('Hudson true it is that my lord Cooke hath soe reported the lawe to be but that it is in a case by the way').

[81] *Manby* v. *Scot* (1660) 1 Keble 69, 69–70. *Cf.* Alverstone CJ's insistence in 1911 that it was not open to him to treat an opinion of Lord Halsbury's as *obiter dictum* because the opinion was 'upon a cognate point'. *Guardians of Hackney Union* v. *Kingston upon Hull Incorporation for the Poor* [1911] 1 KB 748, 761.

obiter.[82] '[T]hough I must give reverence to the opinions of the judges', Bridgman CJ stated in 1662, 'I make a difference between [opinions and] cases adjudged upon debate.'[83] An *obiter* opinion was not necessarily an opinion from the past: judges, by this point, were sometimes self-consciously producing *obiter dictum* – making it clear that something they said in court was to be treated as distinct from the judgment.[84] The year 1671 marks the first reported appearance of '*obiter dictum*',[85] though only in the eighteenth century did lawyers begin to use the term (and *obiter dicta*) regularly.[86] *Obiter* itself was not always the preferred

[82] For exceptions, see *Bayley* v. *Edwards* (1792) 3 Swanston 703, 709 ('yet that was a single case, and only a *dictum*'); *R* v. *Wooton* (1834) 1 Ad & El 232, 236 *per* Patteson J.

[83] *Beckman* v. *Maplesden* (1662) Bridg O 60, 78.

[84] See, e.g., *Payne* v. *Barker* (1662) Bridg O 18, 20–1 *per* Bridgman CJ ('Myself and two of my brethren . . . agree, . . . but there is some difference amongst us touching our reasons . . . [I]f I have occasion to speak my single opinion on any thing, I shall accordingly deliver it as my single opinion, and not *authoritative*') (emphasis in original). This manner of signalling has persisted ever since: see *Bosworth* v. *Farrand* (1665) Carter 96, 111 *per* Bridgman CJ; *R* v. *Jones* (1846) 8 QB 719, 728 *per* Williams J; *Jenkins* v. *Jackson* [1891] 1 Ch 89, 96 *per* Kekewich J ('I cannot help thinking that . . . something ought to be done . . . That, however, I have nothing more to do with than to make these extrajudicial remarks'); *Russian Commercial and Industrial Bank* v. *British Bank for Foreign Trade Ltd* [1921] 2 AC 438, 450 *per* Lord Dunedin ('I can only hope that my remarks will be taken as *obiter dicta* and that when the occasion next arises they will be considered on their merits'); *RTS* v. *Müller* [2010] UKSC 14 at [4]; *MSM* v. *Secretary of State for the Home Department* [2016] EWCA Civ 715 at [35] *per* Beatson LJ; *Telchadder* v. *Wicklan* [2014] UKSC 57 at [47] *per* Lady Hale.

[85] *King* v. *Melling* (1671) 2 Levinz 58, 59 (Levinz, the reporter and one of the barristers in the case, arguing that a technical point about inheritance dealt with in *Wild's case* (1599) 6 Co Rep 16[b] 'was not judicially before the Court, but an *obiter dictum*'). See also *Robinson* v. *Robinson* (1756) 1 Burrow 38, 41. The late seventeenth century also appears to mark the first occurrence of the term in a non-legal English text: see the collection of biographies (written in Latin) by the Presbyterian minister, William Bates, *Vitae selectorum aliquot virorum qui doctrinâ, dignitate, aut pietate inclaruere* (London: Wells, 1681), 367 ('Let us (and this is *obiter dictum*) in keeping with the memory of [the sixteenth-century Italian humanist, Gian Vincenzo] Pinelli').

[86] The terms remain in use to this day. *Cf. Re Singh*, High Court (QBD), transcript, 19 October 1999 (WL 1953237), *per* Turner J: 'it seems to me . . . that what Woolf J said . . . may not have been necessary for the decision which he was then making; in old language that would be called an *obiter dictum*'. The suggestion that '*obiter dictum*' is 'old language' was presumably made in light of the Lord Chancellor's department having determined, in the lead-up to the implementation of the Civil Procedure Rules (SI 1998 3132) in April 1999, that various Latin terms and other legalese should no longer be used in the courtroom. However, although the access to justice reforms targeted some specific Latin terms for replacement with English ones, the objective was never to remove Latin entirely from the English legal lexicon (see, e.g., *Access to Justice: Final Report to the Lord Chancellor on the Civil Justice System in England and Wales* (London: HMSO, 1996), s. 5, ch. 20, para. 13) and *obiter dictum* appears never to have been listed for retirement.

designation for something stated by the way: from the second half of the seventeenth century through to the end of the nineteenth, 'extrajudicial' was used to describe opinions expressed by judges in as well as out of court.[87]

By the late seventeenth century, judges and lawyers were regularly identifying opinions expressed in cases as 'merely' *obiter* or extrajudicial. The usual, perhaps the most enduring, reason for doing this was to dismiss a legal opinion outright – to declare that the opinion, not being legal authority, had no bearing on how the case before the court was to be decided. The opinion is 'extrajudicial ... and therefore not to be regarded', one judge asserted in a case of 1695.[88] Assertions of this nature were to become common in the law reports.[89] Yet, even in the late seventeenth century, judges were not always clear as to whether or not they thought *obiter dicta* had any distinct value. One judge suggested in 1694 that a legal argument had no merit if, besides not being vindicated

[87] See, e.g., *Holland* v. *Fisher* (1662) Bridg O 181, 206 ('that case in itself was but ... an extrajudicial opinion'); *Dean and Chapter of Windsor* v. *Gover* (1669) 2 Saunders 302, 304 ('*Jewel's case* ... was ... no resolution in the point, but at the end of the case an extrajudicial opinion on the point'); *Baxter* v. *Doudswell* (1674) 3 Keble 498, 499 ('an extrajudicial opinion ... this question never came in judgment'); *Earl of Darby's case* (1678) T Jones 237, 242; *Thompson* v. *Leach* (1690) 3 Modern 301, 307 ('this distinction made by my Lord Coke is founded upon no manner of authority; it is only his extrajudicial opinion'); *Wedderburn's case* (1746) Fost 22, 37 *per* Holt CJ ('this extrajudicial opinion weigheth very little with me in the present question'); *Thellusson* v. *Woodford* (1799) 4 Ves Jr 227, 251 ('no more than an extra-judicial opinion'); *Allen* v. *Bradshaw* (1835) 1 Curteis 110, 117 *per* Sir Herbert Jenner ('But whatever may have been the extrajudicial opinion of other judges or eminent writers as to the soundness of that decision, there is not to be found a single case in which a contrary decision has been pronounced; whilst there are, as I have already said, several in which it has been followed'). From the seventeenth century onwards, *obiter* and extrajudicial are regularly taken to mean the same thing (for an early example, see *R* v. *Richardson* (1757) 2 Kenyon 85, 105), though sometimes judges would refer to an opinion as '*obiter* and extrajudicial' to indicate both the status of the opinion as *dicta* and that the judge who offered the opinion did so out of court: see, e.g., *Doe* v. *Martin* (1790) 4 Term Rep 39, 48; *Sill* v. *Worswick* (1791) 1 H Bl 665, 683; also Blackstone, 2 *Commentaries* 238. By the twentieth century, 'extrajudicial' nearly always means either judicial opinions expressed out of court or – less frequently – opinion offered by legal experts who are not judges (or not commenting in a judicial capacity), though the use of the term as a synonym for *obiter* still crops up from time to time: see, e.g., *Grant* v. *Edmondson* [1931] 1 Ch 1, 5; *A-G* v. *Sport Newspapers Ltd* [1991] 1 WLR 1194, 1215.

[88] *R* v. *Kendal & Row* (1695) 1 Ld Raym 65, 65.

[89] See, e.g., *Marshall* v. *Collett* (1835) 1 Y & C Ex 232, 237 *per* Denman CB ('I can only treat it as a *dictum*, not as a judicial authority'); *Re Wright* (1883) 23 ChD 118, 128 *per* Jessel MR ('[I]t appears to me not necessary in the present case to examine the modern *dicta*, for they are nothing more than *dicta*').

by legal authority, it stood unsupported by extrajudicial opinion.[90] But what if the argument had, if nothing else, some *obiter dicta* on its side? Could it then have any merit? The question was left hanging in the air.

There is, in fact, much about the history of *obiter dicta* from around 1700 onwards that seems unclear. A simple message is repeated from one legal generation to the next: *obiter* opinions are not binding on a court. But this is hardly the whole picture. The interest that judges and lawyers have showed in *dictum*, in so far as they exhibit interest in it at all, often concerns the uses to which it might be put, and the quandaries posed by its existence, rather than whether it qualifies as a material source of law. Not until the twentieth century do English judges begin to entertain, and then only exceptionally to entertain, the notion that some *dicta* are to be followed much as precedents are to be followed. While modern judges have very occasionally accorded *dicta* precedent-like status, none has gone so far as to assert – and one would certainly be wrong were one to assert – that *obiter dictum* is a primary legal source. Yet, since a judge is a producer of *dictum* (with aspirations, perhaps, for some of his own produce), he is likely to understand other judges' motivations to pronounce *obiter*, and to be willing to take their pronouncements into account, even if he rejects the proposition that some *dicta* ought to be followed.

If judges accept that *dicta* do not bind them, but also believe that *dicta* should sometimes be taken into account, what status are they according *dicta* when they do take them into account? When a judge entertains particular *dicta*, he will sometimes be treating them as what Hart termed '"permissive" legal sources' – observations which the judge thinks it 'perfectly proper', and so chooses, to rely on 'as "good reasons" for decision', as opposed to 'formal' or 'mandatory' legal sources 'determin-[ing] the case before him'.[91] The mandatory source is the applicable law whereas permissive sources are secondary materials – such as *obiter dicta* – to which judges might resort when determining how the applicable law is to be applied. Hart appreciated that the distinction between permissive and mandatory sources – between, in the case of *obiter dicta*, asserting that a judge's decision in favour of *X* was compelled by statute, and asserting that *dicta* pertaining to the interpretation of the statute persuaded the judge that it applies in favour of *X* – 'may be blurred

[90] *R* v. *Bishop of London and Burch* (1694) 1 Show KB 413, 417.

[91] Hart, *The Concept of Law*, 294 n.

in actual practice'.[92] While, furthermore, mandatory and permissive legal sources might be distinguishable in so far as the former are and the latter are not binding in accordance with a legal system's criteria of validity, there seems – we will return to this point in Section 11 – to be nothing equivalent to a rule of recognition facilitating a distinction between *dicta* which provide Hart's 'good reasons', and are therefore considered persuasive, and *dicta* which are, as it were, mere *dicta*.

Not only is the concept of *obiter dicta* somewhat slippery, but any neatly compartmentalized history of the concept is likely to be a misleading one, not the least because the attitudes that the courts and the profession have towards *obiter* statements are rarely if ever amenable to being categorized as belonging to distinct points in time. A perspective on *dicta* widespread among late-twentieth century judges, for example, might also be in evidence as an anomalous observation discoverable in a few nineteenth and possibly even eighteenth-century law reports. The fact that attitudes towards *obiter dicta* can be seen spanning generations does not mean that the concept has been immune to revision. Anyone familiarizing themselves with the employment, application, and reception of *obiter dicta* in the English courts, certainly from the early nineteenth century to the early twenty-first, could be forgiven for forming the impression that, throughout this period, every new cohort of lawyers has been inclined to make some slightly stronger claim for *dicta* than generations before them had – almost as if, notwithstanding the perennial proclamation that *dictum* must not be mistaken for law, each generation has within it a constituency intent on prompting the next generation to declare *dictum* that little bit more law-like than they themselves had declared it to be. There are no distinct moments at which common-law suppositions about *obiter dicta* profoundly alter; indeed, the suppositions never do *profoundly* alter. Nevertheless, certainly by the twentieth century, the concept of *obiter dicta* bears connotations which it did not carry two centuries earlier. In particular, twentieth-century English judges can occasionally be seen committing to a proposition which their predecessors were reluctant to endorse explicitly: that even though *obiter dicta* are formally only ever permissive legal sources, there are instances where they are to all intents and purposes binding on a later court – where a court could only be making the wrong decision were it to choose not to follow the *dicta*. Even this proposition is not entirely unarticulated before the twentieth century.

[92] Ibid.

Moreover, although, by the end of that century, English judges are now and again to be found according particular *dicta* a more elevated status than anyone would openly have ascribed to any *obiter* observation two hundred years earlier, the story of *dicta* in the courts is not entirely, or even principally, one of how they become legally more significant over time. Rather, an account of *dicta* in the courts mainly concerns what judges have understood *dicta* to be, how lawyers and judges have used and abused them, judges' reasons for commending *dicta*, their reasons for eschewing them or treating them cautiously, and what it means to say that, as with Orwell's animals, some *dicta* are more equal than others.

4 *Dicta* Depicted

The word '*dicta*' is a synonym for 'comments', 'remarks', or 'observations'. In the law reports, its prefix, when it has one, will sometimes be something other than *obiter* – *dicta* can be, among other things, casual, loose, tentative, judicial, persuasive, authoritative, even (we will see in Section 11) binding – though, irrespective of whether the word appears with a prefix, *dicta* are usually delivered and understood to be *obiter dicta*, a term which 'means what the words literally signify – namely, statements by the way'.[93] *Obiter dicta* are judicial statements made in the context of a legal judgment, and which qualify as asides in relation to that judgment because the judgment did not depend on them. Judges, in the course of delivering judgments, sometimes make it clear that an observation is intended as *obiter*. Even when they do not spell out their intentions, the language they use – the presentation of an observation as speculative, for example, or the use of phrases such as 'it is perhaps worth mentioning', 'I might add', 'had the facts been slightly different', 'but that is not for this court', or 'that is for another occasion' – will often betray that the observation is not integral to the judgment. The *obiter* status of a remark might be evident from the fact that a judge is seeking to explain not the court's determination as to the primary legal source governing the matter being decided, but rather how the matter would be decided if the court had determined that a different primary source

[93] *Flower* v. *Ebbw Vale Steel, Iron & Coal Co* [1934] 2 KB 132, 154 *per* Talbot J. See also John Gray, *Lawyers' Latin: A Vade Mecum* (Marlborough: Hale, 2006), 100. The straightforward equation of *dictum* with (either binding or non-binding) judicial observation is fairly common in the Scottish courts: see, e.g., *Logan* v. *McRostie* 1908 SC 196, 201; *Graham* v. *Paterson* 1938 SC 119, 133; *Trusts Inn Ltd* v. *City of Glasgow Licensing Board* [2014] LLR 861 at [48].

applied. A judge might even offer *obiter dictum* in the form of speculation as to how a matter would be decided were the court to rule on the basis of reasoning contained in a secondary legal source – such as when judges consider, often sympathetically, juristic arguments in favour of legal conclusions unsupported by statutory or common-law authority.[94] As often as not, discerning that an observation is *obiter dictum* is a matter not of picking up on signals that it was intended thus, but rather of inferring from context that this is what the observation must be.

Normally, an observation is identified as an *obiter dictum* not by the judge who uttered it but rather retrospectively, by someone taking stock of what that judge said. The judge who, in an opinion, prefaces one of her observations with the words 'I personally take the view . . .', for example, might not provide any indication as to whether the observation was intended to form part of the court's judgment or whether it was intended as an aside. But another judge, when considering the opinion, might conclude that those words indicate that the observation is *obiter dictum*.[95] Since *dicta* have an infinite variety, there can be no checklist facilitating their identification. The most common manifestations of *dicta* do, nevertheless, seem to fall into a number of core categories: comments incidental to or stretching beyond the facts before a court, reflections on how some alteration to the facts would have yielded a different legal result, observations on a point of law similar to but distinct from the one applicable to the case at hand, remarks on a legal argument which was ultimately not treated as a ground for decision, and comments on how some legal matter beyond the remit of the current case will very likely, in due course, have to be addressed either by judges or the legislature (and how it might be dealt with once it is). Assessments of *dictum* are as varied as *dictum* itself. A judge might, in one context, treat *obiter dictum* as a valuable secondary legal source and, in another (not necessarily

[94] See, e.g., *Schuler* v. *Wickman* [1974] AC 235, 262 *per* Lord Wilberforce; *Agip* v. *Jackson* [1990] Ch 265, 286–7 *per* Millett J; *Twinsectra* v. *Yardley* [2002] UKHL 12 at [105] *per* Lord Millett ('There is powerful academic support for the proposition that the liability of the recipient [for knowing receipt of property procured through breach of trust] is . . . strict but subject to a change of position defence'); *Makdessi* v. *Cavendish Square Holdings* [2015] UKSC 67 at [36] *per* Lords Neuberger and Sumption.

> There is a case to be made for taking this course [*sc.*, abolishing the rule on the validity of contractual penalty clauses]. It . . . has some powerful academic support . . . We rather doubt that the courts would have invented the rule today if their predecessors had not done so three centuries ago. But this is not the way in which English law develops, and we do not consider that judicial abolition would be a proper course for this court to take.

[95] See *Hammersmith & Fulham LBC* v. *Monk* (1991) 61 P & CR 414, 423 *per* Slade J.

very different) context, deem it unworthy of consideration.[96] In *Russell* v. *Russell* (1897), Lord Herschell intervened during counsel for the appellants' argument to bring 'some *dicta*' from *Mackenzie* v. *Mackenzie*[97] – a case decided by the House of Lords in 1895 on appeal from the Scottish Court of Session – to their attention.[98] Yet when, in *Russell*, the barristers for the respondent sought to refer the House to 'multitudinous questions … raised *obiter dicta*' by Lord Brougham in the House of Lords' decision in *Paterson* v. *Paterson*[99] – another case heard on appeal from the Court of Session – Herschell cut them short, making it clear that he 'decline[d] to be bound by anything except the actual decision'.[100]

Although the standard description of *obiter dicta* is that they are comments made in passing, English judges and lawyers, while accepting this description, depict them in other ways besides. These depictions are themselves not all to be understood in the same way. When *dicta* are discounted, it is usually because they are considered to have no greater significance now, in the case before the court, than they had back then, in the case where they were pronounced. When judges or counsel consider particular *dicta* to be unreliably reported, apocryphal, or fabricated – to be what Willes CJ once termed *nunquam dicta* – the argument is that these *dicta* (or versions of them)[101] were of no value from the start and must always be dismissed.[102] Likewise, when judges castigate an *obiter*

[96] '*Dicta* are … a known-unknown – something the occurrence of which is perhaps predictable, but whose impact is not.' Niccolò Ridi, '"Mirages of an Intellectual Dreamland"? *Ratio, Obiter* and the Textualization of International Precedent' (2019) 10 *Jnl Int'l Dispute Settlement* 361, 363.

[97] *Mackenzie* v. *Mackenzie* [1895] AC 384.

[98] *Russell* v. *Russell* [1897] AC 395, 409.

[99] *Paterson* v. *Paterson* (1850) 12 D (HL) 24.

[100] *Russell* v. *Russell* at 416.

[101] Not necessarily every version. Different renderings of the same *dictum* might be received differently. See, e.g., *Studebaker* v. *Charlton Steam Shipping Co* [1938] 1 KB 459, 465–6 *per* Goddard J.

> [*Walters* v. *Rank*] is reported both in *The Times LR* and in *Lloyd's List Reports*. The learned judge [Bailhache J] certainly gave an opinion, which he expressly stated was only *obiter*, upon the very point I am now considering. Unfortunately, the two reports flatly contradict one another. In *Lloyd's List Reports* the judge is reported as saying that he thought the clause was not inconsistent with the [US Harter] Act [1893], and in *The Times LR* that it was. I must say that I prefer *The Times* report, prepared as it was by a learned and most experienced reporter.

[102] See *Ellis* v. *Smith* (1754) 1 Ves Jr 11, 13 *per* Willes CJ ('[T]he *obiter dicta* … in many cases were *nunquam dicta*; but barely the words of the reporters; for upon examination I have found many of the sayings ascribed to that great man, Lord Chief Justice Holt, were never

dictum as verbiage, or as self-indulgent, they are invariably asserting that this is the only characterization befitting the *dictum* – that it would be better if the *dictum* had never been uttered, or reported, in the first place.[103] But when judges pay attention, and when counsel urge judges to pay attention, to *obiter dicta*, they normally do so because they accept, or hope to gain acceptance for, the proposition that these *dicta* acquire, in the context of the case now before the court, some resonance or relevance that they did not have in the case in which they were set forth: the earlier decision contains *dicta* which have gravitational force in today's case – this is the essence of what is being accepted or argued – even though today's case lies outside the orbit (is not governed by the *ratio decidendi*) of that earlier decision.[104]

Consider the example of 'loose' *dicta*. When judges dismiss *dicta* as loose, they sometimes mean that the *dicta* reveal the utterer's ignorance of the law. Should *dicta* be discredited on this basis, the verdict seems always to be that they ought to be treated as discredited for all time.[105] More commonly, however, when judges disparage loose *dicta* they mean that the *dicta* were casually 'thrown out'[106] by the utterer. When judges designate *dicta* as casual, they quite often characterize them in other ways as well, such as that a *dictum* is both too loose and 'too wide' (too expansively worded to form part of the *ratio* of the decision in which it appears), or that – a term to which we will turn in a moment – a *dictum* was tentative as well as loose.[107] 'The authority ... is a *dictum* of Sir

said by him'); *Mansell* v. *Mansell* (1732) Cas t Talbot 252, 257; *King* v. *Turner* (1833) 1 My & K 456, 462–3 *per* Brougham LC; also Fry J's scepticism over *dictum* cited from Siderfin's reports in *Robinson* v. *Singh* (1879) 11 ChD 798, 831–2; and Hamilton J's lengthy excursus in *A-G* v. *Reynolds* [1911] 2 KB 888, 930–3.

103 See, e.g., *Great Western Rail Co* v. *Goodman* (1852) 12 CB 313, 318 ('That statement ought not to have appeared in the case'); *Whelan* v. *Palmer* (1888) 39 ChD 648, 651 ('With all deference the Vice-Chancellor might have omitted the whole passage. It is purely *obiter dictum*'); *Rosefield* v. *Provincial Union Bank* [1910] 2 KB 781, 804 *per* Fletcher Moulton LJ; also Quintin Hogg (later Hailsham LC), 'The Gaming Muddle', *Punch* 14 February 1968, 232 at 233 ('In the meantime it is to be hoped that the Courts will remember the golden rule for judges in the matter of *obiter dicta*. Silence is always an option').

104 See Ronald Dworkin, *Taking Rights Seriously* (London: Duckworth, 1977), 110–12.

105 See, e.g., *Giles* v. *Grover* (1832) 1 Cl & F 72, 85 *per* Patterson J; *Stedman* v. *Webb* (1839) 4 My & C 346, 350; *Clarke* v. *Carfin Coal Co* [1891] AC 412, 421 *per* Lord Watson.

106 See, e.g., *Giles* v. *Grover* at 115; *The Vrow Henrica* (1803) 4 C Rob 343, 343; *A-G* v. *Wilson* (1817) 3 Price 431, 436 ('merely a hasty *dictum* thrown out at *nisi prius*, without having undergone discussion'); *Britt* v. *Britt* [1955] 1 WLR 1272, 1274.

107 See, e.g., *Lord Advocate* v. *Jaffrey* [1921] 1 AC 146, 160 *per* Viscount Cave ('I am disposed to think that the argument based upon Lord Cranworth's *dictum* – which was general and tentative in form – has been carried too far'); *Beswick* v. *Bewick* [1968] AC 58, 105 *per*

Matthew Hale', Lord Loughborough remarked in 1788, 'but though I entertain the highest respect for the authority and character of that great judge, yet it would be doing injustice to his memory, to take every hasty expression of his at *nisi prius* as a serious and deliberate opinion'.[108] Some *obiter dicta* might 'even . . . be called *solemniter dicta*', Kenyon CJ remarked two years later.[109] Like others then and since, he was not of the opinion that *dicta* routinely deserved this label.[110]

Yet others rejected the label altogether. *Dicta* 'are always to be taken rather as illustrations than as authorities in law', Abbott CJ insisted in the early nineteenth century, 'for we all know that they are constantly made without the same consideration and care as those which belong to the point in judgment'.[111] Abbott's position entails a common presumption, discernible in English law at least since the seventeenth century, that *obiter dicta* are always to be treated as casual because judges, when they produce them, are making observations additional to the ones which their judicial oath – to decide cases according to the applicable laws and usages of the realm – requires them to make. '[T]he persons who pronounce' the 'decisions of courts of justice . . . are upon their oaths to judge according to the laws of the kingdom', Hale wrote in his *History of the Common Law*, because 'they have a great weight and authority in expounding, declaring, and publishing what the law of this kingdom is', and in determining how it shall 'bind . . . as to the particular case in question'.[112] An *obiter* opinion 'is no judicial opinion', is 'no . . . more than a *gratis dictum*', the Chief Justice of the Common Pleas, John Vaughan, maintained in 1672, for, unlike 'an opinion . . . concluding to the judgment', it is not 'delivered under the sanction of the judges' oath, upon deliberation, which assures it is, or was, when delivered, the opinion of the deliverer'.[113] An *obiter dictum* does not even necessarily

Lord Upjohn; *Re Lehman Brothers International* [2017] UKSC 38 at [82] *per* Lord Neuberger.

108 *Steel* v. *Houghton et Uxor* (1788) 1 H Bl 51, 53.

109 *R* v. *Eriswell* (1790) 3 Term Rep 707, 724.

110 See, e.g., *Grant* v. *Gould* (1792) 2 H Bl 69, 88 ('merely an extrajudicial *dictum* dropped in conversation'); *Ashton* v. *Turner* [1981] QB 137, 141 *per* Ewbank J ('casual observations about other matters').

111 *Barough* v. *White* (1825) 4 B & C 325, 328–9.

112 Matthew Hale, 'The History of the Common Law of England', in Matthew Hale, *On the Law of Nature, Reason, and the Common Law: Selected Jurisprudential Writings*, ed. G. J. Postema (Oxford University Press, 2017), 127–55 at 147. *The History of the Common Law* was first published posthumously in 1713 (Hale died in 1676).

113 *Bole* v. *Horton* (1672) Vaughan 360, 382.

represent a judge's opinion, he added, 'unless every thing spoken at pleasure must pass as the speaker's opinion'.[114]

But casually thrown-out *dicta* are not always presumed to be inherently insignificant. Judges who commend *obiter dicta* when they believe them to be, and dismiss them when they consider them not to be, 'relevant'[115] or 'applicable'[116] are expressing a view on whether those *dicta* now deserve a more meaningful day in court. In the case in which they appeared, the *dicta* had no consequence, but they might be of consequence in the case about to be decided. Certainly *dicta* may be dismissed for good because they were casually formulated, just as they will almost inevitably be dismissed for good if they are borne of legal ignorance.[117] But whereas *dicta* are unlikely ever to be redeemed if they show a judge to be in error as to the law, a thrown-out *dictum*'s day might come: a court might be persuaded that what was a loose legal observation in the context of the precedent is a tighter, more pertinent, legal observation when directed to the matter for decision today.[118]

The judicial statement which can be seen in retrospect to have been prophetic – to have anticipated the course of legal development, possibly even to have been made into law – is perhaps the most obvious example of how, over time, the status of a *dictum* can change. Evershed MR's observation in 1951 that something 'said as an *obiter dictum* in one case

[114] Ibid.

[115] See, e.g., *Peele* v. *Northcote* (1817) 7 Taunt. 478, 483; *Dixon* v. *Caledonian Railway* (1880) 5 App Cas 820, 836 ('the *dictum* was not relevant'); *Wolfe* v. *Surrey CC* [1905] 1 KB 439, 451 *per* Kennedy J ('we are by no means sure that rightly understood the *dictum* is really relevant to the matter we are considering'); *R* v. *Gallagher* (1974) 59 Cr App R 239, 244 ('In the judgment of this court, neither of these cases, in both of which the observations were *obiter dicta*, are relevant in the present case'); *R* v. *Ishaque* [2006] EWCA Crim 2538 at [9] *per* Latham LJ ('It can immediately be seen that ... that *dictum* was directly relevant').

[116] See, e.g., *R* v. *Taylor* (1824) 3 B & C 502, 510; *Gosling* v. *Veley* (1850) 12 QB 328, 394 *per* Parke B ('I cannot ... unless I have some sufficient authority for so holding: that is, some decision, or *dicta*, or analogy, clearly applicable to such a case'); *Willson* v. *Love* [1896] 1 QB 626, 630 *per* Esher MR ('there are many *dicta* by eminent judges applicable to it'); *Burt* v. *Cousins* [1971] 2 QB 426, 451 *per* Sachs LJ ('In my judgment that *dictum* [*per* Holt CJ in *Hern* v. *Nichols* (1701) 1 Salk 288] is applicable here'); *RCC* v. *Benchdollar Ltd* [2009] EWHC 1310 (Ch) at [48] *per* Briggs J ('the *dictum* is not strictly applicable, since that was a case about an estoppel').

[117] See, e.g., *Lucena* v. *Craufurd* (1802) 3 Bos & P 75, 86 ('nothing more than a note of an *obiter dictum* much too loose to form the ground of any decision'); also *Jacobs* v. *Seward* (1871–2) LR 5 HL 464, 466; *Bush, Beach & Gent* v. *Road* [1939] 2 KB 524, 530–1; *Kendall* v. *Lillico* [1969] 2 AC 31, 69–70; *O* v. *A* [2015] UKSC 32 at [39].

[118] See, e.g., *Birch* v. *Pease* [1941] 1 KB 615, 620; *Shogun Finance Ltd* v. *Hudson* [2003] UKHL 62 at [47]; *Gibb* v. *Maidstone and Tunbridge Wells NHS Trust* [2010] EWCA Civ 678 at [25].

may be relied upon on some other occasion'[119] was illustrated the following year by Hodson LJ who, sitting alongside Evershed, noted that although certain remarks contained in a case from the 1920s were speculative when the case was decided, they could be relied upon today because they had subsequently been affirmed by the Court of Appeal.[120] It would be a mistake to treat an *obiter dictum* which Scrutton LJ ventured in 1920 as anything other than 'of undoubted authority' today, Evans LJ observed in 1997, given that the *dictum* became the rule enacted as Section 35 of the Sale of Goods Act 1979.[121] The observation, if interpreted strictly, seems slightly awry: the 'undoubted authority' was the statute affirming the *dictum* rather than the *dictum* itself. Presumably all Evans meant to claim, and what he would certainly have been correct to claim, is that the status of the *dictum* – a statement of legal authority in 1997 but not in 1920 – had altered. His observation illustrates quite neatly just how easy it is to blur or neglect the distinction between accepting *dictum* as an authoritative statement of law and accepting *dictum* as actual legal authority.

Dicta which most commonly acquire relevance are those which are characterized as inconclusive, provisional, untested, speculative, hypothetical or – the favoured word in many law reports – *tentative* legal observations: instances in which judges have offered opinions which would likely need proper legal scrutiny at some point, but which did not need, and possibly could not have received, such scrutiny at the time that they were offered. Not all *dicta* are tentative, for judges can make statements which, though they are *obiter* by virtue of not being integral to the decision in which they appear, concern matters which have been legally resolved. One judge, for example, suggested that it is advisable to avoid using dispositive or non-tentative language when consciously commenting *obiter* ('Caution normally requires the court not to say "never" in any *obiter dictum* pronouncement'), immediately qualified the remark by acknowledging that *obiter dicta* are often observations to the effect that the law on a matter similar but not identical to the one currently before the court is in fact settled.[122] When a *dictum* is tentative,

119 *Cockram* v. *Tropical Reservation* [1951] 2 KB 827, 837.

120 *Bagley* v. *Winsome* [1952] 2 QB 236, 245. See also *Devis* v. *Atkins* [1976] 1 WLR 393, 398 *per* Phillips J ('[Counsel] submits that the observations in that case ... are *obiter dicta*; and I think, on an analysis of the case, that that is right. But the matter does not end there, because that case has been followed, and not merely followed but applied ... in this court').

121 *The Lorico* [1997] CLC 1274, 1286.

122 *R* v. *Avon CC ex p M* [1994] FCR 259, 273 *per* Henry J.

the facts of the case in which it was uttered did not put it to the test as a legal proposition, and there is no source of law that settles the matter to which it relates. A tentative *dictum* is considered relevant or applicable to the case at hand when the facts of that case somehow test it as a hypothetical proposition, and the *dictum* is adjudged to pass the test ('its author had in mind the issue which the court [now] has to decide', and it has proved to be 'of great assistance [to the court] in coming to a conclusion').[123] Yet, as we will see in Section 8, even when *dicta* from earlier cases can be read as credible responses to questions which the courts now have to answer, judges in these courts will not always be inclined to take the *dicta* seriously – precisely because the *dicta* were formulated tentatively.

5 Oblique Strategies

To understand the nature of *obiter dicta* in the common law, and to appreciate how *dicta* are sometimes conceived to be more than merely observations in passing, it makes sense to examine how they have been depicted. For a deeper understanding of *obiter dicta* as a common-law concept, however, it is important to consider the uses to which *dicta* are put. Judges – along with jurists, barristers, and other legal professionals – use existing *dicta* to bolster their own legal arguments. As producers of *dicta*, judges also use them in the sense that they avail themselves of the opportunity to make *obiter* remarks when they want to achieve a particular objective. The distinction between *dictum* as something used and *dictum* as something produced is one which we should be wary of overemphasizing, for not only will the reasons for *dicta* having been uttered in the first place often be no different from the reasons for their having been invoked in a later case, but the receipt of *dicta* typically entails their production: a judicial observation on an earlier judicial observation is likely to be *obiter dicta* (to be a case, as one judge recently put it, of 'piling *obiter* on *obiter*').[124] While judges are both interpreters and producers of *dicta*,

123 *Re McGreavy* [1950] Ch 269, 278 *per* Somervell LJ.

124 *Alpstream* v. *Airfinance* [2015] EWCA Civ 1318 at [259] *per* Christopher Clarke J. Perhaps the most common example of this phenomenon is the judge's *obiter* remark agreeing with or disapproving of an interpretation that counsel for one of the parties, or another judge (usually a judge in another case), has put on *obiter dicta* to be found in an earlier decision. For modern illustrations, see *Greig* v. *Insole* [1978] 1 WLR 302, 333 *per* Slade J; *Re Capital Annuities Ltd* [1979] 1 WLR 170, 197 *per* Slade J; *R* v. *Ayres* [1984] AC 447, 455 *per* Lord Bridge; *Bairstow Eves* v. *Ripley* (1993) 65 P & CR 220, 225–6 *per* Scott LJ; *Dunhill* v. *Burgin* [2012] EWHC 3163 (QB) at [18] *per* Bean J ('*obiter dicta* of the

furthermore, it should be borne in mind that they are not always negotiating *dicta* unprompted. When barristers try to nudge judges into making *obiter* observations – the barristers presumably hoping that the observations might be put to good use in future litigation – their requests, certainly in modern times, have tended to meet with resistance.[125] When judges take into account a *dictum* discoverable in an earlier decision, however, they often do so because counsel has directed them to it. Although nobody but the judges themselves can determine if or how the *dictum* is to bear on their own decision-making in a case before a court today, they might appreciate how it could strike a litigant, and perhaps also a future court dealing with that litigant's appeal, as untoward if they fail so much as to acknowledge a *dictum* which counsel has relied on in making the litigant's legal argument.

In the law reports, it is possible – hardly surprisingly – to find judges using *dicta* in a variety of ways. Consider, first, an outlier illustration: instances in which a barrister introduces *dictum* into an argument and a judge uses its introduction as an opportunity to refer unflatteringly to the opinion of another judge. Though Abinger CB could have rested content with letting counsel's contention – that '[t]he authority cited ... is a mere *obiter dictum* of Eyres J' – pass unchallenged, he chose to add his own gloss: '[i]t was not only an *obiter dictum*, but a very wide divaricating *dictum*'.[126] For Lord Watson, Lord Blackburn's words as cited to court did 'not even amount to *obiter dicta*. They contain no expression of judicial opinion ... One thing seems certain, namely, that his Lordship had not examined the text of Pothier, which contains no such doctrine as his words impute.'[127]

Court of Appeal in one case ... fully considered, and disapproved, by the *obiter dicta* of a majority in a later case').

125 See, e.g., *Davies* v. *Tennant* [1942] 1 KB 119, 124–5 *per* Caldecote CJ; *Stewart* v. *Oriental Fire & Marine Insurance* [1985] QB 988, 1011 *per* Leggatt J ('I decline the invitation ... It is not the function of the courts of first instance to attempt to edify or reassure by *obiter dicta*'); *Preston* v. *Wolverhampton Healthcare NHS Trust* [1997] ICR 899, 923–4 (CA); *Re Z* [2016] EWHC 1191 (Fam) at [27]–[28] *per* Sir James Munby P ('[Counsel for the father] invite me to "pass comment (by way of *obiter dicta*) about the merits of parliamentary review of the scheme of section 54 [of the Human Fertilisation and Embryology Act 2008]" and to "express any view as to the desirability or necessity for future reform as may be considered appropriate" ... I absolutely decline to do any of this').

126 *Sunbolf* v. *Alford* (1838) 3 M & W 248, 251–2.

127 *Scholfield* v. *Earl of Londesborough* [1896] AC 514, 539–40. When *dictum* occasions slight, it is usually either because counsel's doubts over a *dictum* are considered not to be sufficiently resolute or because counsel's case for having a *dictum* taken seriously is

Instances such as these are eccentricities. Only very rarely are judges to be seen playing the man rather than the ball. When judges refer to *dicta*, or respond to counsel's reliance on *dicta*, they nearly always do so either to dismiss the *dicta* as 'mere *dicta*', having no bearing on the court's ruling in the case at hand, or to explain how the *dicta* supply insight into, or how they might have had an effect on, some aspect of the law. *Dicta* deemed insightful and effective are sometimes referred to as authority, meaning not that they have authority as a material source of law, but rather that they are authoritative information about a material source of law. We will leave the broad notion of *dicta* as authority to one side for now, and will concentrate instead some specific propositions concerning their merits and demerits. These propositions, in summary, are: that *dicta* can aid with legal interpretation; that, in some instances, the point of issuing *dicta* is to tidy up loose ends falling outside a court's ruling; that *dicta* can reinforce primary legal authority; and that, by both producing and relying on *dicta*, judges are able to foster, stymie, and disrupt the development of the common law.

Although *obiter dicta* are by definition tangential to a decision, it would be a mistake to think that they are always irrelevant to the decision. Some of the scene setting in a judgment may, strictly speaking, be unnecessary to the judgment itself, yet the judgment might be difficult to understand or contextualize without it. A judge might consider it pertinent to comment *obiter* on particular arguments which are off-point because those arguments closely resemble, and so are worth distinguishing from (even if it is not strictly necessary to distinguish them from), the arguments which are on-point. There may emerge from a ruling some quirk which might naturally invite, even if it does not demand, judicial comment – such as when a judge explains a departure from the standard approach to allocation of costs because one of the parties is found to have mounted frivolous or vexatious litigation.[128] Judges sometimes think it important that the court, irrespective of how it determines the rights and liabilities of the parties to the case,

considered foolish. Very occasionally, however, a barrister's resort to *dictum* is not the cue for judge-on-judge sideswipe, but rather is the root of his own negative verdict on a judge's abilities. Samuel Romilly, arguing before the Court of Chancery in 1817, left no room for doubt as to his estimation of one eighteenth-century Lord Chancellor's capacity to pronounce on matters to do with equity: '[t]he doctrine in *Wake* v. *Conyers* was a mere extrajudicial opinion – a doubt entertained by Lord Northington in consequence of the little knowledge of equity he at that time possessed, and his general prejudice against it'. *Galdwall* v. *Bayliss* (1817) 2 Merivale 408, 411.

128 See, e.g., *Stratton and Stratton* v. *Ford* (1755) 2 Lee 216, 217; *Spelman* v. *Woodbine* (1783) 1 Cox Eq. Cas. 49, 50; *DeVitre* v. *Betts* (1873) LR 6 HL 319, 326 *per* Lord Cairns.

expresses a view – in the form of *obiter dicta* – on some aspect of the parties' (or of one party's) behaviour.[129] A judge could decide in favour of a party while commenting – *obiter* – that, had counsel for the other party pleaded the facts properly or relied on a different legal argument, the decision would have gone the other way. One nineteenth-century judge who considered himself bound to declare a defendant a fraudster could not resist adding *obiter* that he had no doubt he was not.[130]

The commonest commendation of *obiter dicta* in English case law is that they provided the court with valuable guidance. There seem to be three distinct senses in which *dicta* are understood to guide. First, judges and lawyers treat *dicta* as guidance when they rely on them for information about the law. A judge 'ought not ... to follow extra-judicial opinions,' Vaughan CJ insisted in 1672, 'unless he believes those opinions are right'.[131] For Vaughan, following an *obiter* opinion which is 'right' meant – on this he was echoed by others[132] – placing store in *dicta* which, though 'merely explanatory',[133] accurately capture the correct approach to understanding

[129] See, e.g., *Hodgson* v. *Scarlett* (1818) 1 B & Ald 232, 240–1 *per* Lord Ellenborough CJ; *Gluckstein* v. *Barnes* [1900] AC 240, 255 *per* Lord Macnaghten; *Anisminic* v. *Foreign Compensation Commission* [1968] 2 QB 862 (CA), 910 *per* Diplock LJ.

> There are two things in this case which puzzle me much, and I do not suppose that I shall ever understand them ... I do not understand why Mr Gluckstein and his associates were not called upon to refund the whole of the money which they misappropriated ... In the next place, I do not understand why Mr Gluckstein was only charged with interest at the rate of 3 per cent ... Mr Gluckstein has been in my opinion extremely fortunate. But he complains that he may have a difficulty in recovering from his co-directors their share of the spoil, and he asks that the official liquidator may proceed against his associates before calling upon him to make good the whole amount with which he has been charged. My Lords, there may be occasions in which that would be a proper course to take. But I cannot think that this is a case in which any indulgence ought to be shewn to Mr Gluckstein ... He can bring an action at law if he likes. If he hesitates to take that course or takes it and fails, then his only remedy lies in an appeal to that sense of honour which is popularly supposed to exist among robbers of a humbler type.

[130] *Freeman* v. *Pope* (1869–70) LR 9 Eq. 206, 211 *per* James VC ('That is the decision of Lord Westbury. I am bound by that decision, and, therefore, although bound to express my extrajudicial opinion that this gentleman, having regard to his income and his means, had no intention whatever to cheat his creditors at that time, I must judicially declare this settlement to be fraudulent and void as against his creditors').

[131] *Bole* v. *Horton*, 383.

[132] See, e.g., *Walpole* v. *Earl of Cholmondeley* (1797) 7 Term Rep 138, 149 *per* Kenyon CJ; *Kent CC* v. *Lord Gerard* [1897] 1 QB 351, 365 *per* Rigby LJ.

[133] *Eden* v. *Foster* (1725) Sel Cas Ch 36, 38.

the law, or some aspect of the law, applicable to the case at hand.[134] *Dicta* providing explanatory guidance are quite often referred to alongside legal treatises and other forms of juristic commentary considered to be authoritative statements as to the applicable law.[135] The reception of juristic commentary as authoritative guidance might itself be ascribable to a jurist's adoption, elaboration, or even – occasionally – rejection of judicial points made *obiter*. In *Derry* v. *Peek*, the Court of Appeal, holding that liability for fraud might be established by virtue of the fact that there are no reasonable grounds for believing a statement to be accurate, endorsed 'what is said by Mr [Frederick] Pollock in his valuable work on torts', but also noted that Pollock himself, in setting forth his position on liability for negligent misstatements, was drawing on the '*dicta* ... of an eminent common law judge [*sc.*, Maule J] ... [and] an eminent Chancellor [*sc.*, Lord Cairns]'.[136] Whereas Pollock had been following a path cleared

[134] See, e.g., *Jefferson* v. *Bishop of Durham* (1797) 1 Bos & P 105, 130 *per* Heath J (' it may however serve to shew the current opinion of the day'); *Evans* v. *George* (1823) 12 Price 76, 129 *per* Graham B ('I venture to affirm that ... opinion ... on this question, as a general point of law, can be collected from the *obiter dicta*'); *NHS Trust* v. *Y (Official Solicitor)* [2018] UKSC 46 at [58] *per* Lady Black ('[In the Court of Appeal in *Re Briggs* [2017] EWCA Civ 1169] Sir Brian Leveson P ... made some observations about the issue that now concerns this court. Although *obiter*, they are still valuable, not least for their insight into what happens in practice').

[135] See, e.g., *Gibson* v. *Small* (1853) 4 HL Cas 353, 397 ('An examination of the ... *dicta*, and of text-writers on the common law, from which we derive our knowledge of that law'); *Dawkins* v. *Ash* [1969] 2 AC 366, 392–3 *per* Lord Pearson; *DPP* v. *Morgan* [1976] AC 182, 236 *per* Lord Fraser ('Rape being a crime at common law, the proposition as to the state of mind of the doer which is contained in the full definition has to be collected from such judicial *dicta* or other authoritative statements of law as are available'); *Re Blenheim Leisure* [2000] BCC 554, 573 *per* Aldous LJ ('Whether or not the passage ... is *obiter dicta*, it appears to me to set out the law'); *Mexfield Housing Co-operative Ltd* v. *Berrisford* [2011] UKSC 52 at [44] *per* Lord Neuberger MR; *Dory Acquisitions* v. *Frangos* [2020] EWHC 240 (Comm) at [76], [81] *per* Bryan J.

[136] *Derry* v. *Peek* (1887) 37 ChD 541, 581 *per* Sir James Hannen. In describing Maule's and Cairns' *dicta*, Hannen was using the words that Pollock himself had used: Frederick Pollock, *The Law of Torts: A Treatise on the Principles of Obligations Arising from Civil Wrongs in the Common Law* (London: Stevens & Sons, 1887), 191. (When *Derry* v. *Peek* went to the House of Lords, the Court of Appeal's ruling was reversed – much to Pollock's chagrin: see Frederick Pollock, '*Derry* v. *Peek* in the House of Lords' (1889) 5 *LQR* 410.) Maule's observation – that, if fraud could be established, the test to sustain a verdict against the defendant did not entail showing that the defendant knew that he had made false representations – was technically *obiter*: *Evans* v. *Edmonds* (1853) 13 CB 777, 786. But Cairns' observation was part of a *ratio* rather than *dictum*: *Reese Silver Mining Co Ltd* v. *Smith* (1869–70) LR 4 HL 64, 79–80 ('I apprehend it to be the rule of law, that if persons take [it] upon themselves to make assertions as to which they are ignorant whether they are true or untrue, they must, in a civil point of view, be held as

by *obiter dicta*, Francis Newark, in his seminal article on the categorization of nuisance as a tort directed against land rights, was seeking to mark out a route which a *dictum* had blocked. Judges favouring the principle that personal injury damages should be recoverable in negligence have praised Newark for revealing that the opposing principle – that personal injury damages should be recoverable in public nuisance – is located not in judicial precedent but rather is traceable to 'an incautious *obiter dictum* [of Fitzherbert J's] which was let fall in the Common Pleas in 1535' and which 'sent subsequent generations wrong in their law'.[137]

Secondly, a *dictum* might be valued as explanatory guidance because it contains the preferred interpretation of a statutory provision,[138] or because it provides a serviceable definition of a legal concept.[139] Just what 'perils and dangers of the seas' encompasses is somewhat obscure, Langton J remarked in 1937, but it would be even more obscure if it were not for Lord Herschell having once spoken *obiter* on the matter.[140] *Obiter dicta* set forth in *Soar* v. *Ashwell* (1893) – to the effect that the term 'trustee' included dishonest assisters – were followed by judges in a number of late nineteenth- and early twentieth-century cases (including in some which were distinguishable from *Soar* v. *Ashwell*).[141] Sometimes, *dicta* will be valued not because they provide guidance on

responsible as if they had asserted that which they knew to be untrue. Upon that part of the case ... I apprehend that there is no doubt').

137 F. H. Newark, 'The Boundaries of Nuisance' (1949) 65 *LQR* 480, 483. For judicial reception, see *Hunter* v. *Canary Wharf Ltd* [1997] AC 655, 692 *per* Lord Goff; *Corby Group* v. *Corby BC* [2008] EWCA Civ 463 at [31] *per* Dyson LJ (though note also Dyson's qualifying remarks at [20]).

138 See, e.g., *R (Arogundade)* v. *Secretary of State for Business, Innovation and Skills* [2013] EWCA Civ 823 at [18] *per* McCombe LJ ('Clearly, as has subsequently been recognised, Lord Scarman's statements that unlawful residence cannot be "ordinary" were *obiter dicta*, as the students in that case were all lawfully present in the country. However, the statements have been treated as authoritative ever since on the construction of the 1962 Act and on the construction of enactments following a similar structure in this field'); *Belhaj* v. *Straw* [2014] EWCA Civ 1394 at [82] (also [2017] UKSC 3 at [153]).

139 See, e.g., *Re Bettison's* [1956] Ch 67, 70; *Cook* v. *Minion* (1979) 37 P & CR 58, 64 *per* Goulding J; *Morris* v. *Southwark LBC* [2011] EWCA Civ 25 at [52] *per* Lord Neuberger MR.

140 *The Stranna* [1937] P 130, 141 ('There are not many judicial pronouncements upon the term "dangers and accidents of the seas", but we have ... the high authority of Lord Herschell ... Armed with this authoritative *dictum* we can at least proceed with the certainty that the introduction of the term "dangers and accidents" does nothing to cut down the ambit of "perils of the sea"').

141 On the reception of the *dicta* in *Soar* v. *Ashwell* [1893] 2 QB 390, see the observations of Lords Sumption and Neuberger in *Williams* v. *Central Bank of Nigeria* [2014] UKSC 10 at [19], [83], and [86]–[87].

how to read the relevant law but simply because they affirm or reinforce what the relevant law is. 'The observations … are … *obiter*', Hanworth MR remarked in *Nixon* v. *Attorney General* (1930), 'but they express approval of the … authorities … Even if I was minded to differ … I could not venture to do so'.[142]

Judges can be noticeably cautious when relying on *dicta* for interpretive or definitional guidance. The reliability or accuracy of a *dictum* is sometimes treated as apparent, presumptive, or contingent rather than as settled,[143] and it is not unknown for courts to declare *dicta* past their best.[144] *Dicta* setting forth interpretations of statutory provisions are sometimes dismissed as doing more harm than good – statutory interpretation, Shaw LJ once lamented, seems 'bedevilled by history and *obiter dicta*'[145] – and even when *dicta* are accepted as accurate guidance on the construction of a statute, judges are wont to warn against allowing the *dicta* to prevail over the enacted text.[146] It is not unknown for *obiter dicta* to be ineptly reasoned, hastily formulated, *per incuriam*, badly reported, misinterpreted, or read out of context, judges can often be found saying, and therefore the guidance that a *dictum* provides could in all likelihood be poor. '[W]hat fell from him [Lord Mansfield] in the case of *Wilson* v. *Smith* was only an *obiter dictum*', Kenyon CJ remarked at King's Bench in 1797, 'and I confess it does not bring conviction to my mind'.[147] A decade later, Ellenborough CJ remarked on how he had 'not thought it necessary to advert to certain extrajudicial opinions, supposed to have been entertained and expressed by several eminent lawyers … as they

142 *Nixon* v. *A-G* [1930] 1 Ch 566, 597. In much the same vein, see *Bristow* v. *Piper* [1915] 1 KB 271, 277 *per* Avory J ('[I]t was not necessary for the decision, … but it was expressly adopted by the majority of this court in [1905] … as being a correct exposition of the law'); *Swan* v. *Pure Ice Co Ltd* [1935] 2 KB 265, 276 *per* Romer LJ ('*obiter dicta* … amply justified by the authorities'); *Sorrell* v. *Finch* [1977] AC 728, 733; *Hunter* v. *Senate Support Services Ltd* [2004] EWHC 1085 (Ch) at [198] *per* Randall J; *Coventry* v. *Lawrence* [2014] UKSC 46 at [116] *per* Lord Neuberger; *Geys* v. *Société Générale* [2012] UKSC 63 at [124] *per* Lord Sumption.

143 See, e.g., *R* v. *Payne* (1972) 56 Cr App R 9, 11 *per* Megaw LJ ('[T]his court will assume … that the statements … are right. Conceivably some of those statements might have to be considered in another case at another time').

144 See, e.g., *R* v. *Horsham DC ex p Wenman* [1995] 1 WLR 680, 698–9 *per* Brooke J; *Re O* [2005] EWCA Civ 759 at [7] ('It is … apparent to us that judicial *dicta* in some of the early, pre-Children Act cases … do not always seem apt a generation or so later').

145 *The Playa de las Nieves* [1976] 3 WLR 45, 56.

146 See, e.g., *Cenion Finance* v. *Ellwood* [1962] AC 782, 791; *R* v. *Steer* [1988] AC 111, 119; *R (Hart)* v. *Hartlepool BC* [2005] EWHC 840 (Admin) at [51] *per* Sullivan J; *Re Lehman Brothers International* [2017] UKSC 38 at [83] and [103] *per* Lord Neuberger.

147 *Burnett* v. *Kensington* (1797) 7 Term Rep 210, 222.

afford no safe basis for judicial determination, and are contradicted by the actual practice and experience of courts of law'.[148] From around the mid-nineteenth century, judges can frequently be found dismissing *obiter dicta* not because they do not bind – this much was taken for granted – but because they are not 'a correct exposition of the law'.[149] No doubt recalling John Henry Newman, Lord Sumner lamented in 1925 how '[n]o "guidance" is more misleading, no "kindly light" is more of a will-o'-the-wisp than an *obiter dictum* sometimes contrives to be'.[150] In modern times, even parliament appears occasionally to have set its sights on ridding the common law of the effects of erroneous *dicta*.[151]

The third sense in which *dicta* provide guidance is perhaps the most intriguing. Occasionally, a judge's reason for delivering *dicta* will be to warn against assuming that, on a particular issue, the path of the law is marked out. In *Rusbridger* (2003), the House of Lords refrained from declaring section 3 of the Treason Felony Act 1848 incompatible with article 10 of the European Convention on Human Rights (ECHR). The law lords were forthright, nevertheless, in stating *obiter* that section 3 had fallen into desuetude and that it would be an act of folly for a future litigant to try to rely on it.[152] More commonly, *dicta* are said to guide by

[148] *Amey* v. *Long* (1808) 9 East 473, 486.

[149] *Waddell* v. *Kinneil Cannel & Coking Coal Co Ltd* [1931] AC 575, 580–1 *per* Lord Buckmaster. In a similar vein, see *Brune* v. *Thompson* (1843) 4 QB 543, 549; *O'Connell* v. *The Queen* (1844) 11 Cl & F 155, 339–40 *per* Lord Brougham; *Marshall* v. *Bishop of Exeter* (1860) 7 CB NS 653, 706; *Kennedy* v. *Broun* (1863) 13 CB NS 677, 715 ('These *dicta* . . . rest on no solid foundation'); *Sutters* v. *Briggs* [1922] 1 AC 1, 11–12; *Secretary of State for Home Affairs* v. *O'Brien* [1923] AC 603, 629 *per* Lord Atkinson.

[150] *Sorrell* v. *Smith* [1925] AC 700, 743. ('Lead, kindly light, amid the encircling gloom' being the opening words to Newman's poem, 'The Pillar and the Cloud' (1833), which is commonly sung as a hymn.)

[151] Lord Diplock presumed section 13(3) of the Trade Union and Labour Relations Act 1974 to be 'directed against the future acceptance by the courts, as being a correct expression of the law, of certain *obiter dicta* to be found in speeches of individual members of this House' in two decisions from a decade earlier. *Hadmor* v. *Hamilton* [1983] 1 AC 191, 231. The two decisions were *Rookes* v. *Barnard* [1964] AC 1129 and *Stratford & Son* v. *Lindley* [1965] AC 269. Section 13(3) of the Trade Union and Labour Relations Act 1974 (repealed 1992) provided that '[f]or the avoidance of doubt it is hereby declared that . . . an act which . . . is itself not actionable [and] a breach of contract in contemplation or furtherance of a trade dispute . . . shall not be regarded as the doing of an unlawful act or as the use of unlawful means for the purpose of establishing liability in tort'.

[152] *R (Rusbridger)* v. *A-G* [2003] UKHL 38 at [28] *per* Lord Steyn ('[S]ection 3 . . . is a relic of a bygone age and does not fit into the fabric of our modern legal system. The idea that [it] could survive scrutiny . . . is unreal'). See also ibid. at [40] *per* Lord Scott, [60] *per* Lord Walker; and Carissima Mathen, *Courts Without Cases: The Law and Politics of Advisory Opinions* (Oxford: Hart, 2019), 228.

virtue of the fact that they can help judges decide on a direction when a path is not marked out. This point on which I pronounce *obiter*, Holt CJ remarked in *Coggs* v. *Bernard* (1703), is one on which 'the law should be settled', and while 'I don't know whether I ... have settled ... or ... unsettled it', I at least hope 'I have stirred' it so that it might be resolved by 'wiser heads in time'.[153] In the modern era, Patrick Devlin is a notable example of a judge who often made *obiter* pronouncements in the hope that they might in due course help others improve or settle some aspect of the law. 'One of the matters ... canvassed in the course of the argument ... no longer arises', and '[w]hat I have to say about it is, therefore, merely *obiter dictum*', he remarked in *Kwei Tek Chao* v. *British Traders* (1954).

> [B]ut in view of the fact that it is a matter of some importance and that I have had considerable assistance from the researches of [counsel for the defendants] on the point, I think it desirable that I should state, if only so that those who may be concerned in the future may know that the problem arises and has to be solved, what I think is the right answer to it.[154]

Even if a judge was not convinced that his *obiter dicta* yielded the right answer to a currently hypothetical legal point, even if 'he may not be sufficiently convinced of their cogency as to want them to have the full authority of precedent', he may still 'wish to state them', Devlin maintained, 'so that those who later may have the duty of investigating the same point will start with some guidance'.[155]

That *dicta* can shine light into the distance was at least part of the answer, Devlin believed, to those who consider common-law development difficult to square with the rule-of-law requirement that citizens should be able to ascertain, before they act, how the law applies to their intended actions. When a court develops the common law by modifying the rule-formulation of an earlier court, the content that it adds to the

[153] *Coggs* v. *Bernard* (1703) 2 Ld Raym 909, 920. See also *Rahimtoola* v. *Nazim of Hyderabad* [1958] AC 379, 423–4 *per* Lord Denning.

[154] *Kwei Tek Chao* v. *British Traders & Shippers* [1954] 2 QB 459, 485. This manner of using *dicta* is very much evident in transnational courts, one German upper court judge maintains, where judges quite often 'give ... hints ... to indicate what national courts can or should do to prevent future defeats on the transnational level'. Gertrude Lübbe-Wolff, 'Transnational Judicial Interactions and the Diplomatization of Judicial Decision-Making', in *Judicial Power: How Constitutional Courts Affect Political Transformations*, ed. C. Landfried (Cambridge University Press, 2019), 233–49 at 241. For Lübbe-Wolff, '[h]ints by *obiter dictum*', though 'indispensable for cooperative purposes in a transnational context', are '[r]eprehensible ... from other points of view' (ibid.).

[155] *Behrens* v. *Bertram Mills Circus* [1957] 2 QB 1, 24.

common law is applied *ex post facto* to the facts of the case which invites the modification. Those facts predate the ruling, and so the ruling imposes a legal liability which the party that took the liability-incurring action could not have discovered – because it did not exist – at the time of acting. In the stark words of one American legal theorist, common-law courts are, 'with the consent of the State, . . . constantly making *ex post facto* Law', because they are 'constantly in the practice of applying . . . rules which were not in existence and were, therefore, not knowable by the parties when the causes of controversy occurred'.[156] For Devlin, consternation over common-law retroactivity tends to be 'exaggerated'.[157] Significant changes to the common law are very often signalled well in advance, he argued, so that when they do come, those affected by them have had time to prepare for them. The signals usually take the form of *obiter dicta*. 'A judge-made change in the law rarely comes out of a blue sky. Rumblings from Olympus in the form of *obiter dicta* will give warning of unsettled weather.'[158]

If the argument that judge-made law is objectionable on rule-of-law grounds contains an element of exaggeration, surely so too does the characterization of *dictum* as an efficient messaging service. That there will be *dicta* pertaining to one's intended actions, reliably predicting how the law applicable to those actions will have changed when the time comes to take them, will be very much a matter of chance. Such *dicta*, even where they do exist, will not necessarily hold sway in future courts. Certainly *dicta* do sometimes augur what is to come. But until whatever a *dictum* presages becomes law, citizens cannot be sure that it will become law; and so they will be wise to plan their affairs in accordance with the law as it is rather than with a prognostication. Anyone inclined to critique judicial law-making on rule-of-law grounds might even cite *obiter dicta* as part of the problem, for there is the possibility that *dicta* will sometimes be read

156 J. C. Gray, *The Nature and Sources of the Law*, 2nd ed. (New York: Macmillan, 1921), 99–100.

157 Lord Devlin, 'Judges and Lawmakers' (1976) 39 *MLR* 1, 10.

158 Ibid. For a similar American perspective, see Foster Calhoun Johnson, 'Judicial Magic: The Use of *Dicta* as Equitable Remedy' (2012) 46 *Univ. San Francisco L. Rev.* 883, 900.

> When a court desires to overrule . . . it may conclude that justifiable reliance on the court's earlier decisions has been so great that any decision overruling precedent must operate prospectively only. In such circumstances, the court may hold that the parties before it are bound by the earlier case's rule. But the court may also, by means of *dictum*, indicate its disapproval of the earlier decision and suggest that any subsequent reliance on that rule henceforth will be considered unjustified.

not as signals as to how the law is likely to change, but rather as statements as to what the law should now be taken to be. If we were willing to disturb vested rights 'merely on the *obiter dictum* of a judge', without any actual legal authority justifying the disturbance, Abinger CB remarked in 1844, 'the law would become every day more and more unsettled'.[159] In *Attorney-General* v. *Reynolds* (1911), the King's Bench Division affirmed a vested right for which, Hamilton J conceded, there was 'no settled rule upon the authorities' but rather which 'rested ultimately upon a mere *obiter dictum*'.[160] This was not, he insisted, sufficient reason to deny the right: 'rights of property are not to be upset merely because, when historically traced through the reports, they rest on an *obiter dictum*'.[161] But this meant that a litigant incurred a liability not because a local-customary, common-law, or statutory rule imposed it, but because *dicta* could be discovered adverting to the desirability of its imposition. That litigant might fairly have complained that he would never have gone to court had he (or his counsel) known that *dictum* could be made to perform the work of a recognized source of law. In *Leeds Industrial Co-operative Society* v. *Slack* (1924), the House of Lords pointedly avoided repeating the mistake, explaining that the vested right in this instance was being upheld not solely because of the *dicta* to be found in support of it, but because those *dicta* were complemented by prescribed customary practice. 'It is a different question when a practice follows on *dicta*', Lord Dunedin explained. 'A practice it might not be right to disturb, but then it is the practice and not the *dicta* that forms the binding authority.'[162]

Obiter dicta, when they point to paths on which future courts might settle, have the potential to shape the common law. But they can also – to good effect and to bad – inhibit and disrupt as well as contribute to its growth. Consider the case of English judicial review, the development of which has been in significant measure ascribable to *dicta*. In the second half of the twentieth century, judicial observations in support of relaxing one or another restriction on the availability of review were often the impetus for subsequent rulings establishing that misuse of a statutory power by a body responsible for providing a public service was within the supervisory jurisdiction of the Administrative Court.[163] But there has

[159] *Buxton* v. *Cornish* (1844) 12 M & W 426, 429.

[160] *A-G* v. *Reynolds* [1911] 2 KB 888, 930.

[161] Ibid.

[162] *Leeds Industrial Co-operative Society Ltd* v. *Slack* [1924] AC 851, 864.

[163] See Alfred Denning, *Freedom under the Law* (London: Stevens & Sons, 1949), 67–126; also *R* v. *IRC ex p Nati* [1982] AC 617, 641 *per* Lord Diplock ('To revert to technical

also been the potential for *dicta* to leave this area of the law unsettled. It was established by the Court of Appeal in *ex parte Datafin* (1987), for example, that a body might come under the Administrative Court's supervisory jurisdiction if its powers are neither judicial nor governmental yet are in some way woven into the fabric of government regulation – if, for example, the body carries out work which would otherwise have to be undertaken by a government department.[164] Lloyd LJ remarked *obiter* in *Datafin* that had the impugned body (which operated as a surrogate organ of government) been entirely self-regulating, it might – if the body's powers had been such that anyone subject to them had no real choice but to submit to the exclusivity of its authority – still have been amenable to review.[165] In cases decided after *Datafin*, other judges have similarly commented *obiter* on how the decisions of especially powerful private bodies ought to be reviewable.[166]

Dicta of this nature mark out a direction in which an aspect of the common law might develop. But they can also generate uncertainty over the extent to which the common law has already evolved in that direction, and indeed will sometimes prompt judges to make further *obiter* observations not endorsing the original *dicta* but rather in an effort to clarify how far the relevant law actually extends – perhaps hoping that the clarification will dissuade other judges from developing the law (or muddying the waters) even further.[167] Occasionally, neither the *dicta* nor the responses to them

restrictions on *locus standi* ... would be to reverse that progress towards a comprehensive system of administrative law that I regard as having been the greatest achievement of the English courts in my judicial lifetime'); Tom Bingham, *The Business of Judging: Selected Essays and Speeches* (Oxford University Press, 2000), 190.

164 *R* v. *Panel on Take-overs and Mergers ex p Datafin* [1987] QB 815.

165 See ibid. at 845–6.

166 See, e.g., *R* v. *Disciplinary Committee of the Jockey Club ex p Massingberd-Mundy* [1993] 2 All ER 207, 219 *per* Neill LJ (observing that, had he not been constrained by authority, he would have ruled that some decisions of the Jockey Club were judicially reviewable given its position of public importance and its near monopolistic powers in an area in which the general public has an interest and in which many people earn their livelihoods); *R* v. *Jockey Club ex p RAM Racecourses Ltd* [1993] 2 All ER 225, 244 *per* Stuart-Smith LJ (similarly observing that, had the matter been free of authority, he would have held the Jockey Club to be amenable to judicial review).

167 See, e.g., *R* v. *Disciplinary Committee of the Jockey Club ex p Aga Khan* [1993] 1 WLR 909, 932–3 *per* Hoffmann LJ:

> [T]he mere fact of power, even over a substantial area of economic activity, is not enough. In a mixed economy, power may be private as well as public. Private power may affect the public interest and the livelihoods of many individuals. But that does not subject it to the rules of public law. If control is needed, it must be found in the law of contract, the doctrine of restraint

will leave anybody any the wiser. Many an ear pricked in 2005, for example, after Lords Steyn and Hope observed *obiter* that judges might have a common-law power to dis-apply statutory provisions which are considered to violate basic constitutional rights.[168] But while judges (and others) have hardly been diffident about reflecting on these *dicta*, the question of whether such a power exists remains moot.[169]

Judges sometimes resist developing the common law in a particular way because existing *dicta* caution against doing so, or because the *dicta* intimate the pitfalls of so much as rising to the challenge. Some of the *dicta* submitted to the court by the plaintiff's counsel would have us depart from the common-law rule that a lessee cannot compel the lessor to prove good title before he sells the lessee a lease, Coram Richards LCB observed in 1821, but the *dicta* in their entirety were not only not binding but were also 'inconsistent and contradictory, and therefore . . . only tended to make the question [of whether the lessor should be so compelled] still more doubtful'.[170] Beware *obiter dicta* – this is a regular judicial refrain – which conflict with other *obiter dicta*,[171] or which complicate a legal terrain

> of trade, . . . and all the other instruments available in law for curbing the excesses of private power.

See also *R (Mullins)* v. *Jockey Club Appeal Board (No. 1)* [2005] EWHC 2197 (Admin) at [31] *per* Stanley Burnton J.

> [A private body] may wield immense economic power. It is nonetheless a body exercising private functions. It may be that monopolistic bodies exercising powers over the livelihoods of considerable numbers of people should be regulated and subject of [*sic*] review by the courts. The desirability or otherwise of that regulation and review cannot convert a private function into a public function.

168 See *R (Jackson and others)* v. *A-G* [2005] UKHL 56 at [100]–[102] *per* Lord Steyn, [104], [107], and [126] *per* Lord Hope; also ibid. at [159] *per* Lady Hale; and *AXA Insurance* v. *Lord Advocate* [2011] UKSC 46 at [50]–[51] *per* Lord Hope. (Considered in the light of the 2019 constitutional tailspin, the *dicta* seem almost quaint.)

169 For a sample of the (far from uniform) judicial reactions, see *R (Corner House Research)* v. *Director of the Serious Fraud Office* [2008] EWHC 714 (Admin) at [63]–[65] *per* Moses LJ; *Re McCord's Application for Judicial Review* [2016] NIQB 85 at [149], [156] *per* Maguire J; Tom Bingham, *The Rule of Law* (London: Allen Lane, 2010), 167; and Stephen Sedley, *Ashes and Sparks: Essays on Law and Justice* (Cambridge University Press, 2011), xiv, 129–30, 246, 253, 352.

170 *Purvis* v. *Rayer* (1821) 9 Price 488, 497.

171 See, e.g., *General Steam Navigation Co* v. *Guillou* (1843) 11 M & W 877, 887; *Dalton* v. *Angus* (1881) 6 App Cas 740, 812–15; *Hardaker* v. *Idle DC* [1896] 1 QB 335, 352; *Ware & De Freville Ltd* v. *Motor Trade Association* [1921] 3 KB 40, 66; *Best* v. *Samuel Fox & Co Ltd* [1951] 2 KB 639, 650; *Gravesham BC* v. *British Railways Board* [1978] Ch 379, 392; *Beauchamp* v. *Woolworth plc* [1990] 1 AC 478, 488; *IRC* v. *Laird* [2002] EWCA Civ 576 at [52]–[53].

unnecessarily.[172] The refrain is often in evidence in judicial observations concerning how courts will sometimes cherry-pick from a crowd of disparate *dicta* so that particular *obiter* remarks are made not simply to stand out from that crowd but to serve as *rationes decidendi.*[173]

From around the mid-nineteenth century, we start to see barristers explicitly arguing over whether an earlier decision offers up only *obiter dicta* in relation to the case now before a court, or whether certain pronouncements made in that earlier decision are in fact binding authority.[174] This development seems inevitable in retrospect, according to one civil-law analyst of the common-law tradition, because pronouncements contributing to a precedent's *ratio* and pronouncements which are *obiter* are equally capable of occupying 'space which was originally considered to be free of law'.[175] Barristers began, in essence, to exploit the fact that judges, when making judgments, do not normally distinguish between, on the one hand, reasons advanced to fill a gap in the law which has to be filled if there is to be a legal decision, and, on the other, reasons advanced which, though they address a gap (a different gap) in the law, are basically 'textbook-like statements having nothing to do with the decision in the specific case' before them.[176] If a court is persuaded to treat yesterday's *dictum* as today's *ratio*, there is a danger it will end up pressing that *dictum* into performing a service that it cannot properly perform. When courts are persuaded thus, the unfortunate precedent created by the court, Benjamin Cardozo once remarked, might be characterized as 'the spawn of careless *dicta*'.[177]

[172] See, e.g., *R* v. *Roper* (1817) 6 M & S 327, 332–3 *per* Ellenborough CJ ('[B]ecause of some *obiter dicta*, which fell from the Lord Chancellor in his judgment, ... the case is put forward as creating a difficulty upon the present occasion ... But ... there is no such difficulty in the present case'); *Allen* v. *Flood* [1898] AC 1 at 139 *per* Lord Herschell, 153 *per* Lord Macnaghten, and 174 *per* Lord Davey; *Oxford and Cambridge* v. *Eyre & Spottiswoode* [1964] Ch 736, 752 *per* Plowman J; *A-G* v. *English* [1983] 1 AC 116, 139 *per* Lord Diplock ('[T]he criteria for determining where in a particular case the balance lay between fair trial and free press can hardly be said to have been rendered clear-cut by *obiter dicta* to be found in the five separate speeches in this House in *Attorney-General* v. *Times Newspapers Ltd* [1974] AC 273').

[173] See, e.g., *Indyka* v. *Indyka* [1969] 1 AC 33, 96 *per* Lord Wilberforce; *Khan* v. *Birmingham CC* (1980) 40 P & CR 412, 416 *per* Megaw J ('While this statement, when made, may have been *obiter dictum*, it has become authoritative by its adoption thereafter in many cases binding on this court'); *Cruz City* v. *Unitech Ltd* [2014] EWHC 3131 (Comm) at [42] *per* Males J.

[174] See, e.g., *Benson* v. *Benson* (1835) 6 Simons 126, 128–31.

[175] Wolfgang Fikentscher, *Methoden des Rechts in vergleichender Darstellung. Bd II: Anglo-amerikanischer Rechtskreis* (Tübingen: Mohr (Siebeck), 1975), 93.

[176] Ibid.

[177] Benjamin N. Cardozo, 'Law and Literature' (1925), in his *Law and Literature and Other Essays and Addresses* (New York: Harcourt, Brace & Co, 1931), 3–40 at 34.

The characterization is not always apt. Sometimes – common-law judges have hardly been oblivious to this nuance – the unfortunate precedent is accurately ascribed to carelessness not in the formulation of the *dictum*, but in the *dictum*'s reception. Had the judge who embraced the *dictum* paid more attention to what the *dictum* actually says, he would have appreciated that it makes for an unsuitable *ratio*, or contribution to the *ratio*, in the case in which he relied on it – that the *dictum* can be passed off as suitable only if it is read as applying to facts to which it does not, and was never supposed to, apply. '*[D]icta* must be interpreted and applied in the context of the issue that was before the court', Sullivan J insisted in 2004. 'They should not be treated as though they were contained in an enactment of general application.'[178] Loose reception of *dictum*, Rigby LJ had warned a century earlier, can be as troublesome as loose *dictum* itself. 'One danger of treating . . . *obiter dicta* as authorities', he observed, 'is that, if stated only in general terms, one may be applying them to circumstances which the authors never had in mind. In other words, we may be treating as exhaustive what the authors intended only to apply to special circumstances.'[179] Soon after having made this observation, he detected the error in a judgment of Cozens-Hardy J:

> Cozens-Hardy J referred . . . to . . . an *obiter dictum* of Kay J, which he admitted was 'perhaps not necessary for his decision.' The words relied upon were certainly not necessary to the decision: they had nothing whatever to do with it. They only came to this – that if a state of things had arisen, which the learned judge himself considered had not arisen, he might have come to a different conclusion.[180]

When judges do conclude that an *obiter dictum* makes for inappropriate reasoning on a particular set of facts, they need not be dismissing the *dictum* outright. A judge might, for example, eschew reliance on *obiter dicta* brought to the attention of the court, considering them unsuited to the case at hand, but stop short of adjudging those *dicta* unsound in principle. 'So far . . . as . . . the *dicta* [of Brett MR] in *Heaven* v. *Pender* are concerned', Lord Buckmaster ventured in *Donoghue* v. *Stevenson*, 'it is in

[178] *North Devon DC* v. *First Secretary of State* [2004] EWHC 578 (Admin) at [16]. In a similar vein, see *R (Hart)* v. *Hartlepool BC* [2005] EWHC 840 (Admin) at [51] *per* Sullivan J; *Constantin Medien* v. *Ecclestone* [2013] EWHC 2674 (Ch) at [68] *per* Vos J ('The argument . . . is a classic case of over-interpretation of an *obiter dictum* in a judgment on a different topic'); *Sharland* v. *Sharland* [2015] UKSC 60 at [15] *per* Lady Hale.

[179] *Re McCallum* [1901] 1 Ch 143, 157–8 (case decided December 1900).

[180] *Law Union and Crown Insurance* v. *Hill* [1901] 1 Ch 819, 828.

my opinion better that they should be buried so securely that their perturbed spirits shall no longer vex the law'.[181] But he did not consider it inappropriate that counsel for the appellant should have referred to them,[182] and indeed Lord Atkin, in the same case, found Brett's *dicta*, when 'limited by the notion of proximity',[183] to be 'a valuable practical guide'[184] for the purpose of explaining the duty of care owed by manufacturers to consumers. In a 2016 Court of Appeal case, McCombe LJ considered himself constrained from ruling on the basis of 'powerful *obiter dicta*' cited to the court, because the *dicta* did not speak to the matters on which the Court had to decide. But '[h]ad my decision in this case depended upon giving effect to such *dicta*', he added, 'I would have been inclined to do so'.[185] When *dicta* do address issues which are now before a court, judges will sometimes succumb to this inclination. In a rate valuation case before the High Court in 1941, counsel for the applicant argued that none of the judicial opinions relied on by the respondent's counsel belonged to the *ratio* of a binding precedent, and that the application therefore had to succeed. But Singleton J, dismissing the application, not only considered it inaccurate to characterize the cited opinions as *obiter dicta*, but added that even '[i]f they were . . . this court would adopt their view as applicable to this case'.[186]

6 Engines of Confusion

'Decisions are one thing', Lord Diplock insisted, but '*dicta* are quite another'.[187] Courts might be persuaded to rule in accordance with extrajudicial observations, but the observations themselves are never actual precedents – '*stare decisis*' resists being 'pressed so far as to include *obiter dicta*'.[188] By the end of the nineteenth century, none the less, *dictum* had become a valuable commodity in the courtroom. *Obiter*

[181] *Donoghue* v. *Stevenson* [1932] AC 562, 576.
[182] Ibid. at 571–2.
[183] Ibid. at 581.
[184] Ibid. at 580.
[185] *R (Brooks)* v. *Independent Adjudicator* [2016] EWCA Civ 1033 at [39]. See also *Al-Fayed* v. *Al-Tajir* [1988] QB 712, 730 *per* Mustill LJ ('Although these passages might perhaps be regarded as *obiter dicta* since they were dealing with a proposition which had not been advanced, I would have thought it right to give effect to them, if they had been directly in point').
[186] *R* v. *Heston and Isleworth RA* [1941] 2 KB 146, 157.
[187] *The Antaios* [1985] AC 191, 204.
[188] *Parsons* v. *BNM Laboratories* [1964] 1 QB 95, 110 *per* Sellers LJ.

dicta at variance with a precedent can serve the ends of counsel trying to convince a court that the precedent, though prima facie applicable to the facts of the case at bar, is actually unsuited to passing legal judgment on those facts, and that the precedent therefore ought to be distinguished – its *ratio* narrowed – so that the current case falls outside its scope. Counsel might attempt to sidestep a precedent by seeking to convince a court that what has been assumed to be the precedent's *ratio* is in fact *obiter dictum* – if the court is convinced, the precedent is in effect circumvented.[189] Or counsel might argue that pronunciations in a higher court judgment which could be (or have been) mistaken for *dicta* are better understood as constituting, or contributing to, a *ratio* which overrules an inconvenient precedent. Efforts to turn *dicta* into *ratio* and *ratio* into *dicta* are more often than not rebuffed in court – sometimes mercilessly[190] – though occasionally the rejection comes with a commendation for *chutzpah*.[191] In the law reports, tussles over *dicta*

[189] See Michael C. Dorf, '*Dicta* and Article III' (1997) 142 *U. Pennsylvania L. Rev.* 1997 at 2004–5, 2027, 2029–30, 2037 ('circumventing precedent by abusing the holding/*dictum* distinction'), 2060, and 2065.

[190] 'To suggest', as counsel for the Home Secretary appeared to be suggesting, 'that the highest court of this country has by two concurring opinions ... given the force of law to what is clearly a third member's aside is to go beyond even divination', Sedley LJ remarked in 2008 (though he was more disappointed with the ambiguity of the House of Lords' judgment than he was with counsel's audacity). *SSHD* v. *AF* [2008] EWCA Civ 1148 at [110]. He continued: 'Unless and until the new Supreme Court changes the mode of giving judgment, lower courts and lawyers ought in my respectful view to be able to assume that when their Lordships, or a majority of them, intend to make new law, they say so' (ibid.). Sometimes, the judicial rebuff is aimed at other judges rather than at barristers: see, e.g., Scrutton LJ's pointed observations on Lord Salvesen's apparent effort to evade the *ratio* of a binding precedent (by labelling it *obiter dicta*) in *Wilcock* v. *Pinto* [1925] 1 KB 30, 47.

[191]

> [T]he learned junior counsel for the appellants, ... with a courage which distinguishes him, roundly asserted that the statements by the judges ... were mere *obiter dicta*, and should be discarded as worthless ... This struck me as remarkable ... [T]o call the phalanx of judicial authority to which I must necessarily refer mere *dicta* is a misnomer altogether.

Keighley Maxsted & Co v. *Durant* [1900] 1 QB 629, 634–5 *per* A. L. Smith LJ. (The 'learned junior counsel' was Thomas Scrutton. Presumably he was referred to as learned because, in the 1880s, he had written books on the law of copyright and on contracts for carriage of goods at sea, and junior because in 1900, unlike his co-counsel, he had not yet taken silk (though he would do so the following year). Scrutton was appointed as a judge of the King's Bench Division in 1910 and was promoted to the Court of Appeal in 1916.) For further instances of counsel trying their luck, see, e.g., *Christopherson* v. *Bare* (1848) 11 QB 473, 476; *Buckley* v. *National Electric Theatres* [1913] 2 KB 277, 279; *Furniss* v. *Dawson* [1984] AC 474, 494; *Cream Holdings Ltd* v. *Davenport* [2010] EWHC 3096 (Ch) at [131]; *R (Evans)* v. *A-G* [2014] EWCA Civ 254 at [68].

abound. Consider the following piece of parry-and-riposte from the Administrative Court's ruling in *Youngsam* (2017): after counsel for the defence relied on a statement made by Lord Neuberger in *Whiston* (2014) as legal authority, counsel for the claimant contended that the statement must have been *obiter* because, in *Whiston*, Baroness Hale had characterized it thus, and Neuberger, though he referred to Hale's judgment, did not take issue with that characterization. But defence counsel retorted that Lord Neuberger's statement in *Whiston* still did not have to be treated as *obiter* in *Youngsam*, because 'Baroness Hale's observation as to the *obiter* status of' the statement 'is, in itself, *obiter*', and therefore the court was not obliged to consider the characterization valid.[192] In *The Hannah Blumenthal* (1982), the subject of *dicta* seemed to have Lord Denning arguing with himself. 'The task of distinguishing between [*dicta* and *ratio*] is formidable', he observed, '[e]specially when there are four or five speeches and they each gave different reasons'.[193] Yet moments later he would maintain (echoing Lord Reid) that distinguishing *dicta* from *ratio* is more difficult when a court has produced a single unanimous judgment, since the natural inclination is to treat the entire judgment as if it has statute-like authority whereas judgments composed of *seriatim* opinions have to be interpreted more judiciously.[194] 'Time after time', he observed the following year,

> in cases of first importance, there has only been one judgment. Time after time the lower courts have felt bound by that one judgment and by all the sayings in that judgment. They are called *obiter dicta*. They are really

[192] *R (Youngsam)* v. *Parole Board* [2017] EWHC 729 (Admin) at [18]–[19].

[193] *The Hannah Blumenthal* [1982] 3 WLR 49 (CA), 56.

[194] Ibid. at 56–7. *Cf. Broome* v. *Cassell & Co Ltd (No. 1)* [1972] AC 1027, 1084–5 *per* Lord Reid.

> With the passage of time I have come more and more firmly to the conclusion that it is never wise to have only one speech in this House dealing with an important question of law. My main reason is that experience has shown that those who have to apply the decision to other cases and still more those who wish to criticise it seem to find it difficult to avoid treating sentences and phrases in a single speech as if they were provisions in an Act of Parliament.

On Reid's view that single composite judgments are, as compared with judgments composed of separate opinions, more likely to be read as akin to statutory text, see also Essay II (Section 8). The view tends to be reported approvingly, or at least uncritically, yet it seems contestable. Perhaps the language of an opinion will, generally speaking, be more statute-like if judges are agreeing upon a text. Whether the opinion is treated as statute-like is a matter for its readers, however, rather than the judge, or judges, who produced it. The readers – at least those readers who make use of judgments in courts – will presumably seek to subject any type of judicial opinion to close interpretation when doing so fits with their legal argument.

sayings just by the way, as if an aside. Yet they are treated as binding. I do not think that is right.[195]

The law reports are hardly short of exasperated judges chiding barristers for playing fast-and-loose with *dicta* – cherry-picking them, presenting '*obiter dicta* . . . blown up into a statement of principle',[196] citing them out of context, emphasizing them in preference to a *ratio decidendi*, and the like. In disputes between divorced parents over their children's surnames, Ormrod LJ complained in 1980, 'the bandying about of *obiter dicta*' by barristers 'has been going on far too long. Sometimes it would be quite useful if counsel looked at the facts of cases when they are citing them.'[197] *Dicta* may not be binding, but a barrister might still try to argue that a judge's failure to take into account an *obiter* observation made in a higher court is a ground for appeal.[198] The gambit might well meet with success, for, as will become clear in Section 11, some modern judges have cast a degree of doubt over the proposition – for a long time treated as straightforwardly authoritative[199] – that a higher court's *dicta* do not trump a lower court's precedent where the *dicta* and the precedent are in conflict. In *Al-Skeini* (2005), the Court of Appeal accepted that *dicta* offered by Lord Bridge in the House of Lords and relied on by counsel for the appellants were compelling, even if not binding, and that if the correctness of the *dicta* was to be challenged then 'it should be for the House of Lords', not the Court of Appeal, to make that challenge.[200] '[W]here a higher court has decided a question of principle,

195 Lord Denning, *The Closing Chapter* (London: Butterworths, 1983), 48.

196 *Thomas* v. *Pascal* (1969) 20 P & CR 1081, 1084 *per* Harman LJ.

197 *Horsey* v. *Harris*, Court of Appeal (Civil Division), transcript, 30 July 1980 (WL 612771). See also *Murray* v. *Express Newspapers* [2007] EWHC 1908 (Ch) at [31] *per* Patten J. In *Barrington* v. *Lee* [1972] 1 QB 326, 333, Denning MR suggests that the claimant's learning of an *obiter* remark made by Sachs J four years earlier prompted her (unsuccessful) action for recovery.

198 See, e.g., *Darby* v. *Richmond LBC* [2017] EWCA Civ 252 at [8] ('[Counsel's] principal ground of appeal is that the judge failed to take into account *obiter dicta* of Lord Scott . . . '); also *R (M)* v. *CICAP* [2001] EWHC 720 (Admin) at [82].

199 See, e.g., *Direct Exeter, Plymouth and Devonport Railway Co* (1851) 5 De G & Sm 117, 120 ('Although . . . Lord Cranworth and the Lord Chancellor may have expressed doubts their observations were extra-judicial and ought not to overrule in this court'); *Latham* v. *R Johnson & Nephew Ltd* [1913] 1 KB 398, 408 *per* Farwell LJ; *Charles R Davidson & Co* v. *M'Robb* [1918] AC 304, 322 *per* Lord Dunedin. A lower court cannot dismiss a statement as *obiter dictum* if a higher one has decreed it to belong to a *ratio*: *Barton* v. *Wycombe* [1926] 2 KB 3, 26 *per* Atkin LJ.

200 *R (Al-Skeini)* v. *Secretary of State for Defence* [2005] EWCA Civ 1609 at [148] *per* Brooke LJ, also [211] *per* Richards LJ. The House of Lords duly obliged: *Al-Skeini* v. *Secretary of State for Defence* [2007] UKHL 26 at [20], [22], and [136].

albeit *obiter*, for the purpose of clarifying the law' and a lower court disagrees with the higher court's reasoning, Moore-Bick LJ ventured in *Sayce* v. *TNT* (2011), then, even though the reasoning does not 'form[] part of the *ratio decidendi* and' is 'therefore . . . not binding on the [lower court] judge, . . . he ought to . . . follow[] and appl[y] it' rather than 'disregard . . . parts of' the higher court's 'speeches . . . on the grounds that they are *obiter*'.[201]

This last, startling and somewhat thorny, contention – that there are circumstances in which *dictum* should be followed even though it is not legal authority – cannot go unanalysed, though consideration of it must wait until later. At this point, it is worth reflecting on the fact that *obiter dicta* should occasion so much fancy legal footwork. The reason that they should is perhaps obvious: modern judges and lawyers grasp that logomachy over *obiter dicta* and *ratio decidendi* can be a skirmish worth the effort, because there are instances where nobody can be sure that their arguments as to whether particular statements are *obiter* or *ratio* are the ones which will prevail. The law reports offer up numerous instances in which a judge seems uncertain as to whether some statement made in a previous case is best categorized as *obiter dictum*.[202] Categorization of statements as *dicta*, furthermore, is something over which judges often disagree. '[T]his opinion . . . is considered by one of the learned judges of the court below as altogether extrajudicial', Vaughan B remarked in 1830, '[b]ut with great respect for the opinion of that very able judge, I cannot consider the opinion . . . extrajudicial'.[203] Vaughan had offered the same assessment of another opinion the previous year after one of his fellow

[201] *Sayce* v. *TNT Ltd* [2011] EWCA Civ 1583 at [24]. If the higher court's *dicta* 'was clearly intended to clarify the law in relation to what had become a vexed question', he continued, the lower court 'judge ought to' leave 'it to this court to decide whether it could and should depart from it' (ibid.).

[202] See, e.g., *Bagshaw* v. *Spencer* (1743) 2 Atk 570, 581 *per* Fortescue MR ('[King's LC's opinion being] a sort of extrajudicial opinion'); *Vaughan* v. *Taff Vale Railway Co* (1858) 3 Hurl & N 743, 747 *per* Bramwell B ('The observation appears to be extrajudicial'); *Browne* v. *Barber* [1913] 2 KB 553, 575 *per* Vaughan Williams LJ ('a sort of *obiter dicta* . . . '); *Smith* v. *Metropolitan Properties* [1932] 1 KB 314, 333 *per* Talbot J ('Those statements . . . are probably more or less *obiter dicta*'); *R* v. *Westminster CC ex p Ermakov* (1996) 28 HLR 819, 829 *per* Hutchison LJ ('The judge in the present case characterised the passage . . . as an *obiter dictum*. It is, on the basis of the facts to be gleaned from the report, not altogether easy to determine whether or not this is correct').

[203] *R* v. *Westwood* (1830) 4 Bli N S 213, 243. See also *Nedby* v. *Nedby* (1839) 4 My & C 367, 375 *per* Cottenham LC ('[I]t is not at all right to say that the opinion expressed in that case was an extra-judicial opinion . . . It was not extra-judicial at all'); *R* v. *Labouchere* (1884) 12 QBD 320, 322–3 *per* Coleridge CJ.

judges had declared it 'certainly extrajudicial'.[204] In 1844, a House of Lords divided equally on a matter of episcopal law was unable to agree on which prior cases were authority and which merely provided *obiter dicta*.[205] These sorts of disagreements are by no means unique to the nineteenth century.[206] Judges with a penchant for common-law creativity might try to take advantage of the fact that a past judicial observation has unsettled status by arguing for confirmation of its status one way or the other.[207] An advocate before a court, recognizing that earlier judges have been unsure, or have disagreed over, whether an observation belongs to a *ratio decidendi*, will very likely see no harm in trying to get the court to accord the observation the status suited to the outcome that she seeks.

The point has been made already in this Essay that the identification of *obiter dictum* as a secondary legal source poses a peculiar difficulty because, unlike other secondary legal sources, it is embedded in a primary legal source. There is no need to become exercised over the distinction between the reasons provided by members of a legislature in support of enacting a law and other statements made by those members in the process of debating the enactment of that law, because the reasons for deciding to make a text a statutory rule are of secondary legal status just as are any other observations made in the process of coming to that

[204] *Harding* v. *Pollock* (1829) 3 Bli N S 161, 179 *per* Littledale J ('This reasoning of Lord Holt ... is certainly extrajudicial') and 210 *per* Vaughan B ('I cannot ... consider the opinions delivered by Lord Holt ... as *obiter* and extrajudicial *dicta*').

[205] *R* v. *Millis (George)* (1844) 10 Cl & F 534.

[206] See, e.g., *Macbeth* v. *Maritime Insurance* [1908] AC 144, 153 *per* Lord Collins ('This weighty utterance was put aside ... as a mere *dictum* ... But is it fair to say that this pronouncement in its context was merely an *obiter dictum*? I think not'); *Vestey* v. *IRC (No. 1)* [1980] AC 1148, 1192 *per* Lord Edmund-Davies ('Your Lordships were invited to hold that these passages were merely *obiter dicta* and, as such, need not now be applied. But it is an invitation that, for my part, I find it impossible to accept. On the contrary, they appear to me to contain the true *ratio decidendi*'); *The Al Wahab* [1984] AC 50 at 55–7, 72; *County Leasing Asset Management Ltd* v. *Hawkes* [2015] EWCA Civ 1251 at [19]–[25] *per* Briggs LJ; *Southern Gas Networks plc* v. *Thames Water Utilities Ltd* [2016] EWHC 1669 (TCC) at [26] *per* Bowdery J ('Both parties considered Lord Justice Buxton's observations ... to be *obiter dicta* ... I am not so sure').

[207] See Michael Abramowicz and Maxwell Stearns, 'Defining Dicta' (2005) 57 *Stanford L. Rev.* 953, 1021 (uncertainty as to whether an observation is *dicta* or *ratio* 'affords [today's] judges with considerable latitude to select among various paths that lead from facts to judgment'); Cass R. Sunstein, *One Case at a Time: Judicial Minimalism on the Supreme Court* (Cambridge, Mass.: Harvard University Press, 1999), 43 ('[T]he line between holding and *dicta* ... gives subsequent courts a good deal of authority to say that earlier cases, properly understood, have left many things undecided').

decision. Statutory law is canonical text, and anything pronounced by the legislators responsible for that text – the reasoning which was necessary as well as observations which were not necessary to the legislature's decision to enact it – has, at most, epistemic authority. When today's judges and lawyers take advantage of the fact that earlier judges have hesitated or disagreed over whether an observation is *obiter dictum*, they are profiting from a distinct predicament: that the reasoning necessary to a judicial decision is (unlike the reasoning necessary to a legislative decision) a primary source of law, that the judicial decision is likely to be accompanied by *obiter dicta*, and that it is not always easy to separate the reasoning necessary to a judicial decision from some of the *dicta* delivered alongside it. Statutes are law, whereas cases contain law. Interpreting statutes is in at least one sense a less tricky proposition than reading cases, Edward Levi once observed, because the interpreter of a statute can presume against surplusage, whereas the reader of a case invariably has to sort wheat from chaff.[208]

Not only does *obiter dictum* appear in a decision, but the decision itself could be very long, composed of multiple parts (with different authors), and might have been supplemented by case law containing judicial commentary on the *dictum*. It is only to be expected that judges should sometimes be unsure whether an earlier judicial observation is *obiter*, given how much *obiter* judicial observation exists. '[N]ine tenths' of recorded case law, Jeremy Bentham insisted, 'is notorious falsehood'[209] – notorious because its status as falsehood is never sealed, because nobody can guarantee that supposedly non-binding statements contained in judicial decisions will never be read as legal authority. The common law is, for Bentham, 'nothing less than the entire and indiscriminate collection of whatever has been written on the subject';[210] and the law reports, in turn, are 'magazines of lies, and engines of confusion',[211] their contents

> long ago immense . . . and . . . still increasing . . . If any one thinks a heap of materials thus immense too great . . . let him say how much and what he will exclude: between what is to be admitted and what is to be rejected let

[208] Edward Levi, *An Introduction to Legal Reasoning* (University of Chicago Press, 1949), at 6–7, 28.

[209] Jeremy Bentham, *A Comment on the Commentaries and a Fragment on Government*, ed. J. H. Burns and H. L. A. Hart (London: Athlone Press, 1977 [*c.*1774–*c.*1776]), 195. As we saw in the Prologue, he was not always quite so harsh.

[210] Ibid. at 211.

[211] Ibid. at 195.

> him draw the line . . . The individual acts (judicial decisions) are acts of Judges; they are acts of authority. But the rules of Law . . . are conclusions drawn from the . . . individual acts: and these conclusions are what are formed by any one who happens to bestow his thoughts upon the subject.[212]

The categorization of judicial remarks as *obiter dicta* is, from this perspective, essentially an exercise in information-management: a determination that some statements appearing in cases which form part of the record of the common law are not themselves common law. Bentham famously disparaged case law as something devised out of the blue and imposed on citizens retrospectively.[213] Lawyers and others can only watch – precedents do not enable them confidently to predict – how judges will develop the common law, for recorded judicial decisions reveal case law to be 'unfathomable'.[214] Part of the explanation for its unfathomability, in Bentham's eyes, is that the case reports and records contain so much information additional to, though not always readily distinguishable from, the decisions themselves that nobody can be sure (let he who maintains otherwise 'draw the line'!) just what will and what will not be extracted from the stock of reported judicial wisdom and treated as legal authority.

It is barely surprising that English judges have not lined up to endorse Bentham's denunciation of the common law.[215] They are, after all, the very people responsible for producing all the noise that he deplored. To summarize what seems to be a fairly common judicial sentiment: the noise might not always be welcome, but it would be wrong to think that it is always unwelcome. Lord Goff, for example, was by no means inclined to romanticize *obiter dicta*. He warned, much as François Gény did, of how judges acquire an unwarranted general lawmaking power if their observations on hypothetical questions are binding on future

[212] Ibid. at 331.

[213]
> It is the Judges . . . that make the common law:– Do you know how they make it? Just as a man makes laws for his dog. When your dog does any thing you want to break him of, you wait till he does it, and then beat him for it . . . What way then has any man of coming at this dog-law? Only by watching [Judges'] proceedings: by observing in what *cases* they have hanged a man, in what *cases* they have sent him to jail, in what *cases* they have seized his goods, and so forth.

Jeremy Bentham, *Truth* versus *Ashhurst; or Law as it is, contrasted with what it is said to be* (London: Moses, 1823 [1792]), 11–12 (emphases in original).

[214] Bentham, *A Comment on the Commentaries*, 331.

[215] 'I never thought anything of Jeremy Bentham', Alfred Denning once observed with something not quite verging on restraint. 'He was the most pretentious person that ever lived.' Lord Denning, *What Next in the Law?* (London: Butterworths, 1982), 17.

courts.[216] But he also cautioned against the codifier's 'temptation of elegance'.[217] If judges are to 'guard against stating principles in terms which do not allow for the possibility of qualifications or exceptions as yet unperceived',[218] he contended, they should not only avoid articulating those principles with code-like precision but also be willing to pronounce *obiter* on what is as yet unsettled about a principle's reach, so that future courts might have something on which to build when the time for the 'adaptation'[219] of that principle comes. '[I]t is better to have a feast . . . festering with ideas, than a single hygienic package wrapped in polythene, insulated . . . from . . . differences in analysis and on points of detail which may later prove to be important.'[220] A judge might be more amenable to elegance than Goff held himself out to be and still value *dicta* much as he did. Lady Arden, for example, besides advocating and welcoming various statutory codification initiatives,[221] has argued that the judiciary ought to produce 'more concise and clear' (and more single majority in preference to *seriatim*) judgments.[222] Like Goff, however, she is not in favour of judges renouncing *dicta*: '*obiter dicta* . . . are valuable',[223] she has maintained, not least because there is a certain 'type of judgment' – the example she cites is that of where a litigant challenges a legal rule on the basis that it contravenes treaty norms implemented within the national jurisdiction – in which a court 'may be required to explain the [legal] position in greater detail than it would have done before' a challenge was made.[224]

[216] See *R* v. *Secretary of State for the Home Department ex p Wynne* [1993] 1 WLR 115, 120.

[217] Robert Goff, 'The Search for Principle' (1983) 69 *Proc. Brit. Acad.* 169, 174.

[218] Ibid.

[219] Ibid. at 183.

[220] Ibid. at 175. Goff's argument here is primarily intended (as the phrase 'single hygienic package' indicates) as a justification of *seriatim*-opinion judgments in preference to single judgments, though his point is not only that *seriatim* judgments allow for dissent but also, more broadly, that they enable judges to 'express their separate views in different ways' (ibid.).

[221] See Mary Arden, *Common Law and Modern Society. Keeping Pace with Change: Volume II* (Oxford University Press, 2015), 189–236.

[222] Ibid. at 5; also (on preference for single majority over *seriatim* judgments) ibid. at 246 and 254.

[223] Ibid. at 251.

[224] Ibid. at 47. For a recent illustration, see *Re Northern Ireland Human Rights Commission's Application for Judicial Review* [2018] UKSC 27, which contains no small amount of *obiter dicta* concerning how the Court might have addressed the question of the compatibility of Northern Ireland's current abortion law with articles 3 and 8 of the ECHR had the Commission's appeal to bring proceedings been allowed.

English judicial assessments of *obiter dicta* might never have been truly Benthamite, but there are plenty of instances in which judges can be found frowning upon *dicta* as unsightly or potentially harmful clutter, and endeavouring to make the legal landscape look less (or stop it becoming more) untidy. Usually the endeavour takes the form of self-censorship – indeed, a common judicial ploy is to avoid commenting on a legal matter by declaring that the commentary would be *obiter* ('it is not for me to say; it would be extrajudicial for me to express an opinion upon that').[225] On a multi-member panel, a judge delivering a leading judgment might anticipate that the fewer *dicta* she produces, the less likely it will be that her colleagues will be moved to offer *obiter* observations of their own; any judge hoping that other judges will follow her judgment with the simple words, 'I agree' will bear in mind that *dicta* can beget *dicta*. Sometimes, judges offer *dicta* in an attempt to clear up a mess caused by others, such as when one judge makes an *obiter* observation correcting another judge's legally inaccurate *obiter* observation.[226] Now and again, judges seek to curtail or negate the potential effects of their own *dicta* by offering new and improved formulations of them.[227] Occasionally, they explicitly renounce them. A *dictum* 'I ventured on'

[225] *R* v. *Feist* (1858) Dears & B 590, 598–9 *per* Willes J. See also *Temple* v. *Walker* (1820) 3 Phillimore 394, 402 ('[T]he question is whether that point is ripe for discussion; we are not likely to give an extrajudicial opinion upon it'); *Cooke* v. *Bishop* (1831) 5 Bli NS 103, 105 *per* Lord Tenterden ('I shall abstain from expressing an opinion which would be extrajudicial, and which might be quoted as indicating my view of the case upon the future investigation of this very important case when it is again brought before the Court below'); *ex p Coombs* (1862) 3 B & S 296, 303 *per* Cockburn CJ ('On this question we can only speculate, as the legislature has not pronounced on it: we should be only groping our way in the dark, and it is therefore better to abstain from giving any extrajudicial opinion'); *Smith, Gale and French* v. *Richardson* (1878) 4 CPD 112, 115 *per* Denman J; *Re Whitaker* (1887) 34 ChD 227, 232 *per* Cotton LJ ('that particular question does not arise now, and any opinion one might give would be extrajudicial'); *Cox* v. *Hakes* (1890) 15 App Cas 506, 535–6 *per* Lord Herschell; *Scott & Co Ltd* v. *Barclays Bank* [1923] 2 KB 1, 10 *per* Bankes LJ; *Etri* v. *NMB* [1987] FSR 389, 393 *per* Sir Nicolas Browne-Wilkinson; *Hoare* v. *National Trust* (1999) 77 P & CR 366, 384 *per* Schiemann LJ.

[226] See, e.g., *Foster* v. *London, Chatham & Dover Rly Co* [1895] 1 QB 711, 715 *per* Lord Halsbury; *Duke of Marlborough* v. *A-G* [1945] Ch 145, 157 *per* Morton LJ ('[W]e do not desire to make any observations on it which would necessarily be *obiter dicta*. At the same time, we do not wish it to be thought that we agree with the view of the learned judge on this part of the case').

[227] For an example of a judicial panel re-evaluating *obiter dicta* which it had offered in an earlier case, see *Middleton* v. *Denderowicz* [1998] 1 WLR 1164, 1168 ('correcting [and] ... clarifying' *dicta* which the same Court of Appeal judges had set forth in a composite judgment (*Bannister* v. *SGB* [1998] 1 WLR 1123) only six weeks earlier).

five years ago 'was tentative enough', Lord Atkin remarked in 1948, 'but it was ill-advised, especially in a field where *obiter dicta* have added enough difficulty to decided cases'.[228] He was not the first judge candidly to disown his own *obiter dicta*, nor would he be the last.[229]

Avoidance of clutter, or a desire not to add to the clutter, might be the top and bottom of why a judge avoids making *obiter* observations.[230] The more common reason that judges forgo commenting *obiter*, however, is that they do not want to say something they may come to regret – something which may tie their own hands or, perhaps worse still, the hands of the entire court. Occasionally, a judge will try to box clever, delivering *obiter dicta* with a purported get-out clause.[231] Judges who come to lament their *dictum* soon after pronouncing it have been known

[228] *London Brick Co Ltd* v. *Robinson* [1943] AC 341, 349.

[229] See, e.g., *A-G* v. *Clapham* (1855) 4 De GM & G 591, 655 *per* Cranworth LC ('what I said was merely an *obiter dictum*, and I wish not to let this case pass over without noticing it, so that if ever the question should arise, I may not have that *dictum* of mine quoted without having this also quoted at the same time, that I wish to withdraw it'); *The Minerva* [1933] P 224, 232 *per* Bateson J; *Scholl* v. *Clifton* [1967] Ch 41, 48 *per* Harman LJ; *Binks* v. *Huss* [1971] 1 WLR 52, 57 *per* Ashworth J ('[S]ome words which, ill-advisedly, I myself used in giving judgment in *Dunsford* v. *Pearson* [1970] 1 WLR 222 . . . were *obiter dicta*, and like many *obiter dicta* they provide cause for subsequent regret, and they were wrong'); *R* v. *Immigration Appeal Tribunal ex p Subramaniam* [1977] QB 190, 206 *per* Bridge LJ ('I stand in a respectable judicial tradition in keeping a white sheet in my wardrobe and I gladly wear it this morning . . . [M]y *obiter dictum* . . . was wrong'); *Brooks* v. *BT* [1992] Pens LR 45, 56 *per* Sir Christopher Slade ('Though Balcombe LJ has referred with approval to an *obiter dictum* of mine . . . I would not now wish to adhere to that *dictum*').

[230] See *Phyn* v. *Royal Exchange Assurance Co* (1798) 7 Term Rep 505, 507 *per* Kenyon CJ ('As so many observations have been made in the argument of this case on the different expressions used by the several judges in the cases cited, I will take care not to hazard an extrajudicial opinion now'); *Aubert* v. *Maze* (1801) 2 Bos & P 371, 375 *per* Heath J; *Webb* v. *Whiffin* (1871–2) LR 5 HL 711, 738 *per* Lord Cairns.

> Now, we were pressed very much with this question: but how is the official manager to adjust and define the sum he is to call for from the ex-members of the company? My Lords, I think it is important that it should be borne in mind that any opinion that your Lordships, or any of your Lordships, might express upon this subject, cannot upon this appeal become the order of the House, and cannot, therefore, have the effect of a decision of that question; and in many respects I should have desired not to express even a passing opinion upon the subject, because if it should ever hereafter come in controversy, and be brought before your Lordships, I desire that it should come perfectly unaffected as regards any decision of this House by any extrajudicial expression of opinion which may now take place.

[231] See, e.g., *Impey* v. *Secretary of State for the Environment* (1984) 47 P & CR 157, 159 *per* Donaldson LJ ('Those . . . matters . . . fall outside our purview today, and I would merely express preliminary and *obiter dicta* views – views that, if the matter ever came before me in a real form, I might depart from in the light of full argument').

to seek appropriate redactions to the text of the judgment before it finds its way into a law report.[232] When threnody comes too late, *dicta* can end up being disowned. 'If I am correctly reported in the *Law Times* report', Humphreys J protested in 1944, 'I can only say, first, that that was an *obiter dictum*, and, secondly, that I think it was wrong. I have no recollection of saying anything of the sort, and I cannot believe that I said it.'[233] But the standard strategy for judges not wishing to be bedevilled by their *dictum* is to avoid foisting it on the world in the first place. 'I do not feel myself called on to express any decided opinion (extra-judicial as it would necessarily be) on these points', Cranworth LC observed in 1855, for 'this question does not arise in the case now before me for decision, and I desire not to be considered as binding myself on the subject'.[234] Three decades later, Bowen LJ declared himself

> extremely reluctant to decide anything except what is necessary for the special case, because I believe by long experience that judgments come with far more weight and gravity when they come upon points which the judges are bound to decide, and I believe that *obiter dicta*, like the proverbial chickens of destiny, come home to roost sooner or later in a very uncomfortable way to the judges who have uttered them, and are a great source of embarrassment in future cases.[235]

Cranworth and Bowen (who appears to have his chickens mixed up)[236] were perhaps not quite of the same mind. Bowen's worry was that he might one day have to dissociate himself from the *dicta* he once proffered and now regretted. But Cranworth feared that the *dicta* he now regretted would be *dicta* from which he could not extricate himself. *Dicta* might not bind tomorrow's courts, but the authors of *dicta*, perhaps still sitting

[232] Henry Cecil, *The English Judge* (London: Arrow, 1972 [1970]), 160 ('If, on consideration, the judge thinks that his . . . *obiter dictum* was doubtful, or even wrong, he may delete . . . or modify it. And the altered version will appear in the law report').

[233] *Brentnall & Cleland* v. *London CC* [1945] KB 115, 120–1 (case decided November 1944). See also *Cox* v. *Coleridge* (1822) 1 B & C 37, 50 *per* Bayley J ('I wish not to be considered as bound by the *obiter dictum*, which I am reported to have used in the case cited').

[234] *Coape* v. *Arnold* (1855) 4 De GM & G 574, 589.

[235] *Cooke* v. *New River Co* (1888) 38 ChD 56, 70–1. See also *Re Trepka* [1963] Ch 199, 225 *per* Donovan LJ; *R* v. *D* [1984] AC 778, 787 *per* Lord Bridge.

[236] A chicken of destiny is one which has not yet come to be – which is best not counted before it has hatched: to avoid pitfalls associated with presumptuousness over one's destiny, some actions are best not taken until events warranting those actions have transpired. Chickens which come home to roost are – notwithstanding their future-orientation (avoid taking actions which may well rebound on you later) – the proverbial chickens of regret rather than of destiny.

on those courts, might both rue and feel shackled by what they said. The colleagues of those authors, moreover, while perhaps no more enamoured of the *dicta* than the authors themselves, might consider it indelicate to criticize *obiter* remarks made by judges among their number. One of the lessons to be learned from studying *obiter dicta* is that some past judicial pronunciations are not legal authority and yet cannot easily – perhaps simply cannot – be dismissed by today's judges when they apply the law. Just as this lesson might actually provide judges with an impetus to speak *obiter*, so too it is a reason – here Cranworth and Bowen clearly were of the same mind – for judges to stay silent where they sense the danger of *dicta* returning to torment them or inconvenience their colleagues.

7 The Necessity Test

Judicial self-censorship is a decidedly limited strategy. It is difficult, as has been observed already in this Essay, to envisage an actual common-law judge being capable of refraining altogether from making *obiter* observations. Moreover, given the value that a judge might attach to being able to make such observations – given that *obiter dictum* is the main medium through which a judge can try to resolve statutory and other legal ambiguities, suggest how the law might apply to matters yet to be litigated, disapprove of particular legal developments, make suggestions regarding legal reform, and so on – it seems as unrealistic to conceive of judges wanting to renounce *dictum* as it is to believe them to be capable of renouncing it. *Obiter dictum* is, for better and for worse, a feature of the common-law landscape.

A judge might limit the negative effects of *obiter dicta* by leaving them out whenever in doubt about what the repercussions of delivering *dicta* might be. But the most obvious safeguard against the potentially adverse consequences of *dictum* is not judges limiting how much of it they produce but rather judges, as interpreters of *dictum*, invoking a rule of recognition. *Dictum* need not be an inordinate worry – certainly it need not be if the worry is that it might be mistaken for law – so long as there is a test of recognition which enables judges to distinguish the binding *ratio* of an earlier decision from the non-binding *dicta* which sit alongside it. We know that judges will not always be in agreement as to what makes for a decision's *ratio* and which elements of an opinion are merely *dicta*, and that they will sometimes be unsure as to whether a particular judicial statement is the one thing or the other. So can there be, embodied in the rule of recognition, a test for distinguishing *ratio* and *dicta*?

Judges have been understandably diffident when answering this question. For Lord Denning, any effort to distinguish the *ratio* from *dicta*, certainly in a lengthy *seriatim* judgment, 'must be somewhat speculative'.[237] '[T]he rule', Asquith LJ bluffed, 'is quite simple: if you agree with the other bloke, you say it's part of the *ratio*; if you don't, you say it's "*obiter dictum*," with the implication that he is a congenital idiot.'[238] But it would be a mistake to infer from comments such as these that there cannot be a test of validity setting *ratio* apart from *dicta*. Judges and lawyers will accept particular tests of validity as part of the rule of recognition, Hart maintained, but the tests are likely to be evidenced not by their authoritative formulation – they might be unstated – but 'by reference to actual practice: to the way in which courts identify what is to count as law'.[239] Since the eighteenth century, and possibly earlier, there has operated in the courts one particular test 'the precise content and scope of' which 'may not admit of a clear or determinate answer'[240] – one which, as with any test, might be misapplied, or incite disagreements, or be a source of confusion – but which has been 'generally accepted ... in practice'[241] and on which a judge, when negotiating precedent, will typically, even if not always confidently, rely 'for identifying what is to count as law in his court'.[242]

The relevant test, as is well known, is used for identifying the *ratio decidendi* of a case. Everything *obiter* in a case is understood to be so by negative inference: if we can point to the case content that constitutes the *ratio*, then the rest of the content, not belonging to the *ratio*, is *obiter dictum*. The standard – though not the only – formulation of the test posits the *ratio* as the reasoning necessary to the decision.[243] When

237 *The Hannah Blumenthal*, 56 (quoting from *Dicey and Morris on the Conflict of Laws*, 2 vols., 10th ed., ed. J. H. C. Morris et al. (London: Stevens & Sons, 1980), II, 942). See also Richard A. Posner, *How Judges Think* (Cambridge, Mass.: Harvard University Press, 2008), 192–3.

238 Lord Justice Asquith, 'Some Aspects of the Work of the Court of Appeal' (1950) ns 1 *JSPTL* 350, 359.

239 Hart, *The Concept of Law*, 108.

240 Ibid. at 109.

241 Ibid. at 110.

242 Ibid. at 105.

243 See, e.g., Fikentscher, *Methoden des Rechts in vergleichender Darstellung*, 92 ('The reason, or reasons, on which a decision is based define the *ratio decidendi*. And so *obiter dicta* can be defined as alternative, general remarks on substantive law, comparisons with other legal cases not yet in the foreground and which are not actual rulings of the court, but possible solutions to which are implied').

a judge involved in a case expresses a legal opinion which is, or forms part of, the reasoning on which the court's decision is based, that judge's opinion is, or is 'a material ingredient in',[244] the *ratio decidendi*. Judicial observations which are not integral to the *ratio*, which could be removed without the reasoning supporting the decision being affected, are (to borrow a favoured nineteenth-century description) 'gratuitous'.[245] This way of thinking about extrajudicial or *obiter* observations – as observations addressing matters which it was unnecessary for a court to address when it made its ruling – can be traced at least as far back as the late seventeenth century.[246] To this day, judges can be seen assessing statements cited from earlier decisions according to whether those statements were necessary to the decisions – the statements being considered binding *ratio* if they were and non-binding *dicta* if they were not.[247]

The middle part of the twentieth century witnessed a flurry of juristic literature agonizing over, and usually taking to task, the proposition that the reasons necessary to a decision constitute its *ratio decidendi*.[248]

244 *Olive* v. *Smith* (1813) 5 Taunt 56, 60 *per* Gibbs J ('And this is not an *obiter dictum*, but made a material ingredient in the judgment').

245 See, e.g., *Giles* v. *Grover and Pollard* (1832) 6 Bli N S 277, 383 *per* Gaselee J ('the observation ... was a mere gratuitous *dictum*'); *McEwan* v. *Smith* (1849) 2 HL Cas 309, 329 *per* Lord Campbell.

246 See, e.g., *Company of Taylors in Exeter* v. *Clarke* (1695) 2 Show K B 349, 357; *Jones* v. *Earl of Strafford* (1730) 3 P Wms 79, 88 *per* King LC and Raymond LCJ ('that part of the case was at least an extrajudicial opinion not necessary to be determined'); *Bagshaw* v. *Spencer* (1748) 1 Ves Sen 142, 148 ('it was not necessary for Lord King to give that opinion; it being extra judicial'); *White* v. *Warner* (1781) 3 Douglas 4, 6 ('This question, however, could not arise in [the case] ... and therefore the opinion of Popham [J] was extrajudicial'); *Auriol* v. *Mills* (1790) 4 Term Rep 94, 97; *R* v. *Wallis & Barrs* (1793) 5 Term Rep 375, 377 ('those opinions were extrajudicial, and were by no means necessary to the decision of the case'); *Gwynne* v. *Muddock* (1808) 14 Ves Jr 488, 489; *Kitchen* v. *Bartsch* (1805) 7 East 53, 56; *Hutchison* v. *Birch* (1812) 4 Taunton 619, 626; *R* v. *Giles* (1820) 8 Price 293, 359; *Hinton* v. *Dibbin* (1842) 2 QB 646, 666; *Warrender* v. *Warrender* (1835) 2 Cl & F 488, 518 ('The observations attributed to a noble and learned Lord, in the latter case, were not necessary for the decision of that case, and can only have the authority of an extrajudicial *dictum*'); *Skynner* v. *Spilsbury* (1843) 10 Cl & Fin 340, 358; *Gray* v. *R* (1844) 11 Cl & F 427, 460 *per* Gurney B ('There are expressions used by very learned judges, ... but these *dicta* were foreign to the point upon which the judges were called to decide'); *Ellis* v. *Griffith* (1846) 16 M & W 106, 107; *Occleston* v. *Fullalove* (1874) LR 9 Ch App 147, 160; *Palmer* v. *Wick and Pulteneytown Steam Shipping Co Ltd* [1894] AC 318, 320.

247 See, e.g., *Secretary of State for Work & Pensions* v. *Deane* [2010] EWCA Civ 699 at [31]–[33] *per* Ward LJ; *Ghani* v. *Secretary of State for the Home Department* [2018] EWCA Civ 2708 at [12] *per* Leggatt LJ; *West London Law Ltd* v. *Sandhu* [2019] EWHC 828 (Ch) at [31].

248 The best-known critique of the proposition being Arthur Goodhart's (A. L. Goodhart, 'Determining the *Ratio Decidendi* of a Case' (1930) 40 *Yale LJ* 161), a critique which was

Judges before that time and since, by contrast, have more often than not embraced the necessity test, regularly categorizing pronouncements made in earlier cases as *ratio* or *obiter* according to whether the pronouncements strike them as necessary to the decision that was reached. But embracing the test has not always translated into enthusiasm for it: some judges have clearly regarded it as a blunt instrument. We all agree that a statutory duty on landlords to keep premises 'in all respects reasonably fit for human habitation' does not mean that they should be liable for injuries which a tenant sustains as a consequence of property defects which were not within a landlord's knowledge, Atkin LJ observed in *Morgan* v. *Liverpool Corporation* (1926), and we need agree on nothing more in this instance. But it is a pity, he added, that the Court of Appeal could not agree – as part of its *ratio* – on an interpretation of the statutory duty so as to settle the scope of a landlord's liability for repair.

> I agree that the appeal should be allowed ... and I agree upon the only ground, unfortunately, upon which all three of us are agreed – namely, that notice is required before the liability of the landlord to repair in this case exists. The result is that we have embarked, and are embarking, upon a series of *obiter dicta* in respect of the other parts of the case, which I trust will be useful, but which so far as I can see will not be authoritative.[249]

Perhaps the more typical judicial lament over the necessity test is that the characterization of certain observations as *obiter* might not do them justice, even if it is true that a decision did not depend on them. The logic of the necessity test compels us to conclude that a dissenting opinion must be *obiter dictum* in its entirety, Roxburgh J once observed, yet not only are there instances when it would seem 'disrespectful' to dispose of a dissenting opinion by labelling it *dictum* (not the least because dissenting judges will sometimes make a point of endorsing some of the majority reasoning that forms the *ratio decidendi*), but there is also something 'unrealistic' about labelling it thus, given that lawyers and judges – who quite often find *obiter dicta* in dissenting opinions[250] – clearly do not consider *dictum* and dissent to be one and the same thing.[251] Foreign

itself subjected to a range of objections (see, e.g., Julius Stone, 'The *Ratio* of the *Ratio Decidendi*' (1959) 22 *MLR* 597; A. W. B. Simpson, 'The *Ratio Decidendi* of a Case' (1959) 22 *MLR* 453).

249 *Morgan* v. *Liverpool Corporation* [1927] 2 KB 131, 144.

250 For modern examples, see e.g., *Percy* v. *Hall* [1997] QB 924, 938 *per* Simon Brown LJ; *Swynson* v. *Lowick Rose* [2015] EWCA Civ 629 at [14].

251 *Abbott* v. *Philbin* [1959] 1 WLR 667, 676 *per* Roxburgh J ('Jenkins LJ ... was in a minority and, therefore, what he says ... may, in one sense, be *obiter dictum*; but

precedents similarly cast light on the test's blunt edge. A foreign precedent may, judged according to the necessity test, yield a *ratio decidendi*. Yet the reasoning necessary to the foreign court's judgment only ever has the status of *obiter dictum* in English courts, as English courts are not bound by the decisions of foreign courts.[252]

The test also entails a presumption which appears not to be readily accepted by many judges: that the correct categorization of a comment as either *obiter* or as (part of the) *ratio* depends not on what the judge responsible for the comment – or any other individual – thought it to be, but on whether the comment was, objectively speaking, necessary to the decision. Judges occasionally do, as we have seen, take it upon themselves to indicate that they are commenting *obiter* – and indeed will sometimes indicate that their comments are not to be read as *obiter*,[253] or that it is possible to envisage future cases in which their comments will warrant serious consideration.[254] Presumably they send out such signals because they believe that their subjective assessments of the status of their

I should be both disrespectful and unrealistic if I lightly disposed of what he said on that ground'). See also *Allen* v. *Hornchurch UDC* [1938] 2 KB 654, 671 *per* Hewart CJ.

252 Likewise a lower domestic court decision: the decision will yield a *ratio*, but a higher court is of course not bound by that *ratio* (lower court judgments are occasionally referred to as *dictum* by virtue of having been reversed: see, e.g., *Re Western Counties Steam Bakeries* [1897] 1 Ch 617, 622; *Peacock* v. *Del Seatek* [2019] EWHC 2867 (Admlty) at [16], [19]). When English judges refer to *obiter dicta* pronounced in a foreign court, they sometimes mean observations which a foreign judge offered in the course of delivering a judgment and which do not belong to the *ratio* of that judgment (see e.g., *Smith* v. *Desmond* [1965] AC 960, 976; *Oppenheimer* v. *Cattermole* [1976] AC 249, 273; *Grupo Torras* v. *Al-Sabah* [1999] CLC 1469, 1521), while on other occasions they mean that the actual foreign precedent is (in an English court) tantamount to *dictum*. In *Woodland* v. *Swimming Teachers' Association*, Laws LJ's reference to '*dicta* of high persuasive authority which are very much in point in this appeal' seems, at first glance, muddled, for *dicta*, being *obiter*, are not normally described as 'in point'. The *dicta*, however, are very much in point in the appeal, but have the status of *dicta* because they form part of the reasoning in a decision made by the High Court of Australia. See *Woodland* v. *Swimming Teachers' Association* [2012] EWCA Civ 239 at [11]; also *Rahmatullah* v. *Ministry of Defence* [2014] EWHC 3846 (QB) at [98]–[99] and [149] *per* Leggatt J.

253 See, e.g., *North & South Trust Co* v. *Berkeley* [1971] 1 WLR 470, 478 *per* Donaldson J ('whether right or wrong, my views are not *obiter dicta*').

254 See, e.g., *Westdeutsche Landesbank Girozentrale* v. *Islington LBC* [1996] AC 669, 716 *per* Lord Browne-Wilkinson ('Although the resulting trust is an unsuitable basis for developing proprietary restitutionary remedies, the remedial constructive trust, if introduced into English law, may provide a more satisfactory road forward . . . However, whether English law should follow the United States and Canada by adopting the remedial constructive trust will have to be decided in some future case when the point is directly in issue').

comments should have a bearing on, indeed might determine, how the comments are received by other judges and by counsel.

The principal difficulty which most judges identify with the necessity test is that of establishing that a reason provided in an earlier decision was actually necessary to the decision. The best-known illustration of the difficulty is the precedent which contains two or more independent and equally supported lines of reasoning sustaining the court's ruling, and which therefore yields no clear majority *ratio*. The United Kingdom's final appeal court has on numerous occasions been criticized for producing this type of precedent – the criticism coming mainly from the courts where such precedents bind – and some of its members, certainly in recent years, have been mindful of the importance of striving to avoid doing so.[255] The difficulty, in its simplest form, is illustrated by an argument which Neville QC put to the Court of Appeal in 1890. Although a Divisional Court ruling on which he was relying 'went on two grounds', the two Divisional Court judges' shared 'opinion on one [ground] cannot', he insisted, 'be treated as extrajudicial merely because the case might have been disposed of on the other ground alone'.[256] Bowen LJ, delivering the Court of Appeal's judgment, simply dismissed the Divisional Court's ruling as one with which '[w]e do not agree',[257] thereby sidestepping the questions posed by Neville's argument: if providing either ground sufficed to support the Divisional Court's decision, which of the two grounds was the *ratio*? Did the case in fact have two *rationes*? Or, if either ground could be removed without the decision being compromised, was there no *ratio* to be found?

While these questions seemed not to trouble late-nineteenth-century English judges, they did touch a nerve with some lawyer-contemporaries across the Atlantic – particularly at the Harvard Law School, where the method of legal instruction initiated in the 1870s under Christopher Columbus Langdell's deanship posited an intimate connection between aptitude as a law student (and future lawyer) and the careful study of leading common-law cases.[258] Could law schools impart legal knowledge and skills effectively – could legal education meet with Langdell's vision

[255] See Alan Paterson, *Final Judgment: The Last Law Lords and the Supreme Court* (Oxford: Hart, 2013), at 102, 136–7, 210–11.

[256] *Re Standard Manufacturing Co* [1891] 1 Ch 627, 636 (case decided October 1890).

[257] Ibid. at 644.

[258] See Christopher Columbus Langdell, *A Selection of Cases on the Law of Contracts* (Boston: Little, Brown & Co, 1871), viii.

of legal science – if it was impossible to find distinct *rationes* in some of these cases? The notion that some cases might indeed lack *rationes* was certainly not anathema at Harvard in the late nineteenth and early twentieth centuries. Eugene Wambaugh joined the faculty in 1892 and, in that year, set forth a version of the necessity test which echoed a claim put to the Court of Common Pleas by Vaughan CJ in 1672: that if a judicial proposition can be turned on its head without the decision of the court being affected, 'then, however excellent the original proposition may be', it must be *obiter dictum.*[259] Although Wambaugh endorsed this test, he also espied a difficulty with it: what if a case contained two or more propositions which individually sufficed to justify the court's decision? In such a case, any one of these propositions could be turned on its head without the decision being altered: none of them would be a binding *ratio*, 'for it is impossible to say that the court considered any particular one of them conclusive'.[260] A case of this type would, judged according to the necessity test, be a case decided by *obiter dicta*. Edmund Morgan, who joined Harvard from Yale on Wambaugh's retirement in 1925, was candid on this matter: '[t]here are many cases where a hypercritical examination of the opinion might lead one to say that none of the several propositions enunciated by the court constitutes decision, but all must be classed as *dicta*'.[261] The necessity test dictates that some cases have no *rationes,* for if a case contains two or more propositions which independently and equally justify the court's decision – so that none of them can be said to be a majority's *ratio* – the meaning of any of those propositions could be reversed and (so long as any one of them remained not reversed) the decision could still be reached.

[259] Eugene Wambaugh, *The Study of Cases* (Boston: Little, Brown & Co, 1892), 5–6 ('Let him then insert in the proposition a word reversing its meaning. Let him then inquire whether, if the court had conceived this new proposition to be good and to be the point upon which the case ought to turn, the decision could have been the same. If the answer be affirmative, then, however excellent the original proposition may be, the case is not a precedent for that proposition'). See also *Bole* v. *Horton*, 382 ('An opinion given in Court, if not necessary to the judgment given of record, but that it might have been as well given if no such, or a contrary, opinion had been broach'd is no judicial opinion').

[260] Wambaugh, *The Study of Cases*, 33.

[261] Edmund M. Morgan, *Introduction to the Study of Law* (Chicago: Callaghan & Co, 1926), 109–10. The sentence had already appeared in a typescript of the same title which Morgan produced for his first-year Yale students in the 1910s: Edmund M. Morgan, *Introduction to the Study of Law* (Yale Law School, *c.*1910–*c.*1919), 41.

Necessity might seem, therefore, to make for an inauspicious test for the purpose of distinguishing the *ratio* of a case from the *dicta* contained within it. More often than not, however, modern English judges at least implicitly accept the test, and tend to be pragmatic and creative when confronted with precedents lacking majority *rationes*. Alternative reasons to be found in a precedent, it is sometimes suggested, need not be equally compelling reasons: if an earlier court provided, say, two reasons for its decision and one of those reasons explains the decision more convincingly than the other one does, the stronger reason is to be treated as the *ratio decidendi* and the weaker one as *obiter dictum*.[262] This argument held no truck with Lord Simonds. '[T]here is', he insisted in 1950,

> no justification for regarding as *obiter dictum* a reason given by a judge for his decision, because he has given another reason also. If it were a proper test to ask whether the decision would have been the same apart from the proposition alleged to be *obiter*, then a case which *ex facie* decided two things would decide nothing.[263]

In such a case, Simonds maintained, both reasons are to be treated 'as forming the ground of the judgment', and therefore 'neither ... is a *dictum*'.[264] The necessity test, of course, decrees otherwise: neither reason – so long as both are present – is necessary to the judgment, and so neither can be the *ratio decidendi*. Confronted by just such a judgment – the House of Lords' decision in *Dodd's case* (1973), in which 'the reasons for ... decision ... appeared to be divided two to two' – Stephenson LJ, in *Harper* v. *NCB* (1974), conceded that there was no 'discernible *ratio decidendi* common to the majority' of the House.[265] But this did not mean that *Dodd's case* decided nothing. Where a precedent 'has no majority *ratio decidendi*', Lords Toulson and Hodge agreed in 2015, '[i]t stands as authority for the point which it decided, ... but nothing more'.[266] This had been Stephenson LJ's central point in *Harper*: since *Dodd's case* has no *ratio*, he contended, '[w]e are ... bound by the decision of the

262 See, e.g., *Re Wykes* [1961] Ch 229, 244, where Buckley J deems one element of Harman J's reasoning in *Re Gillingham Bus Disaster Fund* [1958] Ch 300 (affirmed by the CA: [1959] Ch 62) to be an *obiter dictum* as opposed to an alternative ground of decision.

263 *Jacobs* v. *London CC* [1950] AC 361, 369.

264 Ibid. 370. For support for Simonds' position, see *Rama Corp* v. *Tin & General Investments* [1952] 2 QB 147, 150; *Penn-Texas* v. *Muray Anstalt (No. 2)* [1964] 2 QB 647, 654–5.

265 *Harper* v. *NCB* [1974] QB 614, 622–3. (*Dodd's case* = *Smith* v. *Central Asbestos Co Ltd* [1973] AC 518.)

266 *Bilta* v. *Nazir* [2015] UKSC 23 at [154]. See also *Singularis Holdings* v. *Daiwa Capital Markets* [2017] EWHC 257 (Ch) at [185]–[186] *per* Rose J.

House of Lords affirming the decision of this court [*sc.*, the Court of Appeal] but not by the reasoning in the speeches of their Lordships'. However, he somewhat audaciously took his contention a little further: since the House of Lords was affirming the Court of Appeal ruling, and since the Court of Appeal relied on only one ground in making that ruling, anyone seeking the *ratio* in *Dodd's case* should turn not to the House of Lords' decision but rather 'to . . . this court and the *ratio* of its decision'.[267]

When judges find fault with the necessity test, their difficulty usually concerns not the reasons actually given in an earlier case, but rather reasons which were not, but which could have been, given. Although the way in which a court arrives at a decision may depend on the presence of a certain set of reasons, there could be another way, or other ways, of arriving at that decision – a way, or ways, which the court did not entertain – which would not depend on the presence of those (or all of those) reasons. Are we to treat a reason as necessary to a court's decision, Kay J wondered in 1889, if that reason, though 'a link in the chain of reasoning' on which the judgment was based, could have been omitted had the court reached its decision by a different route?[268] In *Dunnachie* v. *Hull* (2004), Sedley LJ endeavoured to demonstrate that even if a judge, when making a decision, could have stuck to the route that she took while omitting a particular reason which she treated as a necessary step (therefore shortening the route), it is still understandable why lawyers and other judges, when interpreting that decision, might treat that reason as part of the *ratio decidendi* rather than as *obiter dictum.*

> It is often possible to proceed to a conclusion X either by the progression A -⟶ B -⟶ X or by the progression A -⟶ B -⟶ C -⟶ X. Here step C is by definition not objectively essential; but the judge who takes it has elected to integrate it into his or her reasoning. Does an assenting judgment in such a case include assent to C or not?[269]

The judge who integrates C into his or her reasoning might not have elected to include it but rather might have thought it necessary to include it – to have thought it objectively essential. This, on the application of the necessity test, would have to be adjudged a mistake: C, not being an objectively necessary step to X, is *obiter dictum.* Yet if the judge who relied on C considered it necessary to the judgment, and if, in the same case, another judge (or other judges) assented to that judgment without suggesting that C might not be a necessary step to X, it is understandable why, in later cases,

[267] *Harper* v. *NCB* at 623.
[268] *Westrup* v. *Great Yarmouth Steam Carrying Co* (1889) 43 ChD 241, 245.
[269] *Dunnachie* v. *Hull CC* [2004] EWCA Civ 84 at [17].

C should be treated – even if, strictly speaking, it ought not to be treated – as belonging to the *ratio decidendi.*

It is certainly easy to envisage a judge, having made a decision incorporating various observations (some of which are necessary to the decision and some of which are not), contesting the assertion that he or she was mistaken as to what the *ratio* of the case required. Judges, when deciding cases, are unlikely to be thinking only in terms – assuming they are thinking at all in terms – of which reasons they actually need to give to justify a ruling.[270] Providing the bare minimum of reasons necessary to justify an outcome, after all, might not make for a particularly convincing decision. In courtrooms as elsewhere, decision-makers typically – which is not to say always consciously – are asking themselves if the necessary reasoning is sufficient to the task. It is difficult to point to evidence of this way of thinking in the law reports, for they contain no stock of judicial confessions to the effect that a decision confined to strictly necessary reasoning had to be avoided given that the austerity of such a decision would likely have rendered it unconvincing to anyone other than the party whom it favoured. However, anyone familiar with reported judgments from common-law courts knows that judges – certainly appeal court judges – normally take a path to a decision rather than simply state what the decision is. Judges taking decisional paths might, besides covering the ground that has to be covered, visit attractions which could have been avoided. When they detour to these spots, it is often because they recognize that those invested or interested in the court's decision (a litigant subject to it, the litigant's legal representatives, the legal profession more generally, legal commentators, and later courts deciding analogous cases) are likely to appreciate them taking, might even expect them to take, a scenic rather than the direct route. While a decision might not depend on a particular location having been visited, a judge delivering or contributing to the court's judgment might for good reason – though by no means always for good reason[271] – believe that, had the location been bypassed, the judgment would have made for a rather less significant source of law.

[270] See Patrick Devlin, *The Judge* (Oxford University Press, 1979), 198–9.

> The judicial function is not just to render a decision ... There are many types who can administer orderly-room justice in a minimum of words ... This is justice, but ... not justice according to law. What the lawyer is uniquely trained to do is to produce the just decision out of the law and to expound the reasons for it in terms that conform with the law and add to it.

[271] See Cass R. Sunstein, 'Incompletely Theorized Agreements' (1995) 108 *Harv. L. Rev.* 1733.

Let us imagine that a decision does not strictly depend on the presence of a particular reason – that the reason is not actually necessary to the result – but that omitting the reason from the process of getting to the result would likely call for an explanation. Imagine, too, that a judge therefore includes this reason in her decision because she realizes that not to include it would somehow make the journey seem incomplete (and, very likely, would make for an unconvincing decision). If a later court, considering the decision, were to identify the reason as part of the *ratio*, it would – on a strict application of the necessity test – be making a mistake. But it is perhaps not surprising that judges should sometimes accord such reasons *ratio*-like status. Although an opinion offered in an earlier case was 'perhaps, in a very strict sense, . . . extra-judicial', Wills J observed in 1890, it 'still . . . was very nearly necessary to the determination of that case', and therefore was one which Wills thought he 'should follow', even though he 'differed from it'.[272] This notion – that a *dictum* might not belong to a *ratio* but nevertheless be akin to *ratio* – is one with which judges have struggled. In the Court of Appeal in 1910, Alverstone CJ took issue with a barrister who, like Wills, appeared to intuit a distinction between reasons which are necessary and ones which are almost necessary to a judgment. Counsel for the defendant, according to Alverstone, sought to dismiss various judicial pronouncements as 'only *obiter dicta,* or, at any rate, [as] not so necessary for the purposes of those judgments [in which the pronouncements appeared] as to amount to binding decisions'.[273] Drawing a distinction between pronouncements which are *obiter* and pronouncements which are not *so* necessary as to be, or be part of, the court's decision meant adopting a position which Alverstone 'could not take'.[274] It is rare to find judges either explicitly defending or dismissing propositions to the effect that *dicta* are to be read as *rationes* because they are somehow close to being (even though they are not actually) necessary to the decisions containing them. But they do commonly accept that some pronouncements, while not *rationes decidendi*, are somehow more than mere *dicta* (Sections 9–10). They can also occasionally be found departing from the necessity test.

When judges eschew the necessity test, it is typically because they favour relevance as a criterion instead. A judicial observation might be deemed irrelevant to the decision containing it just as it might be

[272] *Kenrick* v. *Lawrence* (1890) 25 QBD 99, 106.

[273] *Rogers Eungblut* v. *Martin* [1911] 1 KB 19, 23 (case decided October 1910).

[274] Ibid.

considered unnecessary to that decision – in both instances, the observation is being categorized as *obiter dictum*.[275] When observations are not treated as *obiter*, however, 'relevant' and 'necessary' are not always presumed to be one and the same. Judges, when negotiating precedents, have been known to treat a pronouncement as if it were de facto part of a decision's *ratio* because they consider the pronouncement not necessary to the decision but very obviously relevant to it, or relevant to facts closely analogous to the ones on which the court had to rule. Lord Watson remarked in *Collins* v. *Collins* (1884) that observations made by Lord Fullerton in 1849, on the subject of adultery condoned by a divorcing spouse, had been '*obiter* in th[e] sense' that they were offered in a case concerning legal separation rather than divorce.[276] But in the case before the court today – *Collins* concerned the legal significance of a divorcing husband having condoned his wife's adultery – they are to be treated as *ratio*, Watson pronounced, for while the decision of 1849 had concerned separation rather than divorce, Fullerton's observations 'were nevertheless very relevant to the point which the court had to decide, seeing that the contention of the defender was in substance that forgiveness of cruelty ought to receive the same effect in a separation suit as condonation of adultery in an action for dissolving marriage'.[277]

One of the landmark modern cases on the acquisition of equitable property rights offers up a widely debated example of an observation which is relevant but not necessary to the judgment, but which has been received in the courts much as it would have been received if it had been necessary to the judgment. According to Lady Hale, Lord Bridge's observations in *Lloyds Bank* v. *Rosset* (1990) – the main one being that in sole legal title-holder cases it is doubtful that anything short of 'direct contributions to the purchase price [of the land] ... will readily justify the inference necessary to the creation of a constructive trust'[278] – 'were strictly *obiter dicta*'.[279] The House of Lords ruled that Mrs Rosset did not have an overriding interest – legally binding *in rem* without having to be recorded on the Land Register – because the legal

[275] For *dicta* as observations not strictly relevant to the point of law which the court had to deal with in the case where the observations appear, see e.g., *Doe* v. *Wellsman* (1848) 2 Ex 368, 379–80; *Rylands* v. *Fletcher* (1865) 3 Hurl & C 774, 792 *per* Martin B; *re McC (A Minor)* [1985] AC 528, 549–50 *per* Lord Bridge ('I am not prepared to give any weight ... to the *obiter dictum* of Scarman LJ ... whose mind cannot have been focussed on any such issue').

[276] *Collins* v. *Collins* (1884) 9 App Cas 205, 254.

[277] Ibid. For a similar example, see *R (Deepdock)* v. *Welsh Ministers* [2007] EWHC 3347 (Admin) at [24] *per* Hickinbottom J.

[278] *Lloyds Bank plc* v. *Rosset* [1991] 1 AC 107, 133 (case decided March 1990).

[279] *Stack* v. *Dowden* [2007] UKHL 17 at [63].

title was held and the land purchased in her husband's sole name and Mrs Rosset herself, having made no direct or indirect financial contributions, could not be said to have a property right protected by actual occupation. The House had ruled two decades earlier, in *Gissing* v. *Gissing*, that failure to contribute to acquisition of title precluded establishing a property right.[280] Since Mrs Rosset had made no such contribution and so could not establish a property right, there was no need for Lord Bridge to offer an opinion on the minimum necessary to establish such a right by inference.[281] Given, however, that there had been some difference of opinion in *Gissing* over whether indirect as well as direct contributions should suffice to establish a beneficial entitlement,[282] it was understandable not only that he should have offered *dicta* intended to bring some clarity to the matter but also that the *dicta* – which are included, as if part of the *ratio*, in *Rosset's* headnote – should have been received by later courts as legal authority governing disputes between defendants who are sole legal owners of the land and claimants who rely on constructive trust principles to try to establish an implied beneficial entitlement to the value of that land.[283] In *Collins*, and in case law applying *Rosset* rules, decisions of earlier courts are being treated as binding precedents because of the significance accorded to pronouncements on which the decisions did not depend. When a court makes this manoeuvre – when it treats non-necessary reasoning as authority – it is not

280 *Gissing* v. *Gissing* [1971] AC 886 (case decided July 1970).

281 The courts had no statutory discretion to allocate Mrs Rosset an interest in the land because she and Mr Rosset, though separated, had not divorced.

282 Compare *Gissing* v. *Gissing* at 909 *per* Lord Diplock:

> Where the wife has made . . . no direct contribution . . . referable to the acquisition of the house, there is in the absence of evidence of an express agreement between the parties no material to justify the court in inferring that it was the common intention of the parties that she should have any beneficial interest in a matrimonial home conveyed into the sole name of the husband . . .

with ibid. at 896 *per* Lord Reid:

> when the wife makes direct contributions to the purchase by paying something either to the vendor or to the building society which is financing the purchase, she gets a beneficial interest in the house although nothing was ever said or agreed about this at the time: but . . . when her contributions are only indirect by way of paying sums which the husband would otherwise have had to pay, she gets nothing unless at the time of the acquisition there was some agreement that she should get a share. I can see no good reason for this distinction and I think that in many cases it would be unworkable.

283 Though there is reason to think that Lord Bridge's observations in *Rosset* will not remain authority in the long term: see *Stack* v. *Dowden* at [26] *per* Lord Walker.

relaxing or refining the necessity test but rather is presuming, if only implicitly, that necessity will not always be the test.

8 Cheap Talk

Even when a judicial observation is regarded as *dictum* because it was not necessary to the decision in which it appears, the explanation that it was *obiter* will quite often avoid the language of necessity. Observations are regularly categorized as *dicta*, we saw in Section 4, because they are casually or unreflectively – loosely – formulated. Although the common implication, in these instances, is that an observation was not necessary to the decision, the reason given for categorizing it as *obiter dictum* tends to be not that it was surplus to requirement but rather that adjudicating the outcome was – that adjudicating a legal outcome always is – a serious (solemn) business, and that it would somehow be inappropriate to treat the observation, judged in the context of the decision, as part of the court's effort to carry out that business. American jurists have occasionally adopted a granular nomenclature, characterizing as '*dicta*' serious judicial observations made on legal matters in cases where those matters did not have to be addressed, and distinguishing these *dicta* from '*obiter dicta*' – observations which, unlike *dicta*, are bereft of persuasive authority, being merely 'words dropped along the road, wayside remarks'[284] which are without bearing on the outcome of the case in which they were uttered or on any other legal point. While reported cases provide no indication that this distinction has ever been explicitly adopted in English courts, judges in those courts can occasionally be seen taking issue with the presumption that *dicta* set forth in the course of a decision must always lack the rigour or reflectiveness of the reasoning that forms the decision's *ratio*.

One such judge was Lord Wright. In the 1930s, various *dicta* uttered by Wright came in for perhaps more than their fair share of criticism from

[284] Karl N. Llewellyn, *The Bramble Bush: Our Law and Its Study* (New York: Oceana, 1930), 41. See also his *The Case Law System in America*, trans. M. Ansaldi (University of Chicago Press, 1989 [1933]), 14 ('on another view, well-considered *dictum* is due great respect . . . But when the *dictum* . . . is merely . . . an excursus the opinion writer allows himself for whatever reason, then it is called *obiter dictum* and is of little or no value'); and *cf.* Wambaugh, *The Study of Cases*, 18–19 ('Some . . . attempt to distinguish between *dicta* and *obiter dicta* . . . but . . . the expressions are interchangeable'). Llewellyn's description of *obiter dicta* possibly owes something to the definition of *obiter* to be found in the US Latin dictionary of his day: 'on the way, in going or passing along'. *Harpers' Latin Dictionary* (New York: Harper & Bros., 1879, rev. ed. C. T. Lewis and C. Short 1894) (emphasis omitted).

other judges. In 1938, Greer LJ – a judge who quite often declared himself unimpressed with other judges' *dicta*,[285] and who, according to his *ODNB* entry, tried to guard against producing too much *dicta* of his own[286] – rather pointedly declined to accord significance to an observation which Wright had made in the Court of Appeal two years earlier:

> Goddard J was of opinion that Lord Wright ... expressed the view that this clause ... in regard to constructive total loss of the vessel ... insured only against the risk of freight going into the pockets of the hull underwriters. I do not think Lord Wright did mean to say that. If he did, it was an *obiter dictum*, and one uttered during the period when he had descended from the House of Lords to this more fallible tribunal. And if he did say it, ... I do not agree with him.[287]

Wright, who had been promoted directly from the King's Bench Division to the House of Lords in 1932, spent two apparently unhappy years as one of Greer's Court of Appeal colleagues – standing in as Master of the Rolls while the Prime Minister, Stanley Baldwin, sought a permanent replacement for Hanworth MR (another judge who, in the 1930s, saw fit to cast doubt on the wisdom of a Wright *dictum*).[288] Three months after Wright returned to the House of Lords, he delivered an opinion in which he took aim at various

[285] See, e.g., *Tudor-Hart* v. *British Union for the Abolition of Vivisection* [1938] 2 KB 329, 336, where he ventured that an *obiter dictum* offered during argument by Atkin LJ in 1926 was 'in all probability one ... which' Atkin might have shied away from if he had 'had to give judgment' in the relevant case.

[286] C. T. Le Quesne, 'Greer (Frederick) Arthur, Baron Fairfield (1863–1945)', in *Oxford Dictionary of National Biography* (www.oxforddnb.com) ('Greer's judgments were well arranged and free from digression and from obscurity or artifice in language').

[287] *Robertson* v. *Nomikos* [1938] 2 KB 603, 628.

[288] See *Re Wells* [1933] Ch 29, 48 (case decided July 1932).

> Wright J's ... words are confessedly *obiter*. His attention was not directed mainly to the point upon which he offers the benefit of his opinion. We have had the advantage of a further examination and review of the authorities, and I have failed to find any authority which directly supports the observation of the learned judge. We have failed to find any sufficient reason upon which it can be based.

In 1935, Wright had accepted the demotion – which is very much how he saw it – to the Court of Appeal on condition that it was temporary. That he was not returned to the House of Lords till April 1937 clearly irked him. In the preceding month he complained to Arthur Goodhart, with perhaps more than a modicum of vanity, that 'I am a rather transient [Master of the] Rolls and hope soon to be back permanently to the Lords ... I am better known especially abroad as Lord Wright. People would say who is the Master of the Rolls?' Lord Wright to A. L. Goodhart, 12 March 1937, in Goodhart papers, Bodleian (Special Collections), MS Eng. c. 2891.

early-twentieth-century employer liability cases decided by the Court of Appeal. Whereas Greer had implied that *dicta* attributed to Wright had been the product of insufficiently careful reflection, Wright – in a passage no less pointed than Greer's – lamented that the Court of Appeal's mistake in the employer liability cases had been to presume that when law lords make *obiter* observations they will not have thought seriously about what the implications of their observations might be.

> In the Court of Appeal the[] observations [of Lords Halsbury, Watson, and Herschell in *Smith* v. *Baker* (1891)] were put aside. It was said they were *obiter dicta*, which may in one sense be true, but though the issue was concluded by what happened in the county court, this House thought fit to explain the reason on which the employers could properly be held liable . . . It was said that the observations need not be seriously considered, because the relevant authorities were not cited to their Lordships. It would, however, be strange to imagine that these three great lawyers did not trouble to appreciate the authorities relevant to the principles which they were enunciating.[289]

For Wright, as for Kenyon CJ in the late eighteenth century, *obiter dicta* could be *solemniter dicta*. Their status as *solemniter* might even be strongly presumed, Wright seemed to be claiming, if they emanated from the apex court. It will become clear in the next section that Wright is by no means alone among modern judges in believing that some *dicta* warrant veneration because they are Papinian-like pronunciations made by 'great lawyers', and that others have similarly urged against typecasting all *dicta* as casually thrown-out remarks. It will also become clear that when judges do make the case for recognizing particular *dicta* to be grounded in serious judicial reflection, their point is usually that those *dicta* ought not to be treated as common or garden *obiter dicta*. Before turning to the ways in which modern judges have argued against presuming all *dicta* to have the same status, however, it is worth considering one particular argument in support of the proposition that all *dicta* are, in fact, alike.

The argument – succinctly formulated by Marshall CJ when delivering the opinion of the US Supreme Court in *Cohens* v. *Virginia* (1821) – is that a question before a court has to be investigated with care, whereas *dictum*, notwithstanding that a judge might reflect seriously when formulating it, is seldom subjected to the same level of forensic scrutiny.[290]

289 *Wilsons & Clyde Coal Co Ltd* v. *English* [1938] AC 57, 82.
290 See *Cohens* v. *Virginia* 19 US (6 Wheat) 264, 399–400 (1821).

The 'judge who has not heard a question argued out before him may be less likely to see the full implications and less likely to be entirely accurate in the language which he uses', Lord Reid observed in 1959.[291] Not only does a judge responsible for a particular *dictum* not have to consider its legal implications in relation to actual facts, or worry that it might be overruled by a higher court, but – even if a higher court was willing, in principle, to hear appeals against *dicta* – a losing party will have little if any incentive to challenge an *obiter dictum* given that it has no bearing on the lower court's ruling.[292] In a decision reached at King's Bench five years before Marshall spoke in *Cohens*, counsel can be seen being reprimanded for placing too much store in hypothetical reasoning offered in an earlier case,

> as if the *obiter dictum* of a judge could be taken as affording any fair criterion of what his opinion might be when a subject of this nature should be brought before him, or as if it were probable that any judge would, on an incidental point, step out of his way to give a decision on a question of this magnitude and importance.[293]

Knowing that one's reasoning could become binding law is likely to have a galvanizing effect on a judge: the incentive to make sure that the reasoning is sound will be greater than is the case when the judge ventures an opinion in the abstract. Russell LJ, in a case before the Court of Appeal in 1974, confessed that 'during the course of the argument' he had been 'inclined to ... express a view [on] whether ... the defendants ... ha[d] ... reasonable cause'.[294] After 'having discussed the point with Stamp LJ', however, he 'changed [his] mind', realizing that '[s]uch an expression of view ... would be entirely *obiter dictum*, and, like any other *obiter* expressions of view ... would lack the encouragement to incisive thinking which is supplied by the need to be right'.[295]

291 *Davie* v. *New Merton Board Mills Ltd* [1959] AC 604, 645. The general principle in English law is that judgments are not authorities for legal propositions contained within them but not argued in court: *Baker* v. *The Queen* [1975] AC 774, 788 *per* Lord Diplock; *Barrs* v. *Bethell* [1982] Ch 294, 308 *per* Warner J; *Re Hetherington* [1990] Ch 1, 10 *per* Sir Nicolas Browne-Wilkinson V-C; *FHSC Group* v. *GLAS Trust Corp* [2019] EWCA Civ 1361 at [136] *per* Leggatt LJ.

292 It is conceivable that a party might want to challenge *dicta* which are potentially significant to future litigation. This holds good for a litigant who wins as well as for one who loses (though a victorious party who wanted to appeal against *obiter dicta* would be precluded from doing so by virtue of having won).

293 *Moore* v. *Moore* (1817) 1 Phil Ecc 406, 438.

294 *JJB Sports* v. *Milbro Sports* [1975] ICR 73, 76 (case decided July 1974).

295 Ibid.

All *dicta* are alike, according to this line of argument, in so far as they are observations which, however carefully formulated, are set forth without immediate, very likely without any, cost. Judges, when offering *dicta*, do not have to reckon with the legal implications of what they are saying – are venturing opinions without any expectation that those opinions will be put to the test. In the decidedly harsh words of one nineteenth-century judge, 'that which is said to be the law under circumstances not requiring judicial consideration is of little value'.[296]

9 *Dicta* and *Dicta*

This last line of argument has, certainly since the nineteenth century, been an outlier in English case law. The modern judicial commonplace has it that *dicta* are most definitely not all alike – that 'there are *dicta* and *dicta*'.[297] When judges make this assertion, their point is usually that some *dicta* are superior to others. But sometimes the judicial objective is to emphasize that a *dictum* is lightweight even when judged as *dictum*. Some observations – the types of observation which have now and again inspired American lawyers to distinguish *dicta* and *obiter dicta* – are simply casual asides or flourishes: Lord Denning remarking that 'Broadchalke is one of the most pleasing villages in England',[298] for example, or Megarry J opening his judgment on Errol Flynn's domicile at time of death with the observation that Flynn was a man who, '[i]n his career, in his three marriages, in his friendships, in his quarrels, and in bed with the many women he took there, ... lived with zest and irregularity'.[299] A *dictum* might be deemed flimsy because it is a voice in the wilderness – as, for example, when other judges deciding the case where the *dictum* appears had the opportunity to endorse it but omitted, perhaps deliberately declined, to do so. A remark by Lord Tenterden was 'not to be esteemed an *obiter dictum*', Park J insisted in 1829, 'because the

296 *R* v. *Archbishop of Canterbury* (1848) 11 QB 483, 654 *per* Coleridge J.

297 See, e.g., *West* v. *Dick* [1969] 2 Ch 424, 431 *per* Megarry J; *R (N)* v. *Mental Health Review Tribunal (Northern Region)* [2005] EWHC 587 (Admin) at [29] *per* Munby J; *Crawford Adjusters* v. *Sagicor General Insurance* [2013] UKPC 17 at [146] *per* Lord Sumption.

298 *Lloyds Bank* v. *Bundy* [1975] QB 326, 334.

299 *Re Flynn (No. 1)* [1968] 1 WLR 103, 105. On how the passage in which this remark appears is illustrative of a style of delivery perhaps as much absent from civil law as it is present in common-law judgments, see Hein Kötz, 'The Role of the Judge in the Courtroom: The Common Law and Civil Law Compared' [1987] *Tydskrif vir die Suid-Afrikaanse Reg* 35, 42 ('A Continental lawyer feels like being submerged in an oxygen bath when he reads th[is] opening statement').

other judges differ from him'.[300] Five years earlier, Gifford MR had refused to accord any significance to 'an *obiter dictum*, uttered upon a point totally different from that which the court had then to decide, and by a judge, who, in the discussion in which he uttered them [*sic*], was in a minority'.[301] Judicial observations concerning points of law not argued, or not fully argued, before the court in the case where the observations appear are occasionally referred to as a subclass of *dicta*,[302] as are remarks which judges make during legal argument. 'I distrust *dicta* in all cases,' Jessel MR declared in 1882, 'and especially *dicta* during argument.'[303] Interlocutory judicial observations 'elucidate the argument, ... or ... indicate ... the matters which the judicial spokesman thought needed to be investigated', Simon LC noted in the 1940s, but they are 'not judicial pronouncements' and they certainly do 'not decide anything, even provisionally'.[304] This has been a fairly popular judicial stricture, certainly since the nineteenth century,[305] though some judges – mindful of the fact that judicial interventions delivered impromptu in the course of argument might not always be devoid of wisdom – have urged that it not be treated as an edict.[306]

The more interesting disaggregation of *dicta*, regularly endorsed by modern judges, is the claim that some *obiter* observations are especially weighty. In October 1913, Scrutton J commented sceptically on the

300 *Jones* v. *Bright* (1829) 5 Bing 533, 547.

301 *Purdew* v. *Jackson* (1824) 1 Russell 1, 48. For more recent examples, see, e.g., *R* v. *Honourable Society of the Middle Temple ex p Bullock* [1996] ELR 349, 357 *per* Brooke J; *Cosco* v. *Armada Shipping* [2011] EWHC 216 (Ch) at [28] *per* Briggs J. That a *dictum* was a solitary remark might not count against it, we will see, if the judge responsible for it is considered for some reason or another to deserve special legal respect. Furthermore, comity will presumably quite often inhibit judges from conspicuously distancing themselves from their colleagues' *dicta*. For an illustration of distancing softly with his words, see *Kendall* v. *Lillico* [1969] 2 AC 31, 104–5 *per* Lord Guest ('The rest of the members of the House did not concur in this *obiter dictum* ... and there is nothing [in the decision of the House], in my view, ... to conflict with the decision of the Court of Appeal ... In this situation I am content to follow the Court of Appeal').

302 For recent examples, see *Webber* v. *DPP* [1998] RTR 111, 118 *per* Holland J; *JSC BTA Bank* v. *Ablyazov* [2011] EWHC 2988 (Comm) at [34] *per* Teare J.

303 *Wallis* v. *Smith* (1882) 21 ChD 243, 265.

304 *Per* Viscount Simon LC in *Practice Note* [1942] WN 89 (PC).

305 See, e.g., *Doherty* v. *Allman* (1878) 3 App Cas 709, 727 *per* Lord O'Hagan; *A-G* v. *Logan* [1891] 2 QB 100, 106 *per* Vaughan Williams J; *Re Best* [1904] 2 Ch 354, 357 *per* Farwell J; *Re House Property and Investment Co Ltd* [1954] Ch 576, 596 *per* Roxburgh J; *Al Rawas* v. *Pegasus Energy* [2008] EWHC 617 (QB) at [54] *per* Jack J; *Portsmouth NHS Trust* v. *Wyatt* [2005] EWCA Civ 1181 at [76].

306 See, e.g., *British Northrop Ltd* v. *Texteam Blackburn Ltd* [1974] RPC 57, 66–7 *per* Megarry V-C; also *Oscar TM* [1980] FSR 429, 437–8 *per* Graham J.

decision of the King's Bench Division in *Bruce* v. *Burton*[307] – supported, 'so far as *obiter dicta* can support anything', by nothing apart from 'the *dictum* of Wright J in *Grimes* v. *Lethem*'.[308] Atkin J, in the course of delivering a judgment in the same court in July of the same year, demonstrated a rather more accommodating cast of mind. Various 'judicial expressions' cited to court from a number of earlier decisions (one of which was a decision of the Supreme Court of Western Australia) 'are in the nature of *obiter dicta*', he conceded, yet they 'are . . . of so great weight that I should probably feel compelled to follow them'.[309] The notion that *dicta* might carry weight, we have seen, was not lost on sixteenth-century civilian jurists – the weight of a *dictum* ought to be determined by the quality of reasoning underpinning it, Alciato and Gentili maintained, and should not be dismissed as lacking probable authority just because it is at odds with *communis opinio* (Section 1). Although, apart from Fulbeck, English lawyers seem never to have entertained this civilian notion of weighty *dictum*, judges and counsel have been referring to particular *dicta* in terms of their weight, or lack of weight, at least since the eighteenth century.[310] By the mid-nineteenth century the practice was common, and it remains so even today.[311]

While Atkin might have felt compelled to follow some *dicta* because they were weighty, he knew that he was not actually obliged to follow them; a legal proposition is not binding, he would intimate in *Donoghue* v. *Stevenson*, just because it carries considerable weight.[312] Ever since English judges and lawyers began drawing attention to weighty *dicta*, they have also drawn a distinction between weight and binding force: the

307 *Bruce* v. *Burton* (1901) 4 TC 399.

308 *Furtado* v. *City of London Brewery* [1914] 1 KB 152, 158 *per* Scrutton J (case decided October 1913), referring to *Grimes* v. *Lethem* (1898) 3 TC 622.

309 *Gibson* v. *Gibson* [1913] 3 KB 379, 388.

310 *Nottingham* v. *Lambert* (1738) Willes 111, 115 ('*dicta* of no weight'); *Mutter* v. *Robinson et al.* (1816) 1 Merivale 475, 491 ('a mere extrajudicial opinion of little weight'); *Giles* v. *Grover* (1827) 1 Y & J 232, 242 ('entitled to no weight'); *Houlditch* v. *Marquess of Donegal* (1834) 8 Bli NS 301, 338 ('*dicta* of considerable weight').

311 See, e.g., *Keppel* v. *Wheeler* [1927] 1 KB 577, 591 *per* Atkin LJ ('the words . . . though *obiter dicta*, are of great weight'); *Re P* [1964] Ch 575, 584 *per* Plowman J ('the text and the comment on the text [in *Dicey on the Conflict of Laws*] give more weight to that *obiter dictum* than it properly bears'); *International Drilling Fluids* v. *Louisville Investments* [1986] Ch 513, 521 *per* Balcombe LJ ('*dicta*, *obiter* but nevertheless weighty'); *Shah* v. *Colvia* [2008] EWCA Civ 195 at [22] *per* Lloyd LJ.

312 *Donoghue* v. *Stevenson* [1932] AC 562, 584 ('[I]t is very necessary in considering reported cases in the law of torts that the actual decision alone should carry authority, proper weight, of course, being given to the *dicta* of the judges').

weight of a *dictum* brought to the attention of a court may be such that it would be strange if the court were to ignore it, but this does not mean that the court must take account of it.[313] In 1802, Eldon LC lauded an *obiter dictum* presented to the court as 'carrying as much authority as under any circumstances an extra-judicial opinion can'.[314] A century later, Bruce and Phillimore JJ commended a magistrate for having 'correctly and accurately stated the law, and correctly applied it to the facts of th[e] case', even though the magistrate's decision had been based largely on 'authoritative *dicta*'.[315] But could *dicta* have authority?

In the twentieth century, the notion that weighty *dicta* have authority comes into its own in the English courts. But judges and lawyers, when referring to weighty *dicta* as authoritative, mean not that the *dicta* are binding authorities but rather that they are persuasive authorities. The weight of a *dictum* does not make it a binding legal rule, but it might persuade a court that, in the case to be decided, one rule and not another should control the outcome, or that the rule which controls the outcome should be interpreted in a particular way.[316] Furthermore, the persuasiveness of the *dictum* might depend 'upon the area of discussion within which it is made'[317] – courts might be inclined to accord *dicta* more significance, for example, 'when a problem seems to occur in an authoritative desert, where . . . the judge cannot . . . simply extend the line on an existing graph of authority because there is none'.[318]

313 See *Benfield* v. *Solomons* (1803) 9 Ves Jr 77, 85 *per* Eldon LC ('not a direct authority . . . but . . . very weighty *dicta*'); *Friar* v. *Grey* (1850) 5 Ex 584, 596 ('an extrajudicial expression of opinion entitled certainly to great weight, but not as decisive'); *Brinsmead* v. *Harrison* (1871–2) LR 7 CP 547, 550; *R* v. *Bond* [1906] 2 KB 389, 404 *per* Kennedy J; Bentham, *A Comment on the Commentaries*, 151 ('Weighty authority, as it is deemed, but of itself not absolutely conclusive').

314 *Wright* v. *Simpson* (1802) 6 Ves Jr 714, 728.

315 *Fulham Vestry* v. *Minter* [1901] 1 QB 501 at 509, 506.

316 See, e.g., *Phipps* v. *Rochester Corp.* [1955] 1 QB 450, 468 *per* Devlin J ('I could adopt the general principle that adults and children are to be treated alike only if I were to disregard the persuasive *dicta* to the contrary of Lord Atkinson . . . Lord Sumner . . . and Jenkins LJ . . . For myself, I much prefer the flexibility afforded by these *dicta* and I think that I am free to follow them'); *Pallister* v. *Clark* (1975) 30 P & CR 84, 90 *per* Megaw LJ ('[T]hat passage might strictly have to be treated as *obiter dictum* . . . Even, however, if it were to be treated as *obiter dictum*, I would respectfully agree with it and follow it. There is nothing in any of the other authorities to which we have been referred which to my mind casts any doubt or puts any qualification on the principle there stated').

317 *Re Levick's WT* [1963] 1 WLR 311, 317.

318 Bingham, *The Business of Judging*, 39. For examples which seem to come close to what Bingham has in mind, see *Alcock* v. *Chief Constable of South Yorkshire* [1992] 1 AC 310, where the House of Lords, ruling on the question of liability for psychiatric harm

The term 'persuasive authority' appears to enter the English legal lexicon in the first half of the twentieth century.[319] 'There is ... a decision, not ... binding on this court,' Greene MR observed in the Court of Appeal in 1946, 'but of great persuasive authority.'[320] An interpretation which 'the text-book writers' had put on a statutory provision, counsel for the defendants argued before the same court in *Re Wellsted* (1949), 'must have some persuasive authority'.[321] Devlin J may have been the first judge to apply the term specifically to *obiter dicta*. In various mid-twentieth-century judgments, he made a point of characterizing weighty *dicta* as persuasive authorities rather than as *obiter* observations.[322] By the 1960s, other judges can be seen using the term.[323] An observation made by Bayley J 'was, no doubt, *obiter*', Lord

suffered by secondary victims of the Hillsborough disaster, relied on various observations, some of them *obiter*, made by Lord Wilberforce in *McLoughlin* v. *O'Brian* [1983] 1 AC 410, 421–3; and *McDonald* v. *DCLG* [2013] EWCA Civ 1346, where the Court of Appeal appeared to choose to follow observations made by Hale LJ in one of its earlier decisions, acknowledging that the observations may well have been 'technically *obiter*' (ibid. at [58] *per* McCombe LJ, and see also [110] *per* Dyson MR).

319 According to H. Patrick Glenn , 'Persuasive Authority' (1987) 32 *McGill LJ* 261, 275–6, 'persuasive authority' is present in English private law by 'the eighteenth century, if not earlier', and, by the nineteenth century, persuasive authorities were sometimes accepted as actual law. Glenn's argument seems to be that, before the twentieth century, the 'notion' (ibid. at 264) of persuasive authority – meaning secondary or 'non-formal sources of law' (ibid. at 296) – was present in English law, rather than that lawyers were already using the term of art.

320 *Hodd-Barrs* v. *IRC* [1946] 2 All ER 768, 769.

321 *Re Wellsted's WT* [1949] Ch 296, 300. See also *Murdoch Lownie Ltd* v. *Newman* [1949] 2 All ER 783, 785 *per* Slade J ('That any decision of the [Scottish] Court of Session is of the greatest persuasive authority goes without saying').

322 '[C]ounsel for the plaintiff may be right in saying that it was *obiter dictum*', he remarked in 1949, '[b]ut the conclusion which I have reached is greatly strengthened' not only 'by the high persuasive authority of such a *dictum*' but also by virtue of the fact that '[t]his appears to be the only place in the authorities in which the point has been considered'. *Irvin* v. *Hine* [1950] 1 KB 555, 568 (case decided November 1949). See also *Everett* v. *Ribbands* [1952] 1 KB 112, 118 *per* Devlin J ('There is ... no *obiter dictum* on which the plaintiff here can rely as being of persuasive authority'); *Bank voor Handel* v. *Slatford* [1953] 1 QB 248, 261 *per* Devlin J ('What I propose to do is to ascertain whether there are any *dicta, obiter* or otherwise'); *Longhurst* v. *Guildford, Godalming & District Water Board* [1961] 1 QB 408, 419 *per* Devlin LJ. The fact of his characterizing a *dictum* as persuasive authority did not necessarily mean that he would follow it. 'I agree that the appeal fails, and I add a few words only because we are differing from the *obiter dicta*', he observed in a case decided in 1951, though, he added, they are '*obiter dicta* which, of course, have high persuasive authority'. *Pentecost* v. *London District Auditor* [1951] 2 KB 759, 767.

323 See, e.g., *Rookes* v. *Barnard (No. 1)* [1963] 1 QB 623 (CA), 630; *Sheldon* v. *Sheldon* [1966] P 62, 78 *per* Salmon LJ ('There are many *obiter dicta* of persuasive authority in that case.

Salmon remarked in 1978, but it came 'from such a master of the common law' as to 'deserve[] to be treated ... as being of the highest persuasive authority'.[324] Today, judicial statements to the effect that an opinion was 'clearly ... persuasive authority'[325] are not at all unusual.

It is also not unusual, we will see, for modern English judges to refer to unqualifiedly 'authoritative', as opposed to persuasively authoritative, *dicta*. Usually, when judges describe a *dictum* as authoritative, they are according it the same status they attribute to *dicta* of persuasive authority: the two terms mean the same thing. Whether judges always take the terms to mean the same thing is not entirely clear. In certain other common-law jurisdictions, judges can be found referring to authoritative *dicta* as a distinct legal category. English judges acknowledge no such category but, as will become evident in Section 11, they occasionally treat particular *dicta* as if they do.

Let us confine ourselves for the moment to the concept of persuasive authority. *Dicta*, when deemed weighty because persuasively authoritative, are being treated as a valuable source of information – as epistemic rather than as binding legal authority. But when *dicta* are treated in this way, are they not better described simply as persuasive rather than as persuasive authorities? 'Authorities are followed because they are authorities, not because their reasoning is admired.'[326] I might not be persuaded by the reasoning behind what you say, yet still act in accordance with what you say because you speak as an authority, just as I might admire

There is, however, nothing in the actual decision which would bind us'); *DPP* v. *Smith* [1961] AC 290, 327; *Hughes* v. *Griffin* [1969] 1 WLR 23, 32 *per* Cairns J; *Janov* v. *Morris* [1981] 1 WLR 1389, 1392 *per* Dunn LJ ('*obiter dicta* ... which are ... of persuasive authority in this court, although not binding upon us').

324 *Hoskyn* v. *Commissioner of Police* [1979] AC 474, 496 (case decided April 1978). As we saw in the Introduction to this Essay, it was Salmon who, in 1980, professed to doubt that *dicta* had legal value.

325 *Croke* v. *Secretary of State for Communities and Local Government* [2016] EWHC 2484 (Admin) at [29] *per* HHJ Robinson. See also *A-G* v. *Sports Newspapers Ltd* [1991] 1 WLR 1194, 1200 *per* Bingham LJ ('[counsel] relied on principle, judicial and other *dicta* of high persuasive authority, statute, decided authority and the opinion of textbook writers'); *Commercial Union Life Assurance Co Ltd* v. *Moustafa* [1999] L & TR 489, 494 *per* Smedley J ('*obiter dicta*, but none the less of persuasive force'); *Clinch* v. *Dorset Police Authority* [2003] EWHC 161 (Admin) at [33] *per* McCombe J ('[I]n the light of the arguments and the decisions and *dicta* of persuasive authority before me, I propose to follow the *dicta* of Latham J'); *Joint Stock Co Aeroflot* v. *Leeds* [2017] 1 WLR 4537, 4543 *per* Warren J ('*[O]biter* conclusions and reasoning can frequently be of enormous assistance to another judge grappling with the same issues ... [A]lthough not a binding authority, [they] ... can properly be described as a persuasive (if it is) authority').

326 J. D. Heydon, 'Threats to Judicial Independence: The Enemy Within' (2013) 129 *LQR* 205, 210.

your reasoning, and be persuaded by what you say, while knowing that your words carry no authority.[327] An *obiter dictum* cannot be a persuasive *authority* (just as judges cannot declare themselves sceptical of the wisdom of a legal rule and, on that basis, decline to apply it) if it is in the nature of an authority that it controls a judicial decision – if it provides a reason for deciding which cuts off the possibility of a judge making the decision by relying on her own reasoning. That a legal source could be a persuasive authority – both persuasive reasoning and a binding authority – is not impossible. The foreign judgment referred to in a national court, for example, may be merely persuasive in that court while being authority – a binding precedent – in the courts of the jurisdiction from which it emanates. But a *dictum*, unlike a foreign judgment, is authority nowhere rather than authority in one place and potentially persuasive somewhere else. The proposition that *dicta* can be persuasive authorities seems to make sense only if one interprets 'authoritative' to mean 'trustworthy': the *dicta* can be trusted as sources of information about the law relevant to particular cases, and so judges might choose or be convinced – though the fact that a *dictum* is not genuinely authority means they have no obligation – to rely on them when determining how the law is to apply in those cases.

The immediate question to be asked about weighty *dicta*, then, is not, 'how are they authoritative?' but rather, 'what marks them out as persuasive?' Modern English case law yields a range of answers to this question. None of the answers entails the sorts of nuances detectable in medieval and Renaissance legal writings on the matter of what made for probable authority (Section 1). Rather, judges and lawyers can be found identifying a variety reasons for treating particular *dicta* as weighty, without presuming any of these reasons to be more or less compelling than any of the others. The only obvious concession to nuance is a general acknowledgment that a distinction might be drawn between *dicta* having value and *dicta* having weight. *Dicta* are typically considered valuable because they speak in some way to the case now before a court. That a *dictum* carries weight tends to be a more abstract assessment: it might well bear on the

327

> [I]f an agent is genuinely persuaded of some conclusion because she has come to accept the substantive reasons offered for that conclusion by someone else, then authority has nothing to do with it. Conversely, if authority is genuinely at work, then the agent who accepts the authoritativeness of a directive need not be persuaded by the substantive reasons that might support the same conclusion.

Frederick Schauer, 'Authority and Authorities' (2008) 94 *Virginia L. Rev.* 1931, 1943.

present case, but the characterization of it as weighty need not have anything to do with its relevance to that case.

Various qualities make for weighty *dicta* – qualities which are as often as not considered by judges and lawyers to go hand-in-hand. One of the most commonly identified qualities is reflectiveness: the evident mental effort that has gone into the formulation of a *dictum* may make it especially persuasive. '[T]hese observations have the status of *obiter dicta*', Lord Wilberforce remarked in 1978. 'However, ... they were considered and deliberate observations [made in the House of Lords] after discussion of the same matters had taken place in the Court of Appeal ... We ... should hesitate before disregarding them.'[328] His words echoed those of Williams J who, in 1836, noted that though an opinion cited to court was 'extrajudicial', the court 'should ... hesitate very much before we could come to any conclusion contrary to that opinion', given 'that time was taken before the judgment was pronounced'.[329] In *Slack* v. *Leeds Industrial Co-operative Society* (1923), both Warrington LJ and Sterndale MR commented at length on how some *dicta* 'are not views casually expressed on a point not really adequately considered, but ... are arrived at and expressed with the same care and deliberation as if they had been necessary for the decision of the case'.[330]

The length of, and the detail contained in, an *obiter* passage might make it persuasive.[331] So too might the fact that the passage is endorsed by other, or all of, the judges deciding the case, or the fact that it is complemented or reinforced by *obiter* remarks made by judges in other

328 *Ali* v. *Mitchell* [1980] AC 198, 212 (case decided November 1978). See also ibid. at 229 *per* Lord Salmon ('It was indubitably plain to this House that the *obiter dictum* of the majority of the Court of Appeal, although not binding, would carry great weight. Indeed it was extremely doubtful that any judge of first instance or any division of the Court of Appeal would depart from that *obiter dictum* unless this House disagreed with it'); and, for a cautionary note, *Re M* [2020] EWCA Civ 922 at [91]–[92] *per* Moylan LJ.

329 *Clarke* v. *Spence* (1836) 4 Ad & El 448, 467.

330 *Slack* v. *Leeds Industrial Co-operative Society* [1923] 1 Ch 431, 446 *per* Warrington LJ; see also ibid. at 451 *per* Sterndale MR ('Some *dicta* ... are of a different kind; they are, although not necessary for the decision of the case, deliberate expressions of opinion given after consideration upon a point clearly brought and argued before the court'); *Clark* v. *In Focus Asset Management* [2012] EWHC 3669 (QB) at [25] *per* Cranston J.

331 See *R* v. *Secretary of State for the Home Department ex p Wynne*, 119 *per* Lord Goff; *Begum* v. *Tower Hamlets LBC* [2003] UKHL 5 at [20]; *Williams* v. *Central Bank of Nigeria* [2014] UKSC 10 at [28]; *Kellie* v. *Wheatley & Lloyd* [2014] EWHC 2886 (TCC) at [13]; also the ECtHR's treatment, in *Ali* v. *UK* (2015) 63 EHRR 20 at para. 32, of what it termed the Court of Appeal's 'extended *obiter dictum*' on the effect of ECHR art. 6 in *Adan* v. *Newham London BC* [2001] EWCA Civ 1916.

cases.[332] When judges deciding a case all express the same *obiter* opinion, Lord Mansfield once cautioned, it is important to remember that the opinion is still *obiter.*[333] One should also caution against presuming that consensus of opinion will always carry weight. Ungoed-Thomas J once suggested that a weak shot which hits the mark (such as the ruling of a lower court judge) might carry less authority than a 'battery of howitzers off the target' (such as the convergent *dicta* of numerous law lords).[334] Other judges seemed unconvinced – and with good reason, for an opinion cannot be authoritative on a point, no matter how many (and how eminent are those who) express that opinion, if it misses the point.[335]

The more typical inclination of modern judges has been to posit that when *dicta* are on point and not contradicted by precedent, and when they represent convergent judicial opinion, they should be presumed weighty, and possibly treated as dispositive. Shearman J claimed in 1924 that when the Divisional Court decides a case and, in the course of doing so, *obiter dicta* are 'given unanimously by the three judges', the Court 'ought to follow' those *dicta* if it subsequently has to rule on facts to which the *dicta* pertain; 'it would not be seemly for this Court' to do otherwise, he added, 'even if it wanted to do so'.[336] 'They were all *obiter dicta*', Devlin J remarked apropos of opinions set forth by Bankes, Warrington, and Scrutton LJJ in a Court of Appeal decision of 1925, but they were concurring opinions, and 'a unanimous expression of opinion by

[332] See, e.g., *Re Hawkins* [1952] Ch 881, 884 *per* Wynn-Parry J ('[The point which Esher MR makes at the end of his judgment in *Re Gallard* [1896] 1 QB 68] represents nothing but an *obiter dictum*, but it is an *obiter dictum* to which the greatest respect is due, and it is one which has been before the profession since the year 1896, when the judgment was delivered. So far as the researches of counsel have been able to ascertain, it has met with no criticism whatsoever, and in my respectful view it enunciates a proposition the propriety of which is beyond dispute'); *Chapman* v. *Honig* [1963] 2 QB 502, 519 *per* Pearson LJ ('*obiter dicta*, . . . read together and fairly construed'); *The Harmattan* [1975] 1 WLR 1485, 1494 *per* Scarman LJ ('Lord Thankerton introduced a note of doubt as to the universality of the assertion made by Lord Atkin; and this note of doubt which he introduced has been developed by subsequent *obiter dicta* in our courts').

[333] *Campbell* v. *Hall* (1774) Lofft 655, 716.

[334] *Re Grosvenor Hotel* [1965] Ch 1210, 1222–3 *per* Ungoed-Thomas J ('[I]t is a *dictum* in a speech in which all the other Lords concurred . . . A battery of howitzers off the target is more impressive than a pop-gun on it').

[335] See ibid. at 1257 *per* Salmon LJ ('This is undoubtedly true, but a battery of howitzers off target sometimes does great damage to what is intended to be preserved'); also *Whittaker* v. *Kinnear* [2011] EWHC 1479 (QB) at [28] *per* Bean J.

[336] *Mills* v. *London CC* [1925] 1 KB 213, 224 (case decided November 1924).

three Lords Justices carries great weight'.[337] Devlin's observation echoed that of another High Court judge who, in 1907, had noted of a judicial remark that it 'is no doubt *obiter dictum*, but *obiter dictum* of the full Court of Queen's Bench, and we cannot, I think, neglect such an expression of opinion as that'.[338] Though a pronouncement made in an earlier case by 'Cotton LJ, with whom Bowen LJ and Fry LJ concurred', had been an *obiter dictum*, Roskill LJ observed in 1973, it was 'a formidable expression of opinion'.[339] The pronouncement is 'technically not binding on this court', he continued, but 'its correctness has never been challenged and for my part I am not prepared to say that the *obiter dicta* of a Court of Appeal so constituted were erroneous'.[340] *Obiter* opinion is likely to be considered yet more formidable if it was agreed upon by judges in a court higher than the one in which it is being countenanced. In a High Court ruling of 2006, observations made in the Court of Appeal three years previously – concerning how the term 'real risk' should be interpreted for the purpose of assessing the risk of deportees being subjected to treatment contrary to article 3 of the ECHR – were, Munby J accepted, not part of the reasoning necessary to the decision. Yet Munby was not prepared to treat the observations as 'mere *obiter dicta*', for '[t]hey were expressly agreed to ... by [the three judges who made the decision], and represent[ed] the unanimous view of the Court of Appeal as to what the law is'.[341]

The quality and the reception of *dicta* are sometimes bound up with the reputations and abilities of the judges who uttered them: just as there might be *dicta* and *dicta*, there might be judges and judges. Excepting judicial concurrences, dissents, and legal commentary offered by judges outside court, other secondary legal sources seem, as compared with *dicta*, not to yield quite the same intimate link between the standing of the source's producer and the valuation of the source produced. Academic legal analysis possibly provides another exception: the high regard accorded to certain jurists by the judiciary has meant that their writings have proved influential in the courts. Generally, however, the likelihood that a secondary source – including most academic legal

[337] *Biggin* v. *Permanite* [1951] 1 KB 422, 433.

[338] *Casswell* v. *Cheshire Lines Committee* [1907] 2 KB 499, 504 *per* Darling J.

[339] *Steadman* v. *Steadman* [1974] QB 161, 177 (case decided July 1973).

[340] Ibid.

[341] *R (Kpangni)* v. *Secretary of State for the Home Department* [2005] EWHC 881 (Admin) at [8]. See also *Three Rivers DC* v. *Bank of England* [2004] UKHL 48 at [34] *per* Lord Scott.

commentary – will make an impression on judicial decision-making is largely down to luck. Consider, for example, the difference between the status of weighty indigenous *dicta* and the status of foreign precedents: eminent judges in a foreign supreme court have no reason to expect, and in all likelihood will not expect, that their judgments will influence the interpretation and development of legal rules in English courts, even when the legal values and relevant rules in each jurisdiction are broadly alike. Should their judgments prove influential in the English courts, their most likely reaction will be surprise. Highly regarded members of the English judiciary, on the other hand, might set forth a particular *dictum* with every confidence that, because the *dictum* comes from them, it will resonate with barristers and with other judges within the jurisdiction.

When *dicta* are considered weighty because they come from great judicial minds, the minds are quite often identified as thinking alike: the *dicta* are deemed to have elevated status not only because they have venerable sources, but also because they show highly accomplished legal problem-solvers to be in agreement on how a problem should be solved. *Dictum* which, in one case, fell 'from the lips of two distinguished masters of the common law [*sc.*, Diplock LJ and Denning MR]' was, for Mars-Jones J, no mere *dictum.*[342] '*Obiter dictum* . . . or not, I entirely accept it, and intend to decide this case in accordance with its language', Coleridge CJ remarked with regard to an observation set forth in a Privy Council decision of 1860, because the Board responsible for the observation had been composed of 'perhaps as great lawyers as in the year 1860 could have been brought together'.[343] When *dicta* are singled out as special because they were produced by an individual judge, the veneration accorded to the judge might be attributable either to expertise in a particular legal field ('a carefully considered statement by one of the most distinguished commercial judges of the twentieth century')[344] or to abilities across the board ('*obiter dictum* . . . from a source whose *dicta* are very highly persuasive').[345] A commendation might even emphasize how a judge is

342 *Higgins* v. *Arfon BC* [1975] 1 WLR 524, 532. See also *Tombs* v. *Roch* (1846) 2 Collyer 490, 508 *per* Knight Bruce VC; *In the Matter of the Royal British Bank* (1859) 3 De G & J 387, 426 *per* Chelmsford LC ('[T]he opinions expressed upon the subject may be regarded as extrajudicial. Those opinions, however, are very strong, and though not binding as authorities upon my judgment, are entitled to the greatest respect and deference').

343 *Bradlaugh* v. *Newdegate* (1883) 11 QBD 1, 10.

344 *Jindal Iron & Steel Co* v. *Islamic Solidarity Shipping Co* [2004] UKHL 49 at [11] *per* Lord Steyn (the judge being Devlin J).

345 *R (Nasseri)* v. *Secretary of State for the Home Department* [2007] EWHC 1548 (Admin) at [27] *per* McCombe J (the source being Lord Bingham).

both an expert in an area of the law and eminent among lawyers in general. Denning LJ's 'observations were *obiter dicta*', Lord Hoffmann remarked in 2007.

> But there are *obiter dicta* and *obiter dicta* ... This was a learned and carefully prepared reserved judgment (including reference to authorities which had not been cited by counsel) by one of the greatest English judges on a matter close to his heart ... For over forty years, Denning LJ's statement of the law remained unchallenged.[346]

Hoffmann added that the relevant *dicta* had been treated as akin to precedent – 'applied in judgments of lower courts'.[347] Coleridge CJ appeared to be treating the Privy Council *dictum* from 1860 in much the same way. It might be objected that the statement cited to court 'was an *obiter dictum* of Lord Eldon', the Attorney-General, Sir Frederick Pollock, asserted in *R* v. *Millis* (1844), 'but if so, the only observation necessary, in answer to that objection, is, that as he was the most cautious as well as learned judge that ever sat on the bench, his very *obiter dicta*, if so they can be called, are entitled to the weight of the highest authority'.[348] A particular statement cited to court from a contracts textbook was 'not supported by any authority', Lord Hodson observed in 1961.[349] But the fact that Scrutton LJ, dissenting in a Court of Appeal case in 1917, had suggested that he would have treated the statement as good law meant that it was transformed from juristic speculation into 'an authoritative *dictum*, contained as it is in the judgment of a master of the law whose words carry great weight not least in matters appertaining to commercial transactions'.[350] The implication, in all of these instances, seems to be that weighty *obiter dicta* might be accorded precedent-like

[346] *R (Godmanchester Town Council)* v. *Secretary of State for the Environment* [2007] UKHL 28 at [21]–[22]. (The relevant observations are made by Denning in *Fairey* v. *Southampton CC* [1956] 2 QB 439 and concern the meaning of the phrase 'evidence that there was no intention to dedicate'.)

[347] *R (Godmanchester Town Council)* v. *Secretary of State for the Environment* at [22].

[348] *R* v. *Millis (George)*, 573.

[349] *Tsakiroglou & Co Ltd* v. *Noblee Thorl G.m.b.H.* [1962] AC 93, 127 (case decided March 1961).

[350] Ibid. Scrutton's *obiter dictum* preceded the statement in the treatise. In *Tsakiroglou*, counsel for the appellant had relied on the first edition of a c.i.f. (cost, insurance, freight) contracts treatise – by 1961, the work was in its third edition – for the rule that '[i]n the absence of express terms in the contract the customary or usual route must be followed'. A. R. Kennedy, *Contracts of Sale: C.I.F.* (London: Stevens and Sons, 1924), 39. Before the treatise had been published, Scrutton had remarked *obiter* that a statement to this effect was correct in law: '[w]here there is a contract to carry from A to B if the exact route or method of carriage is not specified in the contract, the carriage must be by one of the

status if they speak directly to the facts of the case now before the court. In the twentieth and early twenty-first centuries, we will see, some judges can be seen explicitly adopting this perspective.

But the perspective is not the norm. The predilection, exhibited by many judges, for identifying particular *dicta* as weighty is matched by another judicial inclination: a tendency to emphasize that whatever deference a *dictum* might deserve, it does not bind as law.[351] Indeed, judges have their ways of putting *obiter dictum* in its place. It might have emanated from a legal giant, but it was still very obviously an impromptu remark.[352] Deference need not preclude respectful disagreement.[353] The scales are balanced, with one giant's weight matching that of another.[354] The *dictum* is indeed weighty, but those who have relied on it seem to have had little, if any, grasp of its actual legal import.[355] By far the most common method of reining in a *dictum* is to point out that there is

usual routes and methods of carriage, at the option of the carrier'. *Re Arbitration between L Sutro & Co and Heilbut Symons & Co* [1917] 2 KB 348, 362.

351 See, e.g., *Bonsor* v. *Musicians' Union* [1956] AC 104, 124 *per* Lord Morton; *IRC* v. *Holmden* [1966] Ch 511, 524; *Multiservice Bookbinding* v. *Marden* [1979] Ch 84, 104 *per* Browne-Wilkinson J ('[I]n my opinion Denning LJ's *dictum* is not strictly binding on me. But of course it carries great weight'); *Garry* v. *Gwillim* [2002] EWCA Civ 1500 at [62] *per* Ward LJ.

352 See, e.g., *Hammersmith & Fulham LBC* v. *Monk* [1992] 1 AC 478, 488 *per* Lord Bridge ('Despite the eminence of the author of this observation [Scrutton LJ], I do not feel able to give any weight to it in the absence of any indication of the reasoning on which it is based'); *Al Rawas* v. *Pegasus Energy* [2008] EWHC 617 (QB) at [54] *per* Jack J; *Portsmouth NHS Trust* v. *Wyatt* [2005] EWCA Civ 1181 at [73]–[76].

353 See, e.g., *Re S* [2001] Fam 15, 27–8 *per* Butler-Sloss P ('I recognise that there is distinguished judicial *dicta* [*sic*] to the contrary . . . but . . . I respectfully disagree with [it]').

354 See *Spar Shipping* v. *Grand China Logistics* [2015] EWHC 718 (Comm) at [189] *per* Popplewell J ('In this case *dicta* come from judges on each side with great experience in this area of commercial law and practice, who command the very greatest respect. It would be invidious to seek to ascribe relative weight to the professional reputations of each of those identified'); *Spar Shipping* v. *Grand China Logistics* [2016] EWCA Civ 982 at [27] *per* Gross LJ; and *cf. Myers* v. *DPP* [1965] AC 1001, 1040–1 *per* Lord Pearce ('One is entitled to choose between the individual conflicting *obiter dicta* of two great judges').

355 See, e.g., *Ronson* v. *Ronson* [1966] Ch 603, 618 *per* Stamp J ('[Counsel for the defendant], while conceding that the passage in the judgment of Jenkins J was founded on a concession, which in turn rested on authorities relating to positive and not negative orders or undertakings, urged upon me the persuasive nature of that [*sic*] *dicta*. But, whilst I have the greatest aversion to disregarding any *dicta* falling from the lips of that learned judge, if ever Homer can be excused a momentary nod it is in a passage in an extemporary judgment founded on a concession made by counsel as to the existence of a principle which was in turn founded on authorities which laid down or established a different or more limited principle'); also *Redwood* v. *Francis* [1978] RPC 429, 449 *per* Goff J; *Dornoch* v. *Westminster International Ltd* [2009] EWHC 889 (Admlty) at [79] *per* Tomlinson J; *Patel* v. *Mirza* [2014] EWCA Civ 1047 at [103] *per* Vos LJ.

precedent eclipsing it.[356] 'With the most unfeigned reverence . . . for Lord Cottenham's authority, I cannot act upon even his extra-judicial *dictum*, in opposition to decided cases in which the very point was necessarily before the court', Alderson B insisted in 1840.[357] It is very easy to end up presenting judicial reflections on *dicta* as encompassing a somewhat muddled message: there are *dicta* and *dicta*, but *dicta* are always, ultimately, *dicta.* Yet this manner of presentation would neglect the essence of what it is that certain modern judges can be seen to be trying to do, which is to stop short of according *dicta* the status of binding legal rules while making the case that, in certain instances, superior *dicta* can and should be drawn upon to settle disputes over the interpretation of legal language and to guide the development of aspects of the common law. Not all of these judges have been willing to rest content with the rudimentary observation that some *dicta* are weighty, and are weighty because of their persuasiveness (or persuasive authority). During the twentieth century, as will become clear in the next section, there emerges a distinctly new judicial claim: that if the courts and the legal profession were to settle on a more nuanced nomenclature, it might be possible to capture how some *dicta* are more – considerably more – than mere *dicta*, even if they are not quite *rationes decidendi.*

10 Nearly Law?

The subject of *obiter dicta* sometimes has an air of fashion about it. Particular judges have their favourite lines and styles. Lord Devlin, we

[356] See, e.g., *A-G* v. *Wood* (1828) 2 Y & J 290, 300 *per* Alexander LCB ('I should not think myself at liberty to consider that which is but an *obiter dictum*, and not necessary to the decision of that case, an authority sufficient to over-rule that which was actually done by this Court, upon great consideration'); *In the Matter of The Direct Exeter, Plymouth and Devonport Railway Co* (1851) 5 De G & Sm 117, 120 ('Although . . . Lord Cranworth and the Lord Chancellor may have expressed doubts their observations were extra-judicial and ought not to overrule in this court'); *Prince of Wales Life and Educational Assurance Co* v. *Harding* (1858) El Bl & El 183, 204 ('We are of course bound by the judgment of the House of Lords in that case . . . But we are not bound by the extrajudicial observations of any noble and learned Lord delivered in that assembly, although they are, no doubt, entitled to high consideration'); *The Glendarroch* [1894] P 226, 236 *per* Lopes LJ.

> [I]f the learned Lord had an inclination of opinion at all, it was in favour of that opinion which is put forward by the counsel for the plaintiffs; but the materiality of the whole passage is that the point is not decided at all, and is left for further decision. Therefore, to put an extrajudicial *dictum* of that kind against a practice which has existed for a great number of years would be most undesirable, and would be contrary to all precedent.

[357] *Davies* v. *Quarterman* (1840) 4 Y & C Ex 257, 262.

have seen, liked to characterize weighty *dicta* as persuasive authorities. Mummery LJ often pointedly avoided commenting *obiter*,[358] and Lord Dyson often singled out *dicta* as persuasive owing to the care that went into their formulation.[359] In the 1960s, there was a spate of cases – there have been others since, but none, it seems, before then – in which judges commended particular *dicta* as not just any old *dicta* but as 'powerful' *dicta*.[360] There are, in nineteenth-century law reports, numerous decisions in which tangential issues generating *obiter dicta* are referred to as 'by-points'.[361] Even though it seems unlikely that lawyers suddenly stopped using 'by-points', the term, by around 1910, is no longer in evidence, and from that point seems never again to be in evidence, in reported cases.

One of the more intriguing fashions is 'judicial *dicta*'. Not until late into the twentieth century does any judge start consciously distinguishing *dicta* which were judicial from those which were *obiter* or extrajudicial. The nineteenth-century Chancery judge who purported to see constantly 'cropping up in argument' what he termed 'judicial *obiter dicta*'[362] seemed to be asserting nothing more than that, in the cases coming to court, barristers were regularly relying on judges' *obiter* observations. But from some time around 1900, the concept of judicial *dicta* starts to take on a life of its own. In *Russell* v. *Russell* (1897), Lord Hobhouse questioned whether any judge should be 'so bound by precedent as to compel an innocent husband to take back a wife guilty of

358 *Housden* v. *Conservators of Wimbledon & Putney Commons* [2008] EWCA Civ 200 at [30] *per* Mummery LJ ('In general, it is unwise to deliver judgments on points that do not have to be decided. There is no point in cluttering up the law reports with *obiter dicta*, which could, in some cases, embarrass a court having to decide the issue later on'); *Mayes* v. *HMRC* [2011] EWCA Civ 407 at [40] *per* Mummery LJ.

359 See, e.g., *Harb* v. *Aziz* [2005] EWCA Civ 1324 at [51] *per* Dyson LJ ('Although the observations of the Court of Appeal . . . were in my view *obiter dicta*, nevertheless they were carefully considered and comprehensive'); *R (Lewis)* v. *Redcar and Cleveland BC* [2009] EWCA Civ 3 at [44] *per* Dyson LJ.

360 See *Oliver* v. *Ashman* [1962] 2 QB 210, 229; *Car & Universal Finance* v. *Caldwell* [1965] 1 QB 525, 536; *Goding* v. *Fraser* [1967] 1 WLR 286, 293; *Sion* v. *Sion* [1969] P 122, 134. (The courts had long been commending 'strong' *dicta*: see, e.g., *Roe* v. *Kent* (1783) 3 Doug KB 209, 211 *per* Buller J.)

361 See, e.g., *Price* v. *Williams* (1836) 1 M & W 6, 11; *Doe* v. *Archbishop of York* (1849) 14 QB 81, 104; *Page* v. *Morgan* (1885) 15 QBD 228, 233; *Re Redman* [1901] 2 Ch 471, 474 *per* Kekewich J ('The point, which was distinctly raised in argument, was not a by-point, and what was said by the learned judge cannot possibly be treated as . . . not necessary for the purposes of the case before him'); *Kilgour* v. *Gaddes* [1904] 1 KB 457, 463; *Re Wedmore* [1907] 2 Ch 277, 282.

362 *Duke of Sutherland* v. *Heathcote* [1891] 3 Ch 504, 518 *per* Vaughan Williams J.

falsehood and persecution', and declared himself willing to take account of 'judicial *dicta* and decisions taking a wider range, and quite irreconcilable with the rigid line by which it is now sought to confine the jurisdiction of the court'.[363] Were these 'judicial *dicta*' distinct from *obiter dicta*? Judges can, by this point, occasionally be found stating that the absence of statutory or common-law authority had prompted them to search, or to ask counsel to search (as often as not to no avail), for 'judicial *dicta*' pertinent to the case being litigated.[364] Barristers were often willing to take the initiative unprompted. From the early twentieth century, they can regularly be seen trying to persuade judges to pay attention to judicial *dicta*.[365] Presumably the Court of Appeal would 'not interfere with a long course of judicial *dicta*', one barrister surmised when arguing before it in 1929.[366] The Court disabused him of that presumption by ruling against his client. '[J]udicial *dicta* ... although deserving of respect', Kennedy J maintained in 1906, 'cannot be treated with the weight which attaches to a decision'.[367] While respect for such *dicta* is all well and good, Lord Loreburn cautioned in 1916, they must not – this warning was to be repeated regularly by twentieth-century judges – be used to supply the gaps in a statute.[368]

[363] *Russell* v. *Russell*, 428.

[364] See, e.g., *Re Tollemache* [1903] 1 Ch 457, 465; *Gozney* v. *Bristol Trade & Provident Society* [1909] 1 KB 901, 922–3 *per* Fletcher Moulton LJ; *Jackson* v. *Watson* [1909] 2 KB 193, 206 *per* Kennedy LJ; *A-G* v. *Horner (No. 2)* [1913] 2 Ch 140, 172 *per* Cozens-Hardy MR.

[365] See, e.g., *Simons* v. *Associated Furnishers Ltd* [1931] 1 Ch 379, 382; *Harper* v. *Haden & Sons* [1933] Ch 298, 314; *Rookes* v. *Barnard (No. 1)* [1963] 1 QB 623 (CA), 628–9; also *Custodian for Charities* v. *Mackey* [1985] Ch 168, 185; *Olafsson* v. *Gissurason* [2006] EWHC 3162 (QB) at [20] *per* Mackay J ('[Counsel] for the appellant claims this *dictum* as binding Court of Appeal authority ... In my judgment he puts his case too high'); *Re G* [2014] EWCA Civ 1365 at [15]–[16]; *Re M2 Property* [2017] EWHC 3218 (Ch) at [27], [58].

[366] *Shanks* v. *IRC* [1929] 1 KB 342, 347.

[367] *R* v. *Bond* [1906] 2 KB 389, 404.

[368] See *Herbert* v. *Fox & Co* [1916] 1 AC 405, 408 ('[T]here has arisen a tendency to treat judicial *dicta* ... as though they qualified ... statutory language'); also *IRC* v. *City of London* [1953] 1 WLR 652, 665 *per* Lord Normand ('This is an extreme instance of construing not the Act of Parliament but judicial *dicta*'); *RB* v. *Brighton & Hove CC* [2014] EWCA Civ 561 at [39] *per* Jackson LJ ('Judges have rightly cautioned against glossing the statute with judicial *dicta*'); also Philip Sales, 'The Tort of Conspiracy and Civil Secondary Liability' (1990) 49 *CLJ* 491, 493 n. 15 ('If the language of a judicial decision in a particular case is not to be construed as it if was the language of a statute, that must be doubly true of the language of *obiter dicta*, delivered on the margins of the reasoning in a case, where the pressure for tight and precise formulation is correspondingly diminished').

The twentieth century nevertheless saw judges becoming ever more receptive to judicial *dicta*. Not only is 'this court . . . entitled to have regard to' a judicial *dictum*, Darling J asserted in the early 1920s, but it is obliged to 'look at it in order to see whether or not it lays down a principle which appears to be the right one'.[369] In much the same vein, Macnaghten J maintained in 1940 that he had a 'duty . . . to pay regard to' judicial *dicta*, unless he could 'see good reason to the contrary'.[370] A decade later, Lord Normand observed that '[j]udicial *dicta* . . . of high authority' had 'in some respects clarified' the duties owed by licensors to bare licensees.[371] '[I]n the absence of a direct decision' on the issue of punitive damages, Sachs J remarked a decade later still, 'it is . . . convenient initially to ascertain what guidance can be obtained . . . from judicial *dicta*.'[372]

But what were these cryptic *dicta*? If *dicta* are observations made by judges in the course of reaching decisions – if nobody other than a judge could be the source of an *obiter dictum* – they must always, by definition, be 'judicial'. It is no surprise, therefore, that 'judicial *dicta*' are often just *obiter dicta* by another name: the judge's or barrister's attachment of the word 'judicial' to *dictum* simply indicates that the *obiter* opinion being referred to was attributable to a judge, or to judges.[373] Yet by the middle of the twentieth century there was evidence that 'judicial' was one of various words being used in the courts to indicate that a *dictum* seemed somehow superior to the average *dictum*. Like *dicta* described as weighty, persuasive, strong, powerful, compelling, and the like, judicial *dicta* were 'authoritative statements of law' on particular matters – authoritative pronunciations as to what the relevant law was, or how it was to be construed.[374] When, in 1987, *Norway's Application* returned to the Court

369 *Re la Société Les Affréteurs Réunis* [1921] 3 KB 1, 15.

370 *Nesta* v. *Wyatt* [1941] 1 KB 44, 50 (case decided October 1940). See also *Latilla* v. *IRC* [1943] AC 377, 381.

371 *London Graving Dock Co Ltd* v. *Horton* [1951] AC 737 at 744, 751. See also *Evans* v. *Spritebrand* [1985] 1 WLR 317, 324 *per* Slade LJ ('[J]udicial *dicta* of high authority are to be found in English decisions which suggest that a director is liable for those tortious acts of his company which he has ordered or procured to be done'); *Re Leach* [1986] Ch 226, 235 *per* Slade LJ; *FHR European Ventures LLP* v. *Cedar Capital Partners LLC* [2014] UKSC 45 at [30] *per* Lord Neuberger.

372 *Rookes* v. *Barnard (No. 1)* [1961] 3 WLR 438 (QBD), 447.

373 See, e.g., *FHR European Ventures* v. *Cedar Capital Partners* at [30]; *Re Lehman Bros* [2017] UKSC 38 at [81], [83], and [155].

374 See, e.g., *The Muncaster Castle* [1961] AC 807, 876–7 *per* Lord Hodson ('[The case for the appellants is fortified by the fact that t]he stream of judicial *dicta* . . . flows only in one direction and lends support to the[ir] contention'); *Williams* v. *Williams* [1963] P 212, 224–5 *per* Willmer LJ; *DPP* v. *Morgan* [1976] AC 182, 236 *per* Lord Fraser; *Natwest Bank*

of Appeal, Balcombe and Woolf LJJ ultimately did not accept but nevertheless took very seriously the submission, made by counsel for the deceased's estate, that the Court's judgment at first appeal regarding the correct interpretation of one of the main statutory provisions was 'within the top scale of judicial *dicta* and should only be overruled by the House of Lords'.[375] By this point there had emerged among judges a tendency, still occasionally in evidence today,[376] to use the term 'judicial *dicta*' to denote how, in certain instances, *obiter* observations might be more akin to binding than to persuasive sources: how it made good sense for judges to follow – how it might be untoward of them not to follow – particular observations made in an earlier decision, notwithstanding that those observations did not form part of the *ratio*. There is 'English authority', one American legal commentator has claimed, distinguishing '"by the way" statements' which make for standard *obiter dicta* from '[j]udicial *dicta*', which 'should be followed unless they are erroneous or there are particularly strong reasons for not doing so'.[377] Pollock A-G appeared to be drawing this distinction – without using the term, 'judicial *dicta*' – in *R* v. *Millis* when he declared the *obiter* observation made by Lord Eldon to be entitled to the weight of highest authority (Section 9).

In the twentieth century, the distinction became a commonplace. 'Some *dicta*', Sterndale MR ventured in *Slack* v. *Leeds Industrial Co-operative Society*, 'are of a different kind'[378] – being 'weighty authority', even if not constituting 'a decision ... which binds'.[379] These *dicta*,

v. *Somer International* [2001] EWCA Civ 970 at [36] *per* Potter LJ; *Generics (UK) Ltd* v. *Daiichi Pharmaceutical Co Ltd* [2009] EWCA Civ 646 at [74], [79] *per* Jacob LJ.

375 *Re Norway's Application* [1988] 3 WLR 603 (case decided December 1987), 649 *per* Woolf LJ; and see also ibid. at 648 ('a powerful, succinct and highly persuasive argument') and 631 *per* Balcombe LJ ('a most persuasive argument that, in the absence of any compelling reasons to the contrary, we should follow the considered *dicta* of the first Court of Appeal, leaving it to the House of Lords to put matters right, if necessary').

376 For a recent endorsement see, e.g., *Youngsam* (HC) at [26] *per* Turner J.

377 Robert G. Scofield, 'The Distinction between Judicial *Dicta* and *Obiter Dicta*' (October 2002) 25(7) *Los Angeles Lawyer* 17, 17. The English authority which Scofield cites for distinguishing *obiter* and judicial *dicta* is *Brunner* v. *Greenslade* [1971] Ch 993. As we saw earlier, the distinction had already been alluded to by an American jurist: Llewellyn, *The Bramble Bush*, 40–1 ('The court ... [w]hen it speaks to the question before it, ... announces *law* ... But when it speaks to any other question at all, it says mere words, which no man needs to follow. Are such words worthless? They are not. We know them as judicial *dicta*: when they are wholly off the point at issue we call them *obiter dicta*').

378 *Slack* v. *Leeds Industrial Co-operative Society*, 451.

379 Ibid. at 442.

Warrington LJ elaborated, 'are entitled to such weight that we ought to follow them unless we find that they have been overruled or that they are inconsistent with previous decisions'.[380] Disputes over patents claims are often blighted by a dearth of precedent, Budd J maintained in 1972, and so 'the limits beyond which [a deciding court] must not stray are set by familiar judicial *dicta*'.[381] Though 'judicial' is not the only word that English judges have tagged onto *dicta* of this type when endeavouring to set them apart, it is the one which they have applied most consistently.

One twentieth-century judge, Robert Megarry, bore more than average responsibility for turning, or trying to turn, 'judicial *dicta*' into a legal term of art. Denning J's observations, in *Central London Property Trust* v. *High Trees House*, on defendants being estopped from enforcing their strict legal rights when claimants have reasonably relied upon their assurances that they would not do so, 'must', he remarked in 1967, 'have been *obiter dicta*, or perhaps more properly judicial *dicta*'.[382] Denning's *dicta* are commonly considered to have ensured that the 1937 Law Revision Committee's proposed alterations to the law relating to the necessity of consideration in contracts were judicially implemented.[383] *Dicta* of this nature were judicial rather than *obiter*, Megarry elaborated in 1969, because, rather than being 'mere passing remarks of the judge', they consisted 'of considered enunciations of the judge's opinion of the law upon some point which does not arise for decision on the facts of the case before him'.[384] The following year, he returned to the point again:

380 Ibid. at 446.

381 *Kahn* v. *Stewart* [1972] FSR 620, 628.

382 *Slough Estates* v. *Slough BC* (1968) 19 P & CR 326, 362 (case decided December 1967). See *Central London Property Trust* v. *High Trees House Ltd* [1947] KB 130, 134–5. That the observations were *dicta* was acknowledged by Denning himself: see Lord Denning, 'The Way of an Iconoclast' (1960) 3 *Sydney L. Rev*. 209, 211 ('I rather rashly perhaps . . . went beyond what was necessary for the decision').

383 See, e.g., *Collier* v. *Wright* [2007] EWCA Civ 1329 at [42] *per* Arden LJ (though Longmore LJ (ibid. at [48]) seemed unconvinced). The proposed alterations are contained in the *Sixth Interim Report: Statute of Frauds and the Doctrine of Consideration. Presented by the Lord High Chancellor to Parliament by Command of His Majesty, May 1937*, Cmd. 5449 (London: HMSO, 1945). Denning himself drew on paragraphs 35 and 40 of the Report for support for the proposition that a promise absent consideration might be enforceable by virtue of estoppel: *Central London Property Trust* v. *High Trees House*, 135.

384 *West* v. *Dick* [1969] 2 Ch 424, 431–2. Megarry purported to identify a third, 'innominate' category of *dicta*: judicial statements as to 'what has been done in other cases, not reported' (this category of *dicta* having, he thought, 'the highest authority that any *dictum* can bear'). Ibid. at 432. See also R. E. Megarry, *A New Miscellany at Law*

> A mere passing remark, or a statement or assumption on some matter that has not been argued, is one thing; a considered judgment on a point fully argued is another, especially where, had the facts been otherwise, it would have formed part of the *ratio*. Such judicial *dicta*, standing in authority somewhere between a *ratio decidendi* and an *obiter dictum*, seem to me to have a weight nearer to the former than the latter.[385]

Megarry's judicial *dicta* are invariably the *dicta* of judicial giants. But while he believed that the opinions of eminent judges carry their 'own intrinsic authority',[386] he did not consider the high standing of the judge responsible for a *dictum* to be a reason for calling the *dictum* 'judicial'. A *dictum* deserved this label, in Megarry's view, because the legal point to which it relates did not have to be settled but was nevertheless comprehensively argued in the case in which it was offered, because the *dictum* was formulated in response to adversarial arguments made on this point, and because the point cannot be left unsettled in the case to be decided by today's court. On first glance, there looks to be something fishy about Megarry's claim, in *Royal Bank of Canada* v. *IRC* (1971), that he is setting forth some judicial *dictum* of his own. A judge pays another judge a compliment when he calls his observations 'judicial *dicta*', but is he not indulging in self-aggrandizement if he applies the label to his own remarks? In fact, it is clear – so long as one appreciates what Megarry took the term 'judicial *dicta*' to mean – that this was not a bid to be included in some judicial pantheon. A point which did not arise on the facts in *Royal Bank of Canada* had nevertheless been 'fully argued' before the court by counsel for the Bank, and so – given that counsel's argument had made it possible for Megarry to consider the point thoroughly, and that facts relevant to the point would probably have to be ruled on in a later case – he thought it 'may be helpful' to 'say something' which was to 'be neither of the *ratio* nor merely *obiter dicta* but what for want of a better term may be called judicial *dicta*'.[387]

(Oxford: Hart, 2005), 255; though compare *Viasystems Ltd* v. *Thermal Transfer Ltd* [2005] EWCA Civ 1151 at [28] *per* May LJ.

> I have no doubt but that we should in this instance look at and consider the unofficial reports … I am content also to take it from the unofficial reports that the Court of Appeal's oral judgments in substance contained the passages relied on by [counsel for the claimant] in his muted submission that … Littledale J's *dicta* are binding on this court. I reject that submission because … the passages relied on did not find their way into the Official Reports. Whoever edited them out – perhaps the judges themselves – cannot have regarded them as necessary to the decision, nor worth reporting.

385 *Brunner* v. *Greenslade* [1971] Ch 993, 1002–3 (case decided July 1970).

386 Ibid. at 1003.

387 *Royal Bank of Canada* v. *IRC* [1972] Ch 665, 682–4 (case decided November 1971).

It is difficult to know if any judge other than Megarry has ever taken the concept of judicial *dicta* especially seriously. Yet, it is an interesting concept, because it illustrates a fairly common modern-judicial inclination to treat weighty *dicta* as legal sources which, though secondary, might in certain circumstances come close to being binding authority. The weightiest *dicta* 'are a source of law', Lord Simon claimed in 1973, 'though not a compelling source in the way that the *ratio decidendi* of a case is within the doctrine of precedent'.[388] Lord Dunedin had tried to be more precise on this matter when *Slack* v. *Leeds Industrial Co-operative Society* went to the House of Lords. A weighty *dictum* might be followed as if it were a source of law, he suggested, when there is no genuine source of law directing the court to a legal outcome different from the one suggested by the *dictum*. Whether judges should follow a *dictum* in these circumstances, Dunedin ventured, depends on whether it 'serve[s] to help [them] form [their] own opinion' regarding how the court should rule in the case at hand.[389] If it does not, then the *dictum*, no matter how 'carefully considered', need not so much as be acknowledged, let alone assessed.[390] In the 1860s, Pollock CB had referred to *dicta* which do help judges to form opinions when primary sources fall silent as 'indirect authorities' – sources to be followed in the event that 'there is no direct authority at all'.[391] It seems that barristers were, by this point, quite regularly suggesting to judges that, in the absence of an applicable primary legal source, the court might consider treating a *dictum* as authority *faute de mieux*.[392] In the twentieth century as compared with the nineteenth, the judiciary, we will see in the next section, would be markedly more open to this suggestion. Megaw J, having noted in *Fowley* v. *Gafford* (1967) that 'there appear to be no ... cases' determining if navigators have a right to fix moorings on other peoples' land without permission, proceeded to 'hold that there is no [such] common law right' by relying on 'authoritative *dicta* which are flatly inconsistent with the supposed right'.[393] This modern judicial conviction – that a *dictum* might

388 *Knuller* v. *DPP* [1973] AC 435, 482.

389 *Slack* v. *Leeds Industrial Co-operative Society* [1924] AC 851, 864.

390 Ibid. at 863–4. See also *Re Norway's Application*, 630–1 *per* Balcombe LJ.

391 *Swinfen* v. *Chelmsford* (1860) 5 Hurl & N 890, 918.

392 See, e.g., *Wright* v. *Atkyns* (1810) 17 Ves Jr 255, 258 ('*Chapman's case* ... affords no authority upon this question, except an extrajudicial opinion'); *R* v. *Burdett* (1820) 3 B & Ald 717, 736 ('for which there seems to be no authority, except the extrajudicial opinion of Ashhurst J'); *Taylor* v. *Devey and Graham* (1837) 7 Ad & El 409, 412 ('[T]here is no authority in favour of the custom, except an extrajudicial *dictum*').

393 *Fowley Marine Ltd* v. *Gafford* [1967] 2 QB 808, 822–3.

be enlisted as a surrogate authority where there is no primary source of law to be found – seems, at least implicitly, to treat everything contained in a judgment but not belonging to its *ratio* as a source *sui generis*. Other secondary sources – such as juristic writings, legislative history, and foreign legal decisions – are never treated as anything other than epistemic authorities. Only *dicta* – or rather only *dicta* considered, for one reason or another, to be especially weighty – appear ever to have been accorded the status of a secondary legal source that might do the work of a primary legal source should no actual primary source be available.

Why should judges ever have come to the conclusion that *dictum* might stand in for a material source of law when none of the material sources yields a legal solution? We saw in Sections 6 and 7 that judges, who do not always perceive a clear distinction between a precedent's *ratio* and everything within the precedent that is *obiter*, may be inclined to take particular judicial statements as binding because there is no overwhelming reason to conclude that they are not binding. But there is a difference between a judge mistaking *dictum* for *ratio* and a judge knowing a *dictum* to be *dictum* but nevertheless making it do *ratio*'s work. Why, even if only exceptionally, might judges maintain that *dicta*, unlike other secondary sources, can do this work? In the 1870s, one Court of Appeal judge, Thesiger LJ, proffered an answer. 'I really do not know that there is any definite rule as to what may or may not be cited and acted on as authority', Bramwell LJ remarked in *R* v. *Bishop of Oxford* (1879), '[b]ut to reject the opinion of the head of the law' – he was referring to Lord Chancellor Cairns – 'as to what is the law' while 'admit[ting] the *obiter dictum* of a judge . . . seems somewhat strange'.[394] Bramwell was defending the Court's decision to allow counsel for the appellant to rely on a passage from a parliamentary speech Cairns had made in the House of Lords. Baggallay LJ also defended the decision – if somewhat diffidently.[395] He did so by comparing Cairns' speech with the content of text-books and treatises authored by judges:

> The courts have been in the habit of allowing reference to be made to text-books, the authors of which are living judges, and I am unable to distinguish, in principle, an expression of opinion by a Lord Chancellor as to the

[394] *R* v. *Bishop of Oxford* (1879) 4 QBD 525, 549–50.

[395] Ibid. at 576 ('[W]e allowed the passage to be read, and, though I have since entertained some doubts whether we were right in our decision, which doubts have not been wholly removed, I am, upon the whole, of opinion that there was no objection to the course which we allowed the appellants' counsel to take').

> state of the law upon a particular subject . . . from an expression of opinion upon the same subject by another judge in a treatise published by him.[396]

In *R* v. *Bishop of Oxford*, however, the Court of Appeal did not speak with one voice on this matter. '[A]mong the authorities upon which I rely, I do not count the speech of the Lord Chancellor', Thesiger stated. It cut no ice with him to compare the speech with 'the text-books of living judges', for 'I . . . doubt very much whether the principle upon which such text-books have been admitted as authorities is a sound one.'[397] But what of Bramwell's observation that it seems strange to take this position while being willing to countenance *obiter dicta*? There was, Thesiger believed, a distinction to be drawn. *Obiter dicta*, certainly 'the *obiter dicta* of a judge *in banco*, was a weightier source of authority than a Lord Chancellor's speech to parliament or the text-book of a living judge', he contended,

> for the judge who offers *dicta* in court has the safeguard of a judicial proceeding cast around him; his mind is not likely to be influenced by any considerations beyond those which the law enforces upon him; while when the scene is removed to the area of parliament, political considerations may enter, . . . and may insensibly affect the judgments of even the greatest and wisest of our judges. The sanction and safeguard of judicial procedure are removed, and even the conditions which give the text-book its weight, the exclusive devotion to the legal subject of which it treats, and the calmness with which it is necessarily prepared, may in many instances not exist.[398]

Judges, when writing legal texts or speaking in parliament, are not constrained by legal context – by the net that a judicial proceeding casts around them. But context is everything, Thesiger believed, when judges pronounce *obiter* in the course of deciding cases. *Obiter dicta* are an intrinsically weightier secondary source than juristic speculation and parliamentary intervention because judges produce them while adjudicating – adjudication being a context in which judges understand not only that they must decide according to the law but also that they have to be mindful of the impression that their *dicta* could have on other judicial colleagues deciding the case, on courts ruling on similar disputes in the future, and on barristers and legal commentators (particularly those who might discern an advantage in endeavouring to present the

396 Ibid. at 577.
397 Ibid. at 599–600.
398 Ibid. at 600.

judges' *dicta* as if they were *ratio*). For Thesiger, the courtroom imposes on judges an extra incentive to be on their best professional behaviour, and so the opinions they put forward in that context might be presumed inherently more elevated than legal opinion, even judicial legal opinion, ventured elsewhere.

11 Observation and Authority

Obiter dicta can be the basis for what Ronald Dworkin called theoretical disagreement about law.[399] Judges could agree as to the test distinguishing a *ratio decidendi* from *obiter dicta* yet still, when considering an earlier decision, disagree over what constitutes the former and what are the latter. If the judges do agree as to the test and how it is satisfied for the purpose of yielding the *ratio* of the decision, they in effect invoke the rule of recognition: they accept a standard of legal validity which enables them to treat some of the content of that decision as binding law and the rest of the content as *dicta*, much as they accept criteria of valid enactment when they recognize statutes to be law or a rule of prescription when they recognize a custom as law.

While a rule of recognition yields an answer as to what binds and what is *obiter* within a decision, however, it indicates nothing about the *obiter* content of the decision other than that it is the content which does not count as law. The rule enables judges and lawyers to identify *dicta* as a secondary legal source, but it is irrelevant to their discriminations as between *dicta* which are just *dicta* and *dicta* which carry significant weight. That a *dictum* might be said, in the abstract, to carry such weight – because it is, for example, carefully formulated by an eminent judge in a superior court – places no burden on future courts to acknowledge that weight, or even acknowledge the *dictum* at all, when making decisions on which the *dictum* has a bearing. A norm is a legal norm when it satisfies a test of validity applicable to its type. But there is no test according to which a *dictum* might be upheld as having special epistemic status, or as being suited to play the role of a primary legal source when a decision has to be made on facts to which no such source currently applies.

It is perfectly possible for a jurisdiction's rule of recognition to be altered so that what was once a secondary legal source acquires the status – or in particular circumstances acquires the status – of a primary one. The decisions of the Judicial Committee of the Privy

[399] See Ronald Dworkin, *Law's Empire* (London: Fontana, 1986), 3–6.

Council (JCPC) are a case in point. Since the 1870s, the rule in English law has been that the Judicial Committee's decisions do not bind the domestic courts. But in the second of the Supreme Court's two judgments in *Willers* v. *Joyce* (2016), it was decided – controversially[400] – that once the President of the Supreme Court has appointed a panel of Justices to hear an appeal, 'the members of that panel can, if they think it appropriate, not only decide that [an] earlier decision of the House of Lords or Supreme Court, or of the Court of Appeal, was wrong, but also can expressly direct that domestic courts should treat [a] decision of the JCPC as representing the law of England and Wales'.[401]

There are, in England and some other common-law jurisdictions, instances in which *obiter dicta* appear to have been awarded, or to have come within touching distance of being awarded, the promotion conferred on Judicial Committee decisions. Judges in the United States sometimes treat *dicta*, particularly Supreme Court *dicta*, much as they would a case holding (i.e., a *ratio decidendi*);[402] for evidence, one need look no further than the doctrine of strict scrutiny, which can be traced to a footnote in a case about dairy products.[403] It seems to be generally accepted, nevertheless, that while a court's *dicta* may in certain circumstances have de facto precedential effect because they are followed, and they are followed because they are found to be persuasive rather than because they are (as a holding would be) presumptively

[400] The decision is controversial because it in effect vests in the JCPC the power to change English law, even though it is not a court of the jurisdiction. On the implications of the decision, see the critique by Peter Mirfield, 'A Novel Theory of Privy Council Precedent' (2017) 133 *LQR* 1.

[401] *Willers* v. *Joyce* [2016] UKSC 44 at [21].

[402] See, e.g., David M. Dorsen, *Henry Friendly: Greatest Judge of His Era* (Cambridge, Mass.: Belknap Press, 2012), 217 ('Friendly chose in *Solina* [v. *United States* 709 F.2d 160 (2d Cir. 1983)] to rely on the *dictum* [of Burger CJ in *Holloway* v. *Arkansas* 435 US 475 (1978)] and . . . to apply the *dictum* expansively to . . . the very situation the [Supreme] Court had distinguished'); John Phillip Reid, *Chief Justice: The Judicial World of Charles Doe* (Cambridge, Mass.: Harvard University Press, 1967), 320 ('Doe . . . seldom bothered to distinguish between *obiter dictum* and *ratio decidendi* but cited both indiscriminately'); also Josh Blackman, 'Much Ado about *Dictum*; or, How to Evade Precedent without Really Trying: The Distinction between Holding and *Dictum*', Social Science Research Network (December 2008), papers.ssrn.com (accessed 12 March 2019).

[403] *United States* v. *Carolene Products* 304 US 144, 152–3 n. 4 (1938); Abner J. Mikva, 'Goodbye to Footnotes' (1985) 56 *Univ. Colorado L. Rev.* 647, 649 ('All too often, yesterday's *obiter dictum* becomes tomorrow's law of the land. The classic example, of course, is footnote 4 in *United States* v. *Carolene Products*'). The footnote is contained in the opinion of the Court, which was written by Stone J.

binding.[404] Australia yields a similar lesson as to how *dictum* can on occasions be accorded precedent-like status without the rule of recognition being modified so as to accommodate it as a primary legal source. Since 2007 – after the High Court of Australia criticized the New South Wales Court of Appeal for making a ruling which was 'unsupported by authority' and which 'flew in the face of seriously considered *dicta* uttered by a majority of th[e High] Court'[405] – Australia's intermediate appeal courts 'have tended to regard themselves as under a duty of obedience to High Court *dicta*, at least in certain circumstances'.[406] Canadian lower courts have similarly accepted that *obiter dicta* emanating from the nation's highest court might be presumed binding. In *R* v. *Prokofiew* (2010), Doherty JA, speaking for a unanimous five-judge panel of the Ontario Court of Appeal, suggested that

> [l]ower courts should be slow to characterize *obiter dicta* from the Supreme Court of Canada as non-binding. It is best to begin from the premise that all *obiter* from the Supreme Court of Canada should be followed, and to move away from that premise only where a reading of the relevant judgment provides a cogent reason for not applying that *obiter*. The orderly and rational development of the jurisprudence is not served if lower courts are too quick to strike out in legal directions different than those signalled in *obiter* from the Supreme Court . . .[407]

404 See, e.g., Abramowicz and Stearns, 'Defining Dicta', 957; Marc McAllister, '*Dicta* Redefined' (2011) 47 *Williamette L. Rev.* 161, 161–2; Judith M. Stinson, 'Why *Dicta* Becomes Holding and Why It Matters' (2010) 76 *Brooklyn L. Rev.* 219, 221; and Randy J. Kozel, *Settled versus Right: A Theory of Precedent* (Cambridge University Press, 2017), 73–83. According to Kozel, it is possible to show not only that '[t]he Supreme Court regularly builds frameworks to guide the resolution of future disputes' – frameworks which are typically formulated as *dicta* – but also that an analysis of some of the Court's jurisprudence reveals there are instances in which 'these . . . frameworks appear to exert binding force' (ibid. at 76). The examples on which Kozel draws in order to substantiate this proposition indicate that the notion of *dictum* having binding force could be taken, in this context, to mean two different things: either that a *dictum* is binding because it has to be treated as determinative on a set of facts, or that a *dictum* is binding because it has to be treated as authoritative guidance on how to interpret the law applicable to those facts. His account suggests that, when lower courts conceive of Supreme Court *dictum* as having binding force, the greater likelihood is that they are treating the *dictum* not as binding law but as binding interpretive guidance.

405 *Farah Constructions* v. *Say-Dee* [2007] HCA 22, 69.

406 Matthew Harding and Ian Malkin, 'The High Court of Australia's *Obiter Dicta* and Decision-Making in Lower Courts' (2012) 34 *Sydney L. Rev.* 239, 242.

407 *R* v. *Prokofiew* (2010) 256 CCC (3d) 355 at para. 21 (decision affirmed by SCC: [2012] 2 SCR 639).

That this was an accepted premise was evident, Doherty maintained, from *R* v. *Henry* (2005), where, writing for a unanimous Supreme Court, Binnie J 'recognized that *stare decisis* commands compliance not only with the *ratio decidendi*, but some of the *obiter* from the . . . Court'.[408] Binnie himself was reacting to academic and judicial reception of Chouinard J's observation, in *Sellars* v. *R* (1980), that the Court could sometimes rule on a particular point of law even though ruling on the point 'was not absolutely necessary . . . in order to dispose of the appeal'.[409] For Binnie, the significance of the observation had been exaggerated. No doubt a lower court will occasionally be unwise to disregard a legal opinion endorsed by a majority of the Supreme Court but 'not strictly necessary for the disposition of the case in which it was expressed', he conceded, for disregarding the opinion 'may just precipitate a successful appeal'.[410] But there was no basis for deducing from *Sellars* that 'whatever was said in a majority judgment of the Supreme Court of Canada was binding, no matter how incidental to the main point of the case or how far it was removed from the dispositive facts and principles of law'.[411] While Binnie himself accepted that lower courts might be sensible not to disregard *dicta* produced by the Supreme Court, his own description of a weighty *dictum* – as one 'which is obviously intended for guidance and which should be accepted as authoritative'[412] – seems almost studiedly ambiguous as between lower courts having to take account of a *dictum* as epistemic authority and those courts having to follow a *dictum* because it 'commands compliance'.[413] The ambiguity seems, so far, not to have troubled the

408 Ibid. at para. 18.
409 *Sellars* v. *R* [1980] 1 SCR 527 at para. 4.
410 *R* v. *Henry* [2005] 3 SCR 609 at para. 56.
411 Ibid. at para. 55.
412 Ibid. at para. 57.
413 The tenor of the relevant passage in the judgment seems, if anything, to run against treating *obiter* judicial remarks as akin to primary legal sources:

> All *obiter* do not have, and are not intended to have, the same weight. The weight decreases as one moves from the dispositive *ratio decidendi* to a wider circle of analysis which is obviously intended for guidance and which should be accepted as authoritative. Beyond that, there will be commentary, examples or exposition that are intended to be helpful and may be found to be persuasive, but are certainly not 'binding' . . . The objective of the exercise is to promote certainty in the law, not to stifle its growth and creativity. The notion that each phrase in a judgment of this Court should be treated as if enacted in a statute is not supported by the cases and is inconsistent with the basic fundamental principle that the common law develops by experience (Ibid.).

Canadian lower courts, which, like Australia's, have quite regularly accepted final court *dicta* as binding.[414] In neither Canada nor Australia, however, does there exist anything tantamount to a practice direction placing lower courts under a duty, in particular instances, to follow its *dicta* – the type of duty which the UK's Supreme Court created in relation to Judicial Committee decisions in the second of its judgments in *Willers* – and in both countries the lower courts can occasionally be seen electing not to follow *dicta* produced in the final court of appeal.[415]

As compared with their American, Australian, and Canadian counterparts, English judges had, until recently, been markedly less inclined to put weighty *dicta* on a par with *ratio*. Lord Neuberger set out the orthodoxy in the first of the *Willers* judgments: 'any judicial decision is authority for what it decides, not for *dicta* which plainly go beyond the decision'.[416] Yet, we know, from the ground covered so far in this Essay, that observations which are not integral to the decisions in which they appear but which, for example, capture the unanimous or majority view of a distinguished panel of superior court judges will sometimes be enlisted to do the work of a primary legal source because there is no such source to be applied in the case at hand. By accepting these *obiter* observations as authoritative, a court is usually stating not that it is obliged to follow them, but that it would be injudicious if it did not. Blackburn J captured the attitude in *Pew* v. *Metropolitan Board of Works* (1865), when he observed that '[t]hough we are not bound by the opinion expressed in *The Metropolitan Board of Works* v. *The Vauxhall Bridge Company* ... inasmuch as it was extrajudicial, the respect we feel for its authority makes us reluctant to decide in opposition to it'.[417] Denning MR

[414] See, e.g., *J. K. Read Engineering Ltd* v. *R* [2015] 2 CTC 2023 (Tax Court of Canada) at para. 29.

[415] See, e.g., *Scott* v. *The Queen* (2017) 55 CBR (6th) 252 (Tax Court of Canada) at paras. 94–5; also *ACT* v. *Queanbeyan CC* (2010) 188 FCR 541, 586, where Perram J noted that *dicta* from an Australian High court decision of 1988 'are of considerable persuasive value and, perhaps more importantly, there are no *dicta* to the contrary' but nevertheless maintained that the Federal Court of Australia was not bound to follow them because they were 'neither long-established by authority nor ... seriously considered' by 'a majority of the High Court'. In a similar vein, see *Tim Barr* v. *Narui Gold Coast* [2010] NSWSC 29 at [219] *per* Barrett J; *Mercedes Holdings* v. *Waters (No. 3)* [2011] FCA 236 at [120] *per* Perram J; Harding and Malkin, 'The High Court of Australia's *Obiter Dicta*', 249.

[416] *Willers* v. *Joyce* [2016] UKSC 43 at [151].

[417] *Pew* v. *Metropolitan Board of Works* (1865) 6 B & S 235, 248. See also *Roberts* v. *Crowe* (1872) LR 7 CP 629, 636–7 *per* Willes J ('What fell from Lord Justice James ... was not a mere extrajudicial statement: and, even if it were, coming from such a source, I should feel myself quite safe in relying upon it as an authority for pronouncing judgment for the plaintiff in this case, leaving the matter, if wrong, to be set right elsewhere. Speaking for myself, I adopt it as an authority').

suggested in *Wallersteiner* v. *Moir* (1975) that the word 'tried' should not – when deciding if a party has leave to appeal a case which has been tried – be confined to proceedings which have actually undergone trial in a court, but rather, where evidence and arguments have been heard, might sensibly be extended to summary and interlocutory judgments as well.[418] Order 14 of the Rules of the Supreme Court 1965 in fact did confine 'tried' to completed trials. In 1978, nevertheless, Stephenson LJ followed Denning's *dictum* in preference to Order 14: Denning's suggestion is 'plainly was *obiter*', he conceded, 'but it commends itself to me as, ... sensible, likely to save costs and in accordance with the ordinary use of language'.[419] That a judge should have prioritized an extrajudicial remark over a court rule is unusual. Even though Stephenson did not consider himself bound by the rule, however, nor did he presume himself bound by the *dictum*. He thought it foolish to apply the rule of interpretation given that Denning's reasoning yielded a more common-sense approach, and so he elected to treat the *dictum* as authoritative. But he did not have to treat it as authoritative. Aside from in a handful of modern instances to be considered in a moment, judges in English courts have been careful to stop short of treating, indeed have made a point of not treating, *dicta* as binding authority.

Sometimes, *dicta* are authoritative in the sense that they are the lasting legacy of a judgment. Through *dicta*, judges articulate their understandings of abstract legal principles and their views on how those principles should be valued and rendered explicit or concrete within particular areas of law.[420] When, in the course of delivering judgments, judges formulate these understandings in especially perceptive and perspicuous ways, their observations – even though they might be *obiter* – may be as important as, may even transcend, the judgments themselves.[421] Iconic

[418] *Wallersteiner* v. *Moir* [1975] QB 373, 387.

[419] *Gardener Steel* v. *Sheffield Bros* [1978] 1 WLR 916, 918.

[420] See Neil MacCormick, *Rhetoric and the Rule of Law: A Theory of Legal Reasoning* (Oxford University Press, 2005), 160.

> *[O]biter dicta* are not to be dismissed merely because they are not binding. These after all include judges' discussion of the inherent values of the law, their weighing of principles, and indeed their attempts to formulate principles hitherto more implicit than explicit in the law. Much legal argument concerns matters such as these, and the absence of strictly binding force in such *dicta* is irrelevant to their broader value as an element in legal discourse.

[421] On *obiter dicta* which make otherwise unremarkable cases memorable, see J. A. Jolowicz, 'Les décisions de la Chambre des Lords' (1979) 31 *Revue internationale de droit comparé* 521, 533–4.

cases quite often enjoy iconic status, indeed, not because of their *rationes*, but because of the impact of *dicta* contained within them. Lord Atkin's statement denouncing the majority's interpretation of regulation 18B of the Defence (General) Regulations 1939 in *Liversidge* v. *Anderson* (1942) was clearly not necessary to the House of Lords' decision[422] – not only was Atkin dissenting, but the Lord Chancellor, Viscount Simon, had written to Atkin before delivery of the House's judgment suggesting that Atkin remove the passage from his speech for fear that it might offend the other law lords.[423] Yet, that passage, besides being the most memorable aspect of *Liversidge*, came to be regarded as the correct interpretation of the relevant law.[424]

Some *dicta* come to be accepted not as authoritative interpretations of law, as were Atkin's arresting remarks in *Liversidge*, but – because they provide persuasive answers to unsettled legal points – as de facto

[422] *Liversidge* v. *Anderson* [1942] AC 206, 244–5.

> I view with apprehension the attitude of judges who on a mere question of construction when face to face with claims involving the liberty of the subject show themselves more executive minded than the executive ... In this case I have listened to arguments which might have been addressed acceptably to the Court of King's Bench in the time of Charles I ... The words [in regulation 18B: i.e., 'reasonable cause to believe any person to be of hostile origin or associations or to have been recently concerned in acts prejudicial to the public safety or the defence of the realm'] have only one meaning ... They have never been used in the sense now imputed to them ... I know of only one authority which might justify the suggested method of construction: 'When I use a word,' Humpty Dumpty said in a rather scornful tone, 'it means what I choose it to mean, neither more nor less'.

See also Essay II (Section 8).

[423] See R. F. V. Heuston, '*Liversidge* v. *Anderson* in Retrospect' (1970) 86 *LQR* 33, 43–4.

[424] See, e.g., *Nakkuda Ali* v. *Jayaratne* [1951] AC 66, 76–7 *per* Lord Radcliffe; *IRC* v. *Rossminster* [1980] AC 952, 1011 *per* Lord Diplock ('The time has come to acknowledge openly that the majority of this House in *Liversidge* v. *Anderson* were expediently and, at that time, perhaps excusably, wrong and the dissenting speech of Lord Atkin was right'); *R* v. *Home Secretary ex p Khawaja* [1984] AC 74, 110 *per* Lord Scarman ('The classic dissent of Lord Atkin ... is now accepted as correct not only on the point of construction of regulation 18(b) of the then Emergency Regulations but in its declaration of English legal principle'); Bingham, *The Business of Judging*, 220 ('Lord Atkin was correct in his essential argument on the meaning of the words used in ... Regulation 18B'). For a contrarian perspective, see Lord Denning, *Landmarks in the Law* (London: Butterworths, 1984), 231–3.

common-law rules.[425] In *Hedley Byrne* v. *Heller*, the House of Lords established that damages for financial loss caused by negligent misrepresentation can be recovered in tort.[426] It did so by issuing, in the words of one legal commentator, 'fifty pages of *dicta*' to the effect that the House 'would have found the defendants liable *if* they had not been bankers, *if* they had been negligent, and *if* they had not disclaimed responsibility'.[427] Seen from this perspective, *Hedley Byrne* is a particularly radical example of *obiter dictum* accepted as common law: the opinions of the House of Lords were immediately regarded as having overruled a decision of the Court of Appeal.

More typically, *dicta* accepted as common-law rules, rather than becoming precedents straight away, gradually acquire lives of their own as authoritative statements of general legal principle. Another famous speech by Lord Atkin in another landmark case, *Donoghue* v. *Stephenson*, yields the *ratio* in its penultimate paragraph.[428] But the passage, early in the speech, in which he poses the rhetorical question, 'Who, then, in law is my neighbour?'[429] – a passage which was to prove pivotal to the subsequent development of the law of negligence – is not part of that *ratio*.[430] Denning J's *dicta* in *High Trees* – the ones which Megarry was

[425] See, e.g., *Richardson* v. *Pitt-Stanley* [1995] QB 123, 134–5 *per* Sir John Megaw; *Palatine Graphic Arts* v. *Liverpool CC* [1986] QB 335, 343 *per* Glidewell LJ; *Third Chandris Shipping* v. *Unimarine SA* [1979] QB 645, 650 *per* Mustill J ('[M]any of the observations put forward [by the Court of Appeal in *Rasu Maritima SA* v. *Pertamina* [1978] QB 644 on the availability of *Mareva* injunctions] are in theory *obiter dicta*, but they have always been regarded as authoritative statements of principle, and they have governed the exercise of the discretion in all subsequent cases').

[426] *Hedley Byrne* v. *Heller & Partners Ltd* [1964] AC 465 (overruling *Candler* v. *Crane, Christmas & Co* [1951] 2 KB 164 (CA)).

[427] D. M. Gordon '*Hedley Byrne* v. *Heller* in the House of Lords' (1965) 2 *Univ. British Columbia L. Rev.* 113, 114 (emphases in original). See also Wolfgang Friedmann, 'Limits of Judicial Lawmaking and Prospective Overruling' (1966) 29 *MLR* 593, 605.

[428] *Donoghue* v. *Stevenson* [1932] AC 562, 599:

> a manufacturer of products, which he sells in such a form as to show that he intends them to reach the ultimate consumer in the form in which they left him with no reasonable possibility of intermediate examination, and with the knowledge that the absence of reasonable care in the preparation or putting up of the products will result in an injury to the consumer's life or property, owes a duty to the consumer to take that reasonable care.

[429] Ibid. at 580.

[430] That the passage is not part of the *ratio* is evident from the headnote: see Lord Hodge, 'The Scope of Judicial Law-Making in the Common Law Tradition', speech delivered to the Max Planck Institute for Comparative and International Private Law, Hamburg, 20 October 2019, www.supremecourt.uk/docs/speech-191028.pdf, para. 13 (accessed

minded to label 'judicial' – are similarly illustrative in this regard. So too is what is commonly referred to as 'the rule in *Wheeldon* v. *Burrows*'.[431] In *Wheeldon* v. *Burrows* (1879), *T* owned two adjoining plots of land, one of which was eventually sold to the plaintiff, *W*. The plot retained by *T* enjoyed the benefit of – but *T* had not, at the point of conveyance to *W*, reserved for his plot a right to the enjoyment of – light which passed through windows on *W*'s land and onto *T*'s. *T* subsequently transferred his plot to the defendant, *B*, whereupon *W* boarded over the windows on his own land (through which had passed light which benefited the land now owned by *B*). When *B* removed the boards, *W* successfully sued him for trespass, the Chancery Division of the Court of Appeal holding that *B* had no right to the light from *W*'s windows because there had been no express or implied reservation of such a right when *T*'s conveyance to *W* took place. But what the Court held in *Wheeldon* v. *Burrows* is not what is remembered as the rule in *Wheeldon* v. *Burrows*. That so-called rule, concerning the implied continuation of quasi-easements and contained in a passage of Thesiger LJ's judgment, is technically *obiter*.[432] It is perhaps surprising that 'an *obiter dictum* ... in *Wheeldon* v. *Burrows*' should have settled 'so important a matter as [that] a right of way should be capable of being granted merely by implication in a modern conveyance', Peter Gibson LJ remarked in 1994, 'but Thesiger LJ's proposition has been accepted as correctly stating the law and cannot now be doubted'.[433]

5 April 2020); also Rupert Cross and J. W. Harris, *Precedent in English Law*, 4th ed. (Oxford: Clarendon Press, 1991), 43–5.

431 See, e.g., *Sovnots Investments* v. *Secretary of State for the Environment* [1977] QB 411, 438; *Simmons* v. *Dobson* [1991] 1 WLR 720, 722; *Alford* v. *Hannaford* [2011] EWCA Civ 1099 at [29]–[30] *per* Patten LJ; A. W. B. Simpson, 'The Rule in *Wheeldon* v. *Burrows* and the Code Civil' (1967) 83 *LQR* 240; John West, '*Wheeldon* v. *Burrows* Revisited' [1995] *Conveyancer* 346, 346 ('The rule in *Wheeldon* v. *Burrows* continues to flourish like the proverbial green bay tree. Conveyancers ignore it at their peril').

432 *Wheeldon* v. *Burrows* (1879) 12 ChD 31, 49. The rule, summarized, is that where *A* holds title to land and transfers part of the land to *B*, and *B* informally grants *A* an easement (or quasi-easement) burdening *B's* land and benefiting *A*'s retained plot, then, if *B* subsequently transfers his land to *C*, the easement will still be implied in favour of *A*'s plot so long as (i) *A*'s use of the easement has been continuous and apparent since when he owned all of the land and (ii) the easement is necessary to the reasonable enjoyment of the plot which *A* has retained.

433 *Wheeler* v. *Saunders* [1996] Ch 19, 30–1 (case decided December 1994). Consider also *Twinsectra* v. *Yardley* at [77]–[103] *per* Lord Millett. A charge secured for a specific purpose which gives the lender beneficial entitlement to the repayment of all of the loan plus interest – what English lawyers think of as a *Quistclose* trust – was originally explained by Lord Wilberforce as involving two trust elements: a primary trust for the

The reception of these iconic *dicta* indicates that the judiciary sometimes moves gradually towards accepting particular *obiter* observations as having the status of common-law rules without any judge ever having recommended, or any court having resolved, that this is how the observations should be regarded. But do English judges ever follow the path taken by some of their American, Australian, and Canadian counterparts and deliberately elevate a *dictum* so that it might be treated like precedent? The history of *obiter dicta* in the English courts, it was observed in Section 3, is partly a story about how slightly bolder claims seem to be made in the name of *dicta* from one legal generation to the next. We know, furthermore, that modern judges have not been entirely averse – indeed, over time, seem to have become less averse – to declaring particular *dicta* to carry such weight as to be precedential authority in all but name.

When judges conceive of *dicta* in this way, they do not always understand the *dicta* to be *obiter dicta*. They may be distinguishing, perhaps only implicitly, *dicta* which are *obiter* from *dicta* which are not. The term '*dictum*', it is important to bear in mind, is sometimes used simply to denote 'something that the judge said' – something that need not have been *obiter* but could have been part of the *ratio*. In 1904, Bucknill J professed to be 'accepting ... *dictum*' presented in an 1897 judgment by the President of the Probate, Divorce, and Admiralty Division 'as binding'.[434] But it was the President's decision, not one of his *obiter* observations, that the judge followed. '[T]he *dictum* in *Cook* v. *Ipswich Local Board*, of Blackburn J, ... I think ... is binding on us', Denman J maintained in *Shanklin* v. *Millar* (1880). But the statement which he

purpose of yielding interest and a secondary trust in favour of the lender: *Barclays Bank* v. *Quistclose Investments Ltd* [1970] AC 567, 579–82. But if this is what a *Quistclose* trust was, it could not be a valid trust, for it contained – in the form of its first element – a trust which, being for a non-charitable purpose, offended against the beneficiary principle. In his dissenting speech in *Twinsectra*, Lord Millett, revisiting an argument which he had first advanced in a law review article some seventeen years earlier (P. J. Millett, 'The *Quistclose* Trust: Who Can Enforce It?' (1985) 101 *LQR* 269), dealt with this objection by suggesting that the *Quistclose* trust was a single trust – the borrower holding money on trust for the lender throughout the loan period – with the borrower having a power to use the money for a stipulated purpose. Lord Millett's analysis of the *Quistclose* trust has subsequently been endorsed by the courts in preference to Lord Wilberforce's (see, e.g., *Bellis* v. *Challinor* [2015] EWCA Civ 59 at [53]–[54]), even though Millett, unlike Wilberforce, pronounced *obiter* on the matter. See also Dennis R. Klinck, 'Recharacterizing the *Quistclose* Trust: Lord Millett's *Obiter Dicta* in *Twinsectra*' (2005) 42 *Canadian Business LJ* 427.

434 *Wyke* v. *Wyke* [1904] P 149, 154.

considered binding was not *obiter dictum*: '[i]t was directly applicable in *Cook* v. *Ipswich Local Board*', Denman elaborated, and so 'is as applicable to this case as to that'.[435] In *Natwest* v. *Halesowen* (1972), Lord Kilbrandon professed to have found 'an ample number of expressions of judicial opinion … lending support to' a particular answer to a question which he raised in the course of his speech; 'whether [these expressions are] *obiter dicta* or not', he added, 'seems immaterial'.[436] But the question was one which Kilbrandon had himself raised *obiter*. It is not clear that he would have considered the *obiter* status of the opinions yielding the answer to be immaterial had answering the question been necessary to the court's decision.

Not until some time after 1900 do English judges start seriously to entertain the possibility that particular *obiter* observations might bind as a precedent would bind. In the nineteenth century it was highly unusual – though, as we have seen, not unheard of – for a judge to intimate that courts might sometimes have reasons to treat a *dictum* like a precedent. But by the early decades of the following century, the law reports begin to yield obvious instances of lower court judges considering themselves constrained to follow *obiter dictum* emanating from higher courts when the *dictum* squarely addresses a legal matter not yet resolved by common law or statute. The judge's standard refrain – encountered already[437] – was that the observations might be *obiter*, but, considering the position or status of the court (or judge, or judges) responsible for them, and given the absence of an applicable primary source, I had better follow them as I would a precedent. '[T]hose statements in the judgments of those two learned judges [Esher MR and Lopes LJ] were *dicta* in the sense that they were not necessary for the determination of that case', Farwell J observed in 1935, 'but they are *dicta* which I think I ought to follow'.[438] Forty years later, Dunn J would refer to *obiter dicta* of Denning

435 *Shanklin* v. *Millar* (1880) 5 CPD 272, 278. (Lopes J also characterized Blackburn's remarks as *dictum* but, perhaps because it was '*dictum* with which I do not hesitate to agree' (ibid. at 279), he left the assertion as to its binding force unchallenged.) In a similar vein, see *R (Salford Estates)* v. *Durham CC* [2012] EWHC 2512 (Admin) at [15] *per* Richardson J.

436 *National Westminster Bank Ltd* v. *Halesowen Presswork and Assemblies Ltd* [1972] AC 785, 822.

437 See, e.g., *Gibson* v. *Gibson*, 388 *per* Atkin J and *Mills* v. *London CC*, 224 *per* Shearman J, as considered in Section 9.

438 *Tees Conservancy Commissioners* v. *James* [1935] Ch 544, 560. See also *Re Debtors* [1936] Ch 622, 625 (Bankruptcy Registrar reported as having considered it his 'duty to act in accordance with' *obiter dicta* which had been presented in the Court of Appeal and the

MR's in almost exactly the same way.[439] By this point, lower-court deference to the weight of *dicta* was not at all uncommon.[440] Even though there was a precedent available in *Northern RHA* v. *Crouch* (1984), Browne-Wilkinson LJ chose not to follow it because it was unpublished, it was not supported by any other legal decisions, and there was a body of judicial *dicta* contradicting it. While 'there is no authority directly in point (apart from … [one unreported High Court] decision …) which shows that the view I have adopted is wrong', he concluded, 'the weight of judicial *dicta* supports me in the view that … there are overwhelming reasons why [the sub-contractor] should not be prevented from pursuing its arbitration … Accordingly … [the appeal for] a stay of the arbitration proceedings … should be dismissed'.[441] In *Sayce* v. *TNT* (2011), as we saw in Section 6, Moore-Bick LJ maintained that when the *obiter dictum* of a higher court judge settles a question of legal principle, lower court judges ruling on facts to which that question is relevant ought to follow and apply the *dictum*, even if they are not technically bound by it.[442] Whereas Browne-Wilkinson seemed not to stray beyond the fairly familiar proposition that there are instances when a judge might opt to follow weighty *dicta*, Moore-Bick was advancing a significantly stronger proposition: that following highest court *dictum* is sometimes expected.

Following the higher court *dictum* is expected, according to Moore-Bick, when the issue of principle to which the *dictum* speaks is untouched by precedent. But what if – as was the case in *Crouch* – there is a precedent, albeit a lower court precedent, with which the *dictum* is at odds? Might judges ever be expected to follow the *dictum* in preference to the precedent? It is a truism that, as between the two, precedent prevails. Although judges sometimes opt to follow *dicta*, it would be irregular for a judge to do so (as it was in *Crouch*) if precedent stands at variance with the *dicta*. Until very

House of Lords); also G. W. Paton and G. Sawer, '*Ratio Decidendi* and *Obiter Dictum* in Appellate Courts' (1947) 63 *LQR* 461, 475–6; and Note, '*Dictum* Revisited' (1952) 4 *Stanford L. Rev.* 509, 512.

439 'Counsel … submitted that the passages from the judgment of Lord Denning MR … should … be regarded as *obiter dicta* and not binding upon me. Even if that submission be right … I feel I should follow it [*sic*]'. *Woodcock* v. *South West Electricity Board* [1975] 1 WLR 983, 987.

440 See, e.g., *WEA Records* v. *Benson King* [1975] 1 WLR 44, 52 *per* Brightman J ('I think that I ought to follow the *obiter dicta* in the [Court of Appeal and House of Lords] cases to which I have referred').

441 *Northern RHA* v. *Derek Crouch Construction Co Ltd* [1984] QB 644, 668.

442 See also *Schroder* v. *Birmingham CC* [2014] EWHC 2207 (Admin) at [20] *per* Hickinbottom J ('[A]lthough Lord Millett's comments … might perhaps technically be *obiter dicta*, they are … comments from the highest court').

recently, furthermore, judges have never gone so far as to intimate that a court might in fact be obliged to follow *dicta* instead of precedent.

Yet there has, of late, been some shifting of the sands. Ever more often, judges can be seen contemplating instances in which following *dicta* in preference to precedent might be expected, or even required. Five years before the decision in *Sayce*, the then Chancellor of the High Court, Sir Andrew Morritt, noted that a Court of Appeal precedent on liability for knowing receipt was at variance with a law lord's *obiter dicta* on the same topic. The Court's precedent most likely prevailed, Morritt concluded, but 'given the weight to be attached to the *obiter dicta* . . . I should consider the position if I am wrong in concluding that I am bound by the [Court of Appeal's] decision'.[443] The threshold which Morritt thought about crossing was purportedly crossed by Turner J in *Youngsam* (2017) when, in the Administrative Court, he came 'to the firm conclusion that' although a 'broad statement of principle' which had been made by the then President of the Supreme Court was, 'strictly speaking, *obiter*', it 'was clearly intended to, and now ought to, be followed by all courts of inferior jurisdiction' in preference to applicable precedent.[444]

There was yet more movement six months later. In *Ivey* v. *Genting Casinos* (2017), Lord Hughes, writing for a unanimous Supreme Court, examined the two-stage test for dishonesty established by the Court of Appeal in *R* v. *Ghosh* (1982).[445] He concluded 'that the second leg of the test propounded in *Ghosh*' – whether the defendant was aware that honest and reasonable people would have regarded his behaviour as dishonest – 'does not correctly represent the law and that directions based upon it ought no longer to be given [by judges to juries]'.[446] The test, he maintained, is simply one of whether the defendant was dishonest according to the standards of honest and reasonable people. 'There is no requirement that the defendant must appreciate that what he has done is, by those standards, dishonest'.[447] In *Ivey*, the question for the Supreme

[443] *Charter* v. *City Index* [2006] EWHC 2508 (Ch) at [29].

[444] *Youngsam* (HC) at [40]. The following year, in *Sevilleja* v. *Marex Financial Ltd* [2018] EWCA Civ 1468, counsel for the appellant made a point of arguing that the Court of Appeal was still bound by its own decisions in instances where the decisions had subsequently been contradicted by *obiter dicta* emanating from the Supreme Court. Flaux LJ saw no need to resolve the argument, though he conceded that counsel had raised what had become an '[i]nteresting . . . question of precedent' (ibid. at [64]).

[445] *R* v. *Ghosh* [1982] QB 1053.

[446] *Ivey* v. *Genting Casinos (UK) Ltd* [2017] UKSC 67 at [74].

[447] Ibid. Lord Hughes was in effect displacing the second limb of the *Ghosh* test in favour of Lord Nicholls' reasoning in his judgment for the Judicial Committee in *Royal Brunei*

Court was whether the defendant had cheated within the terms of section 42 of the Gambling Act 2005. The statutory offence makes no reference to dishonesty, so there was no need for the Court to ask if the defendant had been dishonest. Indeed, '[t]he occasion for th[e] ruling [in *Ivey*] owed nothing to the facts of *Ghosh*'.[448] Lord Hughes's conclusion on the second limb of the *Ghosh* test was therefore *obiter*.

A week after the ruling in *Ivey*, a High Court judge maintained that he was still bound by precedent – by *Ghosh*.[449] A month after the ruling, another High Court judge maintained that he was now bound not by *Ghosh* but by Lord Hughes's *dicta*.[450] The question of which bound, the precedent or the *dicta*, was less acute a dilemma for the Court of Appeal: unlike the High Court, it could follow the *dicta* – thereby departing from one of its own precedents – without contravening the doctrine of *stare decisis*.[451] When the question eventually came to the Court of Appeal in *Barton* (2020), Burnett LCJ, delivering the Court's judgment, was in no doubt that its precedent had been superseded by Supreme Court *dicta*.

> The undoubted reality is that in *Ivey* the Supreme Court altered the established common law approach to precedent in the criminal courts by stating that the test for dishonesty they identified, albeit strictly contained in *obiter dicta*, should be followed in preference to an otherwise binding authority of the Court of Appeal . . . [W]e do not consider that it is for this court to conclude that it was beyond their powers to act in this way . . . [W]here the Supreme Court itself directs that an otherwise binding decision of the Court of Appeal should no longer be followed and proposes an alternative test that it says must be adopted, the Court of Appeal is bound to follow what amounts to a direction from the Supreme

Airlines v. *Tan* [1995] 2 AC 378, 389 and the endorsement of that reasoning by Lord Hoffmann in his judgment for the Judicial Committee in *Barlow Clowes International Ltd* v. *Eurotrust International Ltd* [2005] UKPC 37 at [15]. See *Ivey* v. *Genting* at [62].

448 *Ivey* v. *Genting* at [55].

449 *DPP* v. *Patterson* [2017] EWHC 2820 (Admin) at [16] *per* Sir Brian Leveson P ('These observations were clearly *obiter*, and as a matter of strict precedent the court is bound by *Ghosh*, although the Court of Appeal could depart from that decision without the matter returning to the Supreme Court').

450 *GMC* v. *Krishnan* [2017] EWHC 2892 (Admin) at [24]–[28] *per* Sycamore J. The same conclusion was reached in *Yussouf* v. *Solicitors Regulation Authority* [2018] EWHC 211 (Admin) at [65]–[67].

451 On the capacity of the Criminal Division of the Court of Appeal to depart from its own precedents, see *R* v. *Gould* [1968] 2 QB 65, 68–9 *per* Diplock LJ; also (on the Court of Appeal's overruling capacity more generally) *Davis* v. *Johnson* [1979] AC 264, 323–8 *per* Lord Diplock.

> Court even though it is strictly *obiter*. To that limited extent the ordinary rules of precedent (or *stare decisis*) have been modified.[452]

Burnett was, in essence, acknowledging an alteration to the rule of recognition. But the alteration, he appreciated, is modest. The default mantra of English judges is still that *dicta*, even weighty *dicta*, do not bind.[453] Instances in which *obiter dictum* is considered a material source of law are not only exceptional, furthermore, but are also distinguishable from the similar claims made for apex court *dicta* in other common law jurisdictions. The Australian High Court and the Canadian Supreme Court have maintained that lower courts should follow their considered *dicta* unless there is a compelling argument against doing so – the most obvious compelling argument being that a lower court's judgment, though at variance with the final court's *dicta*, is actually supported by authority. The conclusion about final court *dicta* reached by both Turner in *Youngsam* and Burnett in *Barton* is less expansive yet slightly more radical. Lower courts are bound not by final court *dicta* generally but rather only in those instances where the final court issues *dicta* on a specific point of law and clearly (and unanimously) intends that those *dicta* be treated as dispositive in the lower courts henceforth.[454] But when a final court produces *dicta* of this nature – super-*dicta*, as it were – a lower court must apply the *dicta* even if they are at variance with precedent.

The English case law points to another distinction. In *Ivey,* one court's *dicta* are pitted against, and have been considered to override, another court's *ratio*. Could the *dicta* have nullified the *ratio* had both come from the same court? In *Youngsam*, the 'broad statement of principle' with

[452] *R* v. *Barton* [2020] EWCA Crim 575 at [102]–[104].

[453] See, e.g., *Smyth-Tyrrell* v. *Sowden* [2017] EWHC 2331 (Ch) at [6] *per* Paul Matthews J ('I am not strictly speaking bound by *obiter dicta* from the Court of Appeal, though of course they are entitled very great respect'); *Joint Stock Co Aeroflot* v. *Leeds* [2017] 1 WLR 4537, 4541 *per* Warren J ('[A]n *obiter* conclusion, however persuasive, is not binding on a lower court and is one which a court of co-ordinate jurisdiction is free not to follow without needing to be satisfied that the conclusion is clearly wrong'); *Edwards* v. *Simey* [2018] EWCA Civ 1299 at [53] *per* Irwin LJ; *Barlow* v. *Wigan MBC* [2020] EWCA Civ 696 at [47] *per* Bean LJ.

[454] On the unanimity requirement, see *R.* v. *Barton* at [104] ('We emphasise that this limited modification [to the rule of recognition] is confined to cases in which all the judges in the appeal in question in the Supreme Court agree that to be the effect of the decision'); and *cf.* G. R. Sullivan and A. P. Simester, 'Judging Dishonesty' (2020) 136 *LQR* 523, 527 ('It is odd to think that, if a single member of the court sitting in *Ivey* had disagreed . . . *Ghosh* might still be with us'). It is in *Barton* that the unanimity requirement was introduced. Lord Hughes made no such stipulation in *Ivey.*

which Turner J was concerned had been formulated by Lord Neuberger in *Whiston* (2014). Although Neuberger's statement had not been necessary to the decision in *Whiston*, it was endorsed by Lords Kerr, Carnwath, Hughes, and (albeit subject to 'a note of caution about some of the reasoning') by Lady Hale.[455] The statement, Turner maintained, was 'emphatically and unreservedly intended to reverse' conclusions reached by law lords in two earlier judgments.[456] At least since the 1970s it has been accepted that '[i]t is not for any inferior court . . . to review decisions of th[e court of final appeal]',[457] and the decision in *Youngsam* abides by this stricture: '[w]here a majority of the [Supreme Court] Justices have in the clearest possible terms decided that one or more of its previous decisions are not to be followed', it is not open to a lower court 'to seek to emasculate the later decision by reanalysing the earlier case law and reaching a contrary view'.[458] For Turner, Neuberger's statement of principle in *Whiston*, along with the support it received from four other judges, is to be read as just such a decision – it binds as a precedent would bind because it is so clear and emphatic.

But if Neuberger's statement was *obiter dictum*, as Turner insisted it was, it could not – given that *obiter dicta* are statements tangential rather than integral to judicial decisions – be accurately characterized as evidence of the Supreme Court having decided to depart from some of its own precedents. The characterization would only be accurate if it could be shown that English lower courts accept that unequivocal, majority-supported *obiter dicta* emanating from a superior court can bind as decisions within decisions. The Administrative Court, in *Youngsam*, certainly could not ignore Supreme Court precedent. But was it bound to accept conclusions stemming from a review by the Supreme Court of some of the Supreme Court's own decisions if these conclusions were *obiter dicta*? Turner's answer – that, in *Youngsam*, the Administrative Court was required to follow such conclusions – is persuasive only if it is accepted that a final appeal court can issue *obiter* pronouncements to overrule its own binding authorities.

455 *R (Whiston)* v. *Secretary of State for Justice* [2014] UKSC 39. (For the note of caution, see ibid. at [51].)

456 *Youngsam* (HC) at [33]. The judgments being those of Lord Bingham in *R (West)* v. *Parole Board* [2005] UKHL 1 and Lord Brown in *R (Black)* v. *Justice Secretary* [2009] UKHL 1.

457 *Miliangos* v. *George Frank (Textiles) Ltd* [1976] AC 443, 496 *per* Lord Cross.

458 *Youngsam* (HC) at [39].

The difficulty with this answer was circumvented when *Youngsam* reached the Court of Appeal. *Obiter dicta* obviously do not bind, Leggatt LJ observed.[459] But Lord Neuberger's statement, he maintained, is not *obiter dictum*. Rather, it is '*Whiston's* … binding *ratio decidendi*'.[460] Nicola Davies LJ, delivering the main judgment, reached the same conclusion. Her reasoning was that the statement represented the *ratio decidendi* of the case' because 'the majority of the court treated' it 'as a necessary and decisive step in explaining their conclusion'.[461]

Leggatt studiously avoided this reasoning. To affirm Neuberger's statement as *ratio* by relying on the necessity test was, he thought, to create a hostage to fortune.[462] But how then, if not by reference to necessity, could the statement be classified as *ratio*? According to Leggatt, 'the *ratio*' of a case,

> is (or is regarded by the judge as being) part of the best or preferred justification for the conclusion reached: it is necessary in the sense that the justification for that conclusion would be, if not altogether lacking, then at any rate weaker if a different rule were adopted.[463]

As depictions of *rationes decidendi* go, this is perhaps a little too expansive. Judicial reasoning provided in the course of a decision, and which best fits the decision that is reached, will sometimes be *obiter dicta* – as is the case, for example, when the majority's opinion yields the *ratio* of a court's judgment even though superior reasoning in support

[459] *R (Youngsam)* v. *Parole Board* [2019] EWCA Civ 229 at [46] ('[I]t is axiomatic that only the *ratio decidendi* of a case has binding authority and that *obiter dicta* do not. That is the point of the distinction. The doctrine of precedent would be thrown into disorder if it were to be accepted that courts, even the Supreme Court, can in *obiter dicta* overrule otherwise binding decisions').

[460] Ibid. at [68].

[461] Ibid. at [25].

[462] Ibid. at [49].

> '[T]he reference to "a necessary step" in reaching that conclusion … is ambiguous. The word "necessary" is capable of bearing a range of meanings. On one view, it might be taken to suggest that a proposition of law cannot constitute a *ratio* unless it can be said that, had the court not endorsed that proposition, the court would have reached a different result. Yet such a test does not work. For example, it quite often happens that a judge gives rulings on two (or more) separate points of law, either of which would by itself be sufficient to justify the judge's conclusion. It is generally accepted that in such cases each ruling can have the status of *ratio* although it is manifest that the judge would still have reached the same conclusion even if that ruling were reversed'.

[463] Ibid. at [51].

of the judgment is contained in a concurring opinion (Leggatt's own concurring opinion in *Youngsam* is arguably a case in point). Lord Neuberger's statement of principle in *Whiston* should be regarded as *ratio*, according to Leggatt, because it meets with some of the considerations which seem pertinent for the purpose of identifying a *ratio*: in particular, it is a statement which takes account of relevant earlier authorities, which was intended to settle a point of law, and which has not been challenged or qualified in any subsequent case.[464] But these qualities could equally attach to an *obiter dictum*.[465] The conclusion that Neuberger's statement was not *obiter* is not easily squared, furthermore, with an argument which Neuberger himself advanced only months before *Youngsam* was heard in the Administrative Court: that if the Supreme Court is to overrule a precedent, a panel of Justices constituted to hear an appeal has to 'decide that the earlier decision . . . was wrong'.[466] It seems a mischaracterization of his statement in *Whiston* to call it an actual judicial decision to depart from earlier decisions.

Bolder statements might well have been made in the name of *obiter dicta* from one legal generation to the next, but only very exceptionally, and only recently, have judges in English courts seriously countenanced

[464] See ibid. at [60]–[61].

[465] According to Leggatt,

> 'relevant considerations include: (1) the degree of unanimity or consensus among the judges (assuming there was more than one) who decided the precedent case; (2) the clarity or otherwise of the ruling and of the supporting reasoning; (3) whether or to what extent the point on which the court ruled was in dispute and/or the subject of argument; (4) whether or how clearly the court evinced an intention to establish a binding rule; (5) whether and to what extent prior relevant authorities were considered by the court; (6) whether the court would, or sensibly could, have reached the same result if it had not ruled as it did; (7) whether the court's ruling has been applied or approved in later cases; (8) whether the ruling or its underlying reasoning has been criticised by commentators or by judges in later cases; (9) whether the court considered or contemplated the factual situation that has arisen in the current case; and (10) the level in the court hierarchy of the court which decided the precedent case in comparison with the level of the court deciding the current case.'

Ibid. at [59]. The list is not supposed to be exhaustive, and there is no suggestion that a minimum number of these considerations has to be satisfied (or that particular considerations must be satisfied) in order for a statement to qualify as a *ratio decidendi*. Qualification would therefore seem to be in the eye of the beholder, though no doubt judges will often agree – or not significantly disagree – over these (and other) considerations and how they ought to be taken into account.

[466] *Willers* v. *Joyce* [2016] UKSC 44 at [21].

the proposition that, sometimes, *dicta* should be formally binding. Should we expect them to become bolder still? It is difficult to imagine judges venturing much further in this direction, because there are numerous compelling and interlocking reasons for not according *dicta* the status of a material source of law. The concept of *obiter dictum*, we have seen, constrains the lawmaking function of the judge – it is a concept on which judges themselves rely to indicate that particular judicial pronouncements (their own or someone else's) are not to be treated as part of the common law. Removal of this constraint, Lord Salmon once ventured, 'might well lead to chaos'.[467] The initial reaction in the High Court to Lord Hughes's *dicta* in *Ivey* certainly indicated confusion: how could the Court follow the *dicta* without refusing to apply binding authority? If a *dictum* is binding, it becomes subject to the norms of *stare decisis*: judges have to be confident as to the circumstances in which it applies, which courts are bound by it, and when precedent takes (assuming precedent sometimes will take) priority over it.[468] It is impossible to know, at this juncture, if we are on the cusp of an era in which the English courts become reconciled to super-*dicta*. But if we are, it will surely be incumbent on the higher courts, when issuing these *dicta*, to instruct the lower courts on where the *dicta* are to be followed, and, when they are to be followed, to make it clear which authority, or line of authority, has been overruled.

Salmon, when referring to chaos, was contemplating a bleaker scenario: one in which the common law ends up arbitrary as well as indeterminate. If all considered *dicta* could bind as law – if they could have precedential authority (in accordance with the status of the court delivering the judgment containing the *dicta*) even though the issue on which they bear did not arise in the case in which they were delivered – judges could make law in the abstract. A tentative observation could be legally conclusive even though it might not have been argued or investigated in the case in which it was offered; it could be binding authority without anybody having seriously considered what the consequences of the pronouncement being binding authority might be. Judges, particularly judges in the Supreme Court, would be able to produce *dicta* resolving a legal point before any litigant had the opportunity to argue it. Even the judges themselves might be surprised, perhaps occasionally aghast, to

467 *Sakhuja* v. *Allen* [1973] AC 152, 201.

468 Furthermore, the judge who produces the *obiter* but binding pronouncement will want, yet might find it very difficult, to ensure that it does not conflict or compete with other judges' *obiter* but binding pronouncements.

find their past *per le voy* remarks being made to bind as would a carefully wrought *ratio decidendi.* To the consternation of defeated litigants, observations buried in obscure cases could turn out to settle legal liabilities. If the change to the rule of recognition were prospective, past *dicta*, no matter how weighty, would still only be persuasive authority, whereas future, sometimes relatively unimpressive, *dicta* could be binding authority. Yet if the change were to apply to all *dicta*, a person who chose to forgo litigating, because *dicta* did not bind (and only *dicta* supported his case) at the point when his opportunity to litigate arose, might feel cheated on seeing today's litigant succeed by relying on the very sources that were insufficient to sustain his grievance. If the English courts do become more relaxed about the delivery of super-*dicta*, the judges in the highest of those courts will probably need to think carefully about how super they might ever want their *dicta* to be.

12 The Sources Problem

In English law, indeed in any common law system, the instances in which *obiter dictum* is on a par with *ratio decidendi* are exceptional. We do know, nevertheless, that the epistemic authority of *dictum* will sometimes be such that it pulls the levers, as it were, providing the reasons which enable a court to determine that the law relevant to the case should apply in a particular way. There clearly are instances, furthermore, in which courts treat *dicta* as capable of performing as understudies to primary sources – as opinions which can be made to step into a legal void when those sources cannot fill it. Even if we discount those unusual modern instances in which *dicta* are said to bind, therefore, is there not something amiss about the conclusion that *obiter dicta* can only have secondary status? This conclusion, favoured by François Gény (Section 1), was disputed by one of Gény's contemporaries, Theodor Kipp: although '[o]ne speaks about sources of law in a double sense', as 'sources of formation and sources of knowledge', Kipp wrote in 1896, it is important to treat the two types of source as interconnected (*in Verbindung miteinander*).[469] From Kipp's perspective, we would do better to think of primary and secondary legal sources as occupying a continuum rather than as contained in two separate columns, and to acknowledge that some weighty *dicta* might be located closer to the primary rather than to the secondary end of the range.

[469] Theodor Kipp, *Quellenkunde des Römischen Rechts* (Leipzig: Deichert, 1896), 1–2.

This way of thinking about *obiter dicta* has not been lost on comparative lawyers. While *obiter dicta* can be counted among the judicial 'propositions about law that ... rank among the legal formants of a system',[470] Rodolfo Sacco maintains, it is important to draw a 'distinction between those legal formants that are themselves rules of conduct and others that are developed in order to provide ... justifications of rules and conduct'.[471] *Obiter* propositions, though they 'can affect the way in which the operational rules ... are understood and interpreted',[472] are not themselves 'operative rules',[473] according to Sacco, but rather are, at most, 'justifications ... for rules'.[474] While other modern comparative lawyers have been largely receptive to Sacco's notion of legal formants, they have also tended to emphasize that, within a legal system, the status of a formant (source) may change over time and that, among legal systems, the status of particular sources can differ – sometimes quite radically.[475] The judges and lawyers of system *A* may have little regard for foreign precedents as persuasive authorities while routinely according weight to *obiter dicta*, whereas the judges and lawyers of system *B* might barely conceive of *obiter dicta* but regularly turn for legal insight and assistance to the superior court judgments of particular foreign jurisdictions. *Obiter dictum* has never had much significance in some legal systems, while in other legal systems – the English legal system being a case in point – not only might *dictum* be seen to bear weight but judgments as to how much weight it can bear might alter throughout legal generations. It is perhaps not surprising that, from a comparative law perspective, the image of *dicta* occupying a continuum – inconsequential asides at the one end, binding *obiter* pronouncements at the other – holds some appeal.

470 Rodolfo Sacco, 'Legal Formants: A Dynamic Approach to Comparative Law' (pt. I) (1991) 39 *Am. J. Comparative Law* 1, 31.

471 Ibid. at 34.

472 Ibid. at 31.

473 Ibid.

474 Ibid. at 30.

475 See, e.g., Stefan Vogenauer, 'Sources of Law and Legal Method in Comparative Law', in *The Oxford Handbook of Comparative Law*, ed. M. Reimann and R. Zimmermann (Oxford University Press, 2006), 869–98 at 885 ('In most legal systems, ... the conventions as to the determination of the sources of law are far from settled ... Domestic lawyers learn to discern the different strength of the various formants, that is, the difference in weight that is accorded to the respective sources, by years of training and experience. To acquire this ability ... is one of the greatest challenges the comparative lawyer faces when he encounters another system'); also John Bell, 'Sources of Law' (2018) 77 *CLJ* 40, 49.

Not that one need turn to comparative law to unearth doubts over the notion that primary and secondary legal sources are distinct entities. The rule of recognition reveals nothing about *obiter dictum* – it is not supposed to reveal anything about *obiter dictum* – apart from its status as a legal source. Yet that it will tell us even this much is not always guaranteed. We know that a judgment could bind as precedent even though, judged by the necessity test, everything contained within it is technically *obiter*; or that a court might apply a weighty *dictum* in preference to a precedent. It is all very well to point out – as we have (Section 7) – that Hart did not discount the possibility of a test of legal validity being a source of disagreement, being misapplied, or being misunderstood. But if the test is unreliable – if it determines that certain judicial pronouncements do not bind the courts and yet the courts decide on the basis that they do – it is perhaps not the rule of recognition that provides an insight into *dicta*, but rather *dicta* that offer a rather sobering lesson about the rule of recognition.

The lesson itself – that the Hartian version of the rule of recognition inordinately constricts the domain of primary legal sources – is familiar to contemporary legal philosophers. No textbook account of legal positivism would be complete if it did not include the classic Dworkinian critique of Hart's jurisprudence: that a test of validity which focuses on pedigree cannot accommodate principles among the sources of law.[476] The jurisprudential perspective known as legal pluralism is, at core, a plea for a more capacious approach to the identification of legal sources, so that more or less any norms which citizens identify as rules governing their behaviour – including rules enforced by private organizations – might be recognized as binding law.[477] A different critique again can be

[476] See Dworkin, *Taking Rights Seriously*, 39–41.

[477] See, e.g., Brian Z. Tamanaha, *Realistic Socio-legal Theory: Pragmatism and a Social Theory of Law* (Oxford: Clarendon Press, 1997), 116–21; *A General Jurisprudence of Law and Society* (Oxford University Press, 2001), 138 ('Hart's concept of law has been adopted by many "legal pluralists", who assert that society consists in a multitude of "legal" institutions with rule-making and rule-enforcing power, from corporations to universities, to community associations, to sports leagues'), 194 ('*Law is whatever people identify and treat through their social practices as "law"* . . . [T]he distinctive content of particular manifestations of law are determined by the social actors who give rise to them, not by theorists legislating for others based upon an abstract conception of the essential requirements of a singular phenomenon they designate as law') (emphasis in original); Emmanuel Melissaris, *Ubiquitous Law: Legal Theory and the Space for Legal Pluralism* (London: Routledge, 2009), 126 ('[U]nder my argument the concept of law is significantly expanded. Legality can now be discovered everywhere'), 152 ('I see the law as ubiquitous because its sources are to be found in all instances and contexts of people's

attributed to those theorists who maintain that if courts develop the common law then, besides making decisions traceable to existing primary sources, they will generate new rule-formulations based not only on those sources but also on propositions about law expressed as *dicta*, or devised outside the courts, or even, in some instances, formulated entirely independently of legal institutions and communities.[478] According to Frederick Schauer, 'the realm of legitimate legal sources' within a jurisdiction changes – tends to expand – over time, so that, for example, a source once only ever treated at 'authoritative guidance' might be elevated (or occasionally elevated) so that it 'counts as a valid source of law', or the courts begin to treat as epistemic legal authority information which would once have been unequivocally categorized as 'nonlegal'.[479] The rule of recognition comes up short if there are instances in which a source once never identified as binding law now sometimes is identified thus, but there is no criterion of validity making it possible to say exactly when this source is to be identified thus. *Obiter dictum* would seem to be such a source.

This all rather suggests that the history of *dicta* teaches us to beware accepting the thesis that legal systems have rules of recognition. The example of the English legal system, however, shows this to be a simplistic conclusion. Certainly the thesis would be undermined if

association with each other . . . [and] because it governs almost all instances of our lives'). The theorist who is perhaps most often credited for instigating this way of thinking eventually came to concede that there is a difference between a system of law and a system containing law-like rules: compare John Griffiths , 'What Is Legal Pluralism?' (1986) 24 *Journal of Legal Pluralism* 1, 39 ('A situation of legal pluralism . . . is one in which law and legal institutions are not all subsumable in one "system" but have their sources in . . . multifarious social fields . . . so that the "law" which is actually effective . . . is the result of . . . complex . . . patterns of competition, interaction, negotiation, isolationism, and the like') with John Griffiths, 'The Idea of Sociology of Law and its Relation to Law and to Sociology' (2005) 8 *Current Legal Issues* 49, 63–4 ('A few years ago I decided to take advantage of the freedom to define . . . I proposed that "law" should be considered the name of a dimension of variation in social control . . . The proposal . . . encountered . . . withering criticism . . . [F]urther reflection . . . has led me to the conclusion that . . . [s]ociology of law can best be simply considered the study of social control . . . It . . . follows . . . that the expression "legal pluralism" can and should be reconceptualized as "normative pluralism" or "pluralism in social control"').

[478] For the classic modern formulation of this thesis, see Melvin Aron Eisenberg, *The Nature of the Common Law* (Cambridge, Mass.: Harvard University Press, 1991), 154–7.

[479] Frederick Schauer, 'Law's Boundaries' (2017) 130 *Harvard L. Rev*. 2434, 2457; and see also Schauer, 'Authority and Authorities', 1960–1; and Frederick Schauer and Virginia J. Wise, 'Nonlegal Information and the Delegalization of Law' (2000) 29 *Jnl Leg. Studs* 495.

judges subscribed to the proposition that some *dicta* bind as law despite the absence of criteria determining when *dicta* will bind as law. But they do not. When a *dictum* is treated as determinative on particular facts, judges identify reasons for according the *dictum* this status. The *dictum* is determinative because it could just as easily, and perhaps more sensibly, be categorized as one of two or more *rationes* derivable from a judgment, for example, or because the absence of an applicable primary source enables a court to choose to follow the *dictum*, or because an appeal court has settled that, on a particular point of law, its *dictum* is to be preferred over precedent. *Obiter dicta* pose a challenge for the rule of recognition. But it is important not to overestimate that challenge.

It is worth considering also, finally, how *obiter dicta* might sometimes bolster the claim that a legal system embodies standards of validity facilitating the identification of primary legal sources. One of the best-known modifications of Hart's account of the rule of recognition has it that official acceptance of criteria of legal validity may itself depend on judges providing reasons which not only justify the criteria but which also, at least tacitly, show judicial rulings to be in conformity with them.[480] These reasons will often be in the form of *obiter dicta* – observations made (but which did not have to be made) by judges in other cases, and which provide a judge deciding today's case with a justification for applying the law in a particular way. The rule of recognition, from this perspective, justifies a legal ruling not only because it identifies a source as applicable law but also because that law is understood to be underpinned by 'a broader body of reasoning' – some of which may be *dicta* – 'which draws on considerations lying outside the domain of reasoning that is bounded by the rule of recognition'.[481] While some instances of *dicta* pose a challenge to the rule of recognition, in other words, other instances – such as *obiter dicta* explaining how the law is to apply to specific facts – might be said to sustain the concept. Or rather, they sustain it so long as one conceives the rule of recognition to entail both the practice of identifying sources which count as law and the identification of reasons justifying the acceptance of those sources as rules applying to particular disputes in particular ways.

[480] See Neil MacCormick, *Legal Reasoning and Legal Theory*, rev. ed. (Oxford: Clarendon Press, 1994 [1978]), 138–40.

[481] N. E. Simmonds, *Law as a Moral Idea* (Oxford University Press, 2007), 131.

ESSAY II

Dissent

Introduction

'I have touched no question', Justice Benjamin Curtis observed in *Dred Scott* v. *Sandford*, 'which . . . it was not absolutely necessary for me to pass upon' in order 'to arrive at a judgment on the case at bar'.[1] Curtis's reasoning in *Dred Scott* might have been necessary to his own judgment – which was a dissenting opinion – but it was not necessary to the judgment of the United States Supreme Court. A dissenting opinion is, technically speaking, an *obiter dictum.* It is in the nature of an *obiter dictum* that it can be removed from the narrative of a case without the decision in the case being affected. Judges must therefore be pronouncing *obiter* when their contribution to the narrative takes the form of a dissent from the decision. As with *obiter dicta* in general, dissents are not law: '[t]hey have no legal effect in the cases in which they are given', even though they 'may be so obviously right that the courts or Parliament soon steer the law along a better path'.[2] Oliver Wendell Holmes's hypothetical 'bad man' would be not just bad but in all likelihood foolish, certainly reckless, were he to rely solely on dissents (or nearly any other *dicta*) as the source from which to work out the likely legal consequences of his contemplated actions.[3]

[1] *Dred Scott* v. *Sandford* 60 US (19 How.) 393, 633 (1857).

[2] Lord Nicholls, 'Foreword', in *Dissenting Judgments in the Law*, ed. N. Geach and C. Monaghan (London: Wildy, Simmonds & Hill, 2018), xiii.

[3] O. W. Holmes, Jr, 'The Path of the Law' (1897) 10 *Harv. L. Rev.* 457, 460; and see also Mark Tushnet, 'Why Dissent?', in *I Dissent: Great Opposing Opinions in Landmark Supreme Court Cases*, ed. M. Tushnet (Boston: Beacon Press, 2008), xi–xxvi at xiv–xv.

> 'Consider a case in which . . . [you, as a judge, dissent and] conclude that it is unconstitutional to send someone to jail for criticizing the government's policy in vigorous terms, and . . . [the judges that form the majority] conclude that convictions for that offense are perfectly constitutional . . . Suppose a bunch of people agree with you and act on that belief by making exactly the kinds of speech that led to imprisonment in the case . . . What's going to happen to them? In the short run – as long as you continue to be outvoted by your colleagues – they are going to prison'.

Yet there is little to be learned about judicial dissent if a dissent is understood to be but a species of *dictum*. The core attributes of dissent are not shared by, nor are the main questions prompted by dissent relevant to, other *obiter dicta*; indeed, the differences between dissent and other *dicta* are so marked that the concept of dissent and the concept of *obiter dicta* are normally distinguished. Whereas commentary on *dicta* is scant, there is an estimable body of literature attesting to a variety of perspectives on dissent. And while the production of *dicta* is much the same activity in any legal system where judges, when delivering judgments, are accustomed to making pronouncements not connected to the judgments themselves, the question of what it means for a judge to dissent – and of whether, indeed, a judge is allowed to dissent – within any particular system depends on how that system's appellate courts are organized and how those courts make decisions.

This second Essay, like the first, considers a legal concept as it features in English law. Jurisdictional comparisons have slightly more bearing on the concept of dissent than they do on the concept of *dicta*, however, because the meaning and significance (or insignificance) of dissent in any particular jurisdiction are to be understood in relation to the jurisdiction's adjudicative culture. Studies focusing on other court systems yield some interesting and important insights regarding understandings of judicial dissent, possible motives for dissenting, and how dissents are revealed (and whether revelation is preferable to suppression). They also help us to appreciate how judges' own estimations of the value of dissenting are affected by factors such as the size and composition of a court, the types of judgment that a court produces, the size of its caseload, the types of case that it hears, the vulnerability of its decisions to overruling, and whether it can review and invalidate legislation. Yet not only do these studies often need to be treated with circumspection even when considered in relation to the courts and court systems which inspired them, but they typically do not (and are not supposed to) cast any direct light – and might prompt inaccurate conclusions if it is presumed that they do cast direct light – on dissent as an English-court phenomenon. It should become ever more clear as this Essay progresses that dissent can be a difficult activity to bring into focus when, as is the case in the history of the English courts, the norm has not been for majorities to produce single judgments at which dissentients can take aim but rather for judges to deliver separate opinions from which a *ratio* has to be extracted. Even if a *ratio* can be readily extracted from the opinions that make for a court's judgment, a judge might be mistaken for a dissenter because her dissatisfaction with *dicta* delivered along the way is more immediately obvious, and perhaps more noteworthy, than her assent to the judgment's *ratio*. Anyone accustomed to reading English appeals cases not only knows that it is sometimes difficult to ascertain exactly why judges are dissenting or what they are dissenting against, but also might be forgiven for wondering, occasionally, if particular dissenters understood themselves to be dissenting when they delivered their opinions.

Perspectives on dissent, unlike perspectives on *dicta*, can differ quite markedly from one legal system to another. Much of the existing commentary on dissent concerns systems in which judges are forbidden from dissenting expressly, or in which a dissent is typically directed against the majority opinion of a court. Neither of these positions has ever been predominant in English law. The case was made in the first Essay that *obiter dicta* inevitably became a feature of English common-law decision-making once judges began routinely to produce judgments accompanied by reasons. But to claim that dissent was a similarly inevitable feature in the evolution of common-law decision-making would be incorrect. In some circumstances, the appellate judiciary was, and still is, prohibited from issuing dissenting opinions. While judges are accustomed to pronouncing *obiter*, furthermore, an opinion articulated specifically as a dissent is, for at least two reasons, a relatively infrequent occurrence. First, whereas judges can produce *dicta* whether sitting alone or with other judges, they can only ever dissent as members of panels.[4] (Judges sitting alone who renounce their earlier legal opinions in favour of new ones – '[t]he matter does not appear to me now', Bramwell B reflected in 1872, 'as it appears to have appeared to me then'[5] – are changing direction rather than dissenting from themselves.[6]) Secondly, a judge with dissentient inclinations will often avoid producing an unequivocal dissent and, instead, will dissent from only part of a *ratio*, or will deliver an opinion which amounts to a strongly qualified endorsement of the court's decision even though it contains no dissent. As often as not, this type of opinion will be a concurrence – one which (in its standard form)

[4] Though a dissenter might disagree with more than just the panel in preferring a different legal outcome. The panel might, for example, be affirming the decision of a lower court, and the dissent may be at variance with that as well.

[5] *Andrews* v. *Styrap* (1872) 26 LT 704, 706.

[6] For the *locus classicus* on judicial changes of direction, see *McGrath* v. *Kristensen* 340 US 162, 177–8 (1950) (Jackson J, concurring in a judgment which contradicted an opinion he had given when Attorney-General).

reveals a judge to be at variance with a majority over the right path to a conclusion but at one with the majority as to what the conclusion should be – though the categorization of concurrences makes, we will see, for a somewhat murky topic (Section 8).

The first half of this Essay concerns attitudes towards and norms governing dissent, and the prohibition of dissent, across various jurisdictions. There is no central message, perhaps other than that there are reasons to be wary of analyses of dissent which have central messages – messages such as that common law systems tolerate judicial dissent whereas civil law systems do not, that the primary purpose of judicial dissent is to spur legal development, or that judges who dissent are engaging in a distinctively democratic or in a future-oriented activity. Attitudes to dissent have to be understood – even this proposition, it is suggested in Section 5, can be overstated – as bound up with factors such as the status, composition, and case-load of a court and the general approach that the court takes to judgment delivery.

The second half of the Essay focuses specifically on the English appeal courts (along with the Judicial Committee of the Privy Council). There emerges from it an account of not so much judicial dissent in these courts as of an appellate judiciary which prefers unanimous and strong majority judgments, and of judges who are often (more often than is perhaps appreciated) forceful dissenters, but who have nevertheless shown themselves to be adept at delivering opinions which, though minority opinions, are more subtle or dexterous – sometimes more nebulous – than out-and-out dissents. When judges do dissent, their opinions might subsequently be relied upon, by judges and by counsel, as persuasive authorities. But there is a further dimension to the relationship between judicial dissent and legal authority (Section 9). Since dissent is at variance with rather than tangential to a majority's *ratio*, it is potentially authority-sapping as well as being a form of authority in its own right.

Judges, we will see, sometimes remark on how a precedent is regarded as vulnerable to overruling because it is attributable to a majority whose judgment prevailed over dissentient opinion by the slimmest of margins. It is not unknown for judges to question whether the law-altering power of bare judicial majorities ought to be confined. The Criminal Division of the Court of Appeal is subject to a statutory rule which makes the delivery of a dissenting opinion, and therefore a bare-majority decision, almost impossible. This rule, it is often asserted, was enacted out of concern for the sensitivities of defeated criminal appellants rather than the robustness of a court's precedents. As with some of the other claims to be considered in this Essay, the assertion seems somewhat questionable when subjected to close inspection.

1 Some Preliminary Observations on Dissent

This Essay concerns not dissent but judicial dissent. Before we turn specifically to judicial dissent, it is worth reflecting on some of the features of dissent as a general concept. Dissent is normally an action undertaken deliberately. But it is not the case, as some analysts of dissent contend,[7] that it is impossible to dissent unintentionally: some actions are interpreted as dissents, and may in context amount to dissents, even though the actors do not understand themselves to be dissenting when they act. Dissent does have to entail action in some form or another: one is not a dissenter simply by virtue of having the feeling of being in dissent from, or because one internally sympathizes with those who dissent from, a position taken by others. To act on dissentient feeling, however, is not necessarily to dissent. Indeed, judges in English appeal courts, we will see (Section 8), quite often set forth opinions underpinned by dissentient sentiments without going so far as to dissent.

Dissents relate to positions adopted or endorsed – even if only obliquely adopted or endorsed – by others. The so-called Rational Dissenters, for example, were dissenters not because they disagreed (though they did disagree) with William Blackstone, but because they took a stand against the position which Blackstone supported in the fourth book of the *Commentaries*: that, after the passing of the Toleration Act 1689, failure to conform to Church of England opinion remained a crime.[8] Dissenting is different from disagreeing in that I dissent *from* or *against* positions whereas I disagree *with* arguments in support of positions (I only ever dissent *with* in the sense that I agree with others that it is reasonable to dissent from or against a position). It is perfectly logical for me to say that I do not dissent from a position advocated by others and also that I disagree with them over the best way to argue in favour of it. That I dissent, furthermore, does not mean that I must agree with my fellow dissenters. One of the reasons that dissenting judges often produce separate rather than joint dissenting opinions is that their dissents come from different places.

[7] See, e.g., Ronald K. L. Collins and David M. Skover, *On Dissent: Its Meaning in America* (Cambridge University Press, 2013), at 3, 6–7, 11–12.

[8] See Anthony Page, 'Rational Dissent and Blackstone's *Commentaries*', in *Blackstone and His Critics*, ed. A. Page and W. Prest (Oxford: Hart, 2018), 77–96.

A position from which I dissent is likely to be an established one – typically a resolution, conclusion, or outcome. Analyses of dissent often present the dissenter as someone seeking to unsettle or subvert what has been established (or the source of authority for what has been established), and address not the dissent but the manner in which the dissent is expressed: the fact that it takes the form of, say, protest, or insurrection, or ridicule.[9] Resistance to or rejection of particular positions might involve but not be confined to dissent: the characterization of Mahatma Gandhi, Rosa Parks, or Thomas More as dissenters is not inaccurate but nor does it quite capture the dissident as well as dissentient nature of their oppositional actions.

The position against which a dissenter dissents will sometimes be interim or fluid rather than settled. In these instances the dissenter can, in one way or another, be understood to be contributing to a process leading to an outcome, and to be disapproving of a position on what the outcome should be. That position could, owing to the dissenter's initiative, end up being defeated. The dissenter might, like Henry Fonda's character in *12 Angry Men*, be able to persuade other participants in the process that they ought to abandon their initial position, or positions, in favour of another one. A settlement might accord with a dissent simply because a dissenter holds out, and the rules governing the settlement process require participant unanimity if anything other than the dissenter's preference is to prevail. The dissenter's preference could prevail because a favoured position is frustrated rather than defeated: an outcome might, for example, be impossible to implement (as when the chosen appointee turns down the job), so that the second-choice outcome – the dissenter's first-choice outcome – is implemented instead. It is not inconceivable that a dissent might itself be an established position. A dissenting opinion in the wider community might command a majority in a particular sphere or locality – in the church, say, or on the university campus – and advocates of that opinion will sometimes, by virtue of their local majority, be able to secure an outcome which the wider community must respect.[10] Even outside courts, a dissenter's position

[9] See, e.g., Ian Hislop and Tom Hockenhull, *I Object: Ian Hislop's Search for Dissent* (London: Thames & Hudson, 2018), which – reflecting the British Museum exhibition on which it is based – associates dissent with initiatives and artefacts which 'show people questioning the status quo and refusing to accept what they are being told' (ibid. at 12).

[10] See Heather K. Gerken, 'Dissenting by Deciding' (2005) 57 *Stanford L. Rev.* 1745. Consider, for example, the criminal jury as the locality and jury nullification as the dissent: that a defendant is clearly guilty of an offence punishable by statute, and that a judge has directed the jury to this effect, does not preclude the jury (unanimously rather than by majority) from finding the defendant not guilty. See, e.g., *R* v. *Ponting* [1985] Crim L R 318; *Re Randle and Pottle* [1991] 3 WLUK 375; and, for the general principle,

is more often than not defeated, and of judicial dissents it can always be said that they never carry the day in the cases in which they occur; in those cases, they always count as losses.[11] It would be wrong, however, to think that dissenters – judicial as well as other dissenters – never come out on top. The prime motivation for dissenting, indeed, may be the long game, and the conviction that coming out on top is a foreseeable result.

Even though a dissenting perspective will sometimes ultimately be the favoured perspective, the relationship between dissenters and dissented-against is, at the time when the dissent occurs, always asymmetric: the dissenters, at that point, occupy the underdog position (though they are not necessarily a numerical minority), whereas the dissented-against hold the upper hand. In certain contexts, the capacity to dissent is linked to role or status: a company's shareholders might be able to dissent from a proposal that a chief executive be awarded a pay rise, for example, but most likely the company's employees, and certainly members of the public, will be limited to expressing their displeasure at the award. (Whatever the context, expressions of dissent need not be manifest; indeed, they are likely to be concealed or coded when the costs of openly dissenting are high.)

Toleration of certain forms of dissent within systems and communities is often regarded positively. Those who refuse to countenance dissent, John Stuart Mill observed, forsake both the opportunity to reassess their own position in the light of a better-reasoned counterargument and the chance to present that position more convincingly when the counterargument is the weaker one.[12] Dissenters themselves,

Joshua v. *The Queen* [1955] AC 121, 130 (PC); *R* v. *Wang (Cheong)* [2005] UKHL 9 at [18] ('[T]here are no circumstances in which a judge is entitled to direct a jury to return a verdict of guilty'). The landmark decision is *Bushell's case* (1670) Vaugh 135.

11 Overruling is sometimes characterized as a species of judicial dissent. See, e.g., Katalin Kelemen, *Judicial Dissent in European Constitutional Courts: A Comparative and Legal Perspective* (London: Routledge, 2018), 6 ('When the reversal of a lower court's judgment is ... based ... solely on legal interpretation, the nature of disagreement ... does not differ substantially from other forms of judicial dissent'). But when an appeal court overrules a lower court, the overruling counts as a win (it defeats the lower court's judgment), whereas a judge's dissent is always a loss (it is defeated by the opinion of the court).

12

> '[T]he peculiar evil of silencing the expression of an opinion is, that it is robbing ... those who dissent from the opinion, still more than those who hold it. If the opinion is right, they are deprived of the opportunity of exchanging error for truth: if wrong, they lose, what is almost as great a benefit, the clearer perception and livelier impression of truth, produced by its collision with error'.

John Stuart Mill, 'On Liberty' (1859), in John Stuart Mill, *Three Essays* (Oxford University Press, 1975), 5–141 at 24.

furthermore, are often cast (as often as not retrospectively rather than contemporaneously) in a favourable light: as exposers of misfeasance, opponents of injustice, speakers of truth to power, challengers of institutional complacency, and so on.[13] Yet dissent, as a form of behaviour, bears various negative connotations. A dissenter might be the fly in the ointment, thwarting the outcome desired by a majority. Even when a majority outcome prevails, a dissent might weaken it: the people affected by the outcome may have been reconciled to it more easily, for example, had those responsible for it been unanimous. Dissenters are sometimes considered curmudgeons, or troublemakers, or even rule-breakers (as when an expression of dissent is slanderous or amounts to civil disobedience). Just as some dissenters are lauded as courageous, so too others are castigated for being irresponsible, hostile, egotistical, or petulant: sporting and military bodies sometimes attach disciplinary sanctions – fines, points-deductions, discharge, and so on – to displays of dissent. It is certainly not unknown for dissenters to acknowledge – many famous judicial dissents bear this out – that agreement on an outcome is the ideal, and that their having felt moved to dissent, being indicative of a sub-optimal outcome, is a matter for regret.[14] At the beginning of a decision-making process, members of the group responsible for reaching the decision are unlikely to contest a statement from the chair that it would be desirable if consensus could be reached on what should be decided. But these members would probably think it eccentric or even perverse

[13] See, e.g., Neil A. Hamilton, *Rebels and Renegades: A Chronology of Social and Political Dissent in the United States* (New York: Routledge, 2002).

[14] See, e.g., *Shaw* v. *DPP* [1962] AC 220, 272 *per* Lord Reid ('I have had the advantage of reading the speech about to be delivered by my noble and learned friend Lord Tucker, but I regret to say that I find myself in fundamental disagreement with it. I must therefore state my reasons with some particularity'); *Lochner* v. *New York* 198 US 45, 74–5 (1905) (Holmes J) ('I regret sincerely that I am unable to agree with the judgment in this case, and that I think it my duty to express my dissent'); *Ross* v. *The King* (1922) 30 CLR 246, 256 *per* Isaacs J ('I deeply regret there should be any division . . . [b]ut as the conclusion I have formed is clear and distinct, . . . I take the liberty of stating my reasons explicitly'); also O. W. Holmes to Harold J. Laski, 8 June 1930, in *Holmes-Laski Letters: The Correspondence of Mr Justice Holmes and Harold J. Laski 1916–1935*, 2 vols., ed. M. DeWolfe Howe (Cambridge, Mass.: Harvard University Press, 1953), II, 1258–9 ('I regret being called the dissenting Judge in the papers for I don't like to dissent'); Louis Blom-Cooper and Gavin Drewry, *Final Appeal: A Study of the House of Lords in its Judicial Capacity* (Oxford: Clarendon Press, 1972), 83 ('[T]he most apparently poignant judicial tragedy in a legal system . . . is the formal dissenting judgment').

were the chairperson to declare that it would be unfortunate if dissent were not to emerge among the group.

2 The Nature of Judicial Dissent

Judicial dissents share many of the features of other forms of dissent. But it would be wrong to think that they have no unique characteristics. And it would certainly be a mistake to presume that the same characteristics are ascribed to judicial dissents from one legal system to the next. Throughout European systems alone, a range of expressions is used to refer to dissenting opinions – expressions which put various slants on what it means for judges to dissent.[15] In German legal doctrine, a dissent may be referred to either as a special opinion (*Sondervotum*) or as a minority opinion (*Minderheitsvotum*), though in the judgments of the Federal Constitutional Court they are called divergent opinions (*abweichende Meinungen*).[16] In Italy's Constitutional Court, a dissenting opinion is an *opinione dissenziente*.[17] But in various Italian regional civil courts before unification, a dissent was a *voto di scissura* – a vote indicating that the judges involved in a decision had an irreconcilable difference of opinion.[18] In Spanish, a dissenting opinion is a *voto particular disidente* or *discrepante*, the word '*particular*' indicating that disclosure of the opinion is exceptional and subject to the agreement of

[15] See Kelemen, *Judicial Dissent in European Constitutional Courts*, 6.

[16] See Frank Halle, 'Sondervotum und Separate Opinion im Rechtsvergleich', in *Verfassungsrichter. Rechtsfindung am US Supreme Court und am Bundesverfassungsgericht*, ed. B. Großfeld and H. Roth (Münster: Lit, 1995), 141–50 at 141–4; Wolfgang Heyde, *Das Minderheitsvotum des überstimmten Richters* (Bielefeld: Gieseking, 1966), 50–1; Kelemen, *Judicial Dissent in European Constitutional Courts*, 85–6. In decisions of the European Court of Human Rights, a dissent is an *opinion individuelle*, though art. 48 § 2 of the Convention refers to '[a]ny judge' of the Court being 'entitled to deliver a separate opinion', and Rule 74 § 2 of the Rules of Court states that '[a]ny judge . . . shall be entitled to annex to the judgment either a separate opinion, concurring with or dissenting from that judgment, or a bare statement of dissent'.

[17] See Lucia Corso, 'Opinione dissenziente, interpretazione costituzionale e costituzionalismo popolare' (2011) 38 *Sociologia del diritto* 27, 34–6.

[18] See Vittorio Denti, 'Per il ritorno al "voto di scissura" nelle decisioni giudiziarie', in *Le opinioni dissenzienti dei giudici costituzionali ed internazionali*, ed. C. Mortati (Milan: Giuffrè, 1964), 1–20. The *voto di scissura* would not always be published. Nineteenth-century Neapolitan court rules provided that parties to a case could consult the text of a dissent only if they obtained permission from the minister of justice (ibid. at 4). Tuscan civil procedure established in 1771 provided that judicial dissents could be recorded as footnotes to the court's opinion (ibid. at 5).

the entire court.[19] Portuguese judicial convention characterizes the dissent as a vanquished vote (*voto de vencido*).[20] English-speaking lawyers in common law systems refer to judges either offering 'dissenting opinions' or 'dissenting'. It is perfectly understandable that the terms should be used synonymously, for while it is not uncommon (even if it is sometimes bewildering)[21] that common-law judges involved in cases should state no more than that they concur with the decisions in those cases, it is highly unusual – though not unheard of – for judges to dissent from decisions without offering reasons for doing so.[22]

It is sometimes argued that external communication is integral to judicial dissent: that one cannot speak meaningfully of a judge dissenting if, despite her disagreement with other members of the court over how a case should be decided, the disagreement is concealed and the majority's opinion is presented as the court's unanimous opinion.[23] This is certainly not an argument to be dismissed summarily. Consider the case of the judge who confesses extrajudicially that a decision in which she participated was not to her liking but, because the decision had to be unanimous, there was nothing she could do but join with the opinion of the court. Lord Wright appeared to offer such a confession in 1955 in his tribute to a Canadian judge who, eighteen years earlier, had produced an opinion which Wright now revealed he had considered correct but which the Judicial Committee of the Privy Council – on which Wright had sat and which, until 1966, forbade publication of dissenting opinions – had

[19] See Francisco Javier Ezquiaga Ganuzas, *El voto particular: Estudio introductorio* (Madrid: Centro de Estudios Constitucionales, 1990), 94.

[20] See Heyde, *Das Minderheitsvotum des überstimmten Richters*, 49; António Lopo Martinez, 'Voto de vencido: causas e aversão. Uma análise dos votos de vencidos no Tribunal Constitucional português' (2018) 67 *Scientia Iuridica* 21.

[21] See Roderick Munday, 'Judicial Configurations: Permutations of the Court and Properties of Judgment' (2002) 63 *CLJ* 612, 646–8.

[22] For examples, see the second part of Roderick Munday's two-part essay, 'Reasoning Without Dissent; Dissenting Without Reason' (2004) 168 *Justice of Peace Notes* 968, 991. During his time as a Justice of the United States Supreme Court, William O. Douglas regularly took what has been described as an 'utterly reckless' approach to dissenting in tax cases: there are numerous instances in which he 'alone dissented, and dissented without explanation, without a word'. Bernard Wolfman, Jonathan L. F. Silver, and Marjorie A. Silver, 'The Behavior of Justice Douglas in Federal Tax Cases' (1973) 122 *Univ. Pennsylvania L. Rev.* 235 at 272, 328. See *Angelus Milling Co* v. *Commissioner* 325 US 293, 299 (1945); *Bulova Watch Co* v. *United States* 365 US 753, 761 (1961); *Healy* v. *Commissioner* 345 US 278, 285 (1953); and *Commissioner* v. *Estate of Noel* 380 US 678, 684 (1965), where, in each case, it is simply reported that 'Mr Justice Douglas dissents'.

[23] 'The public character [of judicial dissent] is essential. Otherwise, like the proverbial tree that falls in the forest, dissent won't make a noise'. Collins and Skover, *On Dissent*, 21.

overruled.[24] Wright's revelation is often referred to as a de facto judicial dissent.[25] But he was neither dissenting nor admitting 'that he had dissented',[26] for the Judicial Committee had decided – had no choice but to decide – unanimously. Wright was intimating, rather, that he disagreed with the Judicial Committee's decision, and that he might have articulated this disagreement as a dissent had it been permissible to do so.[27]

Dissent cannot be identified as a feature of judicial practice when a court, or court system, is effective in enforcing a convention of keeping judicial deliberations entirely secret, for the convention makes it impossible to establish if judges, when deciding cases, ever express dissenting opinions privately to other judges involved in those cases. In France from the mid-fourteenth century until the early years of the Revolution, judges were subject to a duty ('imposed . . . as a sacred rule . . . by the oath taken when entering into office')[28] to

24 Lord Wright, 'Rt Hon. Sir Lyman Poore Duff, G.M.C.G.: 1865–1955' (1955) 33 *Can. Bar Rev.* 1122. The essay is an obituary for the judge whose Canadian Supreme Court decision was overruled by the Judicial Committee in *Attorney-General for Canada* v. *Attorney-General for Ontario* [1937] AC 326. The case concerns s. 92 of the British North America Act 1897, which assigned matters of 'property and civil rights' exclusively to the legislatures of Canada's provinces. Lord Atkin (delivering the Judicial Committee's judgment) argued that because these matters were assigned thus, they could not be the responsibility of the dominion, which meant that the dominion was not entitled to enact legislation implementing the labour provision in the conventions of the International Labour Organization of the League of Nations (as established under the Labour Part of the Treaty of Versailles 1919), and so the dominion had no authority to enact minimum wage legislation. Wright, who was a member of the overruling panel, made it clear that he thought 'the Privy Council, speaking through Lord Atkin', had interpreted the British North America Act incorrectly (Wright, 'Rt Hon. Sir Lyman Poore Duff', 1126–7).

25 See, e.g., B. J. MacKinnon, Letter to the Editor (1956) 34 *Can. Bar Rev.* 115, 116 ('Lord Wright's apparent dissent'); John Alder, 'Dissents in Courts of Last Resort: Tragic Choices?' (2000) 20 *OJLS* 221, 236 n. 67 ('what amounted to a dissent'); Michael Kirby, 'Judicial Dissent – Common Law and Civil Law Traditions' (2007) 123 *LQR* 379, 396 n. 48 ('a kind of dissent').

26 Peter W. Hogg and Ravi Amarnath, 'Why Judges Should Dissent' (2017) 67 *UTLJ* 126, 132 ('[I]n 1955, Lord Wright . . . disclosed . . . that he had dissented').

27 The pre-1966 single opinion rule makes it impossible to know if Wright disagreed with the Judicial Committee's decision when it was made, or if he only came to disagree with it subsequently. Compare F. R. Scott, 'Labour Conventions Case: Lord Wright's Undisclosed Dissent?' (1956) 34 *Can. Bar Rev.* 114, 115 with Edward McWhinney, 'Labour Conventions Case: Lord Wright's Undisclosed Dissent?' (1956) 34 *Can. Bar Rev.* 243, 243 ('An alternative explanation of Lord Wright's remarks may be . . . that he originally endorsed the opinion of the Privy Council . . . as written by Lord Atkin, but that he has since changed his mind').

28 Manuel-Achille Baudouin, 'Le secret du délibéré et le droit de defense' (1908) 23(1) *Journal des Parquets* 34, 44.

keep all deliberations secret.[29] It is not inconceivable that these deliberations would sometimes result in judges dissenting from the majority of the court. But since deliberations were always kept secret, we cannot be sure that they ever did.

Yet it would be an error to conclude that a judge cannot be said to be dissenting if the dissent is not made public. Consider Spain's judicial system, which, unlike the French system, once adhered to a principle of partial as opposed to complete secrecy: from the fifteenth century to the late twentieth, the Spanish judicial convention was to tolerate expressions of dissent but to require that records of any such expressions be kept confidential (*reservado*).[30] Keeping a dissent confidential did not mean entirely suppressing it: if a decision involving dissent was appealed, the dissenting opinion (or opinions) would be made available to the superior court and to the parties to the case on appeal.[31]

The *voto reservado* illustrates how judges can sometimes be said to have dissented even though the records of the cases in which the dissents occur provide no evidence of them being at odds with the rulings; there are judicial dissents in these cases, but they are stifled by the courts. Other adjudicative cultures provide examples of cases where the dissent is stifled not by the court but by the dissentient, or would-be dissentient, judge. When Louis Brandeis drafted a dissenting opinion he was often, in the first instance, happy to circulate it only among his colleagues on the Supreme Court. If he was convinced that the content, or at least some of the content, of his opinion would be taken on board by the author of the Court's opinion, or if he concluded that delivering the dissent would do more harm than good, he would forgo publishing it.[32] The consequence of Brandeis stifling his dissent is that he did not dissent. It is also possible

[29] According to Baudouin (ibid. at 45–9), the duty originated in a decree issued by Philippe V in 1320 (renewed by Philippe VI in 1344) and endured until 1791, when a law was passed lifting the ban on public deliberations in criminal trials. Two years later, this law was extended so as to apply to all judicial proceedings.

[30] The tradition of the reserved dissenting vote began with the Ordinance of Medina 1489. While the Ordinance allowed judges to write opinions separate from a court's judgment, it provided that the opinions could not be published alongside the judgment but rather had to be recorded in a separate book which was kept secret. See Ganuzas, *El voto particular*, 65. The tradition came to an end in 1985, since when judges in both the ordinary courts and the Tribunal Constitucional have been able to produce separate dissenting or concurring opinions which appear alongside judgments.

[31] See Ganuzas, *El voto particular*, 91–2.

[32] See Philippa Strum, *Louis D. Brandeis: Justice for the People* (Cambridge, Mass.: Harvard University Press, 1984), 369 ('[H]e held his fire when a dissent might hurt his bargaining position; and he used the threat of a dissent as a way of "lobbying"'); Paul A. Freund,

for a judge actually to dissent but to stifle it. Although the rules of the Permanent Court of International Justice permitted dissenting opinions, its judges would occasionally refrain from publishing such opinions for fear of offending other members of the Court. When these judges nevertheless wanted to make sure that their colleagues knew what they thought, they would file their opinions with the unpublished but circulated minutes of the Court's deliberations.[33] In 1970, Germany's Federal Constitutional Court started to allow its judges to publish dissenting opinions. While it is standard practice for those judges to circulate such opinions among colleagues, however, publication is exceptional.[34] There is nothing unintelligible about the proposition that a judge has dissented even though the dissent remains internal to the court.

Transparency in dissent – whether dissent generally or judicial dissent specifically – is a complicated subject. There are, first of all, degrees of transparency. A panel, having made a decision about me, could be open about the fact that, among the decision-makers, there was dissent over the

'Justice Brandeis: A Law Clerk's Perspective' (1978) 68 *American Jewish History* 7, 10–12; John P. Frank, Book Review (1957) 10 *J. Leg. Educ.* 401, 401.

> 'Justice Brandeis used opinions as other men use memoranda. If he wished to persuade his brethren, he occasionally prepared a formal opinion for circulation to the other Justices, and sometimes the turn of events was such that he had no occasion to use it further. Either his views might prevail with someone else writing the opinion of the Court, or, if he was unsuccessful, he might conclude to swallow his dissent'.

33 See Edward Dumbauld, 'Dissenting Opinions in International Adjudication' (1942) 90 *Univ. Pennsylvania L. Rev.* 929, 943. The Permanent Court of International Justice existed from 1922 to 1946. According to Dumbauld, a Court resolution of 1926 brought the practice of filing dissents with the minutes to an end.

34
> 'The well-settled tradition of the Court is to speak as an institution and not as a panel of individual justices . . . Dissenting justices – even if they have circulated written dissents inside the court – usually choose not to publish them or to be identified as dissenters, at least partly out of a sense of institutional loyalty. The prevailing norm seems to be that personalized dissenting opinions are proper only when prompted by deep personal convictions'.

Donald P. Kommers and Russell A. Miller, *The Constitutional Jurisprudence of the Federal Republic of Germany*, 3rd ed. (Durham, NC: Duke University Press, 2012), 28–9. By no means is the norm respected absolutely. Willi Geiger, who served on the Court's second senate from 1951 to 1977, published his dissents as a book: *Abweichende Meinungen zu Entscheidungen des Bundesverfassungsgerichts* (Tübingen: Mohr (Siebeck), 1989). Even before 1970, judges were known to leak dissents to the public. See Philip W. Amram, 'The Dissenting Opinion Comes to the German Courts' (1957) 6 *Am. J. Comparative Law* 108; E. J. Cohn, 'Dissenting Opinions in German Law' (1957) 6 *ICLQ* 540.

outcome. It could be more open still by telling me who dissented. And it could be even more open by letting me know not only who dissented but also what their reasons for dissenting were. How much of this openness I will welcome, indeed whether I will welcome any of it, will depend on the nature and the context of the decision. If the decision about me is adverse, perhaps I will find some comfort in learning that the panel was not unanimous in deciding to turn me down. If the decision can be appealed, it might be to my advantage to know who dissented and what the reasons for dissent were. But if the decision is final, my learning anything about the dissent, even the very fact that there was dissent, might serve only to aggravate me. Parties unconnected to a decision might value transparency in dissent when the decision sets a precedent which could be directed against them: in the event that the precedent is applied against them and they wish to challenge it, it may be to their benefit that they can identify the dissenters and that they have a grasp of the dissentient reasoning. When a decision does not set a precedent, however, both the subject of the decision and those who dissent from it might query the wisdom of revealing that dissent occurred, let alone who dissented and why. Both the successful job applicant and the employees who interviewed her (and are about to become her colleagues) will likely prefer a simple communication of the outcome rather than an indication that the outcome was not unanimous.

Decision-making bodies sometimes conceal internal dissent so as to try to prevent their authority being undermined by external dissent. The principle of collective ministerial responsibility – that ministers must, apart from when a government waives the principle, either resign or face dismissal if they choose to dissent publicly from Cabinet decisions – was once a strategy for dealing with dissent from the Crown. 'It was important to show a united front to the King', according to one constitutional historian, 'because Ministers needed his assent to their measures'.[35] Although the principle has been rendered somewhat fragile of late (and although expressions of dissent from the Crown are no longer an issue),[36] the rationale in support of it still holds good: a Cabinet makes decisions on which individual ministers can often be expected to hold different views – views which, were

[35] G. H. L. Le May, *The Victorian Constitution: Conventions, Usages and Contingencies* (New York: St Martin's Press, 1979), 104.

[36] See Rodney Brazier, *Constitutional Practice: The Foundations of British Government*, 3rd ed. (Oxford University Press, 1999), 143–58. The fragility of the principle was compounded between 2017 and 2019, when a fractured Conservative Party without a working majority had to try to implement a referendum result narrowly favouring the United Kingdom's exit from the European Union.

they to be aired publicly, would enable ministers to dissociate themselves from unpopular policies on which they dissented and which would very likely render the government weak in the face of political opposition. An appellate court can, as compared with a ministerial body, afford to be more tolerant of open dissent among its members because its decisions are not being constantly challenged by the equivalent of an adversary court which would happily see not just the appellate court's decisions undermined but the court's decision-making power removed.

A judicial dissent which is revealed is a dissent made public, but it is not necessarily published. Judges in cases before the International Court of Justice (ICJ) explicitly dissent when they exercise their statutory right to deliver separate dissenting opinions.[37] Sometimes, however, their dissents are not manifest but only discoverable by inference. ICJ judges are permitted but not obliged to provide reasons for dissenting; in some cases they will not produce dissenting opinions, but will nevertheless be known to have dissented because they are not listed among the judges who form the majority.[38] The practice of some courts is to publish dissenting opinions anonymously, or to vest responsibility for formulating them in the judge who writes for the majority (who might also remain anonymous), so as to make it evident that there was dissent but difficult or impossible to discover who was dissenting.[39]

The activity of dissenting might not be entirely transparent even when judges' dissenting opinions are published and attributed. We will see in Section 8 that *seriatim* judgments – ones which are composed of a collection of (typically) individual judicial opinions and which yield no single majority opinion – sometimes contain decidedly oblique dissents, or

[37] Statute of the International Court of Justice (1945), art. 57 ('If the judgment does not represent in whole or in part the unanimous opinion of the judges, any judge shall be entitled to deliver a separate opinion').

[38] International Court of Justice, Rules of Court (1978), art. 95(1) ('The judgment ... shall contain ... the number and names of the judges constituting the majority'). Judges who wish to dissent without providing reasons are entitled, but not obliged, to record their dissents as formal declarations (art. 95(2)).

[39] For German examples, see Kelemen, *Judicial Dissent in European Constitutional Courts*, 85–7; and Jörg Luther, 'L'esperienza del voto dissenziente nei paesi di lingua tedesca' (1994) 25 *Politica del diritto* 241. In Greece, where the publication of dissenting opinions concerning constitutional and other legal matters is compulsory (Constitution of Greece, art. 93(3)), the identity of dissenting judges is not disclosed and a dissenting opinion is written not by the dissentient but by the judge who writes the opinion of the court (Kelemen, *Judicial Dissent in European Constitutional Courts*, 91). According to Luther ('L'esperienza del voto dissenziente', 248), it is conceivable that a dissenting judge in the German Federal Constitutional Court could write the opinion for the majority.

opinions which are close to being but are not quite dissents. Some opinions may be dissents notwithstanding that they contain passages endorsing elements of the majority's reasoning. An opinion might form part of the court's decision, conversely, yet contain a secondary dissenting element – such as when a judge concurs with the majority on the *ratio* but dissents on the appropriate allocation of costs.[40] The dissenting judges in a case sometimes divide into those who dissent entirely from the court's judgment and those who dissent only in part.[41] Dissenters in a case could be the numerical majority but they might disagree among themselves, so that the *ratio* of a decision is settled by the opinions of a minority on the court.[42] There are instances, furthermore, when an opinion's status as a dissent, rather like a *dictum*'s status as *obiter*, is attributable to its reception – as is the case, for example, when a court is unanimous as to what its order should be but one of the judges differs so fundamentally with the majority over some aspect of the judgment that his opinion is commonly treated as a dissent.[43]

[40] See, e.g., *Reynell* v. *Sprye* (1849) 8 Hare 222, 222 *per* Knight Bruce LJ. For a modern example, see *R* v. *Waya* [2012] UKSC 51 at [82]–[125] where Lords Phillips and Reed concurred with the other seven justices in ruling to quash a confiscation order against the defendant but were 'fundamentally at odds' (ibid. at [86]) with the majority's decision to substitute the quashed order for a recalculated one.

[41] See, e.g., *Bank Mellat* v. *HM Treasury (No. 2)* [2013] UKSC 39, where it was held 5:4 that a restriction imposed by the Treasury on the bank was unfair and also 6:3 that the Treasury acted unfairly in not giving the bank notice of its intention to impose the restriction. Only four of the judges agreed with the decision in its entirety. Two of the remaining five agreed that there had been procedural unfairness, one thought that there had been only substantive unfairness, and two were in complete dissent from the decision.

[42] *Neville* v. *London 'Express' Newspaper Ltd* [1919] AC 368, in which Finlay LC's opinion was held to settle the point of law at issue because two of the law lords dissented with one aspect of it and two dissented with another, has been considered to be such a case – see Robert Megarry, *A Second Miscellany-at-Law: A Further Diversion for Lawyers and Others* (London: Stevens & Sons, 1973), 69 – though the decision is recorded as held by a 3:2 majority and is perhaps best understood as one which came down on the side of the two law lords whose position Finlay preferred.

[43] This is true of Lord Steyn's opinion in *R* v. *Mirza* [2004] UKHL 2, for example, in which he joined the majority in dismissing the appeal but dissented on the question of whether the common law rule on secrecy of jury deliberations meant that evidence of what happened among the jurors always had to be inadmissible in court. In the official law report he is referred to as 'dissenting in part' – (2004) 1 AC 1118, 1119 – though his opinion has been considered an all-out dissent: see, e.g., Nicola Monaghan, 'Protecting the Secret Deliberations of the Jury in the Interests of Efficiency – Has the Law "Lost its Moral Underpinning"?', in Geach and Monaghan (eds.), *Dissenting Judgments in the Law*, 343–62 at 362 ('the dissenting opinion of Lord Steyn should be followed rather than the opinion of the majority'). The difference from the majority need not be fundamental: see, e.g., Brice Dickson and Conor McCormick, 'Northern Ireland Dimensions to the First

Judges and legal commentators tend to be interested not so much in the complexities associated with the notion of transparent dissent as in the question of whether transparency is best embraced or abjured: when multimember courts deliver judgments, should judges be allowed to speak for themselves or should they be obliged to speak as one? There is a tendency to distinguish civil law and common law thinking on this matter. Civil law courts are presumed to favour unanimous judgments and common law courts to be more tolerant of judges producing their own (concurring as well as dissenting) opinions. Common lawyers tend to regard the publication of dissent as 'an inescapable feature of judicial independence from one's colleagues', one former Australian judge has written, whereas among civil lawyers 'dissent is regarded as functionally incompatible with the performance by the courts of their essential role in deciding important matters of dispute'.[44] In the United States, the distinction has sometimes been presented in a markedly less neutral fashion. According to one mid-twentieth-century US law professor, 'in contrast with some less fortunate portions of the world, we still insist on public administration that will stand the light of day . . . In judicial administration the concurring or dissenting opinion is simply a part of the light of day'.[45] In 1962, the renowned New York State Court of Appeals judge, Stanley Fuld, remarked on how 'our judges possess a lot more intestinal fortitude, tougher hides, if you will, than their brethren in Europe'.[46]

American veneration of the judicial culture which tolerates open dissent, and disapproval of that which stymies it, is perhaps only to be expected: a judge's right publicly to express dissent from one's colleagues (which is not equivalent to a judge having a right to have the dissent published as a separate opinion alongside a majority judgment) is an obvious example of freedom of speech protected under the First Amendment.[47] Yet instances of veneration can raise wry smiles even

Decade of the United Kingdom Supreme Court' (2020) 83 *MLR* 1133, 1151 where a *dubitante* position (see Section 8) is categorized as '[t]actical dissenting'.

44 Kirby, 'Judicial Dissent – Common Law and Civil Law Traditions', 384.

45 Richard B. Stephens, 'The Function of Concurring and Dissenting Opinions in Courts of Last Resort' (1952) 5 *Univ. Florida L. Rev.* 394, 399.

46 Stanley H. Fuld, 'The Voices of Dissent' (1962) 62 *Columbia L. Rev.* 923, 923.

47 See William O. Douglas, *Points of Rebellion* (New York: Random House, 1970), 1 ('All dissenters are protected by the First Amendment'); Steven H. Shiffrin, *Dissent, Injustice, and the Meanings of America* (Princeton, NJ: Princeton University Press, 1999), 11 ('[D]issent . . . serves to consolidate the values ordinarily associated with the First Amendment'); Collins and Skover, *On Dissent*, 114. According to Little, 'the First Amendment can support at most only a right for judges to express and publicly *note* their dissents, not an additional right to

among American lawyers, for resistance to dissenting is hardly unknown in the US courts. Under the direction of Marshall CJ – and to Thomas Jefferson's dismay – the early-nineteenth-century Supreme Court jettisoned the English *seriatim* style and accepted as normal practice the delivery of single opinions by one Justice (more often than not Marshall himself) speaking for the entire Court.[48] Unanimity in decision – although by no means the near-strict unanimity of the Marshall era – remained more or less the norm until the early 1940s.[49] US judges and lawyers from the late-nineteenth through to the mid-twentieth century often strongly disapproved of judicial dissent,[50] and would occasionally go so far as to endorse the proposition that publication of dissents should be legally prohibited.[51] In 1955, one notoriously truculent appellate judge, Musmanno J, brought an action against the very

publish their rationales for dissenting . . . [T]he First Amendment is generally held not to require the government to subsidize publication of speech'. Rory K. Little, 'Reading Justice Brennan: Is There a "Right" to Dissent?' (1999) 50 *Hastings LJ* 683, 699 (emphasis in original). Though arguably, he adds, the right to publish rationales is constitutionally guaranteed under Article III (ibid. at 700–1).

48 See Melvin I. Urofsky, *Dissent and the Supreme Court: Its Role in the Court's History and the Nation's Constitutional Dialogue* (New York: Pantheon, 2015), 44–9; G. Edward White, 'The Working Life of the Marshall Court, 1815–1835' (1984) 70 *Univ. Virginia L. Rev.* 1, 34–47; M. Todd Henderson, 'From Seriatim to Consensus and Back Again: A Theory of Dissent' [2007] *Supreme Court Rev.* 283, 311–21; John P. Kelsh, 'The Opinion Delivery Practices of the United States Supreme Court 1790–1945' (1999) 77 *Washington Univ. L. Q.* 137, 143–6. When Marshall was away from the Court or had recused himself, Justices would occasionally revert to the *seriatim* style (see ibid. at 144). For Jefferson's dislike of unanimous opinions, see Thomas Jefferson to William Johnson, 27 October 1822, in *The Works of Thomas Jefferson*, 12 vols., ed. P. L. Ford (New York: Knickerbocker Press, 1905), XII, 246–52 at 250 ('For nobody knows what opinion any individual member gave in any case, nor even that he who delivers the opinion, concurred in it himself . . . [H]aving been done in the dark it can be proved to no one').

49 We will see in Section 5 that departure from the norm is often thought to have begun in 1941, when Harlan Fiske Stone became Chief Justice.

50 See, e.g., Henry Wollman, 'Evils of Dissenting Opinions' (1898) 57 *Albany LJ* 74, 75 ('Nothing of any benefit can be gained by a dissenting opinion'); William A. Bowen, 'Dissenting Opinions' (1905) 17 *Green Bag* 690, 693 ('[T]he dissenting opinion is of all judicial mistakes the most injurious'); Walton R. Moore, 'The Habit of Dissent' (1922) 8 *Virginia Law Register* 338, 341 ('The outstanding objection to the habit of dissent is that it weakens and injures the Court with the public'); Ben W. Palmer, 'Dissents and Overrulings: A Study of Developments in the Supreme Court' (1948) 34 *ABAJ* 554, 554 ('The prestige of the Court is threatened, if it has not already been seriously impaired, by recent divisions of opinion'); also Robert Post, 'The Supreme Court Opinion as Institutional Practice: Dissent, Legal Scholarship, and Decisionmaking in the Taft Court' (2001) 85 *Minnesota L. Rev.* 1287 at 1348–9, 1356–7, 1360.

51 As indeed they were in Louisiana's Supreme Court from 1898 to 1921: see Stephens, 'The Function of Concurring and Dissenting Opinions', 400.

court on which he sat when it refused to publish one of his dissenting opinions.[52]

It would be incorrect to detect a rigid distinction between civil law and common law attitudes to dissent. Courts in civil law jurisdictions, we have seen, sometimes allow the publication of dissents. Common law courts – as will become clear when we turn our attention to the English appellate jurisdiction – sometimes forbid it. Just as it is not unheard of for common-law judges to uphold the civil lawyer's preference for unanimous judgments as a virtue, furthermore, civil lawyers can occasionally be found arguing that judges in a jurisdiction's ordinary courts should be allowed to write concurring and dissenting opinions.[53] Although, in some legal systems, dissenting opinions are considered to be a sign of 'democracy and liberty', the Italian jurist, Mauro Cappelletti, wrote in the early 1960s, the ordinary courts of Italy and other major European countries have never been inclined to this view, preferring instead a 'system of collegiality . . . which in our courts acquires, all too often, the character of pure (but cumbersome and costly!) formality'.[54]

[52] The action was unsuccessful. For Musmanno's own account of the episode, see Michael A. Musmanno, 'Dissenting Opinions' (1956) 60 *Dickinson L. Rev.* 139. (See also the tale of the Supreme Court of Mississippi Justice, Oliver E. Diaz, Jr, as recounted by Roderick Munday, 'Suppressing Dissent' (2008) 172 *Justice of the Peace Notes* 830.) Even from Musmanno's own account, it is clear that he revelled in being a thorn in the side of the court on which he sat. On his dyspeptic style, see Megarry, *A Second Miscellany-at-Law*, 154–7; also *Justice Musmanno Dissents: The Dissenting Opinions of Justice Michael A. Musmanno, Associate Justice of the Supreme Court of Pennsylvania, filed during the period January, 1952 to September, 1955* (Indianapolis: Bobbs-Merrill, 1956). Roscoe Pound's remit in writing the introduction to this latter collection presumably would have been to laud it. But he took a dim view of intemperate dissents (see Roscoe Pound, '*Cacoethes Dissentiendi*: The Heated Judicial Dissent' (1953) 39 *ABAJ* 794), and so it is not especially surprising that he should have offered a distinctly restrained, slightly critical assessment of Musmanno's style: Roscoe Pound, 'Introduction', in *Justice Musmanno Dissents* v–ix at ix ('At times Justice Musmanno writes more with the ardor of an advocate than the austerity of a judge speaking the voice of the law').

[53] See, e.g., Hans Georg Rupp, 'Zur Frage der Dissenting Opinion', in *Festschrift für Gerhard Leibholz* (Tübingen: Mohr, 1966), 531–49; Pascal Piconnaz and Pierre Scyboz, 'Les *dissenting opinions* dans les jugements: une innovation à craindre?' (2002) 98(15) *Schweizerische Juristen-Zeitung* 377; Anne Langenieux-Tribalat, *Les opinions séparées des juges de l'ordre judiciaire français* (PhD thesis, Faculté de droit et des sciences économiques, Université de Limoges, 2007). The latter study supports the proposition that France's ordinary courts would do well to replicate the common-law practice of allowing the publication of *seriatim* opinions, though the author starkly admits that '[t]he French judicial system does not know separate opinions' (ibid. at 15) and that there is little if any reason to think that the practice ever will be replicated there.

[54] Mauro Cappelletti, 'Ideologie nel diritto processuale' (1962) 16 *Rivista trimestrale di diritto e procedura civile* 193, 215.

Cappelletti's mentor, Piero Calamandrei, had been expressly critical of this system. In the Italian courts, he observed,

> the judge can think for himself in secret, provided nobody finds out. The judgment is therefore like the formula which closes diplomats' secret meetings: even if we are on the eve of war, the interlocutors reached 'a perfect agreement to the satisfaction of all.' This secrecy may be pleasing to the judge who likes a quiet life, and who prefers to lighten his personal responsibility by hiding behind the screen of collegiality; but in the long run it affects his character like a stupefying drug. It is a typical example of State unanimity, which saves appearances at the expense of conscience.[55]

That civilian jurists are to be found articulating this sentiment seems reason enough to avoid drawing hard-and-fast distinctions between common-law and civil law perspectives on judicial dissent. Yet we should not gloss over the fact that, as between these perspectives, the differences eclipse the similarities. Cappelletti and Calamandrei purported to depict a distinctly continental European (in Calamandrei's case, an Italian) judicial mindset. Pronouncements by mainland European judges sometimes create the impression that they are seeking to conform to the depiction. '[T]he admission of dissenting opinions' – the writing, reading, and discussion of them – 'will cost time', one Dutch Supreme Court judge observed in the 1970s. His point was not that the cost is tolerable even if unwelcome – a refrain typical of common lawyers[56] – but that it justifies upholding a norm of judicial unanimity.[57] Lord Atkin's

[55] Piero Calamandrei, *Elogio dei giudici scritto da un avvocato*, 3rd ed. (Florence: Le Monnier, 1955), 274:

> 'il giudice può pensare colla propria testa in segreto, purchè di fuori non lo sappia nessuno. La sentenza somiglia così alla formula con cui si chiudono le conferenze segrete dei diplomatici: anche se siamo alla vigilia della guerra, gli interlocutori si sono lasciati "riscontrando con sodisfazione il loro perfetto accordo". Questa segretezza può essere gradita al giudice cha ama il quieto vivere, e che preferisce alleggerire la sua responsabilità personale dietro lo schermo della collegialità; ma a lungo opera sul suo carattere come una droga stupefacente. È un esempio tipico di unanimità di Stato, che salva le apparenze a spese delle coscienze'.

[56] See, e.g., Joe McIntyre, 'In Defence of Judicial Dissent' (2016) 37 *Adelaide L. Rev.* 431 at 438, 457–9; also Lee Epstein, William M. Landes, and Richard A. Posner, 'Why (and When) Judges Dissent: A Theoretical and Empirical Analysis' (2011) 5 *Jnl Legal Analysis* 101, 103–4.

[57] Huib Drion, 'Preadvies', in *Handelingen 1973 der Nederlandse Juristen-Vereniging deel 1, eerste stuk* (Zwolle: Tjeenk Willink, 1973), 38 ('[There is] a practical dimension to the admission of dissenting opinions, to be found in its meaning to the judge himself: publication of the diverging opinion will cost time'). Drion adds (ibid.) that the argument is perhaps 'of limited value' when only some minority opinions are published. (I am grateful to Jacco Bomhoff for the translation.)

well-known *dictum* about justice being preferable to finality is in effect turned on its head by Josef Azizi, a former judge of the Court of Justice of the European Union (CJEU), when he laments how a dissent

> contributes to legal uncertainty and . . . will tend to trigger . . . interest . . . in exercising . . . influence on future case law, aiming to overturn the earlier case law on the basis of the additional information given by the dissenting opinion.[58]

Not only do dissenting opinions 'deprive the judgment of the appearance of being the only seriously conceivable solution and way of argumentation',[59] Azizi insists, but they 'have no particular added value' – certainly in the CJEU – given that the 'cybernetic feedback' of 'legal professionals and legal academics' provides the Court with all the help it needs when it seeks 'to pinpoint and eliminate . . . potential weak points and shortcomings' in its reasoning.[60] While some of the arguments in favour of publishing dissents 'have merits',[61] he adds, it would, on balance, 'seem advisable not to abandon, at least in the course of the next decades, the secrecy of deliberations',[62] given the desirability of maintaining the collective agency of the CJEU. A 'decision is deemed to have been taken by the organ as a whole', he observes, and so 'publication of dissenting opinions would . . . seem . . . contrary to the fiction of legal unity of that organ'.[63] This is to conflate legal unity with legal unanimity. Just as a legislator who argues against a bill does not deny that the bill becomes law once the legislature enacts it, a judge who dissents from the

[58] Josef Azizi, 'Unveiling the EU Courts' Internal Decision-Making Process: A Case for Dissenting Opinions?' (2011) 12 *ERA Forum* 49, 61. *Cf. Ras Behari Lal* v. *King Emperor* [1933] All ER 723 (PC), 726 *per* Lord Atkin ('Finality is a good thing, but justice is a better'). Atkin's *dictum* bears comparison with Louis Brandeis' observation that 'in most matters, it is more important that the applicable rule of law be settled than that it be settled right'. *Burnet* v. *Coronado Oil & Gas Co* 285 US 393, 406 (1932) (Brandeis J, dissenting). Brandeis was by no means in favour of stifling judicial dissent for fear of unsettling the law. He was not averse to dissenting himself – his most famous dissent is probably *Olmstead* v. *United States* 277 US 438, 471 (1928) – and he thought it particularly important that judges should have the latitude to dissent in constitutional cases: see Post, 'The Supreme Court Opinion as Institutional Practice', 1351–3.

[59] Azizi, 'Unveiling the EU Courts' Internal Decision-Making Process', 60.

[60] Ibid. at 61–2. See also Gunnar Beck, *The Legal Reasoning of the Court of Justice of the EU* (Oxford: Hart, 2012), 35. For the very opposite argument – that a judicial culture which allows for the publication of judicial dissents has little need for academic critique of judgments – see Antonin Scalia, 'Dissents' [1998] *OAH Magazine of History* 18, 21.

[61] Azizi, 'Unveiling the EU Courts' Internal Decision-Making Process', 61.

[62] Ibid. at 67.

[63] Ibid. at 63.

opinion of the court accepts that the opinion is the court's decision; the fact of my dissenting from a decision, one US Supreme Court Justice once observed, 'does not qualify my duty to respect it as a part of our law'.[64] That a court fails to reach a decision unanimously does not mean that the court, its dissenters included, is not unified over what its decision is.

Some of the views that continental judges express about judicial dissent can seem strange to common lawyers. What these judges dislike about the publication of dissents is quite often exactly what common lawyers extol. The case for secretiveness, moreover, can itself seem somewhat opaque – a claim which is perhaps especially well illustrated by the decision-making culture prevalent in European Union law. The Treaty on the Functioning of the European Union (2007) provides that 'the Union's institutions, bodies, offices and agencies shall conduct their work as openly as possible'.[65] Yet the Treaty exempts the CJEU from this obligation apart from when performing 'administrative tasks',[66] and the rules of the Court require that its judges refrain from being open about how decisions are reached.[67] CJEU judges can be found claiming that trust and loyalty among their number would be undermined if dissenting opinions were published.[68] Yet the claim is rather undermined by the fact that it is not uncommon for the courts of other systems to accommodate the publication of dissents and still remain collegial.[69] It is difficult convincingly to argue that the size of the Court militates against allowing separate opinion-writing, furthermore, for Europe's other main constitutional court, the European Court of Human Rights, does permit its judges to produce separate opinions even though it is constituted by a panel slightly larger than that which makes up the CJEU's Grand Chamber.[70]

[64] *H. L.* v. *Matheson* 450 US 398, 421 (1981) (Stevens J, concurring).

[65] Treaty on the Functioning of the European Union (2007), art. 15(1). See also Treaty on European Union (2007), art. 11(2).

[66] Treaty on the Functioning of the European Union, art. 15(3). See also joined cases C-514/07 P, C-528/07 P, and C-532/07 P, *API* v. *Commission*, CJEU, 21 September 2010.

[67] 'The deliberations of the Court of Justice shall be and shall remain secret'. Statute of the Court of Justice of the European Union (2016), art. 35. See also Alberto Alemanno and Oana Stefan, 'Openness at the Court of Justice of the European Union: Toppling a Taboo' (2014) 51 *Common Market L. Rev.* 97.

[68] See, e.g., Azizi, 'Unveiling the EU Courts' Internal Decision-Making Process', 66.

[69] See Vlad Perju, 'Reason and Authority in the European Court of Justice' (2009) 49 *Virginia Jnl of Int'l Law* 307, 367–9.

[70] One reason that separate opinion writing is permitted in the one context and not the other could be that the issues which come before the CJEU, though varied, tend to be very technical, whereas the issues with which the ECtHR is concerned often involve value judgments on which sincere disagreement is more likely. The difference might also be

The CJEU adopts what is often considered to be an essentially French perspective on judicial independence. Being independent does not, from this perspective, mean being entitled to publish opinions which are out of step with the Court's judgments. Rather, it means having the confidence – when contributing to the formation of those judgments – to express controversial or potentially unpopular views without having to worry that they will be published.[71] Throughout the history of the Court, the judgments themselves – which so often read like statements composed by committee[72] – have been regularly disparaged. '[T]here are . . . some very good judgments emanating from Luxembourg, which are all the more impressive because of the straightjacket imposed by the requirement of compulsory unanimity', the then President of the United Kingdom's Supreme Court observed in 2012. Nevertheless:

> One only has to look at some of the Judgments of the CJEU . . . to see how compulsory unanimity can result in decisions which (i) are incomprehensible, (ii) have internally inconsistent reasoning, (iii) do not answer the issue that has been referred, or (iv) manage to enjoy all these three regrettable characteristics.[73]

One could easily go to town finding fault with a judicial culture which allows dissentient reasoning to be heard in private but not seen in public. This does not mean, however, that the CJEU's commitment to a culture of unanimity is difficult to explain. In 1952, when the Treaty of Paris was signed, none of the major national courts of the six founding states published dissenting opinions – in the ordinary courts of those states, this remains the case to this day. It is hardly surprising that the court established under this Treaty, the original European

partly attributable to the fact that the ECtHR deals only with cases concerning human rights and so, as compared with the CJEU (which has a more diverse case-load), raises a relatively limited range of issues over which judges might find themselves disagreeing.

71 See Perju, 'Reason and Authority in the European Court of Justice', 359–60; and Mitchel de S.-O.-l'E. Lasser, *Judicial Deliberations: A Comparative Analysis of Judicial Transparency and Legitimacy* (Oxford University Press, 2004), 245 ('[T]he ECJ's decisions offer a tempered version of their French counterparts . . . The formalist attributes of the ECJ's decision, including its unsigned, univocal, and collegial form, its relatively short and deductive style, and its clipped, authoritative, and magisterial tone, all contribute to producing a document that bears a distinct family resemblance to its French predecessors').

72 See David Edward, 'How the Court of Justice Works' (1995) 20 *European L. Rev.* 539, 556–7.

73 Lord Neuberger, 'No Judgment – No Justice', BAILII Lecture, 20 November 2012, www.supremecourt.uk/docs/speech-121120.pdf (accessed 23 April 2019), para. 25.

Court of Justice (ECJ), should have followed suit – perhaps especially so given that separate opinion-writing is incompatible with the austere, declaratory, univocal judgment-delivery style of the court to which the ECJ bore the closest resemblance, the French Cour de cassation.[74] The CJEU's aversion to publishing dissents might also be attributable to some of its *sui generis* features. When an appeal court decides a case, a judge who is inclined to dissent from the majority is clear as to what the issues are, because the facts of the case have been established, the arguments for the parties have been canvassed, and there is at least one other lower court in which a judgment has been delivered. But the CJEU, although it hears appeals, is often ruling as a court of first and last instance.[75] Forbidding the publication of dissents where the Court makes such a ruling certainly seems heavy-handed. Yet it is at least understandable why the Court should be averse to judges producing separate opinions in such cases. There is the danger that a dissent – which may have been produced before either a majority or any other judicial opinion was available – might read as a reaction to an inchoate legal picture and would reflect poorly on both the dissenter and the Court. It should also be borne in mind that the working language of the CJEU is French. Allegations of incomprehensibility would perhaps be even more common if the Court required not only that judges whose native language is not French draft French-language judgments, but also

[74] For classic accounts of the Cour de cassation's style, see John P. Dawson, *The Oracles of the Law* (Buffalo, NY: Hein, 1986 [1968]), 409–11; Konrad Zweigert and Hein Kötz, *Introduction to Comparative Law*, 3rd ed. trans. T. Weir (Oxford: Clarendon Press, 1998), 122–3.

[75] Although the Court of Justice hears appeals from the General Court (particularly regarding direct actions against acts of EU institutions), it has sole competence to decide on infringement proceedings against Member States and preliminary references from national courts. The CJEU certainly acts as a court of first and last instance with regard to infringement proceedings (which constitute a fairly small proportion of the Court's docket). It is the only tribunal before which these cases can be brought, and there is no appeal from its decisions. With preliminary references – which make up considerably more of the CJEU's docket – the same holds true in substance but the matter is a little more complex. The Court provides national courts with explanations regarding the validity and interpretation of EU law, and it is, formally speaking, for judges in those courts to apply the law to disputes. But the CJEU tends to be the de facto decision-maker since its explanations leave the national courts with little leeway (though a national court can refer a matter back to the CJEU if it is confused or unconvinced by an explanation).

that non-francophone judges write separate opinions in French if they wish to dissent from or concur with those judgments.[76]

The fact that the CJEU departs from the French legal model by producing not only a judgment on a case but also an Advocate General's opinion has been cited as a further argument in favour of the Court abjuring from publishing dissents. If the point of a judicial dissent is to set out a different perspective on the legal issues at stake in a case, so the argument goes, the dissent might as well be kept secret, because the Advocate General can provide such a perspective.[77] (The force of this argument seems somewhat diminished by the fact that the Court usually agrees with an Advocate General's opinion.[78]) Without enforced unanimity, moreover, it is not inconceivable that CJEU judges – who serve renewable six-year terms – could engage in tactical dissenting: if a judge is eligible for and seeking re-election to the Court by his home state, for example, he might (assuming he need not recuse himself) choose to dissent in those cases where his state is subject to an unwelcome ruling from the majority.[79]

[76] It is unlikely that the problem would be alleviated, furthermore, if the judgments and separate opinions were written in each judge's native language and then translated into French.

[77] See Ditlev Tamm, 'The History of the Court of Justice of the European Union Since its Origin', in *The Court of Justice and the Construction of Europe: Analyses and Perspectives on Sixty Years of Case-law*, ed. A. Rosas et al. (The Hague: Springer, 2013), 9–35 at 18; also Lasser, *Judicial Deliberations* at 160–1, 203–4, 316–17. Advocates-General are not obliged to write their opinions in French.

[78] See Clifford J. Carrubba, Matthew Gabel, and Charles Hankla, 'Judicial Behavior under Political Constraints: Evidence from the European Court of Justice' (2008) 102 *Am. Pol. Sci. Rev.* 435, 448 ('[T]he Court agreed with the AG's opinion on 79% of the legal issues in our data set').

[79] See Andreas Paulus, 'Judgments and Separate Opinions: Complementarity and Tensions', paper delivered to the European Court of Human Rights at Opening of the Judicial Year, Strasbourg, 25 January 2019, www.echr.coe.int/documents (accessed 25 June 2020), 4 ('In systems allowing the re-election of judges, the possibility of dissent may also invite political statements and thus politicise a court'). There is, obviously, no evidence of this behaviour in the CJEU, because it forbids the publication of separate opinions. Nevertheless, the possibility of the Court becoming vulnerable to such behaviour if dissents were published did not go unnoticed in 1973, when there arose – in the context of the UK joining the European Economic Community – the question of whether the Court should embrace the culture of separate opinion-writing. See, e.g., Valerio Grementieri and Cornelius Golden, Jr, 'The United Kingdom and The European Court of Justice: An Encounter Between Common and Civil Law Traditions' (1973) 21 *Am. J. Comparative Law* 664, 669–70 ('The entry of the United Kingdom will . . . cause difficulty in the area of judicial dissent . . . [P]ermitting judges to write dissenting . . . opinions . . . could subject judges to exacting political scrutiny in times of reappointment, perhaps deterring some judges from fully exercising their complete impartiality'). In the ECtHR, elected and (more frequently) ad hoc judges' separate

It is noticeable that some European judges can seem bewildered by what they consider to be their common-law counterparts' disinclination, on the one hand, to regard dissenters as immodest or ill-disciplined and their readiness, on the other, to presume that judicial dissent must somehow be noble, courageous, or indicative of an independent mind.[80] At least pause and reflect – this seems to be the mindset of judges who express such bewilderment – before concluding that, as between suppression and publication of judicial dissent, the latter choice must always be the superior one.[81] The mindset might typify that of a judiciary with a 'civil service character and mentality', one US Supreme Court Justice has observed, but this is no basis for dismissing the proposition that common law judges could 'serve the public better' by being more receptive to 'the values so prized in the civil law tradition'.[82]

3 Without Contraries Is No Progression?[83]

It is perfectly possible for courts to abide by a convention of producing judgments accompanied by reasons but never containing evidence of judicial dissent. The judgments of a court which holds to this convention

opinions do sometimes show them to be taking more benevolent positions when their home country is the respondent state: see Fred J. Bruinsma, 'The Room at the Top: Separate Opinions in the Grand Chambers of the ECHR (1998–2006)' [2008] *Ancilla Iuris* 32, 38–9; also Jiří Malenovský, 'Les opinions séparées et leurs répercussions sur l'indépendance du juge international' (2010) 3 *Annuario Colombiano de Derecho Consitucional* 27, 56–7.

80 See, e.g., Azizi, 'Unveiling the EU Courts' Internal Decision-Making Process', 64–5. By no means is this estimation of the dissenter anathema to all common-law judges: see, e.g., William E. Hirt, 'In the Matter of Dissents *Inter Judices de Jure*' (1960) 31 *Pennsylvania Bar Assoc. Quarterly* 256, 259 ('[The dissenter] turns the spot-light away from the issues in the case and keeps it focused on himself; he tells the world that the law is indefinite, except as expounded by him').

81 See, e.g., Koen Lenaerts, 'The Court's Outer and Inner Selves: Exploring the External and Internal Legitimacy of the European Court of Justice', in *Judging Europe's Judges: The Legitimacy of the Case Law of the European Court of Justice*, ed. M. Adams et al. (Oxford: Hart, 2013), 13–60 at 45–6. Lenaerts, the current President of the CJEU, defends obligatory unanimity as collegial, taking issue with Joseph Weiler's argument that the Court's style is anti-deliberative and authoritarian (see Joseph Weiler, 'Epilogue: The Judicial Après Nice', in *The European Court of Justice*, ed. G. de Búrca and J. H. H. Weiler (Oxford University Press, 2001), 215–26 at 225–6). For Weiler's response (sticking to his guns), see J. H. H. Weiler, 'Epilogue: Judging the Judges – Apology and Critique', in *Judging Europe's Judges*, 235–53 at 250–2.

82 Ruth Bader Ginsburg, 'Remarks on Writing Separately' (1990) 65 *Washington L. Rev.* 133, 150.

83 See William Blake, *The Marriage of Heaven and Hell* (Boston: Luce & Co, 1906 [*c.*1790–*c.*1793]), 7.

cannot be consistently free of *obiter dicta*, however, because it is inevitable that judges, when they explain themselves, will occasionally make observations which form part of the content of yet need not have featured in a judgment. Even if a court avoids publishing reasoning – even if it purports not to allow its judges to pronounce *obiter* – it is unlikely that *dicta* will never find their way into its opinions. In the hierarchy of French ordinary courts up to and including the Cour de cassation, John Dawson remarked in the late 1960s, each opinion 'is phrased with extreme economy and precision, saying no more than seems essential to defend the particular decision'.[84] That these courts should have taken this approach to opinion writing is understandable, given that the Civil Code prohibits judges from making law in the abstract.[85] Yet, even at the time that Dawson wrote, the Cour de cassation had begun – and, in the decades since, has been seen regularly – issuing judgments containing observations (which some jurists consider to be in contravention of the Civil Code) signalling how it would rule on facts different from those in the case being decided.[86] Perhaps all courts, even those which approach

[84] Dawson, *The Oracles of the Law*, 409.

[85] C. Civ., art. 5: 'Judges are forbidden to decide cases submitted to them by way of general and regulatory provisions'.

[86] See Stefan Goltzberg, *L'argumentation juridique*, 3rd ed. (Paris: Dalloz, 2017), 79–80. One of the first such cases was decided in 1969 when, upholding a child maintenance order in favour of the mother of a child born in wedlock, the Cour de cassation observed *obiter* that it would apply art. 342 of the Civil Code so as to rule in the same way were the Court presented with a case identical on the facts apart from the child, or children, being illegitimate: Civ. 1st, 20 Mai 1969, *JCP G* (*Juris-Classeur Périodique – édition Générale*) 1969, II, 16113. For the argument that *obiter* observations contravene art. 5, see Sébastien Tournaux. 'L'obiter dictum de la Cour de cassation' [2011] *Revue trimestrielle de droit civil* 45. According to Tournaux, when the Cour de cassation determines how the law applies to a set of facts before those facts have been litigated, it utilizes *obiter dictum* to achieve a normative rather than a merely pedagogic end: the *dictum* 'added by the judge' (ibid. at 55) stands as a legal rule 'announced outside the scope of the dispute' (ibid. at 54), the judge thereby signalling 'his willingness to assume his status as source of law' (ibid. at 66) and the court 'consolidat[ing] its system of Praetorian norms' (ibid. at 63). For further concerns about Cour de cassation *obiter dicta* and the risk of judicial overreach, see Solenne Hortala, *Les obiter dicta de la Cour de cassation: Étude de la jurisprudence civile* (PhD thesis, École Doctorale Droit et Science Politique, Université Toulouse 1 Capitole, 2017). According to Hortala,

> '*obiter dictum* has not until recently been a common practice [in France], but it could eventually become one. The risk [of overreach] ... could materialize if the Court ... were to engage in a real transformation of its office. By adopting a process of filtering appeals, in order to become a true Supreme Court of Justice, the method of producing case law would inevitably be altered ... The progressive rhythm of the creation of the law,

judgment-delivery in a spirit of austerity, are fated to publish *obiter dicta* from time to time.

But they are not fated to publish judicial dissents. Courts, indeed legal systems, take positions on dissent – not only on whether the publication of dissent should be forbidden or permitted but also, where it is permitted, on whether all or only some multimember panels should be free to publish dissents and how much of (or about) a dissent should be revealed. That the subject of dissent occasions position-taking very likely explains why it has elicited far more juristic analysis than has the subject of *obiter dicta*. Not that all analyses of judicial dissent concern criticisms and defences of the activity; some analysts, for example, are primarily interested in compiling data on the frequency of dissent in particular courts, by particular judges, in particular areas of law, and the like. Nevertheless, the most common approach to studying judicial dissent is the inquiry into reasons justifying the adoption of particular perspectives on dissenting.

The gist of any such justificatory reasoning is that a system of decision-making is better than it would otherwise be owing to the fact that it affirms particular adjudicative values, and that the system's affirmation of those values is at least partly attributable to its policy on dissent. This way of thinking about judicial dissent meets with various objections. A justification for one perspective on judicial dissent might serve equally well as a justification for an opposing perspective; contrary arguments on the topic, as with competing claims about *obiter dicta*, quite often result in an impasse (see Section 4). The connection between the adoption of a perspective and the consequences of adopting the perspective is not always convincingly drawn: toleration of open dissent is sometimes considered to improve the quality of a court's decision-making, for example, even though the improvements associated with its toleration could also be realized on a court which forbids its judges from dissenting. It is also a feature of justification-oriented analyses of judicial dissent that they tend straightforwardly to characterize dissenting as instrumental activity – as

> characterized by the production of case law, would be threatened . . . It is not certain that such a radical change is desirable'.

Ibid. at 510. Similar concerns have been expressed regarding the use of *dicta* in the Conseil d'État: see Maryse Deguergue, 'Les *obiter dicta* dans la jurisprudence du Conseil d'État', in *La pédagogie au service du droit*, ed. P. Raimbault and M. Hecquard-Théron (Toulouse: Presses de l'Université Toulouse 1 Capitole (LGDJ), 2011), 229–45 (arguing that, in recent years, Conseil d'État judges have been inclined to 'participate . . . in the function of the legislator' (ibid. at 231) through the production of *obiter dicta*); and Marie Lannoy, *Les obiter dicta du Conseil d'État statuant au contentieux* (Paris: Dalloz, 2016).

something that judges do in order to achieve particular objectives – even though judges sometimes dissent for no reason other than that they feel conscience-bound to state that they take a different view from the majority on what a legal outcome should be. Arguments for or against transparent judicial dissent need to be approached with caution.

When common lawyers examine these arguments, they often associate the case for unanimity with other adjudicative cultures – particularly with the ordinary courts of civil law countries and the CJEU. Yet the common law itself is not without examples of interdicts on separate-opinion delivery, introduced so as to make it highly unlikely that the decisions of particular courts would ever appear to be anything other than unanimous. Although the common law tradition offers up plenty of arguments in favour of allowing open judicial dissent, furthermore, the arguments are often accompanied by equivocation. Indeed, one of the staples of English commentary on judicial dissent – that judges, even when entitled to dissent, should always be minded to practise abstinence, or at least restraint[87] – reflects the fact that case law reveals even the strongest justifications for delivering dissenting opinions to be tempered by instances which show the justifications to be not entirely clear-cut.

Consider, for example, one of the most regularly and confidently articulated justifications for the publication of judicial dissents: that dissenting opinions can contribute to the development of the law. That dissent proved to be a catalyst for statutory change is a common motif in the history of English appeals. Lord Denning, in his final year as a law lord, rejected the orthodoxy that only those who are party to a contract can sue on it and, dissenting, maintained that third parties should be able to derive enforceable benefits from contracts made by others.[88] If Denning's preferred position was 'to be introduced into our law', Viscount Simonds insisted, 'it must be done by Parliament after a due consideration of its merits and demerits'.[89] The courts never embraced Denning's position – notwithstanding evident reservations over the orthodoxy.[90] But parliament moved towards it: in 1999, it enacted

[87] For recent illustrations, see Neuberger, 'No Judgment – No Justice', para. 27; Thomas Roe, 'Agreeing to Disagree', *NLJ*, 29 January 2016, 15 at 16.

[88] *Scruttons Ltd* v. *Midland Silicones Ltd* [1962] AC 446, 481 (case decided December 1961). For his own estimation of the impact of his dissent, see Lord Denning, *The Discipline of Law* (London: Butterworths, 1979), 289–90.

[89] *Scruttons* v. *Midland Silicones*, 468.

[90] See, e.g., *Swain* v. *Law Society* [1983] 1 AC 598, 611 *per* Lord Diplock; *White* v. *Jones* [1995] 2 AC 207, 262–3 *per* Lord Goff.

a limited third-party right to enforce contractual terms made by other parties.[91] Lord Neuberger expressed much the same sentiment as did Simonds when, in *YL* v. *Birmingham City Council* (2007), he remarked that whether it is 'desirable that residents in privately owned care homes should be given Convention rights against the proprietors' is a question of policy; 'if the legislature considers such a course appropriate, then it would be right [for the legislature] to spell it out'.[92] In *YL*, Lord Bingham and Lady Hale both produced dissenting opinions in which they contended that residents in private care homes already had Convention rights against proprietors when the homes provided care pursuant to a contract with central government or a local authority.[93] The government of the day endorsed the position supported by their opinions as the appropriate course to take,[94] and in 2008 parliament enacted legislation stipulating that independent care home providers perform functions of a public nature when they exercise a statutory local authority duty to provide accommodation and care.[95]

The more common assumption about judicial dissents is that they prompt changes not to enacted law but to judge-made law. As with concurring opinions, dissents illustrate the provisional, revisable nature of common-law rule-formulations.[96] An opinion in dissent from

[91] See Contracts (Rights of Third Parties) Act 1999, s. 1(1); also HL Deb 11 January 1999 vol. 586 col. 29 (Lord Meston) ('[I]n the [Contracts (Rights of Third Parties)] Bill we reach fulfilment of something tenaciously advocated for many years by the noble and learned Lord, Lord Denning'); and Catharine MacMillan, 'Upholding Contractual Intentions', in Geach and Monaghan (eds.), *Dissenting Judgments in the Law*, 79–104 at 102–3.

[92] *YL* v. *Birmingham City Council* [2007] UKHL 47 at [171].

[93] See ibid. at [19] *per* Lord Bingham and at [72]–[73] *per* Lady Hale.

[94] See HL Deb 13 March 2012 vol. 736 col. 233 (Lord Lester) ('In the *YL* case, the then Government argued strongly for the interpretation that Lord Bingham and the noble and learned Baroness, Lady Hale, gave. Both the previous and present Governments have said that they believe that the minority view in *YL* is the correct view').

[95] Social Care Act 2008, s. 145. For a similarly significant dissent from around this time, see Lord Rodger's speech in *Barker* v. *Corus UK Ltd* [2006] UKHL 20 at [66]–[102]. One of the law lords in the majority subsequently observed that the dissent led to the enactment of section 6 of the Compensation Act 2006: Lord Hoffmann, 'Causation', in *Perspectives on Causation*, ed. R. Goldberg (Oxford: Hart, 2011), 3–9 at 8.

[96] See Munday, 'Judicial Configurations', 638 ('[A] legal principle is but a working hypothesis, the best that can be formulated for the time being . . . The dissent . . . illustrates the common law's assumption that the underlying principles of the law are meant to be subject to perpetual, unrelenting re-appraisal'); Matthew Groves, 'Justice Murphy's Dissent in *Australian Conservation Foundation* v. *Commonwealth* (1980): The Birth of Public Interest Standing in Australia?' in *Great Australian Dissents*, ed. A. Lynch (Cambridge University Press, 2016), 189–208 at 190 ('[T]here must be different strands of reasoning within existing principles and cases to fuel the organic growth of the common law. Dissenting judgments

a majority's ruling on a legal matter signals to lawyers and judges that if a court were to revisit the matter, and if it were not bound by the earlier ruling, there is at least one alternative route that it might consider available. Lord Brown captured the point when he observed that the presence of a strong, cogent dissent in a Court of Appeal decision is likely to influence not only a losing party's choice whether to seek to appeal but also the Supreme Court's determination whether the matter of principle which prompted the dissent warrants being scrutinized and expounded upon by a final appellate tribunal.[97] Thus it is that dissenting judges sometimes lose the battle but win the war. In *Hedley Byrne* v. *Heller*, the House of Lords unanimously endorsed Denning's dissenting opinion in *Candler* v. *Crane, Christmas & Co.*[98] Ward LJ's dissent from his colleagues' disapproval of the High Court's judgment in *Oceanbulk Shipping* v. *TMT Asia* was hardly diplomatic,[99] but the Supreme Court readily accepted his reasoning and reversed the Court of Appeal's decision.[100] In *O'Byrne* v. *Aventis Pasteur*, Lord Rodger was alone in considering it 'not beyond reasonable argument' that the proper interpretation of a European product liability directive prevented a claimant from suing after the expiry of a national statutory limitation period.[101] That the law lords were not unanimous as to the scope of the directive meant that the

offer an important source from which judges can adopt new principles or amend existing ones'); Amelia Simpson, 'Treachery or Heroism? The Judgment of Justices Deane and Toohey in *Leeth* v. *Commonwealth* (1992)', in ibid. at 251–71 at 267.

97 Lord Brown, 'Dissenting Judgments', in *Judge and Jurist: Essays in Memory of Lord Rodger of Earlsferry*, ed. A. Burrows, D. Johnston, and R. Zimmermann (Oxford University Press, 2013), 29–37 at 31.

98 *Hedley Byrne & Co Ltd* v. *Heller & Partners Ltd* [1964] AC 465 (overruling *Candler* v. *Crane, Christmas & Co* [1951] 2 KB 164 (CA)).

99
> '[I]f you can use the antecedent negotiations to prove the agreement, to rescind it, or to rectify it, why on earth can you not use the negotiations to establish the truth of what the concluded contract means? Not to do so would strike my mother as "barmy". Perhaps I should simply say it strikes me as illogical . . . What is the justice of a self-imposed rule that one is not allowed to look at the facts which will establish what the parties truly meant by their compromise? . . . I am outnumbered, nay outgunned, by the commercial colossi seated either side of me . . . It goes to prove what every good old-fashioned county court judge knows: the higher you go, the less the essential oxygen of common sense is available to you . . . With, of course, great respect to my Lords, I dissent'.

Oceanbulk Shipping, Trading SA v. *TMT Asia Ltd* [2010] EWCA Civ 79 at [37], [38], and [41].

100 *Oceanbulk Shipping, Trading SA* v. *TMT Asia Ltd* [2010] UKSC 44.

101 *O'Byrne* v. *Aventis Pasteur MSD Ltd* [2008] UKHL 34 at [24].

matter had to be referred back to the CJEU, which confirmed that Lord Rodger's doubt was well founded.[102] When the case returned to the Supreme Court (as it had become), he delivered the judgment allowing the defendant's appeal.[103]

The interplay between judicial dissent and legal development is not entirely captured by instances of legislatures and courts bringing the law into line with positions taken by dissenting judges. Vindicated dissents sometimes come with a sting in the tail: a legislature or final appeal court which creates new law on the back of judicial dissent might subsequently constrain or repudiate that law.[104] Occasionally, dissent will precipitate dissent: the court responsible for today's ruling might eschew an earlier dissenting opinion, for example, yet fail to rule unanimously because at least one of its members was convinced by the dissent and so dissented in kind, as it were, in order to keep alive the possibility of the law ultimately aligning with it.[105] *Chester* v. *Afshar* addressed the question of whether a patient can successfully sue a surgeon if the surgeon omits to warn the patient of the risk of injury, the surgery injures the patient, and the patient is unable, on the balance of probabilities, to say that she would not have consented to the surgery had she been warned of the risk. The High Court, Court of Appeal, and House of Lords judgments all bore the mark of the majority's reasoning in *Chappel* v. *Hart*,[106] in which the High Court of Australia held that the claimant could recover damages even if she could not prove on the balance of probabilities that, had she been told of the risk, she would have forgone the surgical procedure.[107] In the House of Lords, however, one of the two judges in the minority, Lord

102 Case C-358/08 *Aventis Pasteur SA* v. *OB* (Grand Chamber) [2009] ECR I-11305.

103 *O'Byrne* v. *Aventis Pasteur MSD Ltd* [2010] UKSC 23.

104 Evatt J's dissent in *Chester* v. *Council of the Municipality of Waverley* (1939) 62 CLR 1, 23 had an almost immediate impact on the New South Wales legislature, which, on the basis of it, introduced a statutory duty of care for nervous shock victims. In the 1980s, the dissent was endorsed by the High Court of Australia (*Jaensch* v. *Coffey* (1984) 155 CLR 549, 590–1 *per* Deane J). But in 2002 New South Wales enacted a new law which, in contrast to Evatt's dissent, emphasized the responsibility owed by rather than the duty of care owed to the victim. The legislation reined in, even if it did not entirely annul, the impact of the dissent. See Barbara McDonald, 'Justice Evatt and the Lost Child in *Chester* v. *Waverley Corporation* (1939)', in Lynch (ed.), *Great Australian Dissents*, 58–79.

105 On continental European treatment of this observation as a reason for prohibiting publication of dissents, see Kelemen, *Judicial Dissent in European Constitutional Courts*, 83.

106 *Chappel* v. *Hart* (1998) 195 CLR 232.

107 See *Chester* v. *Afshar* [2000] 12 WLUK 682 (HC) at [81]; [2002] EWCA Civ 724 at [48]; [2004] UKHL 41 at [21]–[22] (*per* Lord Steyn), [81]–[83], [88] (*per* Lord Hope) and [99] (*per* Lord Walker).

Bingham, 'adopt[ed] the reasoning of McHugh J', who, 'in his dissenting judgment in *Chappel*',[108] contended that recovery of damages should not be possible if the evidence indicates that the surgeon's failure to alert the claimant to the attendant risk made no difference to the claimant's course of action.[109] The decision of the majority in *Chester* has met with something of a chequered reception in the courts, and it is by no means beyond the realms of possibility that it will one day be displaced in favour of a judgment congenial to Bingham's position.[110] Certainly there are jurists who urge English judges to remain amenable to that position – who contend that, were the courts to adopt it, the law of negligence would be placed on a sounder footing.[111] Even if a dissent, or line of dissents, cannot be said to have resulted in an alteration to the law, it might still have ensured that an area of law remains susceptible to alteration.

There is, then, an argument – a strong argument – to be made to the effect that an adjudicative culture which tolerates advertisement of judicial dissent is likely to facilitate legal evolution. But this culture will not always favour, indeed it will sometimes impede, legal evolution. 'I do not believe that it was ever an important discovery', Lord Radcliffe maintained, 'that judges are in some sense law-makers'.[112] What he thought more interesting yet less frequently remarked upon – though, given the profession from which judges are recruited, not at all surprising[113] – is the judicial capacity for law-conservation: he even went so far as to assert

[108] *Chester* v. *Afshar* [2004] UKHL 41 at [9].

[109] See *Chappel* v. *Hart* at paras. 31–4.

[110] See *Duce* v. *Worcestershire Acute Hospitals NHS Trust* [2018] EWCA Civ 1307 at [84]–[92] *per* Leggatt LJ; also *Correia* v. *University Hospital of North Staffordshire NHS Trust* [2017] EWCA Civ 356 at [28], where Simon LJ maintained that 'if a claimant is to rely on the exceptional principle of causation established by *Chester* v. *Afshar*, it is necessary to plead the point and support it by evidence'. (In *Correia*, counsel for the defendant reserved the right to argue that *Chester* was wrongly decided should the claimant appeal to the Supreme Court.)

[111] See, e.g., Sarah Green, 'Coherence of Medical Negligence Cases: A Game of Doctors and Purses' (2006) 14 *Medical L Rev.* 1 at 7–8, 20–1; and Kristof Zoltan von Csefalvay-Bartal, 'On Good Intentions and Poor Outcomes: A Critical Retrospective on *Chester* v. *Afshar*' (2009) 9 *Univ. College Dublin L Rev.* 46, 48–9. Lord Hoffmann also dissented in *Chester*. Some critics of the decision prefer his dissenting opinion of the two (see, e.g., Robert Stevens, 'An Opportunity to Reflect' (2005) 121 *LQR* 189, 192), and some base their criticisms on neither dissent (see, e.g., Tamsyn Clark and Donal Nolan, 'A Critique of *Chester* v. *Afshar*' (2014) 34 *OJLS* 659).

[112] Lord Radcliffe, *Not in Feather Beds* (London: Hamish Hamilton, 1968), 271. See also ibid. at 215 ('[T]here was never a more sterile controversy than that upon the question whether a judge makes law. Of course he does. How can he help it?').

[113] See ibid. at 71.

that '[t]he very existence of appellate courts tends ... to be a retarding influence on judge-made law'.[114] His thoughts on judicial dissents supply some insight into why he should have taken this view.

Although Radcliffe came to prefer the single court opinion to *seriatim* judgment-writing,[115] he did not favour enforced unanimity and – as is clear from his note to Lord Atkin after Atkin excoriated the majority in *Liversidge* v. *Anderson* – he could be in thrall to a compelling dissent.[116] (Radcliffe himself, we will see in a moment, could be a compelling dissenter.) But a compelling dissent, he appreciated, need not be iconoclastic. A dissent might be powerful not because of the pose that it strikes or its inspirational language – it could well be bereft of such language – but because it reins in the law-altering ambitions of the judges who form the majority.[117] Even though dissents of this type do not persuade the majority that it should refrain from altering the law – they would not be dissents if they did – the majority's decision might still be curtailed or displaced by a later court which, in light of the dissentient reasoning, comes to doubt the wisdom of sticking with the alteration. That a later court will have such doubts – and, as Lord Pearson once observed, that it will be fortified to act on such doubts – seems more likely when the dissentients only just lose to the majority.[118] Just as powerful dissents of

> '[T]here is something rather unusual, something which might be characterised as introverted, about a profession in which the range of learning is, in effect, closed and in which a principle is the more treated as valid the more it can be shown to be ancient and long-established. Such a background should favour a certain conservatism and a certain detachment of outlook ... On the whole I think that this is what our background does'.

[114] Lord Radcliffe, *The Law & Its Compass* (London: Faber & Faber, 1960), 31.

[115] See Radcliffe, *Not in Feather Beds*, 218–19.

[116] Cyril Radcliffe to Lord Atkin, 19 November 1941, James Richard Atkin papers, ATK1/JUD/2/2/41, Gray's Inn Library, London.

> 'I only wanted to say how entirely I agreed with every line of your judgment [in *Liversidge* v. *Anderson* [1942] AC 206] and what a very valuable thing it was that you were there to deliver it. I know how widely the general public responded to the view you took, and I do privately hope that it is the one that will somehow prevail before things go much further'.

[117] Lord Radcliffe, interview with Alan Paterson, cited in Alan Paterson, *The Law Lords* (London: Macmillan, 1982), 101 ('[T]he dissent process ... enable[s] you to try to limit what you regard as an unsatisfactory line by some reasoned and carefully worked out contribution of your own').

[118] Lord Pearson, interview with Paterson, ibid. ('[W]hen the next case arises and it is a little further along the line or a bit short of the line, the dissent may be valuable. There is a difference between a unanimous decision in the House of Lords and a 3:2 conclusion. You look at the dissenting opinions for that reason').

a conservationist bent can be effective in confining or frustrating a majority's efforts to secure a change to the law, furthermore, a dissent in favour of altering the law might entrench a majority's case for maintaining the legal status quo if the dissentient reasoning is so inept as to put that case in an unduly flattering light. Butler J, the sole dissenter in *Buck* v. *Bell* (1927), presumably considered the Virginia statute authorizing involuntary sterilization to be constitutionally invalid. But unlike Holmes J – who wrote with infamous candour for the majority[119] – he did not explain himself.[120] Had he done so, state enactments compelling sterilization – some of which were not repealed until the 1960s – might have been subjected to more extensive judicial scrutiny.[121]

The narrative about judicial dissents precipitating legal developments also meets with the objection that although a legislature or court might change the law in such a way that it corresponds with the position taken in a dissenting opinion, it might be difficult, and may well be impossible, to show that the opinion spurred – or was even one of the reasons which spurred – the change. A third-party right to enforce contractual terms did indeed make its way into law in 1999, but it would be rash to presume that the legislation was attributable, certainly that it was attributable solely, to a dissent by Lord Denning. Not only did Denning produce other notable opinions containing *dicta* criticizing privity of contract doctrine but, more significantly, the enacted law embodied not so much his position (which was essentially a case for abolishing the doctrine) as it did various recommendations made by the Law Commission.[122] Similarly, although

119 *Buck* v. *Bell* 274 US 200, 208 (1927) ('It is better for all the world if, instead of waiting to execute degenerate offspring for crime or to let them starve for their imbecility, society can prevent those who are manifestly unfit from continuing their kind. The principle that sustains compulsory vaccination is broad enough to cover cutting the Fallopian tubes . . . Three generations of imbeciles are enough').

120 The dissent was very likely motivated by Catholic anxieties over eugenics: see Phillip Thompson, 'Silent Protest: A Catholic Justice Dissents in *Buck* v. *Bell*' (2004) 43 *Catholic Lawyer* 125.

121 Although compulsory sterilizations imposed as punishments for crimes were outlawed in *Skinner* v. *Oklahoma* 316 US 535 (1942), judicially initiated sterilizations have never been completely abolished in the United States – and *Buck* v. *Bell* has never been explicitly overruled.

122 Lord Chancellor's Department, *Privity of Contract: Contracts for the Benefit of Third Parties*, Law Com. no. 242, Cmd. 3329 (London: HMSO, 1996). For Denning's *dicta* on privity, see *Smith and Snipes Hall Farm* v. *River Douglas Catchment Board* [1949] 2 KB 500, 514; *Drive Yourself Hire Co* v. *Strutt* [1954] 1 QB 250, 272; *Scruttons* v. *Midland Silicones*, 483; *Beswick* v. *Beswick* [1966] Ch 538, 557. A proposal for legislation enabling third parties to enforce contracts in their own names was made by the Law Revision Committee in 1937: *Sixth Interim Report: Statute of Frauds and the Doctrine of Consideration. Presented by the Lord*

parliament legislated so as to bring the law on contracted-out care home services into line with the position advocated in the dissents of Lord Bingham and Lady Hale in *YL*, the change to the law was primarily a response to arguments advanced by the Joint Committee on Human Rights.[123] A dissenting opinion adjudged to have been vindicated may 'provide nothing more than some quotable support for a decision that would have been the same in any event' – it may have prophesied but not necessarily have led to, or even have contributed to, an alteration to the course of the law.[124] There will not always be, indeed perhaps only seldom will there be, a direct path between dissent and effect.

The notion that there is never a path – of any sort – to be charted between dissent and effect has, rather bizarrely, occasionally been attributed to H. L. A. Hart. One of the many erroneous criticisms directed at Hart's legal philosophy takes him to task for arguing that the judicial dissent is always ineffective.[125] 'A supreme tribunal has the last word in saying what the law is', Hart observed in *The Concept of Law*, 'and, when it has said it, the statement that the court was "wrong"' – a statement which might take the form of a dissenting opinion – "has no consequences within the system: no one's rights and duties are thereby altered".[126]

Hart's point, in so far as it is one about judicial dissents, is that a dissent is not a source of law. His critics took him to be claiming that an apex court's ruling is 'a final authoritative statement of what the law is in a particular case',[127] and that it is therefore pointless for a judge on the court to produce an opinion in dissent from the ruling. Hart's insistence

High Chancellor to Parliament by Command of His Majesty, May 1937, Cmd. 5449 (London: HMSO, 1945). Apparently, the proposal was stymied because of the difficulty of finding space for it in the legislative timetable as the Second World War approached: see Jack Beatson, 'Reforming the Law of Contracts for the Benefit of Third Parties: A Second Bite at the Cherry' (1992) 44 *Current Legal Problems* 1, 10–13.

123 See Joint Committee on Human Rights, *The Meaning of a Public Authority under the Human Rights Act: Seventh Report of Session 2003–04*, HL paper 39, HC 382 (London: HMSO, 2004), paras. 62–7; Joint Committee on Human Rights, *The Meaning of a Public Authority under the Human Rights Act: Ninth Report of Session 2006–07*, HL paper 77, HC 410 (London: HMSO, 2007), paras. 70–110. Although parliament brought the law on care homes into line with the position advocated in the dissents, furthermore, it did not interfere with the general approach that had been taken by the majority.

124 Maurice Kelman, 'The Forked Path of Dissent' [1985] *Supreme Court Rev.* 227, 255.

125 See, e.g., J. Louis Campbell, III, 'The Spirit of Dissent' (1983) 66 *Judicature* 305; also William J. Brennan, Jr, 'In Defense of Dissents' (1986) 37 *Hastings LJ* 427, 429.

126 H. L. A. Hart, *The Concept of Law* (Oxford: Clarendon Press, 1961), 141.

127 Ibid. at 145.

'that dissents have no system-wide consequences'[128] reveals not only his 'bias . . . against dissent',[129] according to one critic, but also his failure to appreciate that dissents, while not sources of law, 'are sources of energy and cogency in law': that dissents have consequences within the legal system because they are 'deployed' by judges in pursuit of 'the goal of system-wide change'.[130]

The criticism is groundless. To claim that rights and duties are not altered by judicial dissent is not to deny the possibility of rights and duties altering because new law is created in response to judicial dissent. When *The Concept of Law* was published in 1961, Hart did not know (though he might have suspected)[131] that, in the United Kingdom, the judicial capacity to respond creatively to dissent was about to change: in its famous *Practice Statement* of July 1966, the House of Lords determined that its rulings did not have to be its last word – that it could overrule its own precedents whenever it decided they were wrong.[132] But even before 1966, judicial opinion at variance with final court precedent was not necessarily inconsequential as regards the future direction of the law, for, as Hart clearly appreciated, a legislature more enamoured of the opinion than the precedent could legislate to deprive the precedent of legal effect.[133]

A striking illustration of the legislature spurning a final court precedent while demonstrating receptiveness to dissenting opinion arose in the years separating *The Concept of Law* and the *Practice Statement.* In *Burmah Oil* v. *Lord Advocate* (1964), a majority of the House of Lords ruled that the appellants (whose Burmese oil installations were razed in 1942 because the British government's wartime policy was to destroy valuable assets rather than let them fall into enemy hands) had a common-law right to compensation from the Crown even though the government's destructive actions amounted to the lawful exercise of a prerogative power.[134] One of the dissenting judges, Lord Radcliffe, professed bewilderment at the decision. It is difficult, he maintained, to discern what the scope of the relevant prerogative is and whether it has

128 Campbell, 'The Spirit of Dissent', 312.

129 Ibid. at 305.

130 Ibid. at 312.

131 Some of his contemporaries certainly did: see, e.g., Gerald Dworkin, '*Stare Decisis* in the House of Lords' (1962) 25 *MLR* 163, 174–5; also the sources cited in Paterson, *The Law Lords*, 144.

132 *Practice Statement (Judicial Precedent)* [1966] 1 WLR 1234.

133 See Hart, *The Concept of Law*, 141.

134 *Burmah Oil Co* v. *Lord Advocate* [1965] AC 75.

ever been asserted before.[135] More importantly, to assert that the common law confers a right to compensation for loss sustained owing to the exercise of this mystical prerogative simply cannot be demonstrated: 'there is no law on the matter to which we can give effect', he concluded, and so the appellant's claim for damages should be dismissed.[136]

That the claim was not dismissed proved contentious. The right to compensation established by the ruling applied to losses suffered by a major oil company but did not extend to those who had been maimed and whose relatives had died as a consequence of the government's policy. Since the Second World War, Burma had been fairly relentless in its pursuit of compensation for losses. After the ruling, colonies which had forsaken this route and accepted modest *ex gratia* payments from the British government had reason to wonder whether it would have paid them to be more vexatious. The ruling affirmed that compensation could be due for losses incurred as a consequence of 'war damage' – offensive destruction intended to frustrate enemy war efforts (such as the targeting of oil supplies necessary for military mobilization). However, defensive destruction, as when buildings are demolished to obstruct the advance of enemy tanks, could not be the basis for a compensation claim because (a distinction which discomfited the other dissenter in *Burmah Oil*, Lord Hodson)[137] it amounted to 'battle damage'. In 1964, the Labour government presented to the commons a bill providing that war-related damage to or destruction of property, whether caused before or after the passing of the bill into law, could not be the basis for a compensation claim against the Crown.

Immediately came the outcry that if parliament were to enact this bill, thereby not only reversing a House of Lords decision but also retroactively altering the rights and duties of the parties to the case, both judicial independence and the rule of law would be imperilled.[138] The Liberal Party and many Conservative backbenchers opposed the bill in the commons, and, when it reached the lords, Liberal peers sought to amend it so that it would only apply prospectively. To enact the bill as *ex post facto* law, one member of the commons contended, would be to determine not that the law needed

135 Ibid. at 113.

136 Ibid. at 135.

137 See ibid. at 142.

138 See, e.g., Lord Devlin, 'Justice in Danger?', *The Observer*, 16 May 1965 at 11; Alan Watkins, 'The Burmah Oil Affair', *The Spectator*, 12 February 1965 at 190.

changing but that the majority in *Burmah Oil*, unlike the Crown's legal advisers, had misunderstood how the common law applied to the facts of the case, and that retroactive legislation was required to remedy the judicial error.[139]

The contention met with two retorts. The first – an objection echoing early seventeenth-century concerns about courts of error being able to overturn judgments which most of the participating judges would prefer to have seen affirmed (see Section 6) – was that the majority in *Burmah Oil* in fact sided with the Crown. The House of Lords held 3:2 that the decision of Scotland's Court of Session – which had ruled 4:1 in favour of the Crown[140] – was to be reversed. The two courts' rulings taken together, one Labour MP observed, yielded a 6:4 majority against holding the government legally bound to pay compensation.[141] Secondly, the legislation was vindicating not the Crown's legal advisers but rather what the Attorney General referred to as the 'remarkably effective' speech of Lord Radcliffe.[142] It is '[c]ertainly a dissenting opinion', one member of the commons conceded, 'but not any less an authority on a matter of this kind'.[143] Much of Radcliffe's reasoning, according to another, 'is clearly to be preferred' to that offered by the majority.[144] Even in the upper chamber, where the government's bill met with the most resistance, members acknowledged the quality and force of Radcliffe's dissent.[145] When the bill returned to the commons, the lords' amendments were rejected.[146] It received royal assent, in its retroactive form, in June 1965.[147] To attribute the enactment of the statute to Radcliffe's opinion would be to overstate matters; it is clear from *Hansard* that other factors were in play. But so too is it clear that various parliamentarians who spoke in favour of the bill were influenced by his dissent.

[139] See HC Deb 3 February 1965 vol. 705 cols. 1149–52 (Jeremy Thorpe).

[140] *Burmah Oil Co (Burma Trading) Ltd* v. *Lord Advocate* 1963 SC 410.

[141] HC Deb 3 February 1965 vol. 705 col. 1152 (Thomas Williams) ('The hon. Member [Mr Thorpe] keeps talking about "all the judges". In fact, of course, the weight of opinion was six judges against four. If one takes all the judges, six of the judges found in favour . . . and only four found for the opposite point of view').

[142] HC Deb 3 February 1965 vol. 705 col. 1210 (Sir Elwyn Jones A-G).

[143] HC Deb 3 February 1965 vol. 705 col. 1099 (Niall MacDermot).

[144] HC Deb 3 February 1965 vol. 705 col. 1118 (Dick Taverne).

[145] See, e.g., HL Deb 25 March 1965 vol. 264 cols 749–50 (Viscount Dilhorne).

[146] See Lord Ogmore, 'The Law and the Lawmakers: The Burmah Oil Company Affair' [1965] *Contemporary Rev.* 30, 31–3.

[147] War Damage Act 1965.

4 Stalemates and Motivations

It is easy, perhaps somewhat too easy, to depict legal change positively – to assume that legal evolution is primarily a story of how legal systems improve over time, and that deliberate lawmaking initiatives are always intended to work, and for the most part will work, to the good. One might equally easily, on the basis of this depiction, seek to justify judicial dissent: judges should be allowed to dissent because a legal system will usually benefit from, rather than be disadvantaged by, the types of modification that dissents facilitate. This justification, we have seen, entails an unduly straightforward connection between dissent and legal change. Even if it is reasonable to assume that changes to the law are usually changes for the better, the existence of dissent will sometimes be an impediment to legal change, and, when the law does change so as to align with dissenting opinion, the presumption that the change is in some way attributable to the dissent might be speculative or mistaken.

Some of the other commonly deployed arguments about judicial dissent are similar in form to that which connects dissent to legal change. Indeed, it is striking just how much normative commentary on judicial dissent ends in stalemate, with jurists often committing to a perspective while failing properly to take account of how it runs up against an equally valid counter-perspective. Counter to the familiar argument that dissents foster legal uncertainty runs the observation that courts' judgments can produce the same – that a judge's very reason for dissenting, indeed, might be to try to limit the damage that a destabilizing judgment could inflict.[148] Dissent, on one account, is evidence of a lack of discipline on the bench.[149] Dissent, even potential dissent, is conducive to discipline, according to another, because members of a judicial majority will probably be inclined to take a co-ordinated approach to opinion writing, perhaps settling on a single opinion, if they expect their reasoning to be

[148] See, e.g., *The Golden Victory* [2007] UKHL 12 at [1] *per* Lord Bingham ('I have the misfortune to differ [from the majority]. I give my reasons for doing so, unauthoritative though they must be, since in my respectful opinion the existing decision undermines the quality of certainty which is a traditional strength and major selling point of English commercial law, and involves an unfortunate departure from principle').

[149] See Learned Hand, *The Bill of Rights* (Cambridge, Mass.: Harvard University Press, 1958), 72; A. W. B. Simpson, 'Lord Denning as Jurist', in *Lord Denning: The Judge and the Law*, ed. J. L. Jowell and J. P. W. B. McAuslan (London: Sweet & Maxwell, 1984), 441–53 at 451 ('undisciplined individualism'); and *cf.* Susan Kiefel, 'The Individual Judge' (2014) 88 *Australian LJ* 554, 558 ('Dissenting judgments allow the most individualistic style of writing. With dissents, much greater liberty is possible and less care need be taken').

compared with dissentient reasoning.[150] Judges who dissent on points of law should (unless they have had a change of heart) continue to dissent in cases which revisit those points of law, it is sometimes argued, because repeated dissents can turn out to be effective judicial campaigns, particularly against courts which have kept faith with dubious precedents.[151] Others take the view that persistent dissent on a point of law is disrespectful to *stare decisis*.[152] Others again contend that repetitive dissent tends to prove counterproductive – that serial contrarians are often considered broken records who show themselves to be perpetually incapable of persuading enough, if indeed any, of their colleagues that they are

150 See Alan Paterson, *Lawyers and the Public Good: Democracy in Action?* (Cambridge University Press, 2012), 159–60; Stephens, 'The Function of Concurring and Dissenting Opinions', 403–4 ('The . . . dissenter . . . cannot . . . change the result . . . but his power to assert inadequacy or inaccuracy . . . is a weapon that puts the other judges on their mettle'); Clarke Rountree, 'Instantiating "The Law" and its Dissents in *Korematsu* v. *United States*: A Dramatistic Analysis of Judicial Discourse' (2001) 87 *Quarterly Jnl of Speech* 1, 20.

151 See Brennan, 'In Defense of Dissents', 436–7; Richard M. Re, 'Promising the Constitution' (2016) 110 *Northwestern Univ. L. Rev.* 299, 349–51; Frederick Schauer, '*Stare Decisis* – Rhetoric and Reality in the Supreme Court' [2018] *Supreme Court Rev.* 121, 132–5; Andrew Lynch, 'Dissent: The Rewards and Risks of Judicial Disagreement in the High Court of Australia' (2003) 27 *Melbourne Univ. L. Rev.* 724, 758–67. There appears to be broad agreement that persistent dissent is antithetical to *stare decisis*: see, e.g., Schauer, '*Stare Decisis*', 132 ('The tissue-thin character of the *stare decisis* constraint in the [US] Supreme Court is . . . exemplified by the general unwillingness of dissenting Justices to abandon their dissents in subsequent cases'); Lynch, 'Dissent', 759 ('persistently rejecting the . . . majority . . . imbue[s] . . . dissent with a character . . . hostile to the values of *stare decisis*'). But it is not clear that *stare decisis* always will be countered by persistent dissent. A judge's continual dissent on a legal point could, for example, amount to her observing (a) that like cases should be treated alike, (b) that the court on which she sits, whenever it rules on that legal point, follows a specific precedent, and (c) that, whenever she is involved in these rulings, she tries – but so far has always failed – to convince the majority that the precedent which is followed is distinguishable. This particular persistent dissenter does not, certainly does not intend to, disrespect *stare decisis*. She is arguing, rather, that the majority has misunderstood the constraint – that it has made a precedent bind in an instance in which it should not bind.

152 See, e.g., *Gertz* v. *Welch* 418 US 323, 354 (1974) (Blackmun J, concurring) ('If my vote were not needed to create a majority, I would adhere to my prior view. A definitive ruling, however, is paramount'); *Ring* v. *Arizona* 536 US 584, 613 (2002) (Kennedy J, concurring) ('Though it is still my view that *Apprendi* v. *New Jersey* 530 US 466 (2000) . . . was wrongly decided, *Apprendi* is now the law, and its holding must be implemented in a principled way'); also *Gibson* v. *United States* [2007] UKPC 52 at [37]–[40] where Lord Hoffmann (along with two other dissenters) contended that, out of respect for *stare decisis*, *Cartwright* v. *Superintendent of Her Majesty's Prison* [2004] UKPC 10 should have been followed – even though the majority, in not following *Cartwright*, was vindicating the dissenting opinion which Hoffmann (along with Lord Rodger) had delivered in that case.

right.[153] To analyse justificatory perspectives on dissent is to board a carousel of competing assertions. Dissents enhance the authority of a court,[154] often inspire public inquisitiveness about law,[155] tend to sharpen legal decisions,[156] and can console defeated parties and over-ruled judges.[157] Dissents diminish the authority of a court,[158] rarely if

153 See, e.g., Ruth Bader Ginsburg, 'Speaking in a Judicial Voice' (1992) 67 *NYU L. Rev.* 1185, 1191; Claire L'Heureux-Dubé, 'The Dissenting Opinion: The Voice of the Future?' (2000) 38 *Osgoode Hall LJ* 495, 515; Richard A. Posner, 'Introduction', in *The Essential Holmes: Selections from the Letters, Speeches, Judicial Opinions, and Other Writings of Oliver Wendell Holmes, Jr*, ed. R. A. Posner (University of Chicago Press, 1992), ix–xxxi at xiv ('Modern judges are quick to dissent in the hope of being anointed Holmes's heir . . . Most of them do not realize that the power of Holmes's dissents is a function in part of their infrequency; he was careful not to become a broken record'). The critical stance adopted by a serial dissenter will sometimes cut little ice with the judiciary but be admired by legal academics: see Post, 'The Supreme Court Opinion as Institutional Practice', at 1360–2, 1365–6.

154 See Scalia, 'Dissents', 22; Kirby, 'Judicial Dissent – Common Law and Civil Law Traditions', 394; Stephens, 'The Function of Concurring and Dissenting Opinions', 396 ('a dissenting . . . opinion . . . is some showing of the extent to which the author has fulfilled his judicial duty to consider and decide, and some indication, too, that other members of the court have considered and rejected, not merely ignored, the views expressed by him').

155 See Lani Guinier, 'The Supreme Court, 2007 Term – Foreword: Demosprudence Through Dissent' (2008) 122 *Harv. L. Rev.* 4.

156 See Robert W. Bennett, 'A Dissent on Dissent' (1991) 74 *Judicature* 255, 259–60 ('By challenging the ideas of others, the dissent helps sharpen the reasoning of those others . . . [T]he prospect of eventual publication must cause those ideas to be taken more seriously than . . . if the norm were to withhold publication'); Brennan, 'In Defense of Dissents', 430 ('[T]he dissent . . . often . . . safeguards the integrity of the judicial decision-making process by keeping the majority accountable for the rationale and consequences of its decision . . . [V]igorous debate improves the final product'); L'Heureux-Dubé, 'The Dissenting Opinion', 510–11; Kirby, 'Judicial Dissent – Common Law and Civil Law Traditions', 396–7; Alder, 'Dissents in Courts of Last Resort', 240; also *Steadman* v. *Steadman* [1974] QB 161, 182 *per* Scarman LJ ('Were it not for the fact of judicial dissent I would have been content simply to voice my concurrence . . . but, as it is, I propose to make some comment on the interesting arguments addressed by both counsel to this court').

157 See McIntyre, 'In Defence of Judicial Dissent', 444 ('A dissent reassures the losing party that their view has been heard; that at least one judge agreed with them'); Blom-Cooper and Drewry, *Final Appeal*, 89 ('[J]udges . . . like to feel that there is some support from above for their overturned decision . . . [T]he losing litigant likes to know that someone would have found for him'); Henderson, 'From Seriatim to Consensus', 339–40; Bader Ginsburg, 'Remarks on Writing Separately', 143.

158 The argument is often built from the presumption that disagreements on a court, like disagreements in a marriage, tend to be more damaging when tensions are already running high. Pressure to avoid dissent, or open dissent, might be elevated when a court's decision will be controversial come what may. Reed J originally intended to dissent and Jackson J went so far as to produce a draft concurring opinion in *Brown*

ever inspire public inquisitiveness about law,[159] tend to blunt legal decisions (or need not be disclosed in order for them to have a sharpening effect),[160] and might rub salt into a loser's wound.[161] Over and again, claims about judicial dissent can be seen colliding against and neutralizing one another.

Two of the most commonly invoked arguments in defence of judicial dissent are among the most contestable. The first of these connects judicial dissent to one or another aspect of democracy. One version of this argument posits as a feature of democracy the acceptance of judicial as well as political dissent. Just as '[o]ne cannot imagine a judge of a Communist court dissenting against the decrees of the Kremlin', William O. Douglas observed, it is inconceivable that a genuinely democratic political system could censor the expression of outlier judicial opinion.[162] Another version holds that toleration of judicial dissent is

v. *Board of Education* 347 US 483 (1954), but Warren CJ persuaded them both that it was important for the Supreme Court to deliver a unanimous judgment on the issue of segregation: see Tushnet, *I Dissent*, 136. Other decisions on sensitive issues which could have reflected badly on the Supreme Court had there been judicial dissent include *United States* v. *Nixon* 418 US 683 (1974) and *Clinton* v. *Jones* 520 US 681 (1997). See Matthew P. Bergman, 'Dissent in the Judicial Process: Discord in Service of Harmony' (1991) 79 *Denver Univ. L. Rev.* 79, 88–9; Henderson, 'From Seriatim to Consensus', 337. Two years before *Brown*, a proposal that Germany's new Federal Constitutional Court allow dissents was rejected on the basis that public confidence in the Court's authority would be jeopardized if its judges openly disagreed over politically sensitive matters: see Arthur von Mehren, 'The Judicial Process: A Comparative Analysis' (1956) 5 *Am. J. Comparative Law* 197, 208–9 n. 42.

159 See Urofsky, *Dissent and the Supreme Court*, 407; *Northern Securities Co* v. *United States* 193 US 197, 400 (1904) (Holmes J, dissenting) ('I think it useless and undesirable, as a rule, to express dissent'); Blom-Cooper and Drewry, *Final* Appeal, 88.

160 See Mark A. Kadzielski and Robert C. Kunda, 'The Origins of Modern Dissent: The Unmaking of Judicial Consensus in the 1930s' (1983) 15 *Univ. West LA L. Rev.* 43, 54–5; Andrew Lynch, 'Unrequited but Still Great – The Dissent of Justices Dixon and Evatt in *R* v. *Federal Court of Bankruptcy; Ex parte Lowenstein*', in *Great Australian Dissents*, 39–57 at 56. If judicial dissent does (in any particular case) have this sharpening effect, the dissent might well have proved to be counterproductive. Judges who produce dissenting opinions are normally motivated to do so because they favour a legal outcome different from the one favoured by the majority. Dissent which has a sharpening effect is, essentially, opinion which has enabled the majority to improve its reasoning.

161 This argument is commonly made in relation to losing parties in criminal appeals cases: see Section 9.

162 William O. Douglas, 'The Dissent: A Safeguard of Democracy' (1948) 32 *Jnl American Judicature Soc.* 104, 105. For similar statements by other judges, see Fuld, 'The Voices of Dissent', 926; L'Heureux-Dubé, 'The Dissenting Opinion', 503; Jesse W. Carter, 'Dissenting Opinions' (1953) 4 *Hastings LJ* 118, 123 ('Freedom of speech … is an essential ingredient of any democracy. It applies no less to the dissenting judge than it does to the average citizen').

likely to bolster public conviction that the legal system itself is democratic. 'Dissent democratizes law, throws open the doors of law, to those who are its clients'; would-be litigants who consider specific legal rules, or interpretations of rules, unsatisfactory when judged according to their own 'visions of justice' might be more convinced that it is worth engaging with the legal system in the hope of securing appropriate legislative or interpretive changes if there exists estimable judicial dissent sympathetic to the arguments that they advance.[163] A third version of the argument maintains that judicial dissent democratizes the judicial process. The gist of this argument, which has various formulations, is that there is a stronger likelihood that a multi-member panel's deliberations on the plurality of values and interests at stake in a case will be more democratically attuned – more akin to a legislature's deliberations – if its members have been able to articulate disagreements in separate opinions.[164] Courts might not be conduits for democracy in the way that legislatures are, but permitting judges to express diverse legal viewpoints – by, among other things, tolerating overt judicial dissent – might, Alder has suggested, be regarded as a modest but still significant compensatory manoeuvre:

> the practice of dissent helps to offset the democratic deficit in the common law. The judges represent ... an array of incommensurable values and interests each of which deserves respect but which are in permanent competition.[165]

The primary difficulty with arguments connecting judicial dissent to democracy is that some of the purported connections are either slight or

[163] Arthur J. Jacobson, 'Publishing Dissent' (2005) 62 *Washington & Lee L. Rev.* 1607, 1632. See also Henderson, 'From Seriatim to Consensus', 339–40.

[164] See, e.g., Lynch, 'Dissent', 736; L'Heureux-Dubé, 'The Dissenting Opinion', 503; Kevin Stack, 'The Practice of Dissent in the Supreme Court' (1996) 105 *Yale LJ* 2235, 2246 ('[T]he consistency of the [US Supreme] Court with our democratic commitments ... depends in part on the Court reaching its judgments through a deliberative process. That dependence ... grounds the justification for dissent. Simply put, ... dissent is necessary to expose the deliberative character of the Court's decisionmaking'); also, for a Chilean formulation of the argument, Sergio Verdugo, 'Aportes del Modelo de Disidencias Judiciales al Sistema Político. Pluralismo Judicial y Debate Democrático' (2011) 18(2) *Revista de Derecho Universidad Católica del Norte* 217, 252–5. If judges are forbidden from overtly dissenting, furthermore, the point of seeking diversity in judicial appointments might be considered somewhat undermined, for there will be little or no opportunity for judges, certainly when delivering judgments, to express diverse perspectives through opinion writing. See Baroness Hale, 'A Minority Opinion?' (2008) 154 *Proc. Brit. Acad.* 319, 332.

[165] Alder, 'Dissents in Courts of Last Resort', 223.

non-existent. Not all the organs within a system of governance need tolerate dissent in order for the system to be democratic. The fact that judges in the system's courts are not allowed to dissent, moreover, does not mean that the system must be undemocratic. And courts in democracies are democratic institutions, even if they forbid dissent, at least in the trite sense that they form part of a democratic system. Tolerance of judicial dissent certainly means that, on a court as in a legislature, more than one voice can be heard. But it overstates matters to assert that a court functions similar to a legislature – 'represent[ing] not a constituency of electors but one of competing societal values'[166] – by virtue of its willingness to countenance and promulgate dissent.[167] Legislative minorities, unlike judicial ones, will most likely be, and be expected to be, overtly partisan.[168] Legislators who dissent from the legislature's decisions are dissatisfied with an alteration to, or a failure to alter, the law, whereas a judge who dissents is contesting not how or whether the law should change but rather how current law applies to a particular problem.[169] The artificiality of characterizing a court's willingness to countenance dissent as indicative of its legislature-like status as a democratic decision-making organ seems yet more pronounced, moreover, when one considers that the very point of a judge's dissent – many lawyers will recall opinions such as Scalia J's in *Obergefell* v. *Hodges* and Murphy J's in *Korematsu* v. *United States* – will occasionally be to make the case that democracy is in some way undermined by the court's decision.[170]

166 Ibid.

167 See Lord Kerr, 'Dissenting Judgments – Self Indulgence or Self Sacrifice?', Birkenhead Lecture, 8 October 2012, at www.supremecourt.uk/docs/speech-121008.pdf (accessed 17 February 2020), 8 ('I tend to doubt that a judge contemplating dissent is actuated by a burning need to keep the public informed of non-comparable ideals or standards'); also Lynch, 'Dissent', 728.

168 See Kirby, 'Judicial Dissent – Common Law and Civil Law Traditions', 398–9.

169 See Verdugo, 'Aportes del Modelo de Disidencias Judiciales', 233. The analogy between dissent in a final court and dissent against 'a majority of Parliament . . . is not quite perfect', Richard Bethell observed in 1856, because the dissenter in parliament may hope to influence legislators' future lawmaking intentions whereas a dissenting judge in a court of last resort – Bethell presumed the House of Lords to be bound by its own precedents – must accept the 'certainty and fixedness' of the court's decisions. *Report of the Select Committee on the Appellate Jurisdiction. House of Lords Sessional Papers* (London: HMSO, 1856) (264) VIII 401, minutes of evidence, para. 39. See also Section 7.

170 *Obergefell* v. *Hodges* 135 S Ct 2584, 2626 (2015) (Scalia J, dissenting) ('I write separately to call attention to this Court's threat to American democracy'); *Korematsu* v. *United States* 323 US 214, 242 (1944) (Murphy J, dissenting) ('I dissent . . . from this legalization of racism. Racial discrimination in any form and in any degree has no justifiable part whatever in our democratic way of life').

Perhaps the most popular justification for judicial dissent is that it is a platform for the prophetic: through their dissents, judges 'foresee the future before events make it manifest to their contemporaries'.[171] Common-law judges themselves are often the ones endorsing this argument, though the endorsements exist along a spectrum. There is, first of all, the proposition – considered in Section 3 – that today's dissent could be a source of tomorrow's law. In *Kansal*, Lord Hope conceded that his dissent could be considered 'pointless' in light of the clear (privately he depicted it as an exasperating)[172] majority on the court, but he decided not to withdraw it because it sought to answer a question that could arise 'in some future case'.[173] 'A dissenting judgment anchored in the circumstances of today', according to Lord Steyn, 'sometimes appeals to the judges of tomorrow. In that way a dissenting judgment sometimes contributes to the continuing development of the law'.[174] Lady Hale put the point more pithily: '[o]ut of today's minority opinion can sometimes come the orthodoxy of tomorrow'.[175] Lord Neuberger expressed it perhaps a little too pithily: '[t]oday's dissent can often be tomorrow's authority.'[176] Judges sometimes have the satisfaction – as did Lord Griffiths when *Pepper* v. *Hart* was re-argued in the House of Lords[177] – of seeing courts

[171] Alan Barth, *Prophets with Honor: Great Dissents and Great Dissenters in the Supreme Court* (New York: Knopf, 1974), 21.

[172] *Lord Hope's Diaries: House of Lords 1996–2009* (Edinburgh: Avizandum, 2018), 137.

> '[I]n *R* v. *Kansal* . . . the debate . . . centred on whether views expressed by the majority in *R* v. *Lambert* [[2001] UKHL 37] . . . must be followed. Lloyd and Steyn agree with me that it is plainly unsound, but Johan Steyn has refused to accept that we should consider departing from that decision. The position seems to me to be very unsatisfactory, so I have written a very long judgment in draft saying what I think and why I believe we should depart from the majority view in *Lambert*. Lloyd has suggested that the issue should go to a panel of seven Law Lords, but Steyn disagrees with this too . . . As usual, Hutton and Slynn, both desperately slow and neither really engaged . . . have yet to produce their drafts'.

[173] *Kansal (No. 2)* [2001] UKHL 62 at [30]. See also Pound, '*Cacoethes Dissentiendi*', 795 ('a well reasoned dissenting opinion in an important case may play a real part in shaping the law when changed circumstances call for reconsideration of the question of law in new applications').

[174] *Fisher* v. *Minister of Public Safety and Immigration* [1998] AC 673, 686.

[175] Hale, 'A Minority Opinion?', 332.

[176] Neuberger, 'No Judgment – No Justice', para. 23.

[177] *Pepper (Inspector of Taxes)* v. *Hart* [1993] AC 593, 619.

> 'I was in a judicial minority of one at the end of the first hearing of this appeal. It was as a result of the discovery that the Parliamentary history of the legislation gave conclusive support to the construction I preferred that your Lordships agreed that the matter should be re-argued to determine whether it

corroborate their dissents. But only the dissent-corroborating decisions can have precedential authority. The dissents themselves cannot.

These reflections on the future-oriented nature of dissent, all taken from English law, are agnostic: none entails the presumption that the dissent-echoing new law will be either superior or inferior to the old law. Judges from other common-law jurisdictions, particularly the United States, have been more inclined to locate the prophetic dissent on the side of the angels.[178] This might be but an instance of a broader tendency (again, predominantly American) to write rather romantically about judicial dissents as principled challenges to authority – as opinions 'offer[ing] an avenue of representation for perceptions at variance with the dominant vision[,] ... locat[ing] wrong in the majority ... and ... function[ing] analogously to civil disobedience'.[179] '[T]he opinion that voices a dissent', Benjamin Cardozo proclaimed, is that of 'the gladiator making a last stand against the lions', of the judge who 'speaks to the future, ... his voice ... pitched to a key that will carry through the years'.[180] It is difficult to imagine anyone venturing very far into the American literature on judicial dissent before encountering Hughes CJ's remark about the dissent in a court of last resort being

> an appeal to the brooding spirit of the law, to the intelligence of a future day, when a later decision may possibly correct the error into which the dissenting judge believes the court to have been betrayed.[181]

> was permissible to use the Parliamentary history as an aid to the interpretation of the legislation. In my view this case provides a dramatic vindication of the decision to consult Hansard; had your Lordships not agreed to do so the result would have been to place a very heavy burden of taxation upon a large number of persons which Parliament never intended to impose'.

178 See, e.g., Sandra Day O'Connor, *The Majesty of the Law: Reflections of a Supreme Court Justice* (New York: Random House, 2004), 120–2.

179 Campbell, 'The Spirit of Dissent', 307. In a similar vein, see Edward C. Voss, 'Dissent: Sign of a Healthy Court' (1992) 24 *Arizona State LJ* 643, 654; Thomas Healy, *The Great Dissent: How Oliver Wendell Holmes Changed His Mind – and Changed the History of Free Speech in America* (New York: Holt & Co, 2013), 3–5; also Robert Bendiner, 'The Law And Potter Stewart: An Interview with Justice Potter Stewart' (1983) 3 *American Heritage* at www.americanheritage.com (accessed 20 February 2020) ('[W]hen I went to law school we had a professor who said dissenting opinions are nothing but subversive literature').

180 Benjamin N. Cardozo, 'Law and Literature' (1925), in his *Law and Literature and Other Essays and Addresses* (New York: Harcourt, Brace & Co, 1931), 3–40 at 33, 34, 36. See also Richard A. Posner, *The Problems of Jurisprudence* (Cambridge, Mass. Harvard University Press, 1990), 461 ('[J]udicial dissents ... compromise the authoritarian character of the law').

181 Charles Evans Hughes, *The Supreme Court of the United States* (New York: Columbia University Press, 1928), 68.

Observations of this nature, extolling the dissent as a foundation for future law, are by no means entirely ill judged. The path towards which a dissenter points may well be the one that a court eventually takes (the court which is slow to alight on the path, furthermore, is at least able to say that a judicial minority was quick to find it).[182] Sometimes there have been 'three opinions against one', wrote Jefferson – himself no fan of judicial dissent – and 'the reasoning of the one was so much the most cogent as to become afterwards the law of the land'.[183] Even if a dissenting opinion remains the path not taken, the subsequent behaviour of judges and lawyers might still yield evidence of its influence.[184] It would, in short, be foolish to dismiss out of hand the assertion that '[d]issents speak to a future age',[185] that the dissenting judge can hold a 'curious concurrent jurisdiction over the future'.[186]

It is an assertion which can, nevertheless, be easily overplayed. Some of the more enthusiastic pronouncements in favour of the dissenting opinion as prognostication assume that a legal error is rectified once the law aligns with the opinion,[187] as if it were unimaginable that a dissent could be the source of the error and that a dissent-affirming alteration to the law could turn out to be a mistake. There tends also to be built into these pronouncements the assumption that legal alteration is what dissenting judges must want. Yet this need not be the case. Scalia J's dissent in

182 Scalia, 'Dissents', 19 ('When history demonstrates that one of the Court's decisions has been a truly horrendous mistake, it is comforting – and conducive of respect for the Court – to look back and realize that at least some of the justices saw the danger clearly and gave voice').

183 Thomas Jefferson to William Johnson, 27 October 1822, in *The Works of Thomas Jefferson*, XII, 248.

184 See J. D. Heydon, 'Threats to Judicial Independence: The Enemy Within' (2013) 129 *LQR* 205, 211; Bader Ginsburg, 'Remarks on Writing Separately', 143–4; Brennan, 'In Defense of Dissents', 430 ('a dissent sometimes is designed to furnish litigants and lower courts with practical guidance – such as . . . hint[ing] that the litigant might more fruitfully seek relief in a different forum'); L'Heureux-Dubé, 'The Dissenting Opinion', 509; Verdugo, 'Aportes del Modelo de Disidencias Judiciales', 256–9.

185 Ruth Bader Ginsburg, in interview with Nina Totenberg, National Public Radio (USA), 3 May 2002, at www.pbs.org/now/transcript/transcript116_full.html (accessed 26 June 2019).

186 Charles P. Curtis, *Lions Under the Throne* (Boston: Houghton Mifflin Co, 1947), 75.

187 'Dissenting opinions are often the pillars which are ready to take over the burden of supporting a sagging principle of law . . . the shock troops in the battle for justice on the battlefield of reason versus formality and intelligence versus blind technicality'. Musmanno, 'Dissenting Opinions', 152–3. See also Donald P. Lively, *Foreshadows of the Law – Supreme Court Dissents and Constitutional Development* (Westport, Conn.: Praeger, 1992), xxvi.

Lawrence v. *Texas* was prescient: he predicted that same-sex marriage would eventually gain legal recognition in the United States, and this indeed came to pass.[188] But the dissent indicates not his hope but rather his dismayed resignation that the law would move in this direction. Perhaps the most intriguing of all the assumptions embedded in arguments emphasizing the capacity of judicial dissents to speak to the future is the assumption that dissenting opinions are to be singled out in this regard. Future judges and lawyers might well value dissentient opinion as an 'invitation for dialogue about the law's development',[189] because it makes 'visible alternative threads within a legal question',[190] and so on. But there is no reason that they should not value other forms of non-binding judicial pronouncement in exactly the same way. *Obiter dicta*, concurring opinions, contributions to *Festschriften*, after-dinner speeches, and no doubt many other forms of communication provide judges with opportunities to be legal seers. There is no special relationship between the law's future and the dissenting opinion.

If there is an overarching assumption detectable in many of these arguments in defence of dissenting opinions, it is that the source of intellectual inquiry is not the dissent but what motivates dissent. That a judge was moved to dissent need not mean – a point which judges themselves are often eager to emphasize – that the dissent must be understood as instrumental or strategic action. 'I was reluctant to dissent', Lord Denning reflected near the end of his judicial career, '[b]ut . . . [s]o long as I did what I thought was just, I was content'.[191] That dissenters might box more cleverly than this – that they dissent to achieve goals, such as shaping the course of the law, bolstering confidence in the judiciary, providing solace to defeated litigants, and so on – seems

188 *Lawrence* v. *Texas* 539 US 558, 604–5 (2003) (Scalia J, dissenting).

> '[T]he Court says that the present case "does not involve whether the government must give formal recognition to any relationship that homosexual persons seek to enter" . . . Do not believe it. Today's opinion dismantles the structure of constitutional law that has permitted a distinction to be made between heterosexual and homosexual unions, insofar as formal recognition in marriage is concerned . . . This case "does not involve" the issue of homosexual marriage only if one entertains the belief that principle and logic have nothing to do with the decisions of this Court'.

It came to pass in *Obergefell* v. *Hodges* 135 S Ct 2584 (2015).

189 L'Heureux-Dubé, 'The Dissenting Opinion', 508.

190 Marie-Claire Belleau and Rebecca Johnson, 'Ten Theses on Dissent' (2017) 67 *UTLJ* 156, 165.

191 Lord Denning, *The Family Story* (London: Butterworths, 1981), 183.

a fanciful notion, Lord Kerr has suggested, for no judge 'can possibly predict what the effect of a dissenting judgment might be, or indeed if it will ever have any effect'.[192] When, in 2004, Trinidad and Tobago's constitution was interpreted by the Judicial Committee of the Privy Council as not accommodating a discretion to commute death penalty sentences, the position taken by a minority of its members was uncomplicated: the majority's decision was wrong and unjust.[193] The only valid justification for dissenting, Knight Bruce V-C asserted in 1842, is the conviction that one is right and the majority is not.[194] For Kerr, this is the top and bottom of the matter. Judges dissent because of 'their conscience and their conviction' that 'their view is right and . . . the conclusions that their colleagues have reached are wrong . . . It is . . . as prosaic and straightforward as that'.[195] Lady Hale epitomized Kerr's dissenter when, in 2011, she protested that he and other members of the Supreme Court were affirming a position on social care which fell short of the standards of a civilized society.[196] The passion of her opinion was matched by some of the majority's reaction to it.[197]

192 Kerr, 'Dissenting Judgments', 14.

193 *Matthew* v. *State of Trinidad and Tobago* [2004] UKPC 33 at [34].

> 'We consider the decision of the majority to be unsound in law and productive of grave injustice to a small but important class of people in Trinidad and Tobago. It is in our opinion clear that the interpretation of the 1976 Constitution of Trinidad and Tobago which commends itself to the majority does not ensure the protection of fundamental human rights and freedoms, degrades the dignity of the human person and does not respect the rule of law'.

On the ructions behind the scenes, see *Lord Hope's Diaries: House of Lords 1996–2009*, 213–14. The appellant's sentence was, in fact, commuted. The Privy Council had decided in *Pratt* v. *A-G for Jamaica* [1994] 2 AC 1 that defendants in his position had this entitlement. '[I]t would be a cruel punishment', the majority determined in *Matthew*, if the appellant – who, on the basis of *Pratt*, had 'been given the expectation of the possibility of presidential commutation' – were now to be sentenced to death (*Matthew* v. *State of Trinidad and Tobago* at [31]).

194 *Garratt* v. *Cockerell* (1842) 1 Y & C Ch 494, 509 ('A judicial dissent . . . ought to be founded on the clear conviction . . . that the decision is erroneous. Such a clear conviction I do not feel').

195 Kerr, 'Dissenting Judgments', at 22, 16. In a similar if less precise vein, see Michael Kirby, 'Judicial Dissent' (2005) 12 *James Cook Univ. L. Rev*. 4, 10 ('The right and duty to dissent signals that every Australian judge, whatever his or her values, honestly states the law and its application to the case as conscience dictates').

196 *R (McDonald)* v. *Royal Borough of Kensington and Chelsea* [2011] UKSC 33.

197 It is sometimes argued that opinions which tend towards the emotive are more likely to be dissents: see, e.g., Samuel H. Pillsbury, 'Harlan, Holmes, and the Passions of

The motivation to dissent will not always be quite as straightforward as Kerr suggests. Roscoe Pound was mistaken to claim that dissenters, rather than simply satisfying their consciences, must 'afford a useful critique of the opinion of the court'.[198] Purely cathartic dissents are perfectly possible.[199] When judges dissent because they differ fundamentally with a majority over some matter, however, their opinions will often amount to more than merely articulations of the conviction that they have the matter right and the majority does not. Judges might hope that their dissents will have an effect even though they cannot know what, if any, effect their dissents will have. William Brennan's and Thurgood Marshall's repeated dissents in death penalty cases show not only that they considered capital punishment to be incompatible with respect for human dignity, and therefore intrinsically objectionable, but also that they were intent on trying to convince the US Supreme Court that the death penalty was a cruel and unusual punishment prohibited by the Eighth Amendment.[200] While it would be

Justice', in *The Passions of Law*, ed. S. Bandes (New York University Press, 1999), 330–62 at 331; Marie-Claire Belleau, Rebecca Johnson, and Valérie Bouchard, 'Faces of Judicial Anger: Answering the Call' (2007) 1 *European Jnl Leg. Studs* 20, 22 ('[I]t is in dissent that emotion is most apparent because dissent expresses a difference in opinion'). The argument seems questionable. Majority opinions also can be emotional and express a difference of opinion (from the minority). *McDonald* is a case in point. Two of the judges in the majority were very clearly put out by Lady Hale's dissent, though what seemed to irk them most – what one of them 'found nothing short of remarkable' (*McDonald* at [27] *per* Lord Brown) and what another purported to 'deplore' (ibid. at [32] *per* Lord Walker) about the opinion – was not Hale's conclusion (ibid. at [79]) that the majority were affirming a position on social care provision which fell short of the standards of civilized society, but rather the suggestion that the care plan which the local authority wished to maintain, and which the majority was upholding, was irrational. Brown seems, in retrospect, to have wished he had reacted otherwise: Brown, 'Dissenting Judgments', 36. Walker's use of 'deplore' was criticized as intemperate: Robert H. George, 'In Defence of Dissent: *R (McDonald)* v. *Royal Borough of Kensington and Chelsea* [2011] *Elder LJ* 409, 413.

198 Pound, '*Cacoethes Dissentiendi*', at 795, 796. Not only did he think that the critique must be 'useful', but he also insisted that it must address a 'question of law ... of at least considerable importance' (ibid.).

199 See, e.g., O. W. Holmes to Harold J. Laski, 10 November 1923, in *Holmes-Laski Letters*, I, 560 ('I ... have written a short dissent [in *Craig* v. *Hecht*, 263 US 255, 280 (1923)] ... I do not expect to convince anyone as it is rather a statement of my convictions than an argument').

200 See Michael Mello, 'Adhering to Our Views: Brennan and Marshall and the Relentless Dissent to Death as a Punishment' (1995) 22 *Fla. State Univ. L. Rev.* 591, 685–94; also Urofsky, *Dissent and the Supreme Court*, 391–400. In *Matthew* v. *State of Trinidad and Tobago*, one of the dissenters, Lord Nicholls, was similarly intent not only on making clear his view that the majority was wrong but also on emphasizing that the domestic

correct to claim that their dissents were conscience driven, it would be incorrect to assert that they were driven by conscience alone. The presumption that conscience based judicial dissents can have a tactical dimension is particularly evident in the proposition – quite often encountered in American legal literature – that a dissenting judge might be a whistle-blower.[201] Effective whistle-blowers not only indicate where they stand on a matter but also put pressure on those whose judgment decides the matter, as well as on those with the capacity to revisit the matter and rule on it afresh, by credibly representing the judgment as egregious – as when, for example, the whistle-blower shows that considerations relevant to the judgment have been suppressed or distorted.[202] One might question whether dissenting judges really ever are whistle-blowers – the characterization is certainly not one which judges are wont to embrace.[203] In so far as judges ever come close to conforming to the type, however, they are not simply conscientious objectors.

5 Dissents, Decisions, and Courts

A dissent has a context. Factors such as the size and composition of a court, the dispositions of its judges, and the number and the types of decisions that it makes can have a bearing on how frequently dissent occurs, how it is expressed, and how – both on and outside the court – the dissent is likely to be received. The higher the number of judges that hear a case, the greater the probability of dissent (and that several judges will dissent), according to one empirical study, because, as panel size increases, judges minded to dissent are more likely to discover that they are not alone in being so inclined and therefore – knowing or at least expecting that they will not be lone dissenters –

court, having failed to recognize a constitutional discretion to commute the sentence, was 'not fulfilling its proper role as guardian of the constitution' (ibid. at [71]).

201 See, e.g., Frank B. Cross and Emerson H. Tiller, 'Judicial Partisanship and Obedience to Legal Doctrine: Whistleblowing on the Federal Courts of Appeals' (1998) 107 *Yale LJ* 2155; Cass R. Sunstein, *Why Societies Need Dissent* (Cambridge, Mass.: Harvard University Press, 2003), 176–9.

202 See Epstein, Landes, and Posner, 'Why (and When) Judges Dissent', 109.

203 See, e.g., Harry T. Edwards, 'Collegiality and Decision Making on the DC Circuit' (1998) 84 *Va. L. Rev.* 1335, 1337 ('[T]he . . . so-called "whistle blower" hypothesis is the product of sheer speculation, and finds no convincing support in . . . data; . . . the hypothesis is absurd and would be understood as such by anyone familiar with the judges and operation of the DC Circuit').

have less reason to be apprehensive about dissenting.[204] Judges might dissent less – might opt to dissent only when especially inclined to do so – if they serve on courts that have heavy caseloads.[205] There are jurisdictionally specific analyses suggesting that the types of case in which dissent is most likely are those which overrule rather than affirm precedent,[206] which yield no clear *ratio* or hinge upon contentious interpretations of legal sources,[207] and which concern fundamental rights.[208] Dissenters' reputations and opinion-writing styles can affect the reception of their dissents.[209] So too might the nature of a court's judgment. The United States Supreme Court is the source of many impassioned, powerfully reasoned, principled, and articulate dissents.[210] Yet the weight of dissenting opinion in a US Supreme Court judgment will sometimes be attributable not only to the quality of the dissentient reasoning but also to the fact that the case contains more dissent than decision. There are certainly cases in which five-

204 See Epstein, Landes, and Posner, 'Why (and When) Judges Dissent', at 105–6, 120. On greater aversion to dissenting alone, see Rachel J. Cahill-O'Callaghan, *Values in the Supreme Court: Decisions, Division and Diversity* (Oxford: Hart, 2020), at 69–70, 118–19.

205 See Robert G. Richards, 'Writing Separately' (2017) 67 *UTLJ* 149, 150 ('Most appellate judges in Canada have their plates full. We would be sorely challenged to find the time to do a great deal of "separate writing"'); Epstein, Landes, and Posner, 'Why (and When) Judges Dissent', at 104, 131–2; Sunstein, *Why Societies Need Dissent*, 20.

206 See Epstein, Landes, and Posner, 'Why (and When) Judges Dissent', 123–4.

207 See Edvard Hambro, 'Dissenting and Individual Opinions in the International Court of Justice' (1956–7) 17 *Zeitschrift für ausländisches öffentliches Recht und Völkerrecht* 229 at 231 (England), 247–8 (ICJ).

208 Kirby, 'Judicial Dissent', 6–7; also Michael Blackwell, 'Indeterminacy, Disagreement and the Human Rights Act: An Empirical Study of Litigation in the UK House of Lords and Supreme Court 1997–2017' (2020) 83 *MLR* 285. 'Higher levels of human rights discourse', according to Blackwell, 'are associated with greater levels of disagreement' (ibid. at 285). Perhaps the correlation is specifically between the type of discourse and express disagreement. It seems conceivable that whereas, on some legal issues, judges will disagree with other judges but consider it not worth openly dissenting, or even indicating disagreement, the high profile nature of many human rights cases, and perhaps the greater probability that these cases stir judges' consciences, could make it more likely that dissents and disagreements over fundamental rights issues are aired.

209 For two vivid Australian examples, see Simone Degeling and Greg Weeks, 'The Essence of a Fiduciary Relationship: Justice Mason's Dissent in *Hospital Products Ltd* v. *United States Surgical Corporation* (1984)', in Lynch (ed.), *Great Australian Dissents*, 209–28 at 226–7; and A. J. Brown, 'When Liberty Divides: Judicial Cleavages and their Consequences in *Al-Kateb* v. *Godwin* (2004)', in ibid. at 311–34, 313.

210 For three exemplars, see *Plessy* v. *Ferguson* 163 US 537, 552 (1896) (Harlan J, dissenting); *Betts* v. *Brady* 316 US 455, 474 (1942) (Black J, dissenting); and *Dennis* v. *United States* 341 US 494, 581 (1951) (Douglas J, dissenting).

against-four resembles one-against-four, the opinion of the Court hanging like a *piñata* which the dissenters take turns to beat.[211]

There are reasons to be wary of some of the hypotheses connecting particular court-contextual factors to the phenomenon of dissent. While it might be correct to claim that a court's characteristics and practices bear upon its dissent rate, it might be difficult convincingly to test the claim if the attributes of the court suggest that its judges should simultaneously be predisposed and averse to producing dissents (as when, for example, the judicial panel is large but its case-load is very heavy). Opinion-writing styles are unlikely by themselves to have an effect on how judicial dissents are received. Brevity in dissent could be welcomed as pithy or criticized as cryptic, just as judges who dissent at length might be lauded for attention to detail or chided for self-indulgence. What matters, in so far as opinion-writing style matters at all, is not the dissenter's style but her ability, or lack of ability, as a purveyor of that style. It is conceivable that a dissenter's judicial reputation will sometimes bear upon how her dissents are received, and certainly the inverse – that the reception of a judge's dissents has a bearing on her (enviable or unenviable) reputation – is perfectly possible.[212] Within some court systems, it is perhaps also conceivable (though it would surely be difficult to prove) that there are judges who endeavour to enhance or embellish a particular judge's reputation because the judge is responsible for dissentient reasoning which these judges would like to see transformed into precedent.[213]

[211] See, e.g., *Obergefell* v. *Hodges* 135 S Ct 2584 (2015). Oliver Wendell Holmes regularly observed that, whereas the writer of the majority opinion has to negotiate the constraints of representing the Court, dissenters can express themselves with much more freedom: see, e.g., O. W. Holmes to Harold J. Laski, 15 March 1917, in *Holmes-Laski Letters*, I, 69 ('Now I am sketching possible dissents in various directions . . . It is a fine sport as one is freer and more personal than when one is speaking for others as well as for oneself'); also Holmes to Laski, 16 August 1924, in ibid. I at 646–7. The *piñata* effect is less likely to be evident when the Court's holding is derived from a plurality rather than a majority opinion. In plurality cases – cases in which more than half of the Justices on the Court agree on the outcome but, disagreeing on reasoning, choose either to write their own opinion or join with someone else's – the force of dissenting opinion is sometimes enhanced by relative lack of unity among the Justices from whose opinions the holding is derived: see, e.g., *Furman* v. *Georgia* 408 US 238 (1972).

[212] See Richard A. Primus, 'Canon, Anti-Canon, and Judicial Dissent' (1998) 48 *Duke LJ* 243, 259 ('Harlan, Holmes, and Brandeis were great Justices, and, in their opinions, authorship often seems to become authority. A question immediately arises, however, as to why those Justices are considered great in the first place. Is it not at least partly because they wrote great opinions, including, and perhaps especially, great dissents?').

[213] See ibid. at 288–300, also 252 ('By reimagining a dissenting Justice and presenting him as a heroic figure, and by simultaneously reimagining the meaning of that Justice's

Underpinning the contextual approach to dissent is an assumption that judges' attitudes to dissenting – whether they are willing to dissent, on what bases they consider it appropriate to dissent, what they hope to achieve by dissenting, and so on – bear a relationship to the courts on which they sit and the types of decisions those courts make. This is by no means an unwarranted assumption – the point of the next section, indeed, is to show that it is hardly possible properly to explain judicial dissent as a phenomenon in English law without taking into account various details which feature in the history of England's appellate courts. It is, nevertheless, important to bear in mind that observations on the relationship between dissent and court often trade on speculation.

Consider, for example, the not uncommon claim that there is a greater likelihood that a court will tolerate and even condone judicial dissent if it specializes in constitutional adjudication. In continental European countries, express dissent is rarely considered acceptable in the ordinary courts, yet it regularly features in the judgments of many constitutional courts. Various hypotheses have been advanced to try to explain why this should be so. Judges in the ordinary courts can be expected to disapprove of express dissent because they almost always receive their legal training in the ordinary court system itself, one political scientist has maintained, whereas judges in European constitutional courts are often former academics – they used to 'spend much of their day . . . developing theory' – and so they 'could be more amenable to filing dissents', given that doing so enables them 'to advance personal theories or shape the future path of the law'.[214] Another conjecture is that ideological as well as legal-interpretive differences can prompt dissent in European constitutional courts because the judges – who are often appointed to the courts following party-political nominations – sometimes diverge over the politics motivating a challenge to the constitutionality of a statute.[215]

dissenting opinions, courts reshape the constitutional canon and construct authorities on which they can then rely in cases before them').

214 Benjamin Bricker, 'Breaking the Principle of Secrecy: An Examination of Judicial Dissent in the European Constitutional Courts' (2017) 39 *Law & Policy* 170, 176.

215 See, e.g., Chris Hanretty, 'Dissent in Iberia: The Ideal Points of Justices on the Spanish and Portuguese Constitutional Tribunals' (2012) 51 *European Jnl of Political Research* 671; Christoph Hönnige, 'The Electoral Connection: How the Pivotal Judge Affects Oppositional Success at European Constitutional Courts' (2009) 32 *West European Politics* 963, 979 (on politicized dissents in Germany's *Bundesverfassungsgericht*). For the argument that, as regards the Spanish Constitutional Court, the hypothesis is simplistic – that the Court's judges, being from a 'civil law background that traditionally favors consensus and dislikes dissent', tend ultimately to eschew the delivery of

Literature on the US Supreme Court yields similar observations. After the Court held, in 1938, that federal common law would no longer be used to settle disputes between litigants based in diverse jurisdictions,[216] its function as a common law final appeal tribunal diminished significantly and constitutional matters began to dominate its docket. Once the Court started to focus increasingly on difficult, often politically controversial, constitutional issues, the percentage of unanimous decisions that it handed down declined quite markedly.[217] Separate dissenting and concurring opinions began to feature regularly in the Court's decisions after Harlan Fiske Stone was made Chief Justice in 1941.[218] Stone saw virtue in judicial dissent: a decision containing dissent, he observed before the Fourth Circuit Court of Appeals in 1942, provides 'assurance to counsel and to the public that [the] decision has not been perfunctory' and 'sounds a warning note that legal doctrine must not be pressed too far'.[219] He was both uninhibited about writing and happy to see others write – was possessed of a leadership style which could prompt others to write – dissenting opinions.[220] Stone's leadership style was attributable both to his temperament, it has been claimed, and to his 'academic pedigree': as 'the first academic appointed to hold the position of Chief Justice' – Stone served as Dean of Columbia Law School between 1910 and 1923 – he was, in comparison with others on the Court, 'more likely to encourage open debate'.[221]

Even if claims connecting judges' dispositions and former academic careers with propensity to dissent are well grounded, they do not necessarily reveal anything specifically about constitutional courts. If judges

dissenting opinions even if it means forsaking the advancement of their own 'ideological goals' – see Nuno Garoupa, Fernando Gómez-Pomar, and Veronica Grembi, 'Judging under Political Pressure: An Empirical Analysis of Constitutional Review Voting in the Spanish Constitutional Court' (2013) 29 *Jnl of Law, Econ. & Organization* 513, 521.

216 *Erie Railroad Co* v. *Tomkins* 304 US 64 (1938).

217 See Henderson, 'From Seriatim to Consensus', 324–5.

218 See ibid. at 325.

219 Harlan Fiske Stone, 'Dissenting Opinions are not Without Value' (1942) 28 *Jnl of the American Judicature Society* 76, 76.

220 See Thomas G. Walker, Lee Epstein, and William J. Dixon, 'On the Mysterious Demise of Consensual Norms in the United States Supreme Court' (1988) 50 *Jnl of Politics* 361; also the quotations attributed to Stone in Alpheus T. Mason, *Harlan Fiske Stone: Pillar of the Law* (New York: Viking Press, 1956), at 608 ('I do not think it is the appropriate function of a Chief Justice to attempt to dissuade members of the Court from dissenting in individual cases'), 628 ('Sound legal principles ... never sprang full-fledged from the brains of any man or group of men. They are the ultimate resultant of the abrasive force of the clash of competing and sometimes conflicting ideas').

221 Henderson, 'From Seriatim to Consensus', 325.

who like to goad other judges or who are quondam academics – or who match both of these descriptions – tend to raise dissent rates when they sit specifically on constitutional courts, we might surmise that the rates are somehow affected by the combination of particular judicial characteristics and the nature of the court. Whatever it is about the nature of the court that contributes to this effect, however, still needs to be identified. If evidence shows that dissent rates tend to rise when judges exhibiting one or both of these qualities serve on courts which do not specialize in constitutional adjudication as well as on ones which do, the indication is that it is the nature of the judge rather than the nature of the court that explains the predilection for dissent.

The hypothesis that judges on a final court will demonstrate a greater proclivity to dissent when the court enforces the constitution has been regularly explored in US legal literature. Political divisions on the bench are sometimes thought to explain why, on the US Supreme Court as in European constitutional courts, unanimous decisions on particular constitutional questions cannot be reached.[222] There is a greater expectation, it has quite often been suggested, that justices will write separate opinions – whether in dissent or in concurrence – when there exists among them differences over what is and is not constitutionally protected.[223] A constitutional case might, as compared with other cases, more regularly see parties who are interested in but who are not litigating the case file a diverse range of interventions – *amicus curiae* briefs – setting out arguments for particular outcomes, thereby potentially tugging the justices (or at least justices who are willing to take the briefs seriously) in various directions, and so increasing the likelihood that the Court's decision will be accompanied by dissent.[224]

The most commonplace supposition connecting dissents and constitutional adjudication concerns *stare decisis*. In a conversation with Felix

222 See, e.g., Richard A. Posner, 'The Supreme Court 2004 Term – Foreword: A Political Court' (2005) 119 *Harv. L. Rev.* 32, 48–51.

223 See Kelman, 'The Forked Path of Dissent', 248 ('[In] many constitutional cases ... justices form such strong and matured convictions ... that they find it exceedingly hard to make even the limited shift from dissent to temporary accommodation'); William H. Rehnquist, 'The Supreme Court: Past and Present' (1973) 59 *ABAJ* 361, 363 ('It may well be that the nature of constitutional adjudication invites, at least, if it does not require, more separate opinions than does adjudication of issues of law in other areas').

224 See Paul M. Collins, Jr, 'Amici Curiae and Dissensus on the US Supreme Court' (2008) 5 *Jnl of Empirical Legal Studies* 143.

Frankfurter in 1923, Louis Brandeis is reported as observing that judicial dissent has a 'special function' in constitutional cases.

> In ordinary cases there is a good deal to be said for not having dissents. You want certainty & definiteness & it doesn't matter terribly how you decide, so long as it is settled. But in these constitutional cases, since what is done is what you call statesmanship, nothing is ever settled – unless statesmanship is settled & at an end.[225]

The special function that Brandeis ascribes to dissent seems not to exist. If, in these constitutional cases, nothing is ever settled, it is a court's capacity to overrule itself, rather than the ability of its judges to write dissenting opinions, that is significant. Brandeis's core point, articulated rather more strenuously by Daniel J some seventy years earlier,[226] was that Supreme Court precedents are perilous propositions if they settle matters of constitutional interpretation once and for all (or rather, subject only to constitutional amendment), for the Court would never be able to recant from a doctrine – separate-but-equal is perhaps the most obvious example – which it now considers discredited. Where a case concerns the Constitution, Brandeis remarked in 1932, the Court will often prefer 'the force of better reasoning' to the norm of *stare decisis* and so will overrule its own precedent.[227] What this 'usually means', one renowned constitutional lawyer would later observe, is 'that *stare decisis* has no weight when the constitutional law on a particular subject seems, to a majority of the Court, to be in need of correction'.[228] This is a line of argument regarding majority rather than dissenting opinions. It is not

[225] Melvin I. Urofsky, 'The Brandeis-Frankfurter Conversations' [1985] *Supreme Court Rev.* 299, 314. The article is composed mainly of Felix Frankfurter's notes of conversations that he and Brandeis had during the 1922–4 Supreme Court summer recesses.

[226] '[T]his is a matter involving a construction of the Constitution ... [W]herever the construction or the integrity of that sacred instrument is involved, I can hold myself trammeled by no precedent or number of precedents. That instrument is above all precedents, and its integrity everyone is bound to vindicate against any number of precedents if believed to trench upon its supremacy.' *Rundle* v. *Delaware & Raritan Canal Co* 55 US (14 How) 80, 99 (1852) (Daniel J, dissenting).

[227] *Burnet* v. *Coronado Oil & Gas Co* 285 US 393, 406–8 (1932) (Brandeis J, dissenting) ('But in cases involving the Federal Constitution, where correction through legislative action is practically impossible, this court has often overruled its earlier decisions. The court bows to the lessons of experience and the force of better reasoning, recognizing that the process of trial and error, so fruitful in the physical sciences, is appropriate also in the judicial function'). See also *Payne* v. *Tennessee* 501 US 808, 827 (1991); *Randall* v. *Sorrell* 548 US 230, 267 (2006) (Thomas J, concurring).

[228] Henry P. Monaghan, 'Taking Supreme Court Opinions Seriously' (1979) 39 *Maryland L. Rev.* 1, 3.

dissent but rather overruling – a manoeuvre at the disposal of a majority – which has a special function in constitutional cases. Dissent, by contrast, has an ancillary function: keeping in play arguments which are not, but which (were the Court to overrule itself appropriately) some day could be, legally authoritative.

If there is a greater likelihood of judicial dissent in areas of law where precedents are particularly susceptible to alteration, and if constitutional adjudication is an area in which the norm of *stare decisis* holds relatively little sway, it might reasonably be assumed that constitutional matters will generate a disproportionate amount of dissenting opinion.[229] It is far from clear, however, that there is something about a court *qua* constitutional court that makes it a naturally fertile ground for judicial dissent. A constitutional court might, in fact, provide nowhere for dissent to flourish – for the simple reason that its judges are forbidden from publishing separate opinions.[230] The hypothesis which espies a connection between constitutional courts, judicial dissent, and relaxed attitudes to precedent following suggests, furthermore, that the high incidence of dissent on a constitutional court is attributable not to the fact that the court's fare is constitutional litigation, but rather to the fact that, as compared with the ordinary courts, it is more likely overrule its precedents. While constitutional courts certainly often do produce considerable amounts of judicial dissent, explaining why this should be so is not at all straightforward.

6 The Tug of Unanimity in England's Courts

What of the English courts? It would be very surprising if attitudes to dissent in English appeal courts were not somehow intertwined with the characteristics of the courts themselves. Yet the circumspection urged in the previous section applies to England's courts just as it does to those of

[229] Constitutional matters will very likely also spur a relatively high proportion of other types of intervention (concurrences, *dicta*, law review articles, and so on) which, like judicial dissents, have the potential to influence future judicial decision-making.

[230] In European constitutional courts, express dissent is not always an option. Under art. 26 of the Irish Constitution, for example, if the President refers a bill to the Supreme Court for a ruling as to the bill's constitutionality, the Court is obliged to deliver a single judgment: see Constitution of Ireland art. 26.2.2° ('The decision of the majority of the judges of the supreme court shall, for the purposes of this article, be the decision of the court and shall be pronounced by such one of those judges as the court shall direct, and no other opinion, whether assenting or dissenting, shall be pronounced nor shall the existence of any such other opinion be disclosed').

other jurisdictions: beware analyses straightforwardly connecting prevailing attitudes towards dissent to a court's (or court system's) culture and norms.

Take, for example, the claim – advanced by a diverse range of judges and jurists – that central to any satisfactory explanation of English judicial attitudes to dissent is the fact that judges have traditionally delivered judgments extempore. Until recently in the history of the English courts, oral hearings and judgments were routine, with each judge involved in a case delivering his own opinion at the end of the trial.[231] The off-the-cuff judgment produced in response to oral pleadings – none of the deciding judges having been apprised of the facts of the case, considered written submissions on it, brushed up on relevant authorities in preparation for it, or conferred with one another about it – was still standard practice in the second half of the twentieth century.[232] '[I]t is exceptional for the judgments … to be delivered otherwise than extempore and orally', Evershed MR observed apropos the Court of Appeal in 1950.[233] The objective of appointing more judges to the Court in 1934 had been to enable each judge – this was when the Court always sat in panels of three – 'to take a day, as occasion demanded, not sitting in court in order to consider and write reserved judgments'.[234] This is certainly what Evershed had hoped would happen.[235] Yet, by the middle of the century, the plan

[231] It was not feasible for early courts to conduct their business in documentary form. Even if it had been feasible, the practice would have barred illiterate jury members from following legal proceedings. Other than in the House of Lords and the Judicial Committee of the Privy Council, the presentation of written submissions and skeleton arguments remained unusual until it became possible to replicate documents at speed. To this day, a good deal of run of the mill court business is done orally.

[232] See F. H. Lawson, 'Comparative Judicial Style' (1977) 25 *Am. J. Comparative Law* 364, 364–5; Heydon, 'Threats to Judicial Independence', 207–8; Jeffery Bowman et al., *Review of the Court of Appeal (Civil Division): Report to the Lord Chancellor* (London: Lord Chancellor's Department, 1997), 90 (para. 47); Lord Dyson, *Justice: Continuity and Change* (Oxford: Hart, 2018), 182 (on having submissions to the Civil Division of the Court of Appeal in the mid-1970s 'dispatched … in a couple of hours by *ex tempore* judgments'); also Lady Hale, email to author, 24 June 2020 ('[B]y my time in the CA [1999–2003], extempore and reserved judgments were roughly half and half'); and Michael Zander, *The Law-Making Process*, 8th ed. (Oxford: Hart, 2020), 296 n. 26 (data indicating that, by 2014, the proportion of extempore judgments delivered annually in the Court of Appeal had declined to just under one-third).

[233] Raymond Evershed, *The Court of Appeal in England* (London: Athlone Press, 1950), 16.

[234] Ibid. at 14.

[235] Ibid. at 15 ('I do not myself think that we reserve – that we are able to reserve – as many judgments as perhaps we should').

had 'not worked out'.[236] A judge would still hear a case ignorant of its facts before it was called, and would normally deliver an oral opinion immediately or very soon after its conclusion. '[B]efore a case is opened . . . the judges have no knowledge of it. It is the duty of counsel in opening the case to give to the court all the necessary facts and the whole matter is thrashed out in open court'.[237]

It is easy to understand why the judicial culture which Evershed describes is sometimes thought to be conducive to the production of dissents. When the judges on a court are thinking on their feet and delivering individual, unscripted, quite often unreserved opinions without having given much or any consideration to what the other deciding judges have to say, it is, the argument runs, only to be expected that the court's decisions will regularly be accompanied by opinions in dissent from (which does not mean these opinions will always have been formulated as dissents from) the majority. '[T]he English dissenting opinion is not a deliberate "institution"', Gino Gorla claimed in 1965,

> but in its historical formation . . . it is simply the natural product of the oral discussion of the case between judges and lawyers; and therefore it is the natural product of the oral opinion of the judge, rendered at hearing, as it happens and often still happens today in the English courts and in others that follow the example.[238]

Yet Evershed himself, in the course of explaining the workings of the mid-twentieth-century Court of Appeal, cast doubt on this line of argument. The judgments of US appeals courts, he observed, are commonly reserved and scripted.[239] That dissenting opinions are very much a feature of these courts suggests that there is no distinct connection between the practice of judicial dissent and a culture of extempore judgment delivery. He maintained, furthermore, that it is a mistake to conflate the routine production of separate opinions by English judges with the regular production of dissenting opinions. Although *seriatim* might be the norm on the Court of Appeal, 'the benefit of a combined

[236] Ibid. at 14–15.

[237] Ibid. at 25.

[238] Gino Gorla, 'La struttura della decisione giudiziale in diritti italiano e nella "Common Law": Riflessi di tale struttura sull'interpretazione della sentenza, sui "Reports" e sul "Dissenting"' (1965) 117 *Giurisprudenza Italiana* 1239, 1255. See also Kirby, 'Judicial Dissent – Common Law and Civil Law Traditions', 384; Kelemen, *Judicial Dissent in European Constitutional Courts*, 82.

[239] Evershed, *The Court of Appeal in England*, 25.

judicial operation'[240] by the deciding judges – their 'learn[ing] the case together[,] ... hearing the questions of ... [their] colleagues, ... understanding the working upon the matter in hand of two [other judicial] minds'[241] – means that 'dissenting judgments are relatively rare'.[242] The oral tradition, he believed, reveals little about – is perhaps the source of an inaccurate conclusion about – dissent in the English courts.

Explaining dissent specifically as it features in the English courts requires, not surprisingly, that one looks to the somewhat complicated history of the courts themselves. The principle of decision by majority – with a (nowadays theoretical)[243] power to dissent vested in the Crown – appears always to have been accepted by parliament and royal council.[244] An early affirmation of the principle can be found in the security clause of the original Magna Carta. Should the king be alleged to have disobeyed the charter's terms, and a committee of twenty-five barons is convened to determine how or if he should be constrained, then, 'if ... these twenty-five disagree among themselves ..., or if any of them ... should not wish or should be unable to attend, what the greater part of those who are present provide or order, is to be treated as ratified and binding, as if all the twenty-five had consented to this'.[245] Note that the majority decision was to be read as if it were unanimous.[246] Maitland, reflecting on decision-making in medieval townships, wondered if the equation was simplistic. '[T]he corporate One' was considered stronger than 'the plural Many': a right at the disposal of many – such as 'the hidesman's right to feed his cattle on the "common"

[240] Ibid. at 22.

[241] Ibid. at 26.

[242] Ibid. at 27.

[243] The power was last exercised in 1708 when Queen Anne, on the advice of her ministers, refused assent to the Scottish Militia Bill. When, in September 2019, the UK parliament passed legislation compelling executive action at odds with a policy which the Conservative government was committed to pursuing, the Crown was not advised to withhold assent from the bill once it had passed through both houses – even though the government did attempt (though it quickly abandoned) a filibuster in the lords, and even though the Prime Minister went so far as to state that he intended to act in contravention of the bill both before and after it had been enacted as law.

[244] See John Gilbert Heinberg, 'History of the Majority Principle' (1926) 20 *Am. Pol. Sci. Rev.* 52, 62–3; John Baker, *The Oxford History of the Laws of England. Vol. VI: 1483–1558* (Oxford University Press, 2003), 74–5; Chris Young, 'The History of Judicial Dissent in England: What Relevance Does It Have for Modern Common Law Legal Systems?' (2009) 32 *Australian Bar Rev.* 96, 109.

[245] Magna Carta (1215), c. 61. The clause does not appear in subsequent reissues and confirmations of the charter.

[246] See John Locke, *Two Treatises of Government*, ed. P. Laslett (Cambridge University Press, 1988 [1689]), 331–3 (II. viii. 96–8).

land' – could be nullified by a municipal resolution 'carried by a majority of one'.[247] Yet the decision of a bare majority was itself a representation by the many. Why should it prevail over 'the old right of the community'?[248] It seemed to Maitland that, in the middle ages, 'this question was obscured from view'.[249]

> Our habit of treating the voice of a majority as equivalent to the voice of an all is so deeply ingrained that we hardly think that it has a history. But a history it has, and there is fiction there . . . In the earlier middle ages it is unanimity that is wanted; it is unanimity that is chronicled; it is unanimity that is after a sort obtained . . . But until men will say plainly that a vote carried by a majority of one is for certain purposes every whit as effectual as an unanimous vote, one main contrast between corporate ownership and mere community escapes them.[250]

The central royal courts of medieval England were corporate in nature: a decision made by multiple judges was a decision by a unified court. In the earliest law reports, opinions were almost never assigned to specific individuals.[251] Records of medieval court proceedings make it difficult to tell when judges were genuinely unanimous and when the view of a majority prevailed (or how minority views were dealt with when one did prevail).[252] Unanimity on a bench was sometimes Maitland's unanimity 'after a sort'. In 1535, when judges in the Exchequer Chamber could not agree on whether a will of the use of land was void, Henry VIII – who stood to acquire the relevant land if the title-holder was held to have died intestate – coaxed them into unanimously accepting that it was.[253] Such

247 Frederic William Maitland, *Township and Borough* (Cambridge University Press, 1898), 33.

248 Ibid. at 34.

249 Ibid.

250 Ibid. at 34–5.

251 See Paul Brand, 'Introduction', in *The Earliest English Law Reports. Vol. II: Common Bench Reports 1285–1289 and Undated Reports 1279–1289 (SS vol. 123)* (London: Selden Society, 2007), xi–ccxvi at xvi ('In the very earliest law reports it is quite rare for individual speeches or arguments to be assigned to specific individuals, and the practice only became at all common after 1278').

252 'Whether unity imported unanimity is a difficult question to tackle . . . What the record prevents us from knowing is whether dissentients could be overruled or ignored'. John Baker, 'The Changing Concept of a Court', in his *Collected Papers on English Legal History*, 3 vols. (Cambridge University Press, 2014), I, 413–31 at 428.

253 *Re Lord Dacre of the South*, YB Pas 27 Hen VIII 7 (1535) at 7 (pl. 22). More instructive than the Year Book account, which concerns the arguments made in court, is Spelman's report of the judges' meetings with the king and his secretary, Thomas Cromwell: see (1977) 93 Selden Soc. 228–30; also (1977) 94 Selden Soc. 140, 201; John Baker, *Baker and Milsom. Sources of Legal History: Private Law to 1750*, 2nd ed. (Oxford University Press,

externally applied pressure was no doubt highly irregular. What is less clear is whether prospective dissentients commonly encountered pressure inside the court. Certainly there are cases in which judges admit a predisposition to decide in favour of a litigant but declare themselves constrained from doing so by virtue of deference to a majority on the bench. In *Sutton* v. *Forster*, heard in the Exchequer Chamber in 1483, Bryan CJ gave judgment against his own opinion. Though 'the opinion of several judges' who disagreed with him conformed to 'no reason or law that I conceive of', he lamented, 'I must do as the greater part of the judges do'.[254] In a case before the Common Pleas just over a century later, concerning a contract containing an obviously incorrect commencement date, Anderson CJ was of the opinion that the defendant had no obligations under the contract until that date arrived. The three other justices, however, 'were strongly against him to the contrary'[255] and so 'Anderson against his own opinion gave judgment for the plaintiff'.[256]

Before the sixteenth century, unanimity in decision – whether genuine or artificial – was very much *comme il faut* in the English courts. A requirement that juries deliver unanimous verdicts appears to have become established court practice by the mid-fourteenth century – the Court of Common Pleas put the matter beyond doubt in 1367 when it held majority verdicts to be void.[257] That judges themselves were

2010), 131–2. Spelman's reporter records that the Exchequer Chamber was evenly divided but that one of the judges, Port JKB, 'spoke so softly', that his opinion was misunderstood and was counted on the wrong side, making a majority of six-to-four in favour of the king. The king wanted the decision to be unanimous and so, according to the reporter, 'all the justices were commanded to appear before the king; and the king commanded them to assemble in order to agree in their opinions. And those who were of opinion that the will was void would have the king's best thanks'. (*Baker and Milsom*, 132.)

254 *Sutton* v. *Forster*, YB Mich 1 Rich III 1 (1483) at 3 (pl. 2); (1945) 64 Selden Soc 56, 62. See also J. H. Baker, *The Legal Profession and the Common Law: Historical Essays* (London: The Hambledon Press, 1986), 168.

255 *Bishop and Harecourt's case* (1589) 1 Leo 210, 211; *Bishop* v. *Harecourt* (1590) Cro Eliz 210, 210 ('Of that opinion was Anderson . . . The three other justices *contra*').

256 *Bishop* v. *Harecourt*, 210; *Bishop and Harecourt's case*, 211 ('and afterwards judgment was given for the plaintiff').

257 YB Mich 41 Edw III 31 (1367) at 31 (pl. 36) (Assize verdict by majority of eleven rejected by Thorp CJ in Common Pleas, 'for the law was founded that each inquest would be taken by twelve free men, and not by fewer'). Jury verdicts with single dissents had been tolerated up to this point, though dissenting jurors were sometimes punished: see David J. Seipp, 'Jurors, Evidences and the Tempest of 1499', in *'The Dearest Birth Right of the People of England': The Jury in The History of the Common Law*, ed. J. W. Cairns and G. McLeod (Oxford: Hart, 2002), 75–92 at 88.

expected to decide unanimously is indicated by the fact that a bench was usually composed of four members[258] – the possibility of judges finding themselves deadlocked if panels were not odd-numbered seems not to have been a significant concern.[259] Judicial dissent, when it existed, was sometimes kept hidden.[260] By the late-medieval period – once reasoned decision-making started to become part of the judicial function – judges, when they could only establish a majority rather than unanimity on a point of law, would often repeatedly adjourn cases and would even avoid giving judgment altogether.

> [T]hey often did nothing. Judicial indecision on a point of law was not seen as a dereliction of duty, as it would be today, because it encouraged and helped the parties to settle their differences – or induced the plaintiff to give up – when the merits were in balance. And, if the parties settled or abandoned the dispute, the courts were relieved from the embarrassment of having to settle the legal doubt.[261]

Why should unanimity, even the mere appearance of unanimity, have been considered important? Intriguingly, one concern seems to have been that a system of decision by judicial majorities could sometimes result in a judicial minority carrying the day. If four judges unanimous in one court are overruled by four judges unanimous in another, the loser on appeal might at least understand that the tie is resolved by the fact that, of the two courts, the latter is the senior one. Without the requirement of unanimity, however, an appellate majority could overrule a unanimous lower court, leaving the loser on appeal wondering why the opinions of five of England's judges – who, notwithstanding a court hierarchy, were all equal in rank – should count

258 See Blackstone, 3 *Commentaries* 40–1. Blackstone notes that odd-numbered benches were sometimes appointed during the reign of James I. *Maine* v. *Peacher*, discussed below, is an example.

259 See John V. Orth, 'How Many Judges Does It Take to Make a Supreme Court?' (2002) 19 *Constitutional Commentary* 681, 686–7.

260 *Slade's case* (1602) 4 Co Rep 91, for example, which determined that debts could be recovered by the action of *assumpsit*, is commonly reported as a unanimous decision – 'the resolution of all the justices of England' (ibid. at 92) – yet it was a decision by a majority. See *Wright* v. *Swanton* (1604), repr. in *Baker and Milsom* 479–81 at 480 *per* Walmsley J ('the case ... was resolved by the opinion of the greater number'); David Ibbetson, 'Sixteenth Century Contract Law: *Slade's case* in Context' (1984) 4 *OJLS* 295, 303–4; also J. H. Baker, *The Law's Two Bodies: Some Evidential Problems in English Legal History* (Oxford University Press, 2001), 17 ('[I]n *Slade's Case* ... Popham CJ refused to allow the judges to give their reasons in public, lest the dissentients should sound too persuasive').

261 Baker, *The Oxford History of the Laws of England. Vol. VI*, 49.

for less than the opinions of three.[262] For some late Elizabethan and early Stuart lawyers, bare majorities in courts of error were considered to illustrate the difficulty. If four judges deciding in Common Pleas were unanimous in upholding a writ of error and the King's Bench then voted three to one in favour of reversing their judgment, John Manningham maintained in 1602, 'there are five on the one side, and but three on the other, yet those three shall prevail'.[263] In *Maine* v. *Peacher*, which came before the Exchequer Chamber in 1610, Coke CJ insisted that he would 'not have this judgment reversed unless more of us agree to its reversal than there were judges in the King's Bench who gave the judgment'.[264] The five-judge King's Bench had been unanimous. 'If four of us . . . reverse what has been done judicially by five, . . . it would be mischievous'.[265] The Exchequer Chamber was, in this instance, composed of seven judges: four would only be 'the majority', not the whole court.[266] If one took the whole to be both courts, a reversal by four looked even worse: a bare majority in the Exchequer Chamber would have prevailed over two-thirds of the sitting judges. Only one Exchequer Chamber judge, it transpired, favoured reversal. That his dissent put paid to the possibility of a unanimous judgment appeared to irk Coke considerably.[267]

[262] Young, 'The History of Judicial Dissent in England', refers to the loser's 'lingering resentment about the practice of decision-making by majority' (110). What the loser would resent is not decision-making by majority but rather the fact that, when one counts all the judges in all the courts that have heard the case, it is not a majority of those judges that decides it.

[263] *The Diary of John Manningham of the Middle Temple, 1602–1603*, ed. R. P. Sorlien (Hanover, NH: University Press of New England, 1976), 149.

> 'Three mens opinions preferred before five, yf not all togither, as in a writt of error in Kinges benche to reverse a judgment in the Common place. Yf there be three of one opinion to reverse, and the fourth would have it affirmed; nowe regarding the judgment in the Common place, with this mans opinion there are five on the on[e] syde, and but three one [on?] the other, yet those three shall prevaile'.

[264] *Maine* v. *Peacher* (1610), repr. in *Baker and Milsom*, 490–1 at 491.

[265] Ibid.

[266] Ibid.

[267] See ibid. The dissentient, Walmsley J, met with Coke's ire not only because he dissented but also because, in another case, he had given judgment against Coke's chaplain when Coke was unable to sit. On Walmsley's propensity to dissent, see John Baker, 'Judicial Conservatism in the Common Pleas 1500–1560', in his *Collected Papers on English Legal History*, I, 466–80 at 466–8; also David Ibbetson, 'Walmsley [Walmesley], Sir Thomas (1537–1612)', *ODNB* (www.oxforddnb.com) (accessed 23 September 2019) ('Walmsley was undoubtedly a very capable lawyer . . . though he was in a very

One of the reasons for the creation of the Exchequer Chamber was that the House of Lords, which had final jurisdiction over allegations of error, was ill-suited to delivering convincing majority decisions on legal matters. In the medieval period, appeals on the basis that the Common Pleas had made an error on the record (a procedure more akin to modern judicial review than to an appeal on merits) went to the King's Bench, and from the King's Bench to the king in council or in parliament – the king's jurisdiction in due course being subsumed within the remit of the House of Lords. The House of Lords met too infrequently and was too overburdened to operate as an effective tribunal for the purpose of inspecting and ruling on alleged errors in court records, and so, in 1585, parliament established the Exchequer Chamber to hear challenges on grounds of error from the King's Bench – though it remained possible to appeal to the House of Lords from both the King's Bench and the Exchequer Chamber.

That the House of Lords retained its appellate capacity with regard to proceedings in error was not uncontroversial, for a majority settling an allegation of error could be composed mainly, occasionally entirely, of lay peers.[268] In 1783, for example, a judgment of the Common Pleas, affirmed by the King's Bench, was reversed when the House of Lords voted nineteen-to-eighteen in favour of upholding a writ in error brought by the Bishop of London. Seven of the voters in the minority were law lords. Only one law lord voted with the majority, while thirteen of the lords in the majority were bishops.[269] By the mid-nineteenth century, law lords could be found urging lay peers to forgo, and in *O'Connell* v. *The Queen* (1844) it was established that henceforth they would forgo, voting on legal appeals.[270] This was a matter of convention rather than law – lay peers retained the legal right to vote, and until around 1860 appear

conservative mould: he resisted to the end what he regarded as undesirable developments in the common law, sometimes continuing his grumbling opposition long after they had become settled law. He was not a man to succumb to pressure to conform to the opinions of others').

268 See, e.g., *Bertie* v. *Falkland* (1697) Colles 10, where some lay peers were clearly dissenting from the legal judgment (though it is not clear how the case was ultimately decided); also *Ashby* v. *White* (1706) 3 Ld Raym 320, where sixteen lay peers dissented from the House of Lords' decision to reverse a judgment of the Queen's Bench. The last occasion on which an appeal was heard only by lay peers was in 1834: see Thomas Beven, 'The Appellate Jurisdiction of the House of Lords' (1901) 17 *LQR* 357, 369.

269 *Bishop of London* v. *Ffytche* (1783) 2 Bro PC 211. On the lords' vote, see Beven, 'The Appellate Jurisdiction of the House of Lords', 367–8.

270 *O'Connell* v. *The Queen* (1844) 11 Cl & F 155.

occasionally to have sat (without voting) on legal appeals simply so as to make a panel quorate.[271]

The convention seemed to signal an uneasy truce. '[T]he law Lords . . . constitute the Court of Law in this House', Lord Wharncliffe maintained in *O'Connell*, and 'if . . . noble Lords unlearned in the law' were to 'interfere [in the appeal] by their votes, . . . the authority of this House as a Court of Justice would be very greatly lessened throughout the country'.[272] No lay peer voted in *O'Connell*, and one of them, Lord Clanricarde, confessed that he considered it 'infinitely better' that legal judgments be left to the law lords.[273] But he also admitted that, had any lay peer voted on the appeal, he would have done so too.[274] When, in 1856, two eminent legal figures, Romilly MR and Lord Selborne, gave evidence to the House of Lords' select committee on the functioning of the upper chamber as an appellate jurisdiction, each spoke in favour of lay peers actively participating in appeals.[275] Support for lay participation nevertheless dwindled over the second half of the nineteenth century. In 1876, parliament recognized law lords as a dedicated arm of the judiciary – Lords of Appeal in Ordinary – whose status as peers depended upon their continuation in judicial office.[276] Lord Denman, a lay peer and the son of a former Chief Justice of the King's Bench, sought to exercise his legal right to vote in judicial proceedings in 1874 and again in 1883. In both instances, the Lord Chancellor ignored his vote.[277] If there ever had been a truce between lay and legal peers, it had, by the end of the century,

[271] See R. E. Megarry, 'Lay Peers in Appeals to the House of Lords' (1949) 65 *LQR* 22, 24.

[272] *O'Connell* v. *The Queen*, 421–2.

[273] Ibid. at 424.

[274] Ibid.

[275] *Report of the Select Committee on the Appellate Jurisdiction*, at 61 (para. 372), 169 (paras. 1085–9). The committee was set up at the instigation of Lord Derby: see HL Deb 28 February 1856 vol. 140 cols. 1448–78; also Olive Anderson, 'The Wensleydale Peerage Case and the Position of the House of Lords in the Mid-Nineteenth Century' (1967) 82 *English Historical Rev*. 486, 498–9.

[276] Appellate Jurisdiction Act 1876, s. 6.

[277] *Bain* v. *Fothergill* (1874) LR 7 HL 158; *Bradlaugh* v. *Clarke* (1883) 8 App Cas 354; also HL Deb 25 February 1876 vol. 227 col. 918 (Lord Denman). Denman delivered a speech in *Bain* v. *Fothergill*. The official report of *Bradlaugh* v. *Clarke* does not mention him. The report of *Bradlaugh* in *The Times* does not list him as one of the deciding lords but states that he 'heard the arguments' and 'expressed his concurrence' with Blackburn LC, who delivered the judgment: *The Times*, 10 April 1883 at 4 col. 5. According to his *ODNB* entry, Denman was 'a regular frequenter of the House of Lords' and non-practising barrister who 'won notoriety rather from his eccentricities than any eminent qualifications'. William Carr, 'Denman, Thomas Aitchison (1805–1894)', *ODNB* (www.oxforddnb.com) (accessed 13 November 2019).

been resolved in the law lords' favour. By 1905, Halsbury LC could declare unequivocally that '[t]he House when sitting on appeals is confined to the legal members of the House of Lords'.[278]

Although concerns over the quirks and hazards of majority decision-making clearly preyed on some legal minds, there is evidence that, by around the beginning of the seventeenth century, a decision could – unanimity being unachievable – be carried by a majority of the judges present in court when the decision was made.[279] In *Shrewsbury's case* (1609), Fleming CJ, finding that his four fellow King's Bench justices were, like him,

> doubtful which way the judgment should be given, . . . did move them to deliver their several opinions, whether the judgment should be reversed, or affirmed in general . . . [T]here being three against two for the reversal of the judgment, . . . by the rule of the Court, judgment was given, that the former judgment should be reversed.[280]

As early as 1590, the King's Bench can be seen resolving a deadlock – one can only guess as to the machinations behind the scenes – by withholding judgment until a day on which one of the four judges was absent, so that a majority of two could prevail.[281] Eighty years later, in a case in which a four-member King's Bench found itself split three ways – two judges maintaining that the defendant should be discharged, one that he should be bailed, and the other that he should be remanded – Vaughan CJ is reported as saying that 'when the Judges are of three opinions', it is 'the usage of this Court . . . to give the rule according to the opinion of the two which agree'.[282]

278 *Re Lord Kinross* [1905] AC 468, 469.

279 See, e.g., *Simms* v. *Westcott* (1589) Cro Eliz 147, 147 ('[T]he verdict was found for the defendant . . . And so was the opinion of Wray, Schute, and Clench. Gawdy *contra* . . . But Wray said that book was no law, and the contrary had been adjudged in this Court. Afterwards, Gawdy being absent, it was adjudged for the defendant'); *Tibbott* v. *Haynes* (1589) Cro Eliz 191, 191 ('[S]o held Gawdy . . . Fenner *contra* . . . Wray was absent; but afterward being present, he agreed with Fenner: and judgment was given for the plaintiff, against the opinion of Gawdy').

280 *Shrewsbury* v. *Rutland* (1609) 1 Bulst 4, 11; see also *Candish* v. *Shrewsbury* (1610) 1 Bulst 59, 61.

281 *Bartlett* v. *Wright* (1590) Cro Eliz 299, 300 ('Gawdy conceived [title to the land] did pass . . . Popham accorded . . . Clench and Fenner *contra* . . . *Et adjournat* . . . [A]fterwards, in Easter term, 35 Eliz. Popham being absent, it was again moved; and, against the opinion of Gawdy, it was adjudged for the defendant').

282 *Rudyard's case* (1670) 2 Vent 22, 24.

But the unanimous judgment was still very much preferred, and in some cases chief justices would press for one vigorously – if not ruthlessly.[283] Even late into the eighteenth century, Lord Mansfield – who presided for thirty-two years as Chief Justice of the King's Bench – could be seen carrying the flame. James Burrow, who served as the official King's Bench law reporter for the best part of Mansfield's tenure, remarked in his report of *Perrin* v. *Blake* (1770) that it was 'remarkable that, excepting this case and another in this volume, there never has been, from the 6th of November 1756' – when Mansfield took office – 'to the time of the present publication, a final difference of opinion in the Court in any case or upon any point whatsoever'.[284] In the other case which Burrow mentions, *Millar* v. *Taylor* (1769), Mansfield had petitioned for unanimity – it gives 'weight and dispatch to the decisions, certainty to the law, and infinite satisfaction to the suitors'[285] – and professed his disappointment at the inability of the judges to agree a resolution.[286] According to one commentator, Mansfield prized unanimity because – recognizing that the King's Bench, Court of Common Pleas, and Court of Exchequer Chamber 'competed with each other for business'[287] – he correctly anticipated that commercial actors would consider a court with a reputation for delivering unanimous rulings to be the best forum in which to litigate.[288]

283 See, for what might have been an example of ruthlessness, *Nelson & Bugg* v. *Woodward* (1591) Cro Eliz 249, 249 ('[O]f this opinion was Clench, Justice. Wray, Chief Justice, and Fenner *contra* . . . Wray, Chief Justice, said, he had conferred with the justices of his house, and they were of his opinion').

284 *Perrin* v. *Blake* (1770) 4 Burr 2579, 2582.

285 *Millar* v. *Taylor* (1769) 4 Burr 2303, 2395 n.

286 Millar had sued Taylor for breach of a copyright, Millar contending that the copyright was perpetually protected at common law while Taylor maintained that the copyright was subject to a twenty-eight-year limitation period set out in the Copyright Act 1710 – that period having expired. Mansfield joined with two of the judges in considering it protected at common law. Yates J dissented, arguing that the right had prescribed under the statute.

287 Henderson, 'From Seriatim to Consensus', 298.

288 See ibid. at 299–302. According to Henderson,

> 'Mansfield needed a mechanism to deliver certainty. He found it in the "opinion of the court." The reform of the common law of commerce was possible only with an assertion of judicial power through a united court speaking with a single voice. Mansfield's expertise and clarity provided a certain statement of the law that drew cases to his court – no longer would multiple courts and numerous judges produce different opinions subject to nuance and ambiguity. A single court would hear and decide the fundamental issues of commercial law, decide them once and for all without

There are factors other than Mansfield's fondness for judicial unanimity – such as the length of his tenure as Chief Justice, his extraordinary work ethic, and his adeptness as a mercantile lawyer – which might better explain why the King's Bench over which he presided proved particularly attractive to commercial litigants. His successor certainly did not think that esteem for the court depended on its judges sticking to Mansfield's preferred judgment delivery style: Kenyon CJ was untroubled by the prospect of judges on his court delivering individual opinions.[289] The unanimous opinion was in any event, for Mansfield, only ever a strong preference. While he 'always leaned . . . to make cases for the opinion of the Court',[290] in *Millar* v. *Taylor* he conceded that there are instances when unanimity simply cannot be achieved. *Millar* was one such instance: since the judges 'all equally endeavoured at . . . unanimity . . . but . . . continue to differ', he concluded, 'each is bound to abide by and deliver that opinion which he has formed upon the fullest examination'.[291]

Mansfield was, in any case, something of an outlier. By the time that he became Chief Justice, the English courts were routinely considering decisions by majorities tolerable notwithstanding that judicial unanimity was the ideal.[292] Yet there is a distinction to be drawn between willingness to accept that a majority can prevail and willingness to condone the delivery of opinions marking dissent from that majority. *Grindley* v. *Barker*, a King's Bench decision decided nearly thirty years after *Millar* v. *Taylor*, is often cited as the first case affirming that the status of a judgment as legal authority is not affected by the fact that it is accompanied by judicial dissent.[293] But

dispute or ambiguity, and provide the certainty and stability needed for commercial transactions'.

Ibid. at 300.

289 See Thomas Jefferson to William Johnson, 27 October 1822, in *The Works of Thomas Jefferson*, XII, 248 ('When Ld. Mansfield came to the bench he introduced the habit of caucusing opinions. The judges met at their chambers, or elsewhere, secluded from the presence of the public, and made up what was to be delivered as the opinion of the court. On the retirement of Mansfield, Ld. Kenyon put an end to the practice, and the judges returned to that of *seriatim* opinions').

290 *Luke* v. *Lyde* (1759) 2 Burr 882, 887.

291 *Millar* v. *Taylor*, 2395.

292 See Baker, *The Oxford History of the Laws of England. Vol. VI*, 51.

293 See *Picea Holdings Ltd* v. *London Rent Assessment Panel* [1971] 2 QB 216, 222–3 *per* Parker CJ; *Atkinson* v. *Brown* [1963] NZLR 755, 766 *per* North J; *Bruce* v. *Cole* (1998) 45 NSWLR 163, 205E *per* Priestly J; also Michael Kirby, 'Judicial Dissent – Common Law and Civil Law Traditions', 386 ('Below the Parliament and Council, . . . the acceptance of

the case is not quite so straightforward. Since it is debatable 'whether there is policy and good reason on the side of the rule which requires unanimity in a jury', Eyre CJ maintained, it is simplistic to draw an analogy between jury panels and judicial panels and deduce that the requirement of unanimity in the former provides a basis for arguing for the same in the latter. Rather than 'force the analogy' and argue that judges, as with juries, should decide unanimously, it is preferable that the majority opinion of a court be accepted as if it were 'the judgment of all'.

> [T]he whole should be governed by the majority . . . It is impossible that bodies of men should always be brought to think alike: there is often a degree of coercion, and the majority is governed by the minority, and *vice versa*, according to the strength of opinions, tempers, prejudices, and even interests . . . [W]hen all have assembled and communicated to each other the necessary information, it is fitter the majority should decide than that all should be pressed to a concurrence.[294]

In the event of disagreement on an outcome, judges should not, on this account, be coerced into deciding unanimously but instead should determine that the position of the majority carries the day in the expectation that their judgment will be accorded the same precedential status as it would have been granted had the court been unanimous. The King's Bench had no difficulty concluding thus in *Grindley* because the conclusion was supported by some of its own decisions. *Grindley* concerned a panel of six statutorily empowered adjudicators which was split four-to-two. The question was whether, under the act of parliament which conferred the relevant decision-making power, a majority could rule on behalf of the entire tribunal. It is 'now pretty well established', Eyre maintained, that where, as in *Grindley*, the issue for the tribunal's determination is of public concern, and the tribunal is of a type that meets regularly, 'the majority will conclude the minority, and their act will be the act of the whole'.[295] He could not have pronounced quite so

dissenting views and of the fact that the opinion of the majority would prevail, was certainly established by 1798 when *Grindley* v. *Barker* was decided').

294 *Grindley* v. *Barker* (1798) 1 Bos & P 229, 237–8.

295 Ibid. at 236. For authority supporting Eyre's claim, see *Attorney-General* v. *Davy* (1741) 2 Atk 212, 212 *per* Hardwicke LC ('wherever a certain number are incorporated, . . . if all are summoned, and part appear, a major part of those that appear may do a corporate act'); *R* v. *Beeston* (1789) 3 Term Rep 592, 594 *per* Kenyon CJ ('in the instance of corporations the act of the majority binds the whole'); *Withnell* v. *Gartham* (1795) 6 Term Rep 388.

confidently had the case concerned a decision on a private matter: in the mid-sixteenth century, the King's Bench had held that a tribunal ruling must be unanimous – that 'dispensation by the major part only of those individuals [who compose the tribunal] is not sufficient' – when the power to adjudicate derives from a private statute.[296] To interpret *Grindley* as establishing that majority decisions are on a par with unanimous decisions – no matter the adjudicative forum in which the majority is formed – is to overestimate the reach of its *ratio*.

Perhaps a more significant proviso attaching to the decision in *Grindley* is the fact that it concerned a tribunal, the majority of whose members had expressed an opinion but the minority of whom had not. The empowering statute did not permit tribunal members to express no view as to how a matter should be decided and therefore, Eyre and Buller J reasoned, the two adjudicators who did not offer an opinion had to be treated as concurring with the four who did.[297] 'All six must undoubtedly try' to make a unanimous ruling, Rooke J added,

> but does it not [*sic*] therefore follow that they must all decide the same way. Each man is after due examination and inquiry to decide according to the best of his judgment, and the question is to be determined by the opinion of the majority.[298]

None of the deciding judges confronted – the terms of the empowering statute meant that they had no need to confront – the problem of the assertive minority. The judge who keeps his counsel after trying but failing to agree with the majority is a different proposition from one who, after trying and failing, produces an opinion supporting a different decision. *Grindley* is certainly authority for the proposition that a majority's decision stands as 'the judgment of all' notwithstanding a passive judicial minority. The principle commonly associated with the case is, however, somewhat more expansive: that a majority will be treated as tantamount to unanimity even if the minority actively dissents.[299]

[296] *The Case of New College, Oxford* (1565) 2 Dyer 247ª, 247ª. Parker CJ was certainly alive to the distinction when he affirmed *Grindley* v. *Barker* in *Picea Holdings* v. *London Rent Assessment Panel*, though the distinction was of no consequence as the rent assessment panel was empowered by a public statute: see G. J. Hand, 'The Majority Principle: *Grindley* v. *Barker* Again' (1972) 7 *Irish Jurist* 96, 97.

[297] See *Grindley* v. *Barker* at 237 *per* Eyre CJ and 239 *per* Buller J.

[298] Ibid. at 242. (The reporter presumably meant 'it does not'.)

[299] See, e.g., *Picea Holdings* v. *London Rent Assessment Panel*, 223 where Parker CJ maintains apropos of *Grindley* that Eyre's assertion that 'the majority will conclude the minority, and their act will be the act of the whole' is 'the general principle' of the case.

7 Dissent in an Apex Court

Over time, the pull of unanimity weakened in the English appeal courts. But the judges in those courts could never be said to have renounced unanimity – whether in the form of a composite court judgment or separate opinions alighting on a *ratio decidendi* – as an ideal. '[I]n this judgment, we are unanimous', Pollock CB remarked in 1859, 'but ... I alone am responsible for the reasons and the form in which they are presented'.[300] '[W]e are unanimous' was also the conclusion of James LJ in a case before the Court of Appeal two decades later, though he was able to conclude thus only after 'h]aving ... had the advantage of hearing the judgments of my learned brothers'.[301] Judicial expressions of disappointment over absence of unanimity, while not necessarily always sincere, are to be sighted quite frequently in the law reports.[302] 'I regret that we are not unanimous', Cockburn CJ maintained in the Common Pleas in 1858, 'for, I cannot help entertaining great distrust as to the propriety of my own opinion when I find it is opposed to that of my Brother Willes'.[303] I too, Willes responded, 'express my regret that I am unable to assent to the judgment which has just been pronounced by' Cockburn.[304] There is barely anything on which 'the learned judges all agree',[305] Dallas CJ lamented in *Rowe* v. *Young*, because the King's Bench could 'very little depend upon mere authorities'[306] – on one line of precedent the conditional assurance of the promisor was the crux of the case whereas on another it was the qualified acceptance of the promisee. When the case was heard in the House of Lords, Lord Redesdale 'most fully concur[red] in the opinion'[307] of Eldon LC, whose decision to apply the doctrine of qualified acceptance – and so reverse the judgment of the King's Bench –

[300] *Shrewsbury* v. *Scott* (1859) 6 CB NS 1, 222[f].

[301] *Re McLaren* (1879) 11 ChD 68, 77.

[302] See, e.g., *R* v. *Middlesex* (1824) 2 Bing 366, 368 *per* Park J; *Wright* v. *Tatham* (1837) 7 Ad & El 313, 394 *per* Park J ('the Judges then present not being unanimous, as I lament they are not unanimous now'); *Kearney* v. *London & Brighton South Coast Railway Co* (1870) LR 5 QB 411, 413 *per* Cockburn CJ; *Stoomvaart Maatschappy Nederland* v. *Peninsular and Oriental Steam Navigation Co* (1882) 7 App Cas 795, 799 *per* Selborne LC ('[T]his case has been to me one of unusual difficulty. In the Courts below, ... judicial opinion has been ... divided ... I fear that, even in your Lordships' House, there is not unanimity'); *Jay* v. *Budd* [1898] 1 QB 12, 15 *per* Halsbury LC; *Pomfret* v. *Lancashire and Yorkshire Railway Co* [1903] 2 KB 718, 721 *per* Collins MR.

[303] *M'Kune* v. *Joyson* (1858) 5 CB NS 218, 226.

[304] Ibid.

[305] *Rowe* v. *Young* (1820) 2 Bli 391, 424.

[306] Ibid. at 418.

[307] Ibid. at 410.

seemed almost as if settled upon randomly ('the state of the law . . . is such, that it would be infinitely better to settle it in any way than to permit that sort of controversial state to exist any longer').[308]

In the mid-nineteenth century, the judicial House of Lords occasioned a disproportionately high level of overt soul-searching over the virtues and drawbacks of unanimity in judgment and toleration of dissent. Throughout the entire history of the upper house *qua* court, individuality was the norm. Although law lords could concur on a legal outcome, the parliamentary convention requiring peers to contribute to debates by delivering individual speeches militated against, even if it did not entirely rule out, the production of composite judgments.[309] A prohibition on the lords expressing dissenting opinions would (certainly if imposed from outside the House) have been contrary to the guarantee of freedom of speech in parliament under article 9 of the Bill of Rights 1689. Although evidence of lords dissenting in debates on bills can be traced at least as far back as the mid-sixteenth century,[310] it would be another three hundred years before parliament began to authorize the publication of its proceedings. One corollary of the prohibition on publishing parliamentary debates had been a rule making the publication of House of Lords' judicial proceedings a breach of privilege. In the 1800s, this rule was gradually relaxed and eventually abolished.[311] Reports of lords' judgments started to appear more regularly, and the quality of law reporting gradually improved.[312]

These developments served to cast light on an uncomfortable truth: the House of Lords functioned poorly as a court. Mid-nineteenth-century

308 Ibid. at 399.

309 See Louis Blom-Cooper, 'Style of Judgments', in *The Judicial House of Lords 1876–2009*, ed. L. Blom-Cooper et al. (Oxford University Press, 2009), 145–63 at 153–4. The House of Lords produced an explicit composite judgment in an extradition case decided the year before it was replaced by the UK Supreme Court: *Norris* v. *United States* [2008] UKHL 16. There are other cases in which the House of Lords' judgments are not described as composite but were authored by all the participating lords – rather than being the work of one (or some) of them and assented to by the others – and therefore de facto are composite. *Heaton's Transport* v. *TGWU* [1973] AC 15 – a case borne of circumstances which seemed to call for an unequivocal court statement (see Lord Rodger, 'The Form and Language of Judicial Opinions' (2002) 118 *LQR* 226, 233–4) – appears to be of this type. *Forbes* [2001] 1 AC 473 and *Barclays* v. *Mawson* [2004] UKHL 51 certainly are.

310 See Thomas P. Baty, 'The History of Majority Rule' (1912) 216 *Quarterly Rev*. 1, 17–18.

311 See Karl M. ZoBell, 'Division of Opinion in the Supreme Court: A History of Judicial Disintegration' (1959) 44 *Cornell LQ* 186, 189; Theodore F. T. Plucknett, *A Concise History of the Common Law*, 5th ed. (Boston: Little, Brown & Co, 1956), 202–3.

312 The Council of Law Reporting began issuing quasi-official reports in 1865.

decisions would sometimes be the work of a single law lord, nominally assisted by a couple of lay peers.[313] If – as occasionally happened – a case came before two law lords, and they disagreed, the tie would be left unbroken and the lower court judgment from which the case had been appealed would be affirmed.[314] When more than two law lords heard a case together, it was unusual for them to agree.[315] In *Johnstone* v. *Beattie* (1843), five law lords split 3:2 in deciding to uphold an order made by the Court of Chancery. One of the majority, Lord Cottenham, was affirming himself – in 1841, in his capacity as then Lord Chancellor, he had delivered the Court of Chancery's ruling.[316] Lord Brougham, who was among the minority, was unimpressed. There was a clear legal course 'which the Court of Chancery in the present instance ought to have taken', he maintained, 'and not having taken it, I hold that there has been a miscarriage, which this Court is required to correct'.[317] Lyndhurst, Cottenham's successor as Lord Chancellor and one of the majority, was eager to put the matter to rest.

> This appeal was argued at considerable length some time back, but as your Lordships did not agree in opinion as to the judgment proper to be pronounced, it was argued a second time a few days ago; and I am sorry to say that even now, as the result of the second argument, there is a difference of opinion among your Lordships. I entertain the utmost possible respect and deference for the opinions of those noble Lords who differ from the judgment which I have formed; but I think it my duty to move your Lordships that the order of the Court below be affirmed.[318]

The Solicitor-General, Richard Bethell, lamented in August 1855 that, as a court, the House of Lords was 'unsatisfactory in its constitution and inferior to the lowest tribunal in what ought to be the accompaniments of a court of Justice'.[319] Three months earlier, Bethell had acted for the

313 Patrick Polden, 'The Judicial Roles of the House of Lords and Privy Council, 1820–1914', in William Cornish et al., *The Oxford History of the Laws of England. Volume XI 1820–1914: English Legal System* (Oxford University Press, 2010), 518–68 at 534.

314 See HC Deb 7 March 1856 vol. 140 col. 2046 (George Bowyer); HL Deb 28 February 1856 vol. 140 col. 1453 (Lord Derby).

315 See J. B. Atlay, *The Victorian Chancellors*, 2 vols. (London: Smith, Elder & Co, 1908), II, 47; Robert Stevens, *Law and Politics: The House of Lords as a Judicial Body, 1800–1976* (Chapel Hill, NC: University of North Carolina Press, 1978), 39.

316 *Beattie* v. *Johnstone* (1841) 1 Ph 17.

317 *Johnstone* v. *Beattie* (1843) 10 Cl & Fin 42, 97–8. That the majority held the opposite spurred him to deliver a tetchy rejoinder: ibid. at 152–3.

318 Ibid. at 84.

319 HC Deb 10 August 1855 vol. 139 col. 2120. See also HL Deb 13 August 1855 vol. 139 col. 2132 (Lord St Leonards).

appellants in the case of *Shortridge* v. *Bosanquet*, which was heard by Lord St Leonards and Cranworth LC. Between the two lords there was no meeting of minds, so the lower court judgment was confirmed and the appeal dismissed.[320] In March the following year, when Cranworth called Bethell as the first witness to testify before the lords' select committee on its performance as an appellate tribunal, Bethell spoke as if he had a score to settle.

Rather than 'strive to attain to unanimity of judgment', Bethell maintained, the law lords 'made their differences of opinion public; frequently . . . great injury was done by unsettling the law'.[321] Unlike the political dissenter, he elaborated, the judicial dissenter is expected to be impartial, and so there is no equation to be drawn between dissenting over what the law should be and dissenting over what the law is. Whereas we can be certain that a statute is law notwithstanding that dissent was expressed in the debates culminating in its enactment, dissent in a judgment concerning the interpretation of that statute could leave the law in an uncertain state. The law lords, as he saw it, seemed not to appreciate that '[t]here is no analogy between a deliberative body and a judicial body', that 'the object . . . and the end of the two institutions is different'.[322] Indeed, the lords' legal arguments were often – to Bethell's dismay – conducted like political arguments: eschewing 'the gravity or the dignity with which . . . the judgments of this high tribunal ought to be expressed', the dissentient law lord '[f]requently . . . slaps the table with energetic action, precisely as if he were arguing a matter to be enforced before the House in its ordinary sittings'.[323] It would be better, Bethell advised, if the lords were to write their opinions rather than deliver them extempore – better still if they were to forgo separate speeches in favour of a single judgment, even if the judgment should only have the backing of a majority.[324] In the Court of Appeal, judges inclined to dissent have a 'bounden duty to express their opinion', since the dissent may be the losing party's key to a successful appeal.[325] But such a duty does not exist in a court from which there is no further appeal. In a tribunal of last resort, 'in order to accomplish the great end of having certainty and no

320 *Bargate* v. *Shortridge* (1855) 5 HL Cas 297 (*sub. nom. Shortridge* v. *Bosanquet* (1852) 16 Beav 84).
321 *Report of the Select Committee on the Appellate Jurisdiction*, 4–5 (para. 15).
322 Ibid. at 7 (para. 39).
323 Ibid. at 5 (para. 21).
324 Ibid. at 6 (paras. 24–6), also 7 (para. 37), 8 (para. 44).
325 Ibid. at 6 (para. 33).

element of uncertainty in the law, one opinion only should be given, and it should be expressed to be the opinion of the Court'.[326]

The remainder of the evidence proceedings seems to have been somewhat overshadowed by Bethell's blistering testimony. None of the other witnesses matched him for candour, though some of them agreed that dissents should be confined to the Court of Appeal and that a final court does best to issue single composite judgments.[327] 'The public', one respondent reasoned, 'would come to understand that', in the final court, 'when there was a difference of opinion it was not disclosed', and so a unanimous judgment would hardly be legerdemain.[328] Another respondent argued that the judgments of an artificially unified highest court are likely to carry more authority than those of an evidently fragmented one, and that the lords would therefore be well advised to adopt a convention of keeping their legal squabbles private.[329] But not all of the respondents favoured single judgments in the House of Lords. According to one witness, a legal peer is more likely to raise his game when he speaks for himself.[330] Separate opinions, another maintained, have the advantage of revealing whether the peers most knowledgeable about the law relevant to a decision in fact supported the decision that the House of Lords reached.[331] Lord St Leonards, who attended the proceedings as both examiner and witness, seemed piqued by Bethell's assertion that the law lords did not value unanimity. '[I]f there is a difference of opinion', he insisted, 'so far from not striving for unanimity, they communicate to each other their views' in the hope of finding consensus.[332] Suppression of dissent so as to facilitate delivery of a single judgment would nevertheless 'be fatal to the law as a science', he added, given the impossibility of determining 'whose opinions had guided the House' in reaching the judgment.[333] The select committee, perhaps

[326] Ibid. at 7 (para. 35).

[327] See, e.g., ibid. at 55–6 (para. 339), 63 (para. 386) (Roundell Palmer), 91 (paras. 589–91) (James Moncreiff), 167 (para. 1071) (John Romilly).

[328] Ibid. at 91 (para. 594) (James Moncreiff).

[329] Ibid. at 43 (para. 282) (Richard Malins) ('See how the public look at this matter').

[330] See, e.g., ibid. at 156–7 (paras. 1020–3) (Duncan McNeill).

[331] Ibid. at 92 (paras. 596–7) (James Moncreiff).

[332] Ibid. at 178 (para. 1144).

[333] Ibid. at 178–9 (para. 1144). *Cf.* the rejection, by the committee responsible for drafting Germany's original Court Constitution Act (1877), of a proposal that judges minded to dissent from a majority should be entitled to do so openly: 'The development of law and science is fostered by deliberate reflection in study rooms [*Studirstube*]', the committee

unsurprisingly, took the middle ground on the matter: while it may well be true that 'divisions diminish the authority of the tribunal of ultimate resort', it concluded, it seems equally true 'that the great principles of law are best elucidated by separate judgments', and so the delivery of single composite judgments by the lords ought to be 'a matter of discretion, . . . left to be arranged among those who hear and decide the Appeals'.[334]

Yet the committee members could not quite disregard the elephant in the room. Until the early-nineteenth century, the supreme appellate tribunal for the British Empire had been a standing committee of the Privy Council acting in an advisory capacity to the King. In 1833, parliament legislated to bring an end to the jurisdiction of the Privy Council as a whole and to establish a Judicial Committee, wherein the right to hear appeals was confined almost entirely to Privy Counsellors (referred to, in any given appeal, as the Board) with experience of 'high judicial office'.[335] It would be surprising were it not the case – and indeed there is evidence – that Privy Council members who served on the Judicial Committee would sometimes disagree over how a dispute was to be resolved.[336] Their convention, nevertheless, was to keep disagreements concealed: the Judicial Committee adhered to an Order in Council, made during the reign of Charles I, stipulating that 'when the business [of the Privy

maintained, 'but not by violent discussions resulting from expressions of polemically motivated dissenting opinions'. Carl Hahn, *Die gesamten Materialien zu den Reichs-Justizgesetzen. Band 1: Materialien zum Gerichtsverfassungsgesetz*, 2nd ed., ed. E. Stegemann (Berlin: Scientia, 1983 [1883]), 985.

334 *Report of the Select Committee on the Appellate Jurisdiction*, xx (para. 5).

335 Judicial Committee Act 1833, s. 1(2)(a). ('Privy Counsellors' is the modern style. In the nineteenth century, members of the Board were 'Privy Councillors'.)

336 See, e.g., *Beaumont* v. *Barrett* (1836) 1 Moo PC 59, 80–1 ('I [*sc.*, Parke B, writing for the Judicial Committee] must own I have felt some doubt myself upon this part of the case . . . The rest of their Lordships do not feel the doubt to the same extent that I do . . . [T]herefore, it appears to their Lordships that the judgment of the court below ought to be affirmed'); *Tongue* v. *Tongue* (1836) 1 Moo PC 90, 97; *Cowie* v. *Remfry* (1846) 5 Moo PC 232, 251; *Re Mushadee Mahomed Cazum Sherazee* (1852) 7 Moo PC 391, 393 ('[W]e are inclined to think that . . . the course which was taken by the parties, though erroneous, may have been taken *bona fide*, under the belief that it was the proper course. I [*sc.*, Lord Cranworth, writing for the Judicial Committee] cannot say I am myself perfectly satisfied that it was so'); *Sheppard* v. *Bennett* (1872) LR 4 PC 371, 415 ('Upon the whole, their Lordships, not without doubts and division of opinions, have come to the conclusion'); also, for further examples and discussion, Lord Denning, 'New Work for an Old Hand' (1958) 1 *Oxford Lawyer* 7, 9–10; P. A. Howell, *The Judicial Committee of the Privy Council 1833–1876: Its Origins, Structure and Development* (Cambridge University Press, 1979), 201–3.

Council] is carried according to the most voices, no publication is afterwards to be made, by any man, how the particular voices and opinions went'.[337]

Among the mid-nineteenth century Privy Counsellors who favoured this convention were law lords who considered it a virtue that the preferred practice in the House of Lords was delivery of *seriatim* judgments and toleration of open dissent.[338] At the core of this group was Henry Brougham, the reformer primarily responsible for the creation of the Judicial Committee. As a contributor to the lords' judicial business, Brougham seemed untroubled by the prospect of disparate separate opinions thwarting unity in judgment, and he was himself a notable dissenter.[339] Even on the Judicial Committee, he sometimes struggled to stay on message with his colleagues.[340] In 1861, none the less, he reminisced that, when the Judicial Committee was established, acceptance that its members must speak as one was attributable to his having 'proposed a course of proceeding' whereby a single 'judgment with the reasons . . . is delivered as the judgment of the court, or . . . as that of the majority'.[341] When, in 1837, the question was raised as to whether it might be wise to depart from this course, Brougham and various other legal peers concluded that there was nothing about the Judicial Committee's judgment-delivery style that needed altering.[342] After

337 Order in Council, 20 February 1627, repr. in Frank Safford and George Wheeler, *The Practice of the Privy Council in Judicial Matters* (London: Sweet and Maxwell, 1901), 133–4 at 133 (art. XI). The Judicial Committee appears to have treated the Order in Council as binding because the first Registrar of the Judicial Committee, Henry Reeve, pronounced it to be such. In fact, it was not binding: see Howell, *The Judicial Committee of the Privy Council*, 200–1.

338 One of the mid-nineteenth-century Lords of Appeal, St Leonards, disapproved of the Privy Council convention (and never contributed to the work of the Judicial Committee), maintaining that he 'would not sit upon any appeal or other Court in the kingdom, if I were not at liberty to express the opinion which I entertain'. *Report of the Select Committee on the Appellate Jurisdiction*, 178 (para. 1144).

339 Besides Brougham's dissents in *Johnstone* v. *Beattie* and *O'Connell* v. *The Queen*, considered above, see also *Birtwhistle* v. *Vardill* (1840) 7 Cl & F 895, 914–23 and *Lynch* v. *Knight* (1861) 9 HL Cas 577, 588–94.

340 See, e.g., *Doss* v. *Doss* (1836) 1 Moo Ind. App. 67, 85–6; also Howell, *The Judicial Committee of the Privy Council*, 202–3.

341 Henry Brougham, *The British Constitution: Its History, Structure and Working*, 2nd ed. (London: Griffin, Bohn & Co, 1861), 378 n.

342 C. C. F. Greville, *Memoirs*, 8 vols., ed. L. Strachey and R. Fulford (London: Macmillan, 1938), III, 376 (emphasis in original).

> 'Yesterday there was a discussion at the Council Board of the Judicial Committee whether when the Lords differed in opinion they should give

a privately divided Board handed down a unanimous judgment in 1844, the Clerk of the Privy Council, Charles Greville, offered some insight into Judicial Committee thinking:

> Dr Lushington, V-C, K[night] Bruce, Baron Parke, and Lord Campbell concurred with the Judgement; Abinger, Denman, and Brougham were against it; Tindal, who heard the first part of the case but not the last, was not there . . . Nothing can exemplify more the objection there would be to the Judges in our Court giving their opinions *seriatim* than in this case. It would be very unsatisfactory to have so close a division made public; . . . if the Judges were to deliver their opinions, it is abundantly probable that the arguments of the minority would appear the soundest law.[343]

But if *seriatim* was *verboten* on the Judicial Committee, why was it tolerated in the House of Lords? Indeed, why might one and the same person cherish the right to deliver a separate opinion when serving as a Lord of Appeal, yet keep faith with a convention refusing him that right when serving as a Privy Counsellor? These questions were not lost on Richard Bethell when he delivered his evidence to the lords' select committee in 1856. For him, the Judicial Committee was right to commit to the single composite judgment. There would be a 'very great improvement' in the House of Lords' legal decisions could it ever bring itself to do the same.[344]

By the beginning of the twenty-first century, legal peers were quite often to be found maintaining that a court of last resort should aim to produce composite (unanimous or majority) rather than *seriatim* judgments.[345] But it was never on the cards that the House of Lords

judgement *seriatim* or whether the majority should simply carry it and judgement be given by one in the name of all. They were *rather* inclined (that is the majority of them) for giving judgement *seriatim*, though with hesitation and doubt; but we found an old order for proceedings in Council . . . which expressly stated that when there was a difference of opinion . . . judgement was . . . given for the whole, and it was not to be divulged how the several opinions went. This decided the question and they resolved to adhere to the old practice'.

343 Greville, *Memoirs*, V, 164. Greville was reflecting on *Croker* v. *Hertford* (1844) 4 Moo PC 329.

344 *Report of the Select Committee on the Appellate Jurisdiction*, 7 (para. 37). See also ibid. at 6 (para. 25). Roundell Palmer likewise observed that there was 'very easily within your Lordships' reach' a 'remedy' to '[t]he defects of circumstance . . . which . . . affect the authority of the judgments of the House': adoption of 'the Privy Council . . . practice . . . of . . . speak[ing] with undivided authority'. Ibid. at 55–6 (para. 339).

345 For illustrations, see Penny Darbyshire, *Sitting in Judgment: The Working Lives of Judges* (Oxford: Hart, 2011), at 344–5, 388–9; Blom-Cooper and Drewry, *Final Appeal*, 94 n. 2; Paterson, *Lawyers and the Public Good*, 181–2; Rosemary Hunter and Erika Rackley,

would embrace the Judicial Committee's appellate arrangements. It was the Judicial Committee, in fact, which was eventually brought (partly) into line with the House of Lords when its *pas devant les sujets* policy on dissenting opinions was terminated by statutory instrument in March 1966. Since then, any Board member who, on hearing an appeal, finds himself at odds with the majority has been 'at liberty to publish his dissent in open Court together with his reasons'.[346]

This shift of position was a long time coming. Before 1966, dissent on the Judicial Committee, though occasionally revealed in reports of decisions, was for the most part kept under wraps; reasons for dissent certainly were never disclosed.[347] The argument in favour of single composite published opinions was reinforced by the controversial ecclesiastical case, *Ridsdale* v. *Clifton* (1877), in which division on the Judicial Committee was leaked to the press – most likely by a Board member – after Cairns LC had refused the Lord Chief Baron, Fitzroy Kelly, the right to put on record his reasons for diverging from the majority.[348] The

'Judicial Leadership on the UK Supreme Court' (2018) 38 *Legal Studies* 191, 207. The argument is often that the single judgment is to be preferred in particular types of dispute (concerning statutory interpretation, say, or the application of the criminal law).

346 Judicial Committee (Dissenting Opinions) Order 1966 (SI 1966 No. 1100), para. 3. The Order does not expressly authorize the delivery of concurring opinions, though this has not stopped members of the Judicial Committee from occasionally producing them: see, e.g., *Stempson* v. *AMG General Insurance* [2006] UKPC 30 at [30]–[36]; *Raphael Fishing Co Ltd* v. *Mauritius* [2008] UKPC 43 at [35]–[70]. The first Judicial Committee dissent (issued by Lord Morris) appeared within weeks of the Order taking effect: *National and Grindlay's Bank* v. *Dharamshi Vallabhji* [1967] 1 AC 207 (PC), 230 (case decided May 1966).

347 Votes on judgments were – following a procedure resembling the Spanish *voto reservado* (see Section 1) – recorded in 'judgment books', the contents of which were inaccessible outside the Judicial Committee. See John T. Saywell, *The Lawmakers: Judicial Power and the Shaping of Canadian Federalism* (Toronto: University of Toronto Press, 2002), 347 n. 45; Tom Bingham, *The Rule of Law* (London: Allen Lane, 2010), 44 ('members who disagreed could record their dissent in a register which was never seen by anyone'). Privy Counsellors who voted against the majority would occasionally confess to having written up their reasons for having done so, but the judgment books apparently only ever recorded votes: Paterson, *The Law Lords*, at 101–2, 241 n. 64. Most of the books were destroyed in a fire caused by a bombing raid in 1940: Howell, *The Judicial Committee of the Privy Council*, 203–4.

348 *Ridsdale* v. *Clifton* (1877) 2 P D 276. For Kelly's impassioned argument for being granted this right, see Fitzroy Kelly, *A Letter to the Lord Chancellor upon the late Order in Council of the 4th of February 1878* (London: Vacher, 1878). On the ins and outs of the case, see Charlotte Smith, '*Ridsdale* v. *Clifton*: Representations of the Judicial Committee of the Privy Council in Ecclesiastical Appeals' (2008) 19 *King's LJ* 551; David B. Swinfen, *Imperial Appeal: The Debate on the Appeal to the Privy Council, 1833–1986* (Manchester University Press, 1987), 229–32.

following year, the Privy Council, at Cairns' instigation (and to the ire of various members of the Judicial Committee), issued an Order reaffirming the Board's commitment to delivering single judgments without disclosure of dissent.[349] While there appears to be '[n]o rational argument' supporting this reaffirmation, Lord Selborne wrote soon afterwards, '[i]t must be admitted, on all hands, that . . . the reasonable and practical conclusion would seem to be' that the commitment to concealing dissentient reasoning on the Judicial Committee 'ought now to be maintained'.[350]

To detect irrationality in the resolution to persist with this commitment was perhaps a little severe. Nineteenth-century ecclesiastical appeals were a perpetual thorn in the side of the Judicial Committee. Churchmen both on and outside the Board quite often resented the fact that majorities composed of non-ecclesiastical, mainly legal, peers were able to rule on matters of religious conscience and remove the Church from final, binding decisions about its own affairs.[351] In cases of this type, prohibition on open dissent was essentially a form of damage limitation; had it been permissible for members of the Board to air their divisions in public, malcontents minded to impugn the Board's judgments could have had a field day.[352] Various senior British legal figures also took the view that insistence on single Judicial Committee judgments operated as a bulwark against an archetypal colonial subject – often an Indian landowner – who litigated regularly, who was rarely satisfied until his case had been heard by the Board, and who would have pushed hard to challenge any unwelcome decision, no matter which court dispensed it, were it accompanied by dissentient judicial reasoning which would have had him come out on top.[353] The latter conviction – that the Board's

349 Judicial Committee of the Privy Council, Order in Council, 4 February 1878 (PC 2/289). On members' displeasure, see Howell, *The Judicial Committee of the Privy Council*, 202; Swinfen, *Imperial Appeal*, 232. Law lords were, by this point, serving as permanent judges on the Judicial Committee: Appellate Jurisdiction Act 1876, s. 6.

350 Roundell [Palmer, 1st] Earl of Selborne, *Judicial Procedure in the Privy Council* (London: Macmillan & Co, 1891 [*c.*1878–*c.*1880]), at 58, 59–60. (The pamphlet was privately printed in 1881.) Until 1966, the only incident resembling a departure from this commitment seems to have been Lord Wright's revelation, in 1955, that one of his fellow Privy Counsellors had once, within the confines of the Board, delivered a dissenting opinion with which he had been inclined to agree (see Section 2).

351 See Swinfen, *Imperial Appeal*, 227–8.

352 See ibid. at 232, 234.

353 See ibid. at 233–5. On Indian landowners and the Judicial Committee, see *Report from the Select Committee of the House of Lords on the Appellate Jurisdiction. House of Commons Sessional Papers* (London: HMSO, 1872) (325) VII 193, minutes of evidence,

judgments were better received overseas because dissenting opinion was suppressed – persisted into the twentieth century. Cases appealed to the Judicial Committee, one Privy Counsellor observed in 1938, come from a diverse range of jurisdictions and typically concern points of law which have elicited conflicting legal opinions in domestic courts. If these points of law are to be demystified and settled, he maintained, there is 'a special advantage' in having 'an authoritative decision by a Court which does not publish dissenting views'.[354]

The most common explanation for the Judicial Committee's commitment to concealment is that, historically, the Privy Council has not delivered judgments but rather has advised the monarch. Privy Counsellors, the argument runs, must avoid putting the Crown in the difficult position of having to interpret and implement reports containing not only recommendations but also arguments running counter to the recommendations. In short, advice to the Crown must be univocal.[355] The advice is of no effect if the monarch does not accept it, much as a bill cannot become law without royal assent. But the fact that the monarch always does accept the advice – that 'it is unknown and unthinkable' that the Crown would refuse to give effect to a recommendation set forth in a Judicial Committee report[356] – makes the proposition that the Board's pronouncements are not legal judgments seem somewhat unworldly.[357]

para. 65 (Henry Reeve) ('Many of the great landowners of India are extremely proud of their lawsuits. There are many of them who never have less than a dozen great appeals which they cherish and keep alive as a part of their dignity and rank').

354 George Rankin, 'The Judicial Committee of the Privy Council' (1939) 7 *CLJ* 2, 19. (The article is the text of a lecture delivered to the Cambridge University Law Society in October 1938.)

355 See, e.g., Lord Justice Atkin, 'Appeal in English Law' (1927) 3 *CLJ* 1, 9 ('[T]he reason for the rule is historical. The Council are, traditionally, giving advice to the Crown, and it was the advice of the Council as a body which the Crown wanted, not the advice of the several members'); Kurt H. Nadelmann, 'The Judicial Dissent: Publication *v.* Secrecy' (1959) 8 *Am. J. Comparative Law* 415, 417; ZoBell, 'Division of Opinion in the Supreme Court', 188; Kelemen, *Judicial Dissent in European Constitutional Courts*, 54–5; Allen Mendenhall, 'The Corrective Careers of Concurrences and Dissents' (2016) 8 *Faulkner L. Rev.* 49, 53; Kirby, 'Judicial Dissent – Common Law and Civil Law Traditions', 386 ('It was considered that the monarch should not be embarrassed by conflicting advice emanating from the council').

356 *British Coal Corporation* v. *The King* [1935] AC 500 (PC), 511 *per* Sankey LC. See also *Ibralebbe* v. *The Queen* [1964] AC 900 (PC), 913 *per* Viscount Radcliffe ('Such Orders are essentially judicial acts').

357 See Edward McWhinney, 'Judicial Concurrences and Dissents: A Comparative View of Opinion-Writing in Final Appellate Tribunals' (1953) 31 *Can. Bar Rev.* 595, 599; Howell, *The Judicial Committee of the Privy Council*, 36 ('carrying pedantry to extreme lengths').

Were the proposition more than merely technically accurate, there would have been an element of eccentricity, to say the least, to the alteration in Judicial Committee practice in 1966: the effect of the change would have been to enable the Board to tender fragmented advice to the Crown. That the Board in reality issues judgments rather than advice was, in fact, conceded long before 1966: a 'haphazard sort of court' the Judicial Committee may be, Brougham remarked in 1844, but a court it undoubtedly is.[358]

Yet in Brougham's day, and long afterwards, the proposal to allow publication of Judicial Committee dissents was an outright non-starter. What had changed by 1966? In the 1850s, the extent to which, as courts of final appeal, the House of Lords and the Judicial Committee of the Privy Council appeared to be cut of the same cloth had prompted Bethell to ask why the norm forbidding the latter tribunal from publishing dissenting opinions should not prevail in the former one as well. By the 1960s, the question had been inverted: if the House of Lords – and indeed other apex courts – published dissenting opinions, why should the Judicial Committee not do the same? Lawyers and politicians in various jurisdictions under the Judicial Committee's wing had long been murmuring about the inferiority of single judgments.[359] In the early-twentieth century, querulousness might have prompted reform but for the fact that

[358] *Report from the Select Committee on the Judicial Committee Bill, 1844*, House of Lords Papers (London: HMSO, 1844), XIX 34, 82. One commentator has observed that although the fact that the Judicial Committee operates as a court was indeed, before 1966, cited as a reason for allowing publication of dissents, it is important not to forget (i) that Board members could in any event signal to the Crown that there was dissent simply by ensuring that a recommendation was carried by majority rather than unanimously, and (ii) 'that the monarch never received reasons for . . . advice . . . in a given case, let alone dissenting reasons'. Oliver Jones, '*Public Prosecutor* v. *Oie Hee Koi* (1968): Not so Humbly Advising? Sir Garfield Barwick and the Introduction of Dissenting Reasons to the Judicial Committee of the Privy Council', in Lynch (ed.), *Great Australian Dissents*, 116–30 at 125.

[359] See *Minutes of Proceedings of the Colonial Conference, 1907* (London: HMSO, 1907), Cmd. 3523, LV 61, 202–3 (Alfred Deakin, Prime Minister of Australia).

> 'The fact that in the case of the Judicial Committee you get but one judgment has its advantages in the way of simplification, and does not promote doubts which might otherwise arise, but it leaves us absolutely unaware whether that judgment was arrived at by a majority of one or by the unanimous consent of the whole . . . The practice of the House of Lords, which at the sacrifice of some apparent simplicity does afford a great many lights upon every question submitted, often from a number of quite individual standpoints, leads our litigants . . . to prefer that method of disposing of their cases'.

Canada, after reviewing the reception of the Board's judgments among its provincial governments, concluded that forswearing decisions containing disparate opinions was, as an approach to handling appeals in an overseer court of last resort, more beneficial than it was disadvantageous.[360] Other federations seemed to fall into line with the Canadian conclusion.[361]

By the middle of the century, however, Canada had stopped taking appeals to the Privy Council, and so was no longer invested in, or influential over, the Judicial Committee's approach to decision-making.[362] Commonwealth and colonial disquiet regarding the Board's appellate function began to re-emerge. The trend was especially marked in Australia, where judges had long been inclined to query the wisdom of an appeals process which entrusted the power of final judgment on domestic matters – matters increasingly governed by Australian judges' adaptations of English common law principles – to a remote tribunal which condensed its decisions into single opinions, typically authored by judges with little or no first-hand knowledge of Australian law.[363] By the early 1960s, it seemed inevitable that, before long, the Judicial Committee

See also *Minutes of Proceedings of the Imperial Conference, 1911. Dominions no. 7* (London: HMSO, 1911), Cmd. 5743, LIV 103, 231–2 (F. S. Malan, Minister of Education, South Africa) ('[T]here is a feeling that the Judicial Committee is really no court of law at all . . . There is only the one judgment. Counsel have to withdraw, and then judgment is published afterwards . . . [I]f the same practice will be followed in the Judicial Committee that is followed in the House of Lords, that . . . would be satisfactory'); and ibid. at 331 (J. G. Findlay, Attorney-General and Minister of Justice, New Zealand).

> '[I]n New Zealand . . . [i]t is sometimes assumed that the Member of the Committee who has least to do writes the judgment and that there is not very much discussion before the judgment is written . . . [I]n the absence of any other judgment than the one, it is sometimes difficult to pick up from a Privy Council decision the real *ratio decidendi* of the judgment . . . If more than one judgment were delivered, or if dissenting judgments were delivered, it would help to elucidate doubtful points which might be contained in the judgment. I think we, in New Zealand, are in favour of separate judgments'.

360 See Swinfen, *Imperial Appeal*, 237–8; Jones, '*Public Prosecutor* v. *Oie Hee Koi*', 122–3.

361 See Swinfen, *Imperial Appeal*, 238–9; Alder, 'Dissents in Courts of Last Resort', 236.

362 Canada abolished criminal appeals to the Judicial Committee in 1933 and civil appeals in 1949. The last Canadian case to be brought to the Committee, a case concerning a claim initiated just a few days before the civil appeals abolition date took effect (see W. G. Morrow, 'The Last Case' (1978) 16 *Alberta L. Rev.* 1, 13), was not decided until 1959: *Ponoka-Calmar Oils Ltd* v. *Earl F. Wakefield Co* [1960] AC 18 (case decided October 1959).

363 See, e.g., *Skelton* v. *Collins* (1966) 115 CLR 94, 135 (Windeyer J); also Kenneth Keith, 'The Interplay with the Judicial Committee of the Privy Council', in Blom-Cooper (ed.),

would end its commitment to producing only single judgments. Many Commonwealth jurisdictions were by this point developing or had acquired their own juridical identities, and judges in the courts of those jurisdictions were often dissatisfied with a final court judgment delivery style which they not only eschewed when deciding their own appeals but which English judges would never have thought to impose upon themselves.[364] It is impossible to tell how much an itch to go it alone prompted the change in Judicial Committee practice. What is clear is that, when change did eventually come, the catalyst for it was very specific. When, in 1964, Garfield Barwick became Chief Justice of the High Court of Australia, he made his participation in the work of the Committee conditional on Privy Council procedure being amended to

The Judicial House of Lords, 315–38 at 324–6. There was quite often a constitutional angle to Australian wariness over the Judicial Committee's jurisdiction. The country's Constitution forbade appeal of litigation on *inter se* matters (matters concerning constitutional relations between the Commonwealth and Australian States or between Australian States) to the Judicial Committee absent certification by the High Court of Australia: Commonwealth of Australia Constitution Act 1900, s. 74. (Section 74 was rendered otiose by the Australia Act 1986, s. 11, which marked the final stage in the abolition of Australian appeals to the Judicial Committee.) But was litigation concerning the interpretation of section 74 within the Judicial Committee's ambit? In 1907, the High Court held that, unless it chose to follow the guidance of the Board, it would be the ultimate arbiter over questions concerning the meaning of section 74: *Baxter* v. *Commissioners of Taxation (NSW)* (1907) 4 CLR 1087. Part of the justification for the ruling was that most if not all members of the Judicial Committee were, as compared with Australian supreme-court judges, likely to be poorly acquainted with Australia's constitution and history: see ibid. at 1111–12 (Griffith CJ, Barton, and O'Connor JJ).

> 'It could not be predicted of the Board, which would sit to entertain an appeal, that it would be constituted with any regard to the special familiarity of its members with the subject. And no disrespect is implied in saying that the eminent lawyers who constituted the Judicial Committee were not regarded either as being familiar with the history or conditions of the remoter portions of the Empire, or as having any sympathetic understanding of the aspirations of the younger communities which had long enjoyed the privilege of self-government'.

364 See, e.g., Jones, '*Public Prosecutor* v. *Oie Hee Koi*', 130; Kelemen, *Judicial Dissent in European Constitutional Courts*, 55. The sense of dissatisfaction might have been intensified by the House of Lords' own unimpressive effort at single judgment delivery in *DPP* v. *Smith* [1961] AC 290. Kilmuir LC had the House sign up to a composite unanimous judgment (drafted by Parker CJ) which re-defined criminal fault in murder cases so that the test became that of whether, from the evidence, a reasonable person would conclude that death or serious injury was the natural and probable consequence of the accused's action, in which case the death or serious injury was to be regarded as having been caused intentionally. Among Australia's judiciary, the judgment was viewed with incredulity. The High Court declined to follow it: see *Parker* v. *The Queen* [1963] HCA 14 at [17] (Dixon CJ).

allow for the publication of dissenting opinions, and he averred that there were other Commonwealth judges similarly reluctant to contribute to the Board's decisions unless the right publicly to dissent with reasons was granted.[365] Gardiner LC convened the law lords to discuss Barwick's ultimatum, whereupon a majority voted in favour of the amendment.[366]

8 When Is a Dissent Not a Dissent?

Correct though it may be to understand the publication of dissenting opinions as a right in the highest courts – bargained for in the case of the Judicial Committee, long enjoyed and prized in the House of Lords – it was ever the case that the judges of these courts celebrated only the fact that they held this right and not those instances in which they exercised it. Nineteenth-century law lords dissented infrequently;[367] and while dissent rates in final appeals would subsequently rise, they have never risen especially steeply.[368] Analysts of judicial decision-making have tended to

[365] See *A Radical Tory: Garfield Barwick's Reflections and Recollections* (Sydney: Federation Press, 1995), 222 (where he suggests that the reluctance was also shared by some law lords); Garfield Barwick, conversation with Clyde R. Cameron (1981), National Library of Australia (audio), at nla.gov.au (accessed 3 January 2020), session 92, 00.22.44 ('I said I wouldn't sit unless we had the right to publish our minority views . . . [A]nd that meant varying the Privy Council's oath to allow me to make the public disclosure'); David Marr, *Barwick* (London: Allen & Unwin, 1980), 219; Murray Gleeson, 'The Privy Council – An Australian Perspective', in *Advocacy and Judging: Selected Papers of Murray Gleeson*, ed. H. Dillon (Sydney: Federation Press, 2017), 146–57 at 152 ('When Sir Garfield Barwick . . . was invited to sit from time to time on the Privy Council, he accepted on condition that arrangements were made for the publication of dissents'). Barwick's claim that he was not alone among his Commonwealth judicial contemporaries is supported by others (see, e.g., Swinfen, *Imperial Appeal*, 240; Stevens, *Law and Politics*, 417), though it has also been pointed out that Commonwealth judges, even in the 1960s, appeared to contribute to Judicial Committee business without demur (see Jones, '*Public Prosecutor* v. *Oie Hee Koi*', 125; Michael Nash, 'Functions and Future of the Judicial Committee of the Privy Council' (1974) 24 *NLJ* 1171, 1171).

[366] The vote was not unanimous: see Paterson, *The Law Lords*, 252 n. 131; Stevens, *Law and Politics*, 417 n. 74.

[367] See C. A. Hereschoff Bartlett, 'Dissenting Opinions' (1906) 32 *Quarterly Rev. of Jurisprudence* 54, 60; Stevens, *Law and Politics*, 70–1 n. 197; Polden, 'The Judicial Roles of the House of Lords and Privy Council', 540. It is important to avoid the error, Polden observes, of treating the memorability of particular nineteenth-century dissents – he cites the example of the opinions of the minority in *Allen* v. *Flood* [1898] AC 1 – as evidence of regular dissent.

[368] Although dissenting opinions started to feature more regularly in the judgments of the House of Lords in the twentieth century (see Paterson, *The Law Lords*, 100–4), unanimity was still, by the early-twenty-first century, far more common in House of Lords (and, subsequently, Supreme Court) cases than it was in final appeals cases in Canada,

be interested not so much in fluctuations in final court dissent rates as in what the explanations for particular fluctuations might be: that judges with a predilection for dissent join a court,[369] for example, or that a presiding judge's leadership style encourages or discourages dissent,[370] or that the types of legal question increasingly before a court are ones over which judges tend to divide.[371] Today, as ever, the right to dissent is more likely to be exercised with apparent reluctance rather than with enthusiasm.[372] The virtue of restraint in exercising the right, and in reacting to the exercise of the right, quite often features in judges' accounts of their trade.[373] Occasionally, the source of intrigue is that the right was exercised by none of the judges responsible for a particular judgment.[374]

It is not so much the right to dissent that judges have valued, in fact, as the right to offer an individual opinion. By the time that the Judicial Committee had altered its practice in the 1960s, it was becoming quite common for appellate judges to reflect openly on whether – even if only in specific types of case or areas of law – they did better to incline to a 'collectivist' or an 'individualist' approach to judgment writing; particular judges were occasionally, and somewhat impressionistically,

Australia, and the United States. The UK's Supreme Court was reported (in 2010) to have a unanimity rate of 82 per cent, as compared with a US Supreme Court unanimity rate of just below 43 per cent. Chris Hanretty, 'Dissenting Opinions in the UKSC', *UK Supreme Court Blog*, 19 August 2010, at ukscblog.com (accessed 9 January 2020).

369 See, e.g., A. A. Paterson, 'Scottish Lords of Appeal, 1876–1988' [1988] *Juridical Rev.* 235, 249–50; Paterson, *Lawyers and the Public Good*, 171–3.

370 See, e.g., Brice Dickson, 'A Hard Act to Follow: The Bingham Court, 2000–8', in Blom-Cooper et al. (eds.), *The Judicial House of Lords*, 255–75 at 261–2; Paterson, *Lawyers and the Public Good*, 181–2; Hunter and Rackley, 'Judicial Leadership on the UK Supreme Court', 200–5; Cahill-O'Callaghan, *Values in the Supreme Court*, 117.

371 See, e.g., Brown, 'Dissenting Judgments', 34.

> 'The present position could hardly be more different from that faced by generations of Law Lords past: a diet for the most part of black-letter law . . . and very little in the way of public law disputes, let alone human rights appeals. It is surely the case that nowadays, particularly in the highest courts, ever fewer appeals lend themselves to conclusions that can be characterized as plainly right or plainly wrong'.

372 See Neuberger, 'No Judgment – No Justice', para. 28; Paterson, *Lawyers and the Public Good*, 159, also 182 (where it is observed that the UK Supreme Court has issued a far higher percentage of single-judgment decisions than the House of Lords ever did).

373 See, e.g., Hale, 'A Minority Opinion?', 325; John Dyson, *A Judge's Journey* (Oxford: Hart, 2019), 134.

374 For perhaps the most obvious modern example, see *R (Miller)* v. *The Prime Minister* [2019] UKSC 41.

associated with these labels.[375] Nobody – not even the most ardent collectivist – was calling for an end to dissenting opinions. Neither, however, was the case for publishing such opinions much emphasized by individualists.

Consider the case of Lord Reid, an eloquent defender of the *seriatim* tradition. Reid saw no justification for discouraging judicial dissent in final appeals,[376] and he regarded the Judicial Committee's decision to start publishing dissenting opinions as a change for the good.[377] But he did not parade the dissent as a distinctive type of separate opinion. His view of the dissenting opinion seemed to be – certainly if his own dissents are anything to go by – that it is a supple and, indeed, subtle instrument. Emphatic dissents, while not beyond him,[378] were seldom his style. Often, he would deliver not a wholesale dissent but rather would depart from the majority on some particular aspect of the decision or strand of the *ratio*.[379] Sometimes, he would intimate his inclination to dissent and

[375] Lord Diplock, for example, has quite often, and understandably, been depicted as having, with some success, pushed the House of Lords in the direction of producing collective judgments: see, e.g., L. C. B. Gower, 'Reflections on Law Reform' (1973) 23 *UTLJ* 257, 259; Stevens, *Law and Politics*, 567; F. A. Mann, 'The Single Speech' (1991) 107 *LQR* 519, 520. But he seemed less inclined to push in cases which did not involve statutory interpretation. Certainly he was not averse to producing dissenting or concurring opinions himself, and he appeared to share Lord Reid's concern – see Essay I (Section 6) and below – that judicial language is more likely to be read as akin to statutory language when a precedent takes the form of a single judgment: see *D* v. *NSPCC* [1978] AC 171, 220; also Lord Diplock, *The Courts as Legislators* (Birmingham: Holdsworth Club, 1965), 14 ('Judge-made law . . . is pieced together from the statements by individual members of the Courts . . . [T]here is no exclusive linguistic formula in which the rule is expressed. Being thus emancipated from the tyranny of language a rule so made is more flexible'). Lord Bingham was certainly wary of the 'single lapidary judgment' (Bingham, 'The Rule of Law' (2007) 66 *CLJ* 67, 71) and is commonly remembered as a judge more inclined to individualism in final appeals: see Paterson, *Lawyers and the Public Good* at 170–1, 181–2. He nevertheless seemed drawn to collectivism in criminal appeals cases: see Dickson, 'A Hard Act to Follow', 261–2.

[376] See Paterson, *The Law Lords*, 103.

[377] See Lord Reid, 'The Judge as Law Maker' (1972) ns 12 *JSPTL* 22, 28–9.

[378] See *Warner* v. *MPC* [1969] 2 AC 256, 278 ('I dissent emphatically from the view that Parliament can be supposed to have been of the opinion that it could be left to the discretion of the police not to prosecute'); also *Anisminic Ltd* v. *Foreign Compensation Commission* [1969] 2 AC 147, 171 ('dissent[ing] emphatically from' the Court of Appeal on a specific point raised in the case).

[379] See *Sun Life Assurance* v. *Davidson (Inspector of Taxes)* [1958] AC 184, 207 ('I would [unlike the rest of the House] allow the appeals but only to the extent of allowing relief in respect of sums disbursed as brokerage'); *Smith* v. *Austin Lifts* [1959] 1 WLR 100 (dissenting from the majority on the question of whether the appeal should be upheld against the first respondents [ibid. at 109–10], but adding that 'the doubts which

then make a point of producing an opinion which, he would insist, fell short of being a dissent.[380] Quite a few of his dissents – there is not a great number of them – are highly nuanced legal analyses (as often as not in tax appeals) containing little or no clue as to their status.[381] His dissents, in line with the convention of the time, do not refer to the other lords' speeches.[382] That his late-career dissents were indeed dissents is even less obvious owing to the fact that they take first billing in the cases.[383] Many of Reid's dissenting opinions might be better characterized as separate opinions which turn out – on close reading and assessed *vis-à-vis* the other lords' speeches – to be dissents. It is perhaps unsurprising that the justification he gave for the right to dissent should have been his main justification for the convention of separate opinion-writing generally: that a final court provides more scope for the proper development of the common law when it avoids issuing single judgments – the language of

I have . . . are not sufficient to require me to dissent from the conclusion that this appeal as regards the second respondents should be allowed' [ibid. at 113]); *Timber Shipping Co* v. *London & Overseas Freighters* [1972] AC 1, 17–18 (dissent on one specific ground of appeal). Even his famous speech in *Shaw* v. *DPP*, cautioning against reckless judicial legislation, was a dissent on just one of the two counts being appealed.

380 See *Knuller* v. *DPP* [1973] AC 435, 455; *Re Vandervell's Trusts (No. 1)* [1971] AC 912, 930 ('Treating the matter as an ordinary question of construction I would have been inclined to agree with the decision of the Court of Appeal. But if your Lordships think otherwise I am not prepared to dissent on this matter').

381 See, e.g., *London Graving Dock Co* v. *Horton* [1951] AC 737, 773; *IRC* v. *Baddeley* [1955] AC 572, 593; *Adamastos Shipping Co Ltd* v. *Anglo Saxon Petroleum Co Ltd* [1959] AC 133, 168; *Barclays* v. *IRC* [1961] AC 509, 525; *Smith* v. *NCB* [1967] 1 WLR 871, 872; *Heaton (Inspector of Taxes)* v. *Bell* [1970] AC 728, 741; *BSC Footwear* v. *Ridgway* [1972] AC 544, 552.

382 The convention was weakening in the House of Lords by the end of the twentieth century. It is unconvincing to argue that dissents in UK Supreme Court decisions tend to make the decisions less authoritative as precedents, one of its Justices (and more prolific dissenters) maintained in 2012, because, given that the Court had all but abandoned the convention ('[j]udgments of the Supreme Court . . . constantly cross refer'), majorities now often directly address any dissentient 'challenges to their reasoning'. Kerr, 'Dissenting Judgments', 11–12; see also *Daventry* v. *Daventry* [2011] EWCA Civ 1153 at [187] *per* Lord Neuberger MR. Just how far out of favour the convention has fallen it is difficult to say. There are, even in the Supreme Court era, numerous examples of incisive dissents which Justices in the majority have left unaddressed. Kerr's sole dissent in the controversial joint enterprise case, *Gnango* [2011] UKSC 59, is an early example. More recently, there is Lord Carnwath's highly critical dissent from the majority's decision to expand the law of easements in *Regency Villas* v. *Diamond Resorts* [2018] UKSC 57.

383 The convention was to sequence the delivery of speeches according to judicial seniority (the Lord Chancellor always being the most senior judge, the other law lords ranked by order of appointment). Reid became the most senior Lord of Appeal in 1962.

which, Reid thought, is often read as if it were akin to statutory language – and instead produces judgments composed of individual, sometimes quite disparate, judicial pronouncements.[384]

Reid's approach, in so far as he had an approach, to the formulation and deployment of dissenting opinions hardly distinguishes him from many other modern appellate judges. His dissenting opinions were – the opinions of judges in England's appeal courts as often as not are – opinions first and dissents second. It seems no accident, indeed, that judges and lawyers quite often refer not to dissenting but to *minority* judicial opinions – opinions which do not fully assent but nevertheless might not run entirely counter to what a majority has to say. Shortly before the establishment of the UK Supreme Court, one American law professor proclaimed that there are no dissents in English law: since a dissent has a target in the form of the court's judgment, he reasoned, 'there could not as a logical matter be dissents' in English appeals, 'because no appellate panel ever adopts a single judgment as the judgment of the court'.[385] (The reasoning would likely not have impressed the law lord who, a few years earlier, drafted a forceful dissent against a majority before he had even read any of their opinions.[386]) Although Frederick Pollock was in no doubt that law lords do dissent, he complained to Holmes of how insularity was too often their way: they 'do not always look as if they had taken much trouble to appreciate the other

[384] See Reid, 'The Judge as Law Maker', 29; *Gallie* v. *Lee* [1971] AC 1004, 1015; *Broome* v. *Cassell & Co* [1972] AC 1027, 1084–5; also (on the inappropriateness of interpreting common law rule formulations as one might interpret statutory language) *Strick* v. *Regent Oil Co* [1966] AC 296, 313.

[385] Jacobson, 'Publishing Dissent', 1609. See also Voss, 'Dissent', 644–5.

[386] See *Attorney-General* v. *Guardian Newspapers Ltd* [1987] 1 WLR 1248. The case concerned *Spycatcher*, a book by a former MI5 operative, Peter Wright, which chronicles, among other things, the unlawful activities of some of Wright's former security service colleagues. The Attorney-General obtained an interim injunction to prevent sensitive information from the book (which could not be published in the UK) appearing in British newspapers. Around the same time, the book was published in the United States. The Court of Appeal reinstated the injunction after the High Court had discharged it. The House of Lords decided (by a majority of 3:2) that the injunction should continue. Lord Oliver, dissenting, could barely conceal his exasperation over the majority's ruling that it was in the public interest to keep the injunction in place. 'The fact is', he observed, 'that any citizen of this country can buy the book in America and bring it home with him or order the book from America and receive a copy by post' (ibid. at 1284). But he also conceded that he had formulated his dissent before having read the majority's opinions: 'I must accept the disadvantage of expressing my dissent before I have had a chance of reading and at least trying to understand the reasons which your Lordships in the majority are going to give in support of your decision' (ibid. at 1283).

point of view'.[387] A more common lament regarding dissents in English appeals runs to the effect that, in the twentieth century, Holmes was by himself responsible for more dissents of note than were all of the Lords of Appeal put together.[388] Lord Atkin's 'famously powerful protest'[389] in *Liversidge* v. *Anderson* (1941), excoriating the majority for its 'hitherto unheard of "subjective" construction' of a wartime internment regulation,[390] is the only English dissent with which – owing as much to the opinion's reception as to its content – many non-lawyers can be expected to confess any sort of familiarity.

That English law offers up few memorable dissents does not mean that it yields only a meagre crop of powerful dissents. Dissenting opinions in English case law are rather like restaurants in metropolitan neighbourhoods. Anyone who makes the appropriate effort will discover a range of impressive ones, and will probably judge some of them to be a notch above the range – though lists of favourites will differ from one aficionado to the next. A lawyer immersed in English appellate jurisprudence has at least three retorts to anybody who should suggest that the law reports offer up barely any noteworthy dissents. The first is that there is no dearth of reported cases in which judges advance insightful, rigorous, occasionally vindicated, sometimes underappreciated arguments rejecting the position of a majority on matters such as the applicability of particular rules to disputes, the distinctions to be drawn (or not to be drawn) between legal concepts, tenets of legal interpretation, the acceptability of specific inferences from facts, the values and principles central to an area of the law, the nature and scope of particular rights, and the proper role of the judiciary.[391] The second retort is a little more elementary: there is no

[387] *The Pollock-Holmes Letters: Correspondence of Sir Frederick Pollock and Mr Justice Holmes 1874–1932*, 2 vols. (Cambridge University Press, 1942), II, 30.

[388] 'The celebrated dissents of the past which have wrought a change, whether in the law or in public attitude, ... are celebrated at least in part because of their rarity'. Kerr, 'Dissenting Judgments', 14.

[389] *A* v. *HM Treasury* [2010] UKSC 2 at [6] *per* Lord Hope; and see also *R* v. *Secretary of State for the Home Department ex p Khawaja* [1984] AC 74, 110 *per* Lord Scarman ('The classic dissent').

[390] *Liversidge* v. *Anderson* [1942] AC 206, 239 (case decided November 1941). See also Essay I (Section 11). For the argument that Atkin's dissent is not quite the cordite that it is commonly depicted to be, see Susan Keifel, 'Judicial Courage and the Decorum of Dissent', Selden Society Lecture, 28 November 2017, at www.hcourt.gov.au/assets/publi cations/speeches (accessed 26 June 2019), 10; Stephen Sedley, *Law and the Whirligig of Time* (Oxford: Hart, 2018), 148–9.

[391] Leaving aside cases considered elsewhere in this Essay, other instances are: Lord Morton in *Scottish Insurance Corp.* v. *Wilsons & Clyde Coal Co Ltd* [1949] AC 462, 498 (on the

reason to presume that the title of noteworthy dissent has to be reserved for opinions which are passionate or vituperative, or which offer up quotable passages about subsequently vilified majorities, or which read as if directed at the intelligence of a future day. The third is more candid again: if you insist on categorizing as noteworthy only the crystalline, forthright, *Liversidge*-like dissent, and you have found little matching the description apart from what *Liversidge* itself offers up, you need to spend more time with your head in the law reports.[392]

Instances of especially powerful dissent – such as Lord Millett's castigation of a majority struggling to distinguish reading down a statute from legislative amendment,[393] or Lady Hale's condemnation of ante-nuptial agreements as dubious private-governmental devices[394] – are perhaps more common since

interpretation of company articles of association and principles of shareholder entitlement); Lord MacDermott in *Oppenhein* v. *Tobacco Securities Trust Co Ltd* [1951] AC 297, 313 (on the application of the personal nexus test in charitable trusts litigation); Lord Mackay in *Pepper (Inspector of Taxes)* v. *Hart* [1993] AC 593, 613 (on use of legislative history to interpret ambiguous statutes); Lord Millett in *Twinsectra* v. *Yardley* [2002] UKHL 12 at [52]–[146] (on the test for dishonest assistance in breach-of-trust litigation); Lord Neuberger in *Stack* v. *Dowden* [2007] UKHL 17 at [96]–[158] (on the abandonment of the presumed resulting trust in co-ownership cases and on imputation of parties' intentions when inference proves impossible); Lord Mance (along with Lord Bingham's complementary dissent) in *R (Bancoult)* v. *Secretary of State for Foreign and Commonwealth Affairs (No. 2)* [2008] UKHL 61 at [68]–[74] (Bingham) and [137]–[186] (Mance) (on the executive's use of prerogative power); and Lord Sumption (along with Lord Clarke's complementary dissent) in *R (Prudential plc)* v. *Special Commissioner of Income Tax* [2013] UKSC 1 at [114]–[138] (Sumption) and [139]–[149] (Clarke) (on legal advice privilege).

392 So as to discover, e.g., *A* v. *Secretary of State for the Home Department* [2004] UKHL 56 at [96]–[97] *per* Lord Hoffmann; and *A* v. *Secretary of State for the Home Department (No. 2)* [2005] UKHL 71 at [59] *per* Lord Bingham.

393 See *Ghaidan* v. *Godin-Mendoza* [2004] UKHL 30, esp. at [57].

> 'I have the misfortune to be unable to agree with this conclusion. I have given long and anxious consideration to the question whether, in the interests of unanimity, I should suppress my dissent, but I have come to the conclusion that I should not. The question is of great constitutional importance, for it goes to the relationship between the legislature and the judiciary, and hence ultimately to the supremacy of Parliament. Sections 3 and 4 of the Human Rights Act [1998] were carefully crafted to preserve the existing constitutional doctrine, and any application of the ambit of section 3 beyond its proper scope subverts it'.

394 See *Radmacher* v. *Granatino* [2010] UKSC 42, esp. at [137] ('[U]nlike a separation agreement, the object of an ante-nuptial agreement is to deny the economically weaker spouse the provision to which she – it is usually although by no means invariably she – would otherwise be entitled'), [138], [159] ('[T]his Court should not be developing the common law in such a way as to produce an injustice and thus to encourage people to seek a divorce when they would not otherwise wish to do so'), [169] and [189].

1966, when the House of Lords' change of tack over its own precedents improved the chances of a final court dissenting opinion eventually being formulated as law.[395] But anyone seeking out such instances would err were they to confine their attention to *Liversidge* and a scattering of cases which came after it. Coleridge J's erudite, understated, cautionary dissent in *Lumley* v. *Gye* (1853) is integral to the history of tortious interference in English law.[396] Lord Shaw's departure from the majority in *ex parte Zadig* (1917), another wartime internment case, might not scale the heights of Atkin's dissent in *Liversidge*, but it is still often hailed, particularly by civil liberties lawyers, as having packed a considerable punch.[397] Celebrated though Atkin's contribution to *Liversidge* might be, his dissent in *Everett* v. *Griffiths* (1920) – just as eloquent and as passionate, but not as emotive, as the *Liversidge* opinion – might make more of an impression on those who prefer articulations of major differences served undemonstratively.[398]

395 The vast majority of the English judicial dissents considered in two recent studies devoted to the topic appear in post-1966 cases: see Geach and Monaghan (eds.), *Dissenting Judgments in the Law*; Frederic Reynold, *Disagreement and Dissent in Judicial Decision-making* (London: Wildy, Simmonds & Hill, 2013).

396 *Lumley* v. *Gye* (1853) 2 El & Bl 216, 244.

397 *R* v. *Halliday ex p Zadig* [1917] AC 260, 276. For a detailed and sympathetic assessment of Shaw's opinion, see David Foxton, '*R* v. *Halliday ex parte Zadig* in Retrospect' (2003) 119 *LQR* 455, 483–7. Detention and internment cases are also the source of powerful judicial dissents in other jurisdictions: see, e.g., *Korematsu* v. *United States* 323 US 214 (1944); *Al-Kateb* v. *Godwin* (2004) 219 CLR 562.

398 *Everett* v. *Griffiths* [1920] 3 KB 163, 199. Another of Atkin's dissents in same area of law, *East Suffolk Rivers Catchment Board* v. *Kent* [1941] AC 74, 88, is better known: see *Gorringe* v. *Calderdale MBC* [2004] UKHL 15 at [41] *per* Lord Hoffmann; also *Duff* v. *Highlands and Islands Fire Board* 1995 SLT 1362 (Scot. Court of Session, Outer House), 1363 *per* Lord Macfayden ('I do not regard the *East Suffolk* case as very satisfactory … I find the dissenting speech of Lord Atkin … more convincing than the view of the majority'). *Everett* concerned the scope of the duty of care owed by doctors to mentally incapacitated patients. Atkin concludes:

> 'we are dealing with the liberty of persons ill able to protect themselves, paupers, and persons of weak mind who, though sane, may afford to the unthinking or careless mind evidences of insanity. In my opinion it is just as it is convenient that the law should impose a duty to take reasonable care that such persons, if sane, shall not suffer the unspeakable torment of having their sanity condemned and their liberty restricted; and I am glad to record my own opinion, ineffectual though it be, that for such an injury the English law provides a remedy'.

Everett v. *Griffiths*, 223. In the same year as the case was decided, Atkin became President of the Medico-Legal Society, which was concerned with, among other things, issues relating to the ascription of legal liability to those judged to be of unsound mind: see Geoffrey Lewis, *Lord Atkin* (Oxford: Hart, 1999), 159–60.

Given, nevertheless, that dissents deemed especially significant are thin on the ground in the history of English law, it should come as no surprise that – in contrast to some other common-law jurisdictions – the question of what makes for 'great' dissents (and dissenters) features barely at all in the juristic narrative. Nor has much attention been accorded to what is, as regards English appellate decision-making, a rather more intriguing question: why are certain opinions categorized as, or not categorized as, dissents?

Between dissent and non-dissent lies the murky terrain of the quasi-dissent. Judges can be seen admitting to having been a hair's breadth from dissenting,[399] even occasionally withholding opinions which advance particular positions once they realize that the opinions will be dissents.[400] The language of dissent is sometimes used resignedly or apologetically.[401] A judge might concur despite being loath to do so.[402] Occasionally, judges profess not to be dissenting 'formally' – the implication quite often being that the judge's opinion might be considered a dissent in all but name.[403] Thinking up ways of dissenting without using

[399] See, e.g., *Butt* v. *Conant* (1820) 1 Brod & Bing 548, 586 *per* Burrough J; *Oceanic Steam Navigation Co* v. *Sutherberry* (1880) 16 ChD 236, 244 *per* Jessel MR; *Lord Llangattock* v. *Watney, Combe, Reid & Co Ltd* [1910] AC 394, 399 *per* Lord Shaw.

[400] Lord Blackburn concluded his contribution to *Foakes* v. *Beer* with an admission that he had written up the reasons that he originally expected would form the basis for his opinion, but then decided that he would 'not . . . repeat them nor persist in them' – that his opinion would be a concurrence and not a dissent – because they 'were not satisfactory to the other noble and learned Lords who heard the case'. *Foakes* v. *Beer* (1884) 9 App Cas 605, 623.

[401] See, e.g., *London & India Docks Co* v. *Thames Steam Tug & Lighterage Co Ltd* [1909] AC 15, 20 *per* Lord Atkinson ('I do dissent, though I have striven to concur'); *Cooper* v. *Wilson* [1937] 2 KB 309, 349 *per* Macnaghten J; *Schaefer* v. *Schuhmann* [1972] AC 572 (PC), 593 *per* Lord Simon.

[402] See, e.g., *Seed* v. *Higgins* (1860) 8 HL Cas 550, 562 *per* Campbell LC; *Beamish* v. *Beamish* (1861) 9 HL Cas 274, 353 *per* Lord Chelmsford ('[I]t is with very great reluctance that I agree with the opinions which have been expressed'); *Bolton* v. *Stone* [1951] AC 850, 868 *per* Lord Radcliffe ('I agree with regret'); *Wine Shippers (London)* v. *Bath House Syndicate* [1960] 1 WLR 989, 996 *per* Harman LJ; *Rendell* v. *Went (Inspector of Taxes)* [1963] 1 WLR 1085, 1094 *per* Sellers LJ ('With much reluctance, I do not dissent'); *Bushell* v. *Faith* [1970] AC 1099, 1105 *per* Lord Reid; *Jones* v. *Wrotham Park Settled Estates* [1980] AC 74, 106 *per* Lord Salmon; *Reckitt* v. *Borden* [1990] 1 WLR 491, 495 *per* Lord Bridge ('With undisguised reluctance I agree'); *Re Toshoku Finance Ltd* [2002] UKHL 6 at [50] *per* Lord Hobhouse; *Carlco Ltd* v. *Chief Constable of Dyfed Powys* [2002] EWCA Civ 1754 at [25]–[27] *per* May LJ and [30] *per* Clarke LJ; *B (A Child)* [2012] EWCA Civ 1475 at [149] *per* Lewison LJ.

[403] See, e.g., *Smith* v. *London and St Katharine Docks Co* (1868) LR 3 CP 326, 334 *per* Keating J ('I do not feel sufficiently strongly to dissent formally'); *Davey* v. *London & South Western Railway Co* (1883) 11 QBD 213, 220 *per* Manisty J ('I do not feel sufficient confidence in my own opinion as to this case to dissent formally from the decision'); *Comber* v. *Leyland* [1898] AC 524, 533 *per* Lord Morris ('I do not intend to dissent

the word 'dissent' could well be a judicial parlour game.[404] As often as not, the label is attached to an opinion by a law reporter rather than by the dissenting judge.[405] Lord Buckmaster dissented in *Donoghue* v. *Stevenson*: the headnote tells us so, and his reasoning and conclusion facilitate the deduction.[406] Yet he reveals himself as a dissenter not by acknowledging that he dissents, but rather by stating that he 'find[s] it hard to dissent' from an opinion of one of the majority in *Mullen* v. *Barr* – a case which *Donoghue* overruled.[407]

Some opinions are identified as dissents even though it is not clear that they are. According to the headnote to *Clayton* v. *Ramsden* (1942), Lord Wright dissented on one aspect of the *ratio*.[408] But did he? The case concerned a will which made it a condition that the beneficiary marry

formally from the judgment which has been proposed, especially as my dissent would be of no practical value'); *Cope* v. *Crossingham* [1909] 2 Ch 148, 159 *per* Cozens-Hardy MR; *Rookes* v. *Barnard* [1964] AC 1129, 1192 *per* Lord Evershed ('Having regard to the unanimity of your Lordships' view upon this matter I have not thought it right formally to dissent'); *Central Asbestos Co Ltd* v. *Dodd* [1972] 1 QB 244, 267 *per* Edmund Davies LJ ('I do not find it necessary to dissent formally from the contrary view which I gather is so firmly held by each of my brethren'); *R* v. *Chief Constable of North Wales ex p Evans* [1982] 1 WLR 1155, 1165 *per* Lord Bridge ('[I]t would . . . be an empty gesture for me to express a formal dissent on the point'); *L* v. *L* [2010] EWCA Civ 177 at [21] *per* Wall LJ ('I do not propose to take my unhappiness about this application to the extent of a formal dissent from the judgment').

404 See, e.g., *Phillips* v. *Homfray* (1883) 24 ChD 439, 471 *per* Baggallay LJ (dissenting) ('Speaking with much diffidence, as my views in this respect differ from those of my colleagues'); *Lowry (Inspector of Taxes)* v. *Consolidated African Selection Trust Ltd* [1940] AC 648, 693 *per* Lord Romer (dissenting) ('I should, but for the fact that some of your Lordships are of the contrary opinion, have thought it plain'); *Baker* v. *Bowketts Cakes Ltd* [1966] 1 WLR 861, 868 *per* Winn LJ (dissenting) ('With diffidence, I declare myself unable to concur. Since my judgment will have no effect, I will state it succinctly'); *James* v. *Secretary of State for Wales* [1968] AC 409, 443 *per* Lord Morris (dissenting) ('I have the misfortune to differ, with respect, from your Lordships'); *Tilling* v. *Whiteman* [1980] AC 1, 23 *per* Lord Fraser (dissenting) ('I regret that I am unable to agree with the view of my noble and learned friends'); *Deutsche Morgan Grenfell plc* v. *IRC* [2005] EWCA Civ 78 at [298] *per* Buxton LJ (dissenting). By the late-twentieth century, it had become fairly common for judges to indicate that they were dissentients by expressing – usually at the beginning of an opinion – their regret at being 'unable to concur'.

405 The UK Supreme Court has departed from this particular script by identifying dissenters in the 'press summaries' which it issues with its judgments. Modern law reporters are usually attaching the label with the dissenting judge's blessing.

406 See *Donoghue* v. *Stevenson* [1932] AC 562, 567 ('these principles [of negligence liability] cannot be changed nor can additions be made to them because any particular meritorious case seems outside their ambit'), 577 ('it is difficult to see how any common law proposition can be formulated to support her claim').

407 Ibid. at 578.

408 *Clayton* v. *Ramsden* [1943] AC 320, 320 (case decided December 1942).

someone of Jewish faith and parentage. The House of Lords held that the will was void because the condition failed the certainty of objects test. Wright concurred that the Jewish parentage condition was uncertain. But he was 'not . . . disposed' to conclude the same as regards the Jewish faith condition.[409] Given, however, that both limbs of the condition had to be certain if the will was not to be declared void, he saw no point in elaborating on a difference of opinion relating to just one of them.[410] Judges like Wright – amenable to the court's ruling despite disagreeing on an aspect, or aspects, of the reasoning in support of it – do not normally consider themselves to be, nor are they commonly recorded as, dissenters.[411] It would be very easy to tie oneself in knots by seeking to mark out a boundary separating concurring opinions containing elements of dissent (what one commentator calls '"dissenting" concurrences')[412] and dissenting opinions which partly concur.

The history of common-law appellate judgment-delivery indicates that judges who register their differences over decisions in which they participate need not be identified as having either concurred or dissented. Whereas a dissenting opinion is, in essence, a 'No, because . . .' statement, a concurring opinion could be a 'Yes, and . . .' statement (when the judge's reasoning complements but does not form part of the judgment's *ratio*) or a 'Yes, but . . .' statement (when the judge agrees with the judgment but offers partly or entirely different reasoning in support of it).[413] A judicial 'Yes, but . . .' statement will never be a dissenting opinion. But nor will it necessarily be categorized as a concurring opinion. Doubts about my fellow judges' reasoning, Brougham maintained, are a necessary but not a sufficient reason for dissenting from that reasoning: 'I must see far more clearly that all has been error and delusion . . . before

409 Ibid. at 331.

410 See ibid. ('But I do not pursue these questionings. The view I have expressed on the words "Jewish parentage" is sufficient to decide the appeal, with the result that, in my judgment, the whole condition is void').

411 See, e.g., *Great Western Railway Co* v. *Swindon and Cheltenham Extension Railway Co* (1884) 9 App Cas 787, 807 *per* Lord Bramwell; *The Tervaete* [1922] P 259, 275 *per* Atkin LJ; *Rose* v. *Epstein* [1974] 1 WLR 1565, 1574 *per* James LJ; *R* v. *Bow Street Metropolitan Stipendiary Magistrate ex p Pinochet Ugarte (No. 3)* [2000] 1 AC 147, 248 *per* Lord Hope; *R (R)* v. *Durham Constabulary* [2005] UKHL 21 at [24]–[49] *per* Lady Hale (also ibid. at [22] *per* Lord Steyn).

412 James Lee, 'A Defence of Concurring Speeches' [2009] *Public Law* 305, 318.

413 The two types of concurrence sometimes appear alongside the same judgment: see, e.g., *Sevilleja* v. *Marex Financial Ltd* [2020] UKSC 31, which contains both a 'Yes, but . . .' opinion and a 'Yes, and . . .' opinion.

I can so declare it', he observed in *O'Connell* v. *The Queen*.[414] Should such a declaration not be possible, it is better to align with 'the clear opinion of the great majority, than [with] the doubting, uncertain, and hesitating opinion of the small minority'.[415] In common-law case reports, judges who, like Brougham, doubt but do not dissent from a decision are not always identified as having concurred with it. Sometimes, the headnote to or summary of a case records not their concurrence, but the fact of their having expressed doubt: before or after a doubting judge's name there will appear a Latin word, usually the word *dubitante*.[416]

There is much about the history, the use, and indeed the very concept of *dubitante* that is difficult to fathom. The label is by no means unique to English law reporting – judges were being tagged *dubitante* in late colonial America, pre-Confederation Canada, Enlightenment-era Scotland, and in Australia by the beginning of the Federation.[417] One commentator has ventured that the term first appears in English law late in the eighteenth century.[418] It is certainly around this time that the term starts to become more noticeable in law reports – this might be because, after Burrow started to include headnotes in his reports in the 1760s, many other reporters followed suit.[419] But there is evidence of judges and serjeants being recorded as

414 *O'Connell* v. *The Queen*, 334.

415 Ibid. at 345.

416 Very occasionally, reporters have used *hesitante* instead: see, e.g., *Parsons* v. *Loyd* (1772) 3 Wils KB 341, 344; *Roberts* v. *Bell* (1857) 7 El & Bl 323, 323; *Whiteman* v. *Sadler* [1910] 1 KB 868, 877 ('*dubitante* (or *hesitante*) Vaughan Williams LJ'); *Helman* v. *Horsham and Worthing Assessment Committee* [1949] 2 KB 335, 335. Likewise *reservante*: see, e.g., *Bureau Wijsmuller NV* v. *Owners of the Tojo Maru (No. 2)* [1972] AC 242, 243; *General Aviation Services* v. *TGWU* [1975] ICR 276, 294 *per* Orr LJ (identified as *dubitante* by Lord Salmon in *General Aviation Services* v. *TGWU* [1985] ICR 615, 627).

417 See, e.g., *Bernard* v. *Stonehouse* 2 Va Colonial Dec B60, B64 (Va Gen Ct 1737) ('Judgment was given . . . con. Blair [J] *dubitante*'); *Walker* v. *Hunter* (1853) 16 D 226, 226 ('Held (*dubitante* Lord Ivory, *et abs.* Lord Robertson)'); *Gibson* v. *Boyd* (1839) Carswell NB 8, 8; *Commissioner of Railways* v. *Leahy* (1904) 2 CLR 54, 54. In the United States, judges are sometimes identified as concurring but *dubitante*: see, e.g., *Feldman* v. *Allegheny Airlines* 524 F.2d 384, 392–3 (2d Cir. 1975) (Friendly J 'concurring *dubitante*'). Dissenting judges too have been labelled *dubitante*, as if their doubts over the judgment of the court are to be separated from their dissent from it: see, e.g., *City of Fairburn* v. *Cook* 372 S.E.2d 245, 255 (Ga App 1988) ('McMurray PJ and Carley J dissent. Deen PJ dissents *dubitante*'). A judge might even be described as partly concurring, partly dissenting, and partly *dubitante*: see *United States* v. *Walker* 9 MJ 892, 894 (AFCMR 1980) (Mahoney J 'dissenting in part, concurring in part, and *dubitante*').

418 Jason J. Czarnezki, 'The *Dubitante* Opinion' (2006) 39 *Akron L. Rev.* 1, 2 ('No English cases use the term prior to late 1700s cases').

419 See F. H. Newark, 'Headnotes' (1956) 12 *NILQ* 29, 29.

dubito as far back as the late middle ages.[420] By the time of the Restoration, reports of judges doubting the court's judgment had become quite common, and reporters had settled on *dubitante* as the preferred expression for the purpose of indicating that a judge entertained doubts about a judgment but did not consider it so wrong-headed that dissent was in order.[421] The King's Bench held unanimously in *Arnote* v. *Breame* (1704) that scaffolding erected on land enjoyed by the defendant caused a nuisance to the plaintiff and that it therefore had to be removed. But was it within the gift of the plaintiff to remove it? Holt CJ thought that it was.[422] Since it 'does not necessarily appear that the ground was [the defendant's]', he reasoned, the plaintiff might 'pull it down ... without danger of becoming a trespasser'.[423] The decision was *per curiam*, and so the other three judges did not deliver opinions. But the law report records that they did disagree with Holt over the issue of who was entitled to remove the scaffolding: 'Powell, Powys, and Gould, Justices, clearly *contra* [Holt]: for when they declare it to be a nuisance, and that it should be removed, who should remove it but he on whose ground it is?'[424] The report (which Holt probably held in low regard[425]) does not record Holt's response, but simply states that he was '*dubitante ut supra*',[426] presumably meaning that while he agreed with his colleagues in finding for the plaintiff, he remained unconvinced by – but considered it an overreaction to dissent from – their argument that the plaintiff had no right to remove the scaffolding.

420 See *Thurston* v. *Leike*, YB Hil 41 Edw III 4 (1367) at 4 (pl. 11) ('Finchden, *dubito*'); *Fene* v. *Gylmin*, YB Mich 20 Edw IV 10 (1480) at 10 (pl. 8) ('Choke, *dubito*'); also Anthony Fitzherbert [d. 1538], *La Graunde Abridgement* (London: Tottell, 1565), 121.

421 See, e.g., *Stone's Case* (1669) 1 Vent 29, 29 ('The case being moved again, the Court (*absente* Moreton, & *dubitante* Rainsford) granted a writ of privilege'); *Proctor* v. *Newton* (1670) 2 Lev 37, 37; *White* v. *Stringer* (1673) 2 Lev 105, 106 ('Hale Chief Justice, and Wylde held clearly, to which also Rainsford agreed, *dubitante* Twysden'); *Wade* v. *Baker and Cole* (1696) 1 Ld Raym 130, 132 ('[J]udgment was given for the plaintiff by Powell Justice, and Treby Chief Justice, Nevill Justice *dubitante*'); *Williams* v. *Lacy* (1697) 1 Ld Raym 227, 229; *St John Baptist in the Devises* v. *St James in Bishops Cannings* (1724) 2 Ld Raym 1371, 1371.

422 *Arnote* v. *Breame* (1704) 6 Mod 244, 245.

423 Ibid.

424 Ibid.

425 See *Slater* v. *May* (1704) 2 Ld Raym 1071, 1071–2 ('And the Chief Justice [Holt] ... said, upon the observation upon 4 Mod, see the inconveniencies of these scambling reports, they will make us appear to posterity for a parcel of blockheads').

426 *Arnote* v. *Breame*, 245. See also *Culliford* v. *Blanckford* (1692) 12 Mod 26, 26 ('Dolben, Justice, *dubit.*').

It is law reporters, note, who use *dubitante.* Almost never does the text of a judgment contain the word.[427] There is nothing at all unusual about a judge describing an opinion – their own or someone else's – as a concurrence or a dissent. But cases in which judges describe other judges as *dubitante* are rare,[428] and instances in which they identify themselves thus are almost non-existent.[429] Lord Scarman considered Lord Halsbury's opinion in *Scott* v. *Scott* to be '*maxime dubitans*' – to be the epitome, in other words, of *dubitante* judicial expression.[430] Yet Halsbury is not marked as *dubitante* in the case report. Law reporters, even today, are prone to using *dubitante* imprecisely, and sometimes omit to use it when using it would be apt. One report of a case might designate a judge *dubitante* whereas another might not.[431] A judge might not be reported

427 See, e.g., *The Achilleas* [2008] UKHL 48 at [93], where Lady Hale concludes that 'if this appeal is to be allowed, as to which I continue to have doubts, I would prefer it to be allowed on the narrower ground identified by Lord Rodger, leaving the wider ground to be fully explored in another case and another context'. The description of the opinion as *dubitante* is not to be found in the transcript of the judgment; it is only to be found in the headnote for the case at [2009] 1 AC 61.

428 For examples from a limited range, see *Miliangos* v. *George Frank (Textiles) Ltd* [1976] AC 443, 484 *per* Lord Simon; *Total Liban* v. *Vitol Energy* [2001] QB 643, 652 *per* Peter Gross QC (sitting as a Deputy High Court judge) ('In [*Randall's case* (1858) EB & E 84] . . . Wightman J delivered a concurring judgment, albeit *dubitante*'); *R (Laporte)* v. *Chief Constable of Gloucestershire* [2006] UKHL 55 at [97] *per* Lord Carswell and [146] *per* Lord Mance; *Secretary of State for the Home Department* v. *MB* [2007] UKHL 46 at [84] *per* Lord Carswell; *R (Corner House Research)* v. *Director of the Serious Fraud Office* [2008] EWHC 246 (Admin) at [61] *per* Collins J.

429 From an even more limited range, see *University of Strathclyde* v. *Carnegie Trustees* 1968 SC (HL) 27, 47 *per* Lord Wilberforce ('I must . . . rank myself as *dubitans*'); *Re Norway's Application* [1987] QB 433, 488 *per* Kerr LJ ('I feel, frankly, uneasy about my acceptance, *dubitante*, of the very limited evidence in this connection on the present application').

430 *Attorney-General* v. *Leveller Magazine Ltd* [1979] AC 440, 471; and see *Scott* v. *Scott* [1913] AC 417, 442.

> '[W]hile I agree with the Lord Chancellor [Haldane] in the result which he has arrived at in this case, and generally in the principles he has laid down, I wish to guard myself against the proposition that a judge may bring a case within the category of enforced secrecy because he thinks that justice cannot be done unless it is heard in secret. I do not deny it, because it is impossible to prove what cases might or might not be brought within that category, but I should require to have brought before me the concrete case before I could express an opinion upon it'.

431 See, e.g., *West Penwith Rural DC* v. *Gunnell* (1968) 19 P & CR 546 (Edmund Davies LJ recorded as *dubitante*); [1968] 1 WLR 1153 (not recorded as *dubitante*); *Pugh* v. *Savage* (1970) 21 P & CR 242 (Harman LJ recorded as *dubitante*); [1970] 2 QB 373 (not recorded as *dubitante*); *Taylor* v. *Director of the Serious Fraud Office* [1999] EMLR 1 (Lord Lloyd recorded as *dubitante*); [1999] 2 AC 177 (not recorded as *dubitante*).

as *dubitante* despite professing doubt about the court's decision; Lord Brown considered himself *dubitante* in *Yemshaw* v. *Hounslow London Borough Trust*,[432] as indeed he was,[433] but none of the case reports categorizes him thus.[434] Headnotes sometimes attach the label to one doubting judge but not to another – two judges appeared to be *dubitante* in *Re Collie*, Goff J observed in 1971, even though the case report states that only one of them was.[435] Judges are occasionally reported as *dubitante* despite not having expressed any doubt. In two cases decided within a year of one another, Woolf LJ was (in different series of law reports) designated *dubitante* not because he expressed doubts about aspects of the decisions, but rather because he suggested that future courts would be well advised to guard against reading the decisions as if they were precedents amenable to wide application.[436]

432 See Brown, 'Dissenting Judgments', 34–5.

433 'I have already indicated my very real doubts . . . At the end of the day, however, I do not feel sufficiently strongly as to the proper outcome of the appeal to carry these doubts to the point of dissent. I am content that the views of the majority should prevail and that the appeal should be allowed'. *Yemshaw* v. *Hounslow LBC* [2011] UKSC 3 at [60]. Likewise Lord Mance's *dubitante* conclusion to his opinion – identified as *dubitante* in none of the law reports – in *Doherty* v. *Birmingham City Council*: 'I would myself have concluded that the remission could and should go further and cover avowedly the issue whether the . . . notice to quit was invalid as contrary to article 8 of the [European] Convention [on Human Rights] . . . but . . . this may not ultimately matter because the common law . . . should itself be capable of achieving fair and reasonable results'. *Doherty* v. *Birmingham City Council* [2008] UKHL 57 at [164].

434 Some of the newspaper accounts of the case (which received considerable media attention) treated Brown as a dissenter: see, e.g., Jenny McCartney, 'Those Shouts Will Reverberate', *Sunday Telegraph*, 30 January 2011 at 26 ('Lord Brown . . . made clear his misgivings about the majority ruling . . . but . . . did not carry the day'). *Yemshaw* was not a majority ruling. The Supreme Court was unanimous in allowing the appeal.

435 *Re Rushton* [1972] Ch 197, 202 ('[I]n *re Collie* (1876) 3 ChD 481 although James LJ is described as *dubitante*, . . . so really also, I think, was Baggallay LJ') (case decided February 1971). See also *Robinson* v. *Chief Constable of West Yorkshire Police* [2018] UKSC 4, the *Appeal Cases* headnote for which designates Lord Hughes (who doubted that the Supreme Court was correct to uphold the trial judge's finding that the police owe citizens a qualified duty of care governed by ordinary negligence principles) as *dubitante*: [2018] AC 736, 736. Lord Mance, however, is not so designated, even though he 'confess[ed] to the same doubt as Lord Hughes about the judge's finding of negligence' (ibid. at 763).

436 See *Customs and Excise Commissioners* v. *Bell Concord* [1990] 1 QB 1040, 1050 *per* Woolf LJ (*dubitante*) ('I agree . . . subject to two points to which I will now refer, which I do not consider it is necessary to decide for the purposes of this appeal and on which I would prefer to express no concluded view although I regard it as important to draw attention to them since otherwise our decision could be considered to have wider application than I would wish') (case decided February 1989); *Young* v. *Secretary of State for the Environment* (1990) 60 P & CR 560, 565 *per* Woolf LJ (*dubitante*) ('I agree . . . I am

The question of what it is that a judge has done to warrant being deemed *dubitante* is a complicated one. '[T]he opinion entered *dubitante*', Lon Fuller once observed, indicates that 'the judge is unhappy about some aspect of the decision rendered, but cannot quite bring himself to record an open dissent'.[437] In English law reports, it is usually a judge, rather than a judge's opinion, that is referred to as *dubitante*.[438] Entire judicial opinions, usually short statements, matching Fuller's description are certainly issued from time to time.[439] But most *dubitante* pronouncements are not entire opinions but rather *dicta* contained in opinions: the opinion of a *dubitante* judge will often contain a good deal that is not *dubitante*.[440]

The law reports definitely confirm that a *dubitante* judge stops short of dissenting. In *Gillon* v. *Deare* (1845), for example, Erle J, having declared that 'with extreme hesitation and regret . . . I differ from the rest of the court',[441] is identified as *dissentiente*,[442] whereas Maule J, concurring with the judgment but 'entertain[ing] a good deal of doubt',[443] is designated *dubitante*.[444] The reports also show that judges have manifold reasons for choosing doubt over dissent. As is often observed, judges

concerned, however, that it could result in this appeal being construed as having a wider effect than I would intend') (case decided February 1990).

437 Lon L. Fuller, *Anatomy of the Law* (Harmondsworth: Pelican, 1971 [1968]), 132.

438 Very occasionally, more than one judge: see, e.g., *Brickfield Properties* v. *Newton* [1971] 1 WLR 862 (Edmund Davies and Cross LJJ *dubitante* on the same point of law); *Carter* v. *Bradbeer* (1975) 61 Cr App R 275, 276 (Lords Diplock and Kilbrandon); *South Carolina Insurance Co* v. *Assurantie Maatschappij 'de Zeven Provincien' NV* [1987] AC 24, 25 (Lords Mackay and Goff); also *Slater* v. *Worthington's Cash Stores* [1941] 1 KB 488 (Court of Appeal, affirming a lower court judgment, accepting that the judge was correct to be *dubitante* over the defendants' assertion that they could rely on act of God).

439 See, e.g., *Canadian Pacific Steamships Ltd* v. *Bryers* [1958] AC 486, 508 *per* Lord Keith (*dubitante*); *Westwood* v. *Post Office* [1974] AC 1, 9 *per* Lord Wilberforce (*dubitante*) ('[Y]our Lordships . . . are unanimous . . . I defer to this unanimity of view though I have to say that, unaided, I should have difficulty in reaching the same conclusion').

440 See, e.g., *Gay* v. *Matthews* (1862) 4 B & S 425, 436–7 *per* Wightman J (*dubitante*) ('On all points except the last I concur . . . But, with respect to the [last] point . . . I . . . express my doubt').

441 *Gillon* v. *Deare* (1845) 2 CB 309, 317.

442 Ibid. at 309.

443 Ibid. at 316.

444 Ibid. at 309. Likewise *Warrington* v. *Leake* (1855) 11 Ex 304, 308 *per* Pollock CB (*dubitante*) ('Upon the principal matter I entertain great doubt, but upon the whole I think the safest course will be to allow the order setting aside the judgment to stand') and 311 *per* Martin B (*dissentiente*) ('I am sorry that I cannot concur in the opinions expressed by the other members of the Court'); *South Yorkshire Railway and River Dun Co* v. *Great Northern Railway* (1853) 9 Ex 55, 55 ('Pollock CB *dubitante*; and Martin B *dissentiente*').

are more likely to be disposed to forsaking dissent and expressing themselves *dubitante* when they assess that a decision calls for unanimity above all else.[445] Judicial contributions to cases are quite frequently branded *dubitante* because judges admit that they are holding back from delivering their own opinions and instead are aligning with opinions which yield conclusions to which they are not instinctively drawn but which are authored by colleagues better versed in the relevant legal system or area of law.[446] Both of these reasons for preferring to express doubt rather than dissent seem to militate against the proposition – occasionally advanced by jurists and judges[447] – that English judgments tend to be written with the losing party in mind: defeated litigants hardly have cause to be content with judges who are *dubitante* rather than *dissentiente* for the sake of comity, or because the case is beyond their ken. A judge might be awarded the title of *dubitante* by virtue of observing that there could be more to a case than meets the eye, and that, had the facts of the case been established more assiduously, their opinion – perhaps also the opinions of other participating judges – would probably have supported a different outcome.[448] Or a judge might be a doubter rather than a dissenter because he sees no point to the fight that a dissent would entail. In *Kusel* v. *Watson* (1879), a Court of Appeal composed of Jessel MR and Bramwell and Baggallay LJJ unanimously overruled a decision by Bacon VC, who had held that in a dispute between a lessee and a lessor over the length of a lease with an unspecified term of years, the lessee's rather than the lessor's favoured term was the valid one. Baggallay 'incline[d] to the view that [Bacon's] judgment . . .

[445] See, e.g., Alan Paterson, *Final Judgment: The Last Law Lords and the Supreme Court* (Oxford: Hart, 2013), at 182, 184; Paterson, *The Law Lords*, 102; Chris Hanretty, 'The Decisions and Ideal Points of British Law Lords' (2012) 43 *Brit. J. Pol. Sci.* 703, 715; Blom-Cooper, 'Style of Judgments', 153.

[446] See, e.g., *Re Scott and Alvarez's Contract* [1895] 2 Ch 603, 614 *per* Lopes LJ (*dubitante*) ('I bow to . . . the better judgment of my learned brothers, though . . . if I had been left to my own unaided judgment, I should have thought the . . . condition was sufficiently stringent to cover even a bad title'); *Haskins* v. *Lewis* [1932] 2 KB 1, 17–18 *per* Greer LJ (*dubitante*) ('If this case depended solely on my judgment I should have confined the order to an order for possession of the ground floor and the first floor, but inasmuch as my brothers think differently and agree with the view of Swift J, who is a very experienced judge in these matters, I shall have considerable hesitation after this in giving effect to the view which otherwise would have commended itself to my judgment').

[447] See, e.g., Heydon, 'Threats to Judicial Independence', 215–16; Brown, 'Dissenting Judgments', 33–4; also J. Gillis Wetter, *The Styles of Appellate Judicial Opinions: A Case Study in Comparative Law* (Leyden: Sythoff, 1960), 71–2.

[448] See, e.g., *British Railways Board* v. *Herrington* [1971] 2 QB 107, 126–7 *per* Salmon LJ (*dubitante*).

was correct'.[449] But since the lessee did 'not object to a lease in the form proposed by the Master of the Rolls',[450] he chose not to dissent, and was recorded as *dubitante*.[451]

Dubitante pronouncements are always, in essence, 'Yes, but . . .' statements. So how, if at all, are they distinguishable from concurrences containing an element of dissent? One possibility, suggested apropos American case law, is that whereas the judge who delivers a concurrence combined with dissent has reservations about some aspect of a decision, a *dubitante* pronouncement relates to a general legal concept.[452] On this account, a judge is primarily concurring but partly dissenting if, in a case concerning (say) a discretionary trust, she accepts the same definitions of trust certainty as do her fellow judges, agrees with them in so far as she considers three of the four trust provisions to be valid, but is at variance with them in maintaining that the fourth provision is void because it fails the certainty of objects test. The same judge would be expressing herself *dubitante*, by contrast, if she agreed with her fellow judges that the trust was valid in its entirety but also delivered *obiter dicta* doubting whether, as currently applied to discretionary trusts, the certainty of objects test is fit for purpose.

In English case law, this distinction – between qualified concurrence as decision-specific and *dubitante* as pertaining to general legal concepts – is simply nowhere to be found. Judges designated *dubitante* are often ones who disagree with their colleagues (or a majority of them) over how the law applies to a particular aspect of a case, but who see no point in upgrading their disagreement to a full-scale dissent given that, were the dissent to become the opinion of the majority, the outcome of the case would not change.[453] The opinions of judges who concur can

449 *Kusel* v. *Watson* (1879) 11 ChD 129, 135.

450 Ibid.

451 Ibid. at 129.

452 Czarnezki, 'The *Dubitante* Opinion', 2 ('the term is most frequently used to express doubt in general, not to define a judge's disposition in a given case').

453 See, e.g., *Great Western Railway Co* v. *Crouch* (1858) 3 Hurl & N 183, 194 *per* Wightman J (*dubitante*) ('I entertain very great doubt whether the appellants were guilty of any neglect . . . but, however that may be, it seems to me that, as the case stands upon the pleadings, the issue . . . was properly found for the respondent'); *Williams* v. *Atlantic Assurance Co Ltd* [1933] 1 KB 81, 97–8 *per* Scrutton LJ (*dubitante*) ('I am inclined to doubt the correctness of this and to think that the mortgagee can assign the whole interest he has . . . but I am disposed to think this . . . does not afford . . . any defence'); *Wheeler* v. *Mercer* [1957] AC 416, 427–8 *per* Lord Morton (*dubitante*); *London Investment & Mortgage Co Ltd* v. *Worthington (Inspector of Taxes)* [1959] AC 199, 207–8 *per* Lord Reid (*dubitante*); *Associated Newspapers Ltd* v. *Wilson* [1995] 2 AC

often be characterized, we have seen, in the exact same way – as indeed, occasionally, can those of judges who, like Lord Wright in *Clayton* v. *Ramsden*, are identified as part-dissenters. Opinions expressing reluctant assent, furthermore, sometimes are, and sometimes are not, designated *dubitante* (an inconsistency which could be at least partly attributable to law report editors being aware of particular judges' preferences as to how, or whether, *dubitante* should be used). The *Appeal Cases*, for example, do not attach the designation to a short speech, delivered by Lord Wrenbury in 1926, which opens with the admission that 'with the very greatest reluctance ... I concur',[454] whereas they do attach it to an opinion of Lord Russell's, delivered a decade latter, which concludes with the rather abrupt declaration that he was 'prepared to concur, but without enthusiasm'.[455] The assertion that *dubitante* is a distinct kind of judicial utterance is itself, perhaps, *dubitante*.

9 Minorities As Authorities

Much of the first half of this book was concerned with *dicta* as a form of authority. There emerged a complex, at times somewhat murky, picture. In the English courts, we saw, not only is there a distinction to be drawn between *dicta* which are merely *dicta* and *dicta* which are somehow 'weighty', but it appears nowadays to be accepted that there are (distinctly heterodox) instances in which, in the lower courts, final court *dicta* is to be followed as precedent would be followed, possibly even in preference to precedent. The relationship between judicial dissent and legal authority is similarly complicated and invites two broad lines of enquiry. The first concerns judicial dissent as a form of authority. Although judicial dissents can serve as epistemic authority, it would be incorrect to consider them all of a piece with other weighty *dicta*. The second concerns binding authorities which contain dissents. To conceive of a judicial

454, 479 *per* Lord Browne-Wilkinson (*dubitante*) ('I prefer to express no view on the ... issue ... discussed by [Lord Bridge] ... As at present advised I would not share his view on the issue but it is unnecessary to express any concluded view since the decision of this case does not turn on that point'); *R (Spath Holme Ltd)* v. *Secretary of State for the Environment* [2001] 2 AC 349, 407 *per* Lord Hope (*dubitante*).

[454] *Glicksman* v. *Lancashire & General Insurance Co Ltd* [1927] AC 139, 144 (case decided November 1926).

[455] *Lindsey CC* v. *Marshall* [1937] AC 97, 117 (case decided July 1926). In the same vein, see *National Association of Local Government Officers* v. *Bolton Corporation* [1943] AC 166, 181 *per* Lord Thankerton (*dubitante*).

dissent as any kind of authority might seem strange, given that to dissent from a majority whose decision binds as precedent is, in effect, to find oneself out of step with – is essentially to challenge – an authority. Nevertheless, we know from ground already covered in this Essay that a decision might make for a less commanding precedent if it is accompanied by dissent, particularly if the dissent leaves the court deciding by a simple majority. Perhaps the most intriguing line of enquiry regarding the relationship between judicial dissent and legal authority concerns not the reception of particular dissents as secondary sources but rather the capacity for dissents to weaken the precedential status of the judgments (or sequence of judgments) in which they appear.

Judges and lawyers in England have not been much exercised, certainly not explicitly exercised, by judicial dissents *qua* secondary sources. It is not unusual for judges to observe that the dissenter in a case is a legal eminence,[456] nor is it uncommon for jurists to speculate on what the contours of a particular area of law would look like today had the majority in a landmark case been on the side of a dissentient, or had the dissenter's reasoning become *ratio* in the decision of an overruling court.[457] Yet there is a marked, even if not quite a complete, absence of judicial observation and juristic literature advancing claims comparable to those regularly made regarding *dicta* – that some dissents are especially weighty, 'judicial', or authoritative; that there are dissents and dissents. This might simply be because English case law is populated far less by dissenting opinions than it is by regular *dicta*. But it might also have something to do with the fact that judicial dissent makes for a peculiar species of persuasive authority.

An argument often advanced in support of single composite judgments is that it can be difficult to distinguish a concurring opinion from an opinion which contributes to the majority's *ratio decidendi*. *Boys* v. *Chaplin* (1969), in which all the law lords agreed on the outcome but each gave different reasons in support of it, is often considered an extreme illustration of the difficulty.[458] With judicial

[456] See, e.g., *Re Woodburn* (1857) 1 De G & J 333, 350 *per* Cranworth LC; *Berkley* v. *Thompson* (1884) 10 App Cas 45, 48 *per* Selborne LC; also *Report of the Select Committee on the Appellate Jurisdiction*, 92 (para. 597).

[457] See, in particular, Geach and Monaghan (eds.), *Dissenting Judgments in the Law*, most of the contributions to which consider particular dissenting opinions 'as the basis for changing the law ... if the same issue were to come before the Supreme Court in the future' (ibid. at xvi).

[458] *Boys* v. *Chaplin* [1971] AC 356 (case decided June 1969). On the depth of the difficulty (and for a valiant attempt to resolve it), see Adrian Briggs, 'What did *Boys* v. *Chaplin* Decide?' (1983) 12 *Anglo-American L. Rev.* 237.

dissent, by contrast, one knows where one stands: there is no question of opinions expressed as dissent belonging to the *ratio*. But a dissenting opinion, while obviously not part of a *ratio*, is equally obviously *vencido* (Section 2). Within a judgment, all judicial opinions other than dissenting opinions are either supportive (even if only reluctantly supportive) of the outcome or, in the case of most *obiter dicta*, neutral as to the outcome. Dissenting opinions have the distinction of making a case against the outcome – and making it to no avail. As persuasive authority, a dissenting opinion – though it is but one of a range of persuasive authorities that can feature in a judgment[459] – might be considered to have an inbuilt (though, we will see in a moment, by no means insurmountable) handicap: unlike any other content that might serve as persuasive authority it was found, at the point of its promulgation, to be unpersuasive. Counsel will probably be on a sticky wicket if her argument relies very heavily on dissenting opinion. Compared with following precedent or endorsing *dicta*, furthermore, eschewing a precedent in favour of dissent from its *ratio* can be a bold step for a court to take, for the court will often be overruling precedent on the basis that, even if the precedent is considered purely in relation to the law as applicable at the time, the majority responsible for it must be adjudged to have picked the wrong side.[460] That dissents are arguments for votes which lost seems to set them apart from – might, occasionally, make them a slightly riskier choice than – other persuasive authorities.

How, then, do judges (and those who argue before judges) make use of judicial dissents? And what sorts of claims do they make for them? In essence, they resort to dissents much as they resort to *dicta*. English case law yields no distinctive strand of judicial reflection on gradations of authority in dissents comparable to judges' various ruminations on *dicta*. But there is certainly evidence that the notion of dissent as authority is understood to have multiple connotations. The *ne plus ultra* of the authoritative judicial dissent is the dissent brought to life as law by

[459] See *Woolwich Equitable Building Society* v. *IRC* [1993] AC 70, 201 *per* Lord Slynn ('[N]one of the cases cited provides in its *ratio* a decisive basis upon which [the claimant] can rely to support its claim . . . Yet . . . there are in some cases statements of principle . . . which do not form part of the *ratio decidendi* and in others statements in dissenting judgments which it seems to me should be considered when the present question has to be resolved').

[460] The step need not be quite so bold, since a court might be overruling the precedent owing to the fact that today – given subsequent legal developments, that is, rather than the law applicable at the time – the dissentient reasoning makes for a better *ratio* than does the reasoning of the majority.

a legislature or a later court. 'Law as a science would be weakened if we could not resort to the judgments of each judge', Atkin LJ observed before the Cambridge University Law Society in 1926, 'and there have been times when dissenting judgments in the ultimate tribunal have been of the greatest value'.[461] His own opinion in *Liversidge* some fifteen years later is often hailed as the epitome of the authoritative dissent – although among judges there seems to be at least as much enthusiasm for Denning LJ's opinion in *Candler* v. *Crane, Christmas & Co*,[462] which is quite often referred to as an authority in its own right.[463]

Vindicated dissents akin to Atkin's in *Liversidge* and Denning's *Candler* – as well as others already encountered in this Essay (see Section 3) – are not particularly unusual. A court capable of overruling a precedent quite often does so by aligning with dissent accompanying the earlier judgment instead of following the judgment itself.[464] In *Hill* v. *Hill* (1949), for example, a majority of law lords overruled the Court of Appeal's decision *Hyams* v. *Stuart King* because only the dissenting judge, Fletcher Moulton LJ, appeared to have understood the relevant law.[465] The germ of the House of Lords' so-called rule in *Rylands* v. *Fletcher* can famously be traced to Bramwell B's dissent over the case

461 Atkin, 'Appeal in English Law', 9.

462 An opinion some of the judicial plaudits for which could be excerpted to read like the review-snippets which often appear in theatre-show advertisements: see, e.g., *Spartan Steel Alloys Ltd* v. *Martin & Co* [1973] QB 27, 45 *per* Edmund Davies LJ ('blazing the trail which was to lead to *Hedley Byrne*'); *Killick* v. *Pricewaterhouse Coopers (No. 1)* [2000] PNLR 1 at [42] *per* Neuberger J ('legendary').

463 See, e.g., *Peach Publishing Ltd* v. *Slater & Co* [1998] BCC 139, 143; *Electra Private Equity* v. *KPMG Peat Marwick* [2000] BCC 368, 381–2; *McCumm* v. *Treasury Solicitor* [2001] EWCA Civ 1502 at [18].

464 See, e.g., *IRC* v. *Crossman* [1937] AC 26, 71–2 *per* Lord Roche; *R* v. *Smith (Morgan James)* [2001] 1 AC 146, 204 *per* Lord Taylor; *Three Rivers DC* v. *Bank of England* [2001] UKHL 16 at [5]–[6], [61], [85]–[86], and [132]–[133]; *Barclays Bank* v. *Nylon Capital* [2011] EWCA Civ 826 at [33] (*per* Thomas LJ) and [68] (*per* Lord Neuberger) ('It seems to me that the correct position is that identified by Hoffmann LJ in his dissenting judgment (whose authority derives much support from the fact that his view prevailed in the House of Lords)'); *Furnell* v. *Flaherty* [2013] EWHC 377 (QB) at [63] *per* Turner J ('Du Parcq LJ (in a dissenting judgment later vindicated by the House of Lords . . .) rejected this conclusion'); *Re Racal* [1981] AC 374, 390 *per* Lord Edmund-Davies ('I have to say respectfully that the existing law is, in my judgment, to be found in the dissenting judgment of Geoffrey Lane LJ in *Pearlman* [v. *Keepers and Governors of Harrow School* [1979] QB 56] and that the majority view was erroneous'). Geoffrey Lane LJ's dissent in *Pearlman* has since been somewhat cautiously displaced in favour of the majority view: see *R (Privacy International)* v. *Investigatory Powers Tribunal* [2019] UKSC 22 at [74].

465 *Hill* v. *William Hill (Park Lane) Ltd* [1949] AC 530 (overruling *Hyams* v. *Stuart King* [1908] 2 KB 696).

in the Court of Exchequer.[466] Occasionally, judges do not vindicate a dissent but rather remark on how the dissent might have been vindicated, or how its vindication is surely only a matter of time. Had the facts in an earlier case been slightly different, a judge might observe, the *ratio* of the case would likely have been dissenting opinion and the dissenting opinion the *ratio*.[467] Judges can also be found pronouncing *obiter* on how, once facts different from the ones currently under consideration come before the court, there will be an opportunity to endorse dissentient reasoning set forth in an unsatisfactory precedent in preference to the reasoning of the majority.[468]

Whether vindication of a dissent is possible depends, of course, upon which court is considering the dissent and how the rules of *stare decisis* apply to its judgments. Not only had a dissent by Romer LJ 'attracted the support of many', Edmund Davies LJ observed in 1973, but one South African provincial court judge had even made a point of following the dissentient reasoning in preference to the reasoning of the majority. But it is the majority's decision that 'binds us' in the Court of Appeal today, he added, persuasive though the dissent obviously is.[469] A dissenting opinion which had been presented to the Court of Appeal was 'very powerful', Megaw LJ conceded in a case decided some five years later, but it cannot be adopted, given that '[t]his court is . . . bound by the *ratio* of the decision of the majority'.[470]

Transformation of judicial dissents into law is the most obvious, but it is not the only, method of vindication. A judge might co-opt a dissent not in the belief that it provides the right *ratio* for today's case but because it contains an exemplary formulation of a legal principle. Lord Westbury's reasoning in *Ricket* v. *Metropolitan Railway Co* (1867),[471] regarding damage-valuation in public nuisance cases, was not only offered in the

466 *Rylands* v. *Fletcher* (1868) LR 3 HL 330; *Rylands* v. *Fletcher* (1865) 3 Hurl & C 774, 788 (Bramwell B, *dissentiente*). For the details, see Ian Ward, *English Legal Histories* (Oxford: Hart, 2019), 528–30; also A. W. Brian Simpson, *Leading Cases in the Common Law* (Oxford: Clarendon Press, 1995), 213–26.

467 See, e.g., *R* v. *Lyons* [2002] UKHL 447 at [33] *per* Lord Hoffmann.

468 See, e.g., *Sempra Metals Ltd* v. *HMRC* [2007] UKHL 34 at [184] *per* Lord Walker.

469 *Sutcliffe* v. *Thackrah* [1973] 1 WLR 888, 893.

470 *Western Fish Products Ltd* v. *Penwith DC* (1979) 38 P & CR 7, 34 (case decided May 1978). In a similar vein, see *Durrheim* v. *Ministry of Defence* [2014] EWHC 1960 (QB) at [89] *per* Patterson J ('Although there are very strong dissenting judgments which reveal a difference between the minority and majority . . . they are dissenting judgments and I am bound to follow the majority').

471 *Ricket* v. *Metropolitan Railway Co* (1867) LR 2 HL 175, 200.

course of a dissent but can also be seen to be out of step with subsequent authorities, Lord Hoffmann maintained in 2001,[472] yet it 'seems to me as convincing today as it was then'.[473] Given that there is a discernible common-law tradition of discouraging the delivery of dissenting opinions in cases intended to settle disputes over the interpretation of statutes,[474] there is perhaps a measure of irony in the fact that some of the most durable *dicta* setting out principles of statutory construction are contained in judicial dissents. Lord Simon, in the course of a dissent, provided what has come to be regarded as authoritative guidance on plain-meaning interpretation.[475] In establishing how to avoid interpreting a statute which had been superseded by science so that it yields an inconsistency, Lord Bingham, in *Quintavalle* (2003), relied upon 'pertinent ... guidance given by ... Lord Wilberforce in his dissenting opinion'[476] in *Royal College of Nursing* v. *DHSS* (1981).[477] By 2009, Wilberforce's guidance was, according to Lord Walker, 'recognized as [an] authoritative' statutory-interpretive presumption.[478]

There are certainly, in modern appeals, instances in which a judge lauds a dissent to be found in another case as powerful, persuasive, weighty, influential, 'of high authority', commanding 'considerable respect', and the like.[479] The judges paying the compliment are often

472 *Wildtree Hotels Ltd* v. *Harrow LBC* [2001] 2 AC 1 at 9, 11.

473 Ibid. at 17.

474 See, e.g., *Smedleys* v. *Breed* [1974] AC 839, 858–9 *per* Lord Diplock ('[N]o useful purpose would be served by my elaborating the reasons for what would only be a minority opinion, for this appeal comes before your Lordships' House in order to obtain an authoritative ruling as to what must be proved by a defendant to establish a defence under [the statute] ... What matters is that a majority of your Lordships should agree as to the meaning of [the statute] and should express that meaning in terms that are not liable to be misunderstood and are easy to apply to the circumstances of particular cases'); also *Sheddon* v. *Goodrich* (1803) 8 Ves Jr 481, 497 *per* Eldon LC.

475 *Maunsell* v. *Olins* [1975] AC 373, 390; and see Rupert Cross, *Statutory Interpretation*, 3rd ed., ed. J Bell and G. Engle (Oxford University Press, 2005), at 49, 82; Andrew Ashworth, 'Interpreting Criminal Statutes: A Crisis of Legality?' (1991) 107 *LQR* 419, 427. In *Maunsell*, which centred on the interpretation of a statute, Lord Diplock (who generally counselled against dissenting in statutory interpretation cases) concurred with Simon's dissent.

476 *R (Quintavalle)* v. *Secretary of State for Health* [2003] UKHL 13 at [10] (and see also [24]).

477 *Royal College of Nursing* v. *Department of Health and Social Security* [1981] AC 800, 822.

478 *IRC* v. *Ainsworth* [2009] UKHL 31 at [52].

479 See, e.g., *Said* v. *Butt* [1920] 3 KB 497, 499 per McCardie J; *Homburg Houtimport BV* v. *Agrosin Private Ltd* [2003] UKHL 12 at [16] *per* Lord Bingham; *R (A)* v. *Secretary of State for Health* [2017] UKSC 41 at [36] *per* Lord Wilson; *Lynch* v. *Walker Racing Ltd* [2017] EWHC 2484 (QB) at [13] *per* Langstaff J.

themselves dissentients,[480] and some judges stand out as being more than ordinarily sympathetic to dissenting judicial opinion.[481] Yet it is more noticeable with dissents than it is with other types of persuasive authority that a flattering description of the source is often preparatory to a judge's declaration that the source is, for one reason or another, dispensable for the purpose of deciding the case before the court.[482] Notwithstanding that appeal courts do, occasionally, vindicate dissents, the chances that the court will accept counsel's argument that a dissenting opinion should be accepted as if it were binding are close to negligible unless it is shown in the submission that the opinion is complemented by other, ideally stronger, authorities.[483]

480 See, e.g., *Warwick Rural DC* v. *Miller-Mead* [1962] Ch 441, 462 *per* Willmer LJ (dissenting) ('I should, for my part, prefer to follow the powerful dissenting judgment of Atkin J'); *Attorney-General* v. *Guardian Newspapers*, 1320 *per* Lord Oliver (dissenting).

481 Lord Wright is a case in point. See *Glanely* v. *Wightman* [1933] AC 618, 640; *Davies* v. *Powell Duffryn Associated Collieries Ltd* [1942] AC 601, 616; *Summers* v. *Salford Corporation* [1943] AC 283, 292; *General Medical Council* v. *Spackman* [1943] AC 627, 639; *London Passenger Transport Board* v. *Upson* [1949] AC 155, 170–1; also *Charles Osenton & Co* v. *Johnston* [1942] AC 130, 136, where Wright was with the rest of the House of Lords in accepting Simon LC's contention that the judgment of the majority of the Court of Appeal should be reversed and Clauson LJ's dissent affirmed. Wright seemed especially amenable to the dissents of Thomas Scrutton (in whose chambers Wright had served his pupillage): see, e.g., *Sedleigh-Denfield* v. *O'Callaghan* [1940] AC 880, 910; *Luxor* v. *Cooper* [1941] AC 108, 149; *Sovfracht* v. *Van Udens Scheepvaart en Agentuur Maatschappij* [1943] AC 203, 236.

482 See, e.g., *Cox* v. *Evans* [1917] 1 KB 275, 282 *per* Ridley J; *Rose* v. *Ford* [1937] AC 826, 851–2 *per* Lord Wright; *Camden Nominees Ltd* v. *Slack* [1940] Ch 352, 361–2 *per* Simonds J; *Fitzwilliam's Collieries* v. *Phillips (Inspector of Taxes)* [1943] AC 570, 578 *per* Lord Russell; *National Anti-Vivisection Society* v. *IRC* [1948] AC 31, 48 *per* Lord Wright ('I have great sympathy with much that the Master of the Rolls [Greene MR] has said in his powerful dissenting judgment. I have a great love for animals and some familiarity with certain classes. I am sorry that rabbits, a weak and an innocent, but monstrously destructive race, should have to be destroyed in great number as they were and are being, to save our people from qualified starvation. I agree with the Master of the Rolls that rats, beetles and other pests if they have to be destroyed should be destroyed with as little cruelty as possible. But destroyed they must be'); *Unit Construction Co Ltd* v. *Bullock (Inspector of Taxes)* [1960] AC 351, 361 *per* Viscount Simonds; *Bedson* v. *Bedson* [1965] 2 QB 666, 686 *per* Davies LJ.

483 See, e.g., *Du Jardin* v. *Beadman Bros* [1952] 2 QB 712, 716; *Cunningham (Anthony Barry)* [1982] AC 566 at 574–5, 577–9; *Nutting* v. *Southern Housing Group Ltd* [2004] EWHC 2982 (Ch) at [12]–[14] (Evans-Lombe J rejecting counsel's submission that Lord Millett's dissent in *Ghaidan* v. *Godin-Mendoza* be treated as authority); *R (Law Society)* v. *Master of the Rolls* [2005] EWHC 146 (Admin) at [15]. For acceptance of dissenting opinion complemented by authorities see, e.g., *Customs and Excise Commissioners* v. *Air Canada* [1989] QB 234, 244–7; and also Coulson J's comments (on factors to be taken into

Usually, when judges rely on dissents as persuasive authority, they utilize them much as they would any other secondary source. Judges in a majority might acknowledge that dissentient judicial reasoning (drawn, perhaps, from a source which is itself only persuasive authority)[484] has influenced them in formulating their *ratio*. Members of a majority might observe that although dissenting opinion – contained in another case, or in the judgment on the current case when it was heard in the lower appeal court, or to be delivered alongside an impending judgment – did not bear upon their formulation of a *ratio*, it did lead them to consider more thoroughly than they would otherwise have done what the possible outcomes to the case could be.[485] Judges can be found disagreeing over the relevance of dissents just as they can over the relevance of other persuasive sources to the deciding of a case.[486] A court, as often as not urged by counsel, might rely on dissenting opinion as the justification for applying a precedent's *ratio* narrowly.[487] When it seems likely that the law on a litigated matter will be developed if a case goes to appeal, Sedley J suggested in 1998, dissenting opinion can prove especially valuable to stakeholder parties hoping to influence how a higher court develops it.

> Where on the trial of a preliminary issue a court of first instance is bound by higher authority and must leave it to the appellate system to decide whether to change course, the question … must … include a certain margin of appreciation in respect of doctrines of law which are still perceptibly changing or capable of change. Not everything which is currently precluded by authority is unarguable. This will particularly be so where there are in the appellate courts dissenting judgments capable of sustaining the plaintiff's case.[488]

account when deciding whether to accord weight to dissents) in *F Ltd* v. *M Ltd* [2009] EWHC 275 (TCC) at [16].

484 See, e.g., *McLoughlin* v. *O'Brian* [1983] 1 AC 410 at 430 *per* Lord Scarman, 437 *per* Lord Bridge (each acknowledging the influence of Evatt J's dissent in *Chester* v. *Council of the Municipality of Waverley*).

485 See, e.g., *Rees* v. *Darlington Memorial Hospital NHS Trust* [2003] UKHL 52, where Waller LJ's dissent in the Court of Appeal in was very carefully considered but ultimately not adopted by the House of Lords.

486 See, e.g., *Shogun Finance Ltd* v. *Hudson* [2003] UKHL 62, where divergent views are expressed as to the significance of Devlin LJ's dissent in *Ingram* v. *Little* [1961] 1 QB 31, 62 for the purpose of deciding the case.

487 See, e.g., *Westminster Bank Ltd* v. *IRC* [1958] AC 210, 219 (*arguendo*); *Martin* v. *IRC* [2007] EWCA Civ 1041 at [50]; *Macleod* v. *Mears* [2014] EWHC 3140 (QB) at [44]; *Crossman* v. *St George's Healthcare NHS Trust* [2016] EWHC 2878 (QB) at [49]–[50].

488 *Connolly-Martin* v. *Davis* [1999] PNLR 350, 356 (case decided July 1998).

Does this observation hold good for judicial dissents any more than it does for other secondary sources? It does for some dissents. While it is more accurate to think of judges' opinions as providing reasons for decisions rather than as legal arguments (these being the province of counsel), we might somewhat crudely conceive of their dissents as losing arguments. A dissent might be a weak losing argument, a strong losing argument, or a losing argument which (no doubt because it is strong) is turned into a winning argument.[489] Dissents which perform the function which Sedley identifies, or which serve in any other way as persuasive authority, are strong losing arguments – arguments which, by virtue of their strength, make the reasoning in support of a binding decision seem less compelling (there is 'an authority binding upon us', Wightman J declared before Common Bench in 1863, but the dissenting opinion accompanying it 'diminishes its weight').[490] A judge can easily create

[489] One legal theorist, writing about US judgments, has argued that some dissents might, even in the cases in which they appear, be categorized as part of the winning argument: Nina Varsava, 'The Role of Dissents in the Formation of Precedent' (2019) 14 *Duke Jnl of Constitutional Law & Public Policy* 287. Varsava's thesis is that '[i]n the case of a dual-majority decision . . . rationales from the dissenting opinion are judgment-supportive: either the plurality or the concurrence relied on the same rationales (as the dissent) to reach its conclusion in favor of the judgment of the court' (ibid. at 312). She illustrates the thesis thus: *T*, *S*'s mother, supports *S*'s endeavour to become a gymnast because she considers it beneficial to *S*'s well-being. *T*'s friend, *A*, concurs with *T* in supporting *S*'s endeavour, but she supports it because she believes 'that parents should make every effort to ensure that their daughters are popular at school' (ibid. at 294–5). Another friend of *T*'s, *M*, is the dissenter: she thinks that *T* 'should *not* allow her daughter to participate in competitive gymnastics because', like *T*, 'she believes that parents should try to promote their children's physical well-being' (ibid. at 295). Varsava's point is that *M*'s dissentient reasoning supports the judgment of the dual-majority (*T* and *A*). But it is not clear that the scenario yields any *ratio* that could be ascribed to a majority, for *M*'s reasoning seems to be different from *T*'s. If *T* and *M* were judges, *T*'s opinion could summarized as that *S* should be supported in her effort to become a gymnast, the reasoning being that parents should support their children's activities when the activities benefit children's well-being. The gist of *M*'s opinion, by contrast, is that *S* should not be supported in her effort to become a gymnast, the reasoning being that providing such support is inconsistent with the principle that parents should strive to promote their children's well-being. *T* and *M* share the belief that children's well-being is important (it seems likely that *A*, who presumably considers popularity to be conducive to well-being, also shares that belief). But they are not aligned in their reasoning, and *M*'s reasoning – since parents should try to promote their children's well-being, they should not encourage their children to pursue activities which are likely to harm it – does not support (imagine her surprise if she were told that it did support) the judgment of the majority.

[490] *Horrocks* v. *Metropolitan Railway Co* (1863) 4 B & S 315, 324. For (limited) empirical support for the hypothesis that ordinary citizens react to judicial decisions in much the same way – that they are more likely to consider a decision authoritative, even if they disagree with it, if there is no dissent among the decision-makers as to how the law

doubt over a precedent by commenting pointedly on the powerful dissent accompanying it. Be careful what you wish for, Lord Pearce warned counsel for the respondents in *Anisminic*: if you were correct, and the House was bound to apply its decision in *Smith* v. *East Elloe RDC* to the ouster clause in this case, 'I would think it necessary to reconsider' that precedent 'in the light of the powerful dissenting opinions' which accompanied the opinions of the majority.[491]

There were powerful dissenting opinions in *Anisminic* itself – delivered by Lords Reid and Somervell. To characterize these opinions as strong losing arguments does not quite do them justice. They were, more accurately, losing arguments which came very close to being winning arguments. Our second line of enquiry regarding the relationship between judicial dissent and authority concerns not how judicial dissents are a form of persuasive authority, but rather how, in some cases, very little separates authority which binds from authority which persuades. The durability of a precedent typically depends on judicial support for it not only in the case in which the precedent was established but in subsequent cases as well. Just as the dissent associated with a precedent might weaken its authority, absence of dissent can make the source grow stronger. Counsel relies on a decision which, strictly speaking, does not bind us, Baggallay LJ remarked in the Queen's Bench Division in 1879, but the fact that the decision has met with 'no judicial dissent . . . until the judgment from which these appeals are brought' leads us to follow it all the same.[492]

Judges regularly treat as noteworthy the fact that a precedent occasioned more than one dissent.[493] These judges also sometimes, though rather less regularly, maintain that those who supported a precedent's *ratio* make for a questionable majority. This argument, we saw,

should apply to the dispute – see James R. Zink, James F. Spriggs II, and John T. Scott, 'Courting the Public: The Influence of Decision Attributes on Individuals' Views of Court Opinions' (2009) 71 *Jnl of Politics* 909.

491 *Anisminic* v. *Foreign Compensation Commission*, 200–1; and see *Smith* v. *East Elloe RDC* [1956] AC 736. This is not the only occasion on which Pearce sought to pour cold water on a cited authority by drawing attention to its accompanying dissent. See also *Williams* v. *Williams* [1964] AC 698, 758 ('but the sole authority . . . is . . . *Timmins* v. *Tameness* [*sc.*, *Timmins* v. *Timmins* [1953] 1 WLR 757] in which there is a powerful dissenting judgment by Hodson LJ').

492 *R* v. *Bishop of Oxford* (1879) 4 QBD 525, 576.

493 See, e.g., *Milne* v. *Commissioner of Police* [1940] AC 1, 15 *per* Maugham LC; *Fitzpatrick* v. *Sterling Housing Association* [2001] 1 AC 27, 65 *per* Lord Hutton; *R (Burkett)* v. *Hammersmith & Fulham LBC* [2004] EWCA Civ 105 at [10] *per* Carnwath LJ.

surfaced in the aftermath of *Burmah Oil* v. *Lord Advocate* (Section 3) and also preyed on the minds of various late Elizabethan and early Stuart lawyers who disliked bare majorities in courts of error (Section 6). The argument, in essence, is that the judicial majority in the final appeal court is not a majority of all the deciding judges in all the courts taken together.[494] A. P. Herbert put the argument to satirical use in 1933. Spare a thought, he wrote, for 'the weary and impoverished litigant' who loses by a bare majority in the House of Lords – even though '*per capita*, His Majesty's judges were equally divided on the point in dispute'.[495] This litigant will very likely come away from the courts distrusting the reasoning of all of the judges who heard his case, including those who would have had him win, and he will certainly wonder why the judges in the final court should be thought to be possessed of 'superior wisdom'.

> It is not surprising . . . if many appellants present themselves to that House in a reckless or at least a speculative mood, as a gambler who has backed a succession of losers still hopes to recover all by a wild wager on the final race. The Court of Appeal, to one in this mood, must represent a minor handicap taking place at 3.30 . . . When a man keeps two clocks which tell the time differently, his fellows will receive with suspicion his weightiest pronouncements upon the hour of the day, even if one of them happens to be right.[496]

When precedent is associated not with a single case which has progressed through the appeal courts but rather with a series of final court decisions affirming a particular *ratio*, there emerges, Lord Templeman observed in 1988, the prospect of that *ratio* – supported by a genuine judicial majority as opposed to a cluster of dissentients who happened to constitute the greater number – being eradicated by a very small body of judges. His speech in *Craven* v. *White* betrays his

[494] Although, in this Essay, the argument has been considered specifically in relation to English courts, it of course applies to other courts besides. For example, a tally of all the judges throughout the three US courts that heard *Palsgraf* v. *Long Island Railroad Co* 248 NY 339 (1928) has them 7:6 in favour of finding that the defendant owed the plaintiff a duty of care (the final court, New York Court of Appeals, ruled against the plaintiff by a 4:3 majority). See John T. Noonan, Jr, *Persons and Masks of the Law: Cardozo, Holmes, Jefferson, and Wythe as Makers of the Masks* (New York: Farrar, Straus and Giroux, 1976), 144 ('a majority of the judges who heard it . . . thought to constitute a cause of action').

[495] A. P. Herbert, '*Board of Inland Revenue* v. *Haddock*: Why is the House of Lords?' (1933), in his *Uncommon Law: Being Sixty-six Misleading Cases Revised and Collected in one Volume* (London: Eyre Methuen, 1977 [1969]), 255–60 at 259.

[496] Ibid. at 258–9.

exasperation not so much with the respondent's effort to finesse an artificial tax avoidance scheme as with what he considered to be the majority's failure to see that the respondent's defence depended on an inordinately limited interpretation of applicable principle as set forth in a series of House of Lords rulings.[497] Templeman was one of two dissenters. It struck him as unacceptable that a bare majority of the House should, in effect, be able to sidestep a body of its own precedent which had regularly been applied in the lower courts. Were my opinion to prevail, he insisted, 'a knife-edged majority' would have 'no power to limit this principle which has been responsible for four decisions of this House approved by a large number of our predecessors'.[498]

Stare decisis has never been subject to the qualification that, in final appeal court decisions, a majority might be too small to produce a binding *ratio*. Nor has any sustained attention been accorded to the proposition that, exceptionally, a precedent might be reappraised given that, were the panel responsible for it to be reconvened to decide the case today, many in the majority would switch sides so that the minority's preferred outcome would hold sway. Not that this proposition has never been tested in the courts. In *Conway* (2018), counsel for the appellant's argument centred on *Nicklinson*, a Supreme Court case in which five of the nine justices took the view that had the Court wanted to issue a declaration of incompatibility under section 4 of the Human Rights Act 1998 – on the basis that a general statutory prohibition on assisted dying is incompatible with article 8 of the European Convention – it was constitutionally competent to do so.[499] The Supreme Court nevertheless opted, by a 7:2 majority, not to declare section 2(1) of the Suicide Act 1961 to be incompatible with article 8. The two dissenters would have issued a declaration immediately. Three of the justices in the majority concluded that, since parliament was soon to debate a bill proposing the partial decriminalization of assisted dying, the legislature should be given the chance to repeal and replace section 2(1), and only if it failed to do so

[497] An interpretation which, according to Templeman, 'would only revive a surprised tax avoidance industry and cost the general body of taxpayers hundreds of millions of pounds by enabling artificial tax avoidance schemes to alter the incidence of taxation'. *Craven (Inspector of Taxes)* v. *White* [1989] AC 398, 491 (case decided July 1988).

[498] Ibid. A decade earlier, in the Court of Appeal, Cumming-Bruce LJ had remarked on what he considered a similar problem: the inherent weakness of a Court of Appeal majority which, though subsequently followed in cases decided by various combinations of judges, regularly met with dissent: *Davis* v. *Johnson* [1978] 2 WLR 182, 223–4.

[499] *R (Nicklinson)* v. *Ministry of Justice* [2014] UKSC 38.

(or failed to do so satisfactorily) should a declaration be issued. The bill was debated but never put to a vote. In *Conway*, counsel for the appellant submitted to the Court of Appeal that since nothing had come of the bill, the opinions of the justices in *Nicklinson* who favoured deferring, but who in principle supported, a declaration of incompatibility should now be 'added to the dissenting judgments' so that the decision became, in effect, a 5:4 majority in favour of declaring section 2(1) to be Convention-incompatible.[500] The Court of Appeal considered the facts in *Conway* to be distinguishable from those in *Nicklinson* – though even if *Nicklinson* had been followed its majority would not have been recalculated.[501]

Judges are generally unmoved by efforts to redefine or rejig majorities. The same cannot be said, however, of the claim that, with some precedents, the judges in the majority were very nearly not a majority – the dissenters almost came out on top – and therefore the *ratio* attributable to the majority is one over which a court with the capacity to depart from the precedent might at least want to pause. Precedents built on marginal majorities need not be weak authorities.[502] The fact that a slightly differently constituted court might have taken the majority in a different direction, furthermore, is not (by itself) a ground for appeal.[503] The

[500] *R (Conway)* v. *Secretary of State for Justice* [2018] EWCA Civ 1431 at [83].

[501] Ibid. at [133] ('[W]e have not found the dissection of the judgments in [*Nicklinson*] . . . particularly enlightening. [Counsel for the appellant] sought to extract from some of the judgments . . . support for . . . speculative thoughts . . . about the prospects of success of a new application for judicial review should Parliament fail to legalise assisted suicide by the Bill then before Parliament'). The Court of Appeal refused the appellant permission to appeal to the Supreme Court. When the appellant then took the application for permission to the Supreme Court itself, it seems that the determining panel only narrowly upheld the refusal: see Joshua Rozenberg, *Enemies of the People? How Judges Shape Society* (Bristol University Press, 2020), 102–5.

[502] *Boardman* v. *Phipps*, for example, contains two cogent dissents, and the *ratio* attributed to a rather disparate majority (Lord Cohen's reasoning was somewhat different from that contained in the opinions of Lords Hodson and Guest) not only imposes on fiduciaries a markedly strict version of the no-conflicts-of-interest rule but also contains some questionable reasoning: *Boardman* v. *Phipps* [1967] 2 AC 46. But a strict approach to the formulation of the rule was already supported by precedent (*Keech* v. *Sandford* (1726) Sel Cas Ch 61) and by final court *dicta* (*Regal (Hastings) Ltd* v. *Gulliver* [1942] 1 All ER 378, 386 *per* Lord Russell). The apparent fragility of the majority's *ratio*, furthermore, is – as is often the case with long-standing bare-majority precedents – largely offset by the fact that it has regularly been followed in the courts.

[503] See *R* v. *Maxwell* [2010] UKSC 48 at [36] *per* Lord Dyson; *McGuinness* v. *Nursing and Midwifery Council* [2017] EWHC 325 (Admin) at [35] *per* Stephen Davies J ('I am prepared to accept that it is possible that a different panel on a different day might have reached a different conclusion . . . However, that does not mean that the decision which this panel made . . . was . . . wrong').

slimness of a majority, nevertheless, can indicate – sometimes to a judge's disquiet[504] – not only how a decision could easily have gone the other way but also how an area of law might equally easily have been placed on another path. There are, Lord Hoffmann observed in 1998, 'those cases' – he had in mind *McLoughlin* v. *O'Brian*, though many other final appeal court decisions fit the bill – 'in which one feels that a slight change in the composition of the Appellate Committee would have set the law on a different course'.[505] Had the majorities in these cases taken that course (and assuming the final court or parliament did not subsequently depart from it), many controversial moral questions – whether an underage child can agree to contraceptive treatment,[506] whether consent is a defence to sadomasochistic infliction of harm,[507] and so on – would have met with different legal answers.[508] In those cases which leave judges uneasy over the direction of the law having been settled by the slightest of margins, there will also – Jeremy Waldron makes the point regarding constitutional controversies settled by US Supreme Court 5:4 splits – have been a litigant, possibly a category of litigant, for whom the

504 See, e.g., *R* v. *Kearley* [1992] 2 AC 228 at 237 *per* Lord Griffiths, 251 *per* Lord Bridge; also Paterson, *Lawyers and the Public Good*, 174–5.

505 *White* v. *Chief Constable of South Yorkshire Police* [1999] 2 AC 455, 502 (case decided December 1998). Soon after Hoffmann made this point, he was at the centre of a case which illustrated it: *Pinochet (No. 3)* was reheard by a seven-judge panel after the decision of the original five-member panel (which included Hoffmann) was set aside owing to Hoffmann's connection to Amnesty International, which had been given leave to serve as an intervening party. The fresh panel took a more restrictive approach to the definition of extradition as compared with the original panel: see Richard Buxton, 'Sitting *en banc* in the New Supreme Court' (2009) 125 *LQR* 288, 288.

506 *Gillick* v. *West Norfolk and Wisbech AHA* [1986] AC 112 (Lords Brandon and Templeman dissenting).

507 *R* v. *Brown* [1994] 1 AC 212 (Lords Mustill and Slynn dissenting).

508 The twelve-member Supreme Court's readiness (as compared with the House of Lords) to sit as a panel of seven – even nine – might indicate a desire on the part of its members to reduce both the production of bare-majority final-court precedents and speculation over what, in any particular case, the Court's decision might have been had any of the non-participating justices delivered opinions. Yet if the Court truly was motivated thus, one of its recent recruits once suggested, it would be more amenable to sitting as a panel of eleven: see Andrew Burrows, 'Numbers Sitting in the Supreme Court' (2013) 129 *LQR* 305, 308 (at the time that Burrows wrote, the Court had never sat with an eleven-member panel). Some of the Court's decisions would meet with speculation as to what might have been even if it always sat as a panel of eleven: see James Lee, 'Against All Odds: Numbers Sitting in the UK Supreme Court and Really, Really Important Cases', in *Apex Courts and the Common Law*, ed. P. Daly (University of Toronto Press, 2019), 94–139 at 119 ('As long as there is, as there inevitably will be, one justice on the substitutes' rather than the judicial bench, there could still be a concern that any one judge would have made a difference').

judgment is very likely a defeat which seems all the more harsh owing to the narrowness of the verdict.

> [W]e require passionate advocates for one side or the other to put up with a constitutional position that they regard as an abomination simply because one more Justice voted for it than voted for the contrary view. That is a lot of weight to put on a decision-procedure ... We plead with the losers in the name of fairness to their fellow citizens. But what do we offer the losers in five-four judicial decisions?[509]

In some jurisdictions, and certainly in English law, this view of bare majority decisions – that, for losing parties, they are outcomes to which it can be very difficult to become reconciled – is part of the (though not the only)[510] explanation for a discernible negativity towards, and in certain instances the imposition of restrictions on, dissent in criminal appeals. When parliament established the Court of Criminal Appeal in 1907, it determined that the Court's judgment delivery style should resemble that of the Judicial Committee of the Privy Council: apart from in exceptional circumstances, there would be a single 'judgment of the court'.[511]

509 Jeremy Waldron, 'Five to Four: Why do Bare Majorities Rule on Courts?' (2014) 123 *Yale LJ* 1692, 1723.

510 In *Howe*, Lord Griffiths made the case against dissenting opinions – in favour, more specifically, of single composite judgments – on the basis that clarity, certainty, and simplicity are of especial importance in criminal law: see *R* v. *Howe* [1987] AC 417, 438; and *cf.* Reid, 'The Judge as Law Maker', 29 ('For a time it was customary in the House of Lords to have only one speech in criminal appeals. But after the disaster of *Smith* v. *DPP* we changed that: I don't believe that decision would have been so bad if there had been more than one speech'). Restrictions on disclosure of voting on magistrates' panels deciding criminal cases may reflect concern not for losing parties but for the safety of magistrates in their local communities: Alder, 'Dissents in Courts of Last Resort', 235.

511 Criminal Appeal Act 1907, s. 1(5). Separate opinions are permissible when members of the Court are divided on a question of law: Senior Courts Act 1981, s. 59. See, e.g., *Crown Prosecution Service* v. *Eastenders Group* [2012] EWCA Crim 2436, where, on one of the points of law at issue, there was a difference of opinion between the presiding judge, Laws LJ, and Mitting and Edwards-Stuart JJ (who delivered a judgment of their own on the relevant point), though none of the judges is recorded as dissentient. Exceptional cases, in which the Court's judgments are accompanied by dissent, do exist: see, e.g., *R* v. *Kerr* (1921) 15 Cr App R 165 where Darling J delivers the judgment, concluding that he has directed the other judges to 'express their separate opinions' because '[o]ne member of this Court does not agree with my opinion' (ibid. at 168). Avory J then delivers a concurring opinion and Salter J delivers a short dissent (though nowhere in the report is it referred to as a dissent). Various other cases may have involved dissent, though all that is clear from the reports is that they were majority judgments: see D. Seaborne Davies, 'The Court of Criminal Appeal: The First Forty Years' (1951) ns 1 *JSPTL* 425, 440. On the Judicial Committee's practice as having inspired section 1(5), see Herman Cohen, *The Criminal Appeal Act, 1907* (London: Jordan & Sons, 1908), 21–2.

A governmental committee chaired by Lord Donovan reviewed the practices of the Court in 1965 and concluded that although it was far from obvious that the quality of the Court's judgments would suffer were its judges to get into the habit of delivering dissents and separate concurrences,[512] the single-judgment rule had 'worked quite well'[513] since the Court's inception and there was no need to repeal it.[514] The rule, slightly tweaked, is still in force.[515]

The original explanation for the rule – introduced as an amendment to the Criminal Appeal Bill during its passage through the commons – was that separate opinions of any kind risk creating the impression of a court divided, and that it is especially important not to allow this impression to form in relation to a court with primary responsibility for judging appeals concerning the state's imposition of criminal sanctions on its subjects.[516] Judges and lawyers have been inclined, however, to formulate the rationale for the rule in slightly different terms.[517] Given that the Criminal Division of the Court of Appeal (as it is now known) conventionally sits as a panel of three, its judgments, were they not unanimous, would have to be by a bare majority. A rule upholding an extremely strong presumption in favour of single judgments in the Criminal Division was established and has endured, the argument runs, because revealing to the accused that one of the three judges would have upheld his appeal might be considered callous: he is lacerated enough by the application of the criminal law, 'without the

A similar rule of court procedure can be found in Estonian criminal law: see Julia Laffranque, 'Dissenting Opinion and Judicial Independence' (2003) 8 *Juridica International* 162, 166.

512 *Report of the Interdepartmental Committee on the Court of Criminal Appeal*, Cmd. 2755 (London: HMSO, 1965), para. 248.

513 Ibid. at para. 250.

514 Ibid. at para. 251.

515 Senior Courts Act 1981, s. 59.

516 HC Deb 19 July 1907 vol. 178 col. 1061 (Sir John Walton A-G) ('[T]he practice of the Privy Council to have no minority judgment should be followed in criminal matters, so that the executive, in the execution of a sentence, should have the full support of the tribunal'). William Anson argued that the rule should allow for the publication of dissenting opinions but his argument was not accepted (ibid. at col. 1062).

517 Though the original explanation for the rule has not been entirely lost on them: see Roderick J. Munday, '"All for One and One for All": The Rise to Prominence of the Composite Judgment within the Civil Division of the Court of Appeal' (2002) 61 *CLJ* 321, 341 ('In criminal cases, . . . the liberty of the subject is at stake and the courts are channelling the force of the state against its own citizens – it is thought inappropriate for the court to speak with a divided voice').

salt of a favourable but impotent dissenting judgment being rubbed into the wound'.[518]

Unanimity in criminal appeals certainly seems desirable when the appeal court is providing an instruction to a lower court, such as that the lower court's decision be remanded for fresh proceedings or remitted for further consideration. Given that a dissenting judge can, in principle, request that a case be relisted, furthermore, it is not impossible to imagine an appellant preferring a unanimous judgment out of fear that there could be a rehearing were a judge vehemently to dissent against his acquittal.[519] But it seems doubtful that the persistence of the single-judgment rule in criminal appeals can be attributed to a desire to spare losing accused parties from discomfiture. That the rule has persisted is more likely ascribable to the awkwardness of the alterative: allowing a criminal appeals court to uphold convictions by non-unanimous judgments while also requiring that it give accused parties the benefit of the doubt. Even this explanation for the continuation of the rule runs into the obvious objection that it does not account for those criminal cases not covered by it. The rule does not apply to criminal appeals heard in the Court of Appeal when it sits as a Divisional Court. And of course, should a criminal defendant be granted leave to appeal to the final court, the judgment delivered in that forum need not be free of dissent. If the point of the single-judgment rule is to soften blows delivered to defendants, moreover, it seems strange that only criminal defendants should be the beneficiaries of it. Although, in the Civil Division of the Court of Appeal, there will invariably be only one judgment when a case is considered patently unmeritorious or unanswerable, adjudication in civil appeals is not subject to a single-judgment rule, notwithstanding that a civil litigant made to pay substantial damages might be stung by the salt of a dissent every bit as much as might a convicted criminal defendant.[520]

518 Blom-Cooper and Drewry, *Final Appeal*, 81, though *cf.* ibid. at 89 ('[T]he losing litigant likes to know that someone would have found for him'). On the idea of a dissent defeated by a bare majority rubbing salt into a wound, see also Bader Ginsburg, 'Remarks on Writing Separately', 135; Kirby, 'Judicial Dissent – Common Law and Civil Law Traditions', 392 ('the feeling that an unsuccessful prisoner should not be upset by knowing that one judge saw merit in the appeal'); Kelemen, *Judicial Dissent in European Constitutional Courts*, 124 ('out of concern for the accused').

519 Though relisting for re-hearing owing to judicial dissent is a rarity: see *Report of the Interdepartmental Committee on the Court of Criminal Appeal*, para. 19; *R* v. *Shama* (1990) 91 Cr App R 138, 139 *per* Lloyd LJ.

520 Munday, 'All for One and One for All', 333–7, shows that, by the early 2000s, the Civil Division, though not under the yoke of a single-judgment rule, was increasingly inclined

Arguments such as that bare majority judgments can torment losing litigants, and can leave lawyers pondering how the shape of a legal doctrine might have been very different had but one of the judges been replaced by another, certainly should not be discounted. But what, if anything, is to be done about such judgments? In *Craven* v. *White*, we saw, Lord Templeman maintained that a final court knife-edge majority should not have the power to apply a legal principle in a manner inconsistent with how that principle has been applied in a line of final court precedents. But he did not spell out the circumstances in which he would have considered departure from the precedents permissible. Perhaps his point was that the court needed to demonstrate consensus in some form,[521] though it seems more likely that he was not being prescriptive but rather was simply bemoaning the potency of a bare majority. Were the final court determined to avoid bare majorities, it is not clear how it could do so other than by committing to delivering unanimous judgments.

In some jurisdictions with constitutional courts, it has occasionally been argued and even accepted that if judges are to be prohibited from striking down enacted laws apart from in instances of clear legislative error, invalidation of a statute through judicial review should be impossible unless the court's decision is unanimous or by supermajority.[522]

to speak with a single voice, particularly in cases concerning disputes in the public eye, alleged legal impropriety, matters on which it is especially important to give a clear legal answer, and issues demanding judgments which are likely to impact on substantial numbers of future litigants. Munday also observed that when these types of cases came before the Criminal Division, the Court would often make a point of emphasizing its unanimity (ibid. at 342–3). In a complementary paper, published in the same year, he cited as further evidence of the Court's increasing tendency towards unanimity the fact that civil appeals were being heard ever more regularly by panels composed of just two judges: Munday, 'Judicial Configurations', 656. In the current Court of Appeal, dissents are rare and it is unusual for cases to contain more than one judgment.

521 Templeman was attentive to the distinction between the composite judgment of a unanimous court and a sole (single- or co-authored) judgment which meets with complete concurrence. See *IRC* v. *Stype Investments*, transcript of judgment (CA), 7 April 1982 (unpaginated), 1982 WL 222217 ('It is not a unanimous judgment, it is a judgment to which we all subscribed. There is ... a subtle and quite substantial difference').

522 See Evan H. Caminker, 'Thayerian Deference to Congress and Supreme Court Supermajority Rule: Lessons from the Past' (2003) 78 *Indiana LJ* 73; Jed H. Shugerman, 'A Six-Three Rule: Reviving Consensus and Deference on The Supreme Court' (2003) 37 *Georgia L. Rev.* 893; Joon Seok Hong, 'Signaling the Turn: The Supermajority Requirement and Judicial Power on the Constitutional Court of Korea' (2019) 67 *Am. J. Comparative Law* 177.

Enforcement of a supermajority norm is controversial even when the practice is confined to constitutional adjudication: there will be cases in which an impugned law will hold good notwithstanding that a (bare) majority on the court agrees with a complainant that the law should be declared unconstitutional. The proposition that a supermajority norm might govern judgments on any type of litigation before a final appeal court – so that, for example, a non-unanimous UK Supreme Court panel of five would require a majority exceeding 3:2, of seven exceeding 4:3, of nine exceeding 5:4, or of 11 exceeding 6:5 – runs up against numerous objections, the principal of which is that the strongest legal argument and the most deserving of the disputing parties will often not prevail if a final appeals process does not treat bare majority judgments as dispositive. A precedent not founded on unanimity or a supermajority will have a *ratio* ascribable to a minority on the court. A decision could go in favour of a litigant in the High Court and in the Court of Appeal, and then she could lose in the Supreme Court because only a simple majority adjudged her to have the stronger case.[523] Her anger will almost definitely be compounded by the fact that the Supreme Court's bare-majority judgment would once have made her a winner. The list of objections could easily be extended. Extending it would serve no end, however, considering that, in English law, nobody has ever seriously countenanced introducing a supermajority convention into the final appeals process.

10 Are We Agreed?

Although the supermajority idea makes for an eccentric proposal, the reasoning underpinning it is entirely straightforward: the only way to guarantee that an odd-numbered multimember judicial panel does not produce decisions by bare majority is to subject it to a rule which forbids decisions by bare majority. Members of a panel not governed by such a rule might strive to decide cases unanimously, but, given that they will sometimes differ over what they would have unite them, they will still be capable of producing bare majority rulings. Common-law appeal courts can and increasingly do avoid producing such rulings by issuing composite judgments, Dyson Heydon observed in the year before his retirement from the High Court of Australia, but the trend is not necessarily welcome. His principal point was that a culture of composite judgment

[523] She would very likely be no less confounded by the judicial process had the judgments turned out identically apart from that she had lost 2:1 in the Court of Appeal.

delivery might militate against judicial independence.[524] But alongside this point ran a subtler one. To those who dislike judgments composed of separate opinions, who worry over courts appearing divided and producing *rationes* which are barely supported, Heydon issued a challenge: you might prefer that judges come to an agreement and formulate it as a composite judgment, but if you were pushed to explain the nature of their agreement, what would your answer be?

> Who did the work? Did every judge understand the judgment? Did every judge closely examine it? Did a confident 'specialist' assume dominance over nervous 'generalists'? What, if any, compromises were made? It is sometimes said that all members of the court contributed 'equally' to a composite judgment. The intellectual activity involved cannot be measured to that degree of precision. That is an extreme illustration of a fundamental difficulty in composite judgments. The same difficulty exists where a judge delivers a full judgment and the remaining judges say 'I agree.' No doubt the judges do sincerely agree on something, but on what?[525]

Judges in common-law appeal courts, in so far as they can ever be said to exhibit this kind of inquisitiveness, seem generally more drawn to the inverse line of questioning. It is certainly conceivable that, by the time the judges on a panel have finished discussing a case, they will have contrived to eradicate what, at the outset of their discussion, was a graspable majority outcome.[526] But judges' accounts of their deliberations over cases more commonly attest to a different dialectic. Even in medieval courts, we saw, presiding judges can occasionally be seen steering would-be dissentients towards the majority's position (Section 6). While stories of modern judges being strong-armed into unanimity are invariably apocryphal,[527] contemporary legal commentators – often judges

[524] Heydon, 'Threats to Judicial Independence', 221–2 ('Judicial disagreements . . . are better revealed than concealed. The behaviour of those judges who advocate or choose the course of concealment rather than revelation constitutes the most insidious of threats to judicial independence').

[525] Ibid. at 212.

[526] See Peter J. McCormick, '"Was it Something I Said?" Losing the Majority on the Modern Supreme Court of Canada, 1984–2011' (2012) 50 *Osgoode Hall LJ* 93.

[527] See, e.g., Lord Mance, *The Common Law and Europe: Differences of Style or Substance and do they Matter?* (Birmingham: Holdsworth Club, 2007), 4 ('Lord Denning, like Lord Mansfield, two hundred years before, was so towering a figure that dissents were comparatively rare in his court . . . The story goes that, learning of likely disagreement by a colleague in one case, he said "So, you will have to dissent". When the third member of the court indicated that he shared his colleague's view, Lord Denning is reputed to

themselves – regularly observe how the members of a panel might share the first drafts of their opinions with a view to ironing out differences of perspective and identifying a unanimous or majority point of view,[528] how they might find their way to (or be navigated towards) issuing a single judgment,[529] or how some judges try to shape the opinion of the court by endeavouring to disseminate their draft opinions before the other judges have written theirs.[530] Judges who start out as dissentient voices might be convinced into joining or concurring with a majority. Or the quality of their reasoning might be such that they win over that majority. They might even end up speaking for it.[531]

It would be understandable if there indeed is a tendency for judges and lawyers to reflect little on what it means to say that a majority or all of the members of a judicial panel were in agreement. The process of deciding appeals seems more likely, after all, to have judges opting for the opposite line of interrogation: to have them asking what genuine disagreements, if any, exist between them when deciding a case, whether their disagreements concern the outcome or the route to the outcome, and, if it is thought that a disagreement should be brought out into the open, whether it is best articulated as dissent, as concurrence, or even as a combination of the two. Just as cases – to hark back to the Prologue – contain more than just case law, the topic of judicial dissent is not confined to judicial dissents. It also concerns some of the movement off the ball – the framing and negotiation of, and calculations over, the activity as well as the pursuit of the activity itself.

have said: "So you will have to dissent also"'). For another account of the story, see Brennan, 'In Defense of Dissents', 429.

528 See *Lord Hope's Diaries: UK Supreme Court . . . and Afterwards 2009–2015* (Edinburgh: Avizandum, 2019), 150; Paterson, *Lawyers and the Public Good*, 162–6; Tetyana Nesterchuck, 'The View from Behind the Bench: The Role of Judicial Assistants in the UK Supreme Court', in Burrows et al. (eds.), *Judge and Jurist*, 99–110 at 109–10; also Lynch, 'Dissent', 742.

529 See Paterson, *Lawyers and the Public Good* at 159, 182.

530 See Dyson, *A Judge's Journey*, 201. In the final court, this particular practice is now consigned to the past – though the superseding practice has the same aim of securing judicial consensus. Lord Leggatt, email to author, 27 August 2020 ('The practice now is for the presiding judge to allocate someone to write the first judgment at the end of the post-hearing meeting in which everyone gives their provisional view . . . If there are differences of view, the person chosen will be someone who holds the majority view or whose opinion seems likely to be able to achieve broad support. The convention now is that no one else will write unless and until they have read the draft lead judgment').

531 See Paterson, *Final Judgment*, 176–80; Paterson, *Lawyers and the Public Good* at 173–5, 187; also Scalia, 'Dissents', 22–3.

INDEX

Printed in Great Britain
by Amazon

68962399R00169